CAPITALISM AND THE ENVIRONMENT

Rising economic inequality has put capitalism on trial globally. At the same time, existential environmental threats worsen while corporations continue to pollute and distort government policy. These twin crises have converged in calls to revamp government and economic systems and to revisit socialism, given up for dead only 30 years ago. In *Capitalism and the Environment*, Shi-Ling Hsu argues that such an impulse, if enacted, will ultimately harm the environment. Hsu argues that inequality and environmental calamities are political failures – the result of bad decision-making – and not a symptom of capitalism. Like socialism, capitalism is composed of political choices. This book proposes that we make a different set of choices to better harness the transformative power of capitalism, which will allow us to reverse course and save the environment.

Shi-Ling Hsu is the D'Alemberte Professor of Law at the Florida State University College of Law and is the author of *The Case for a Carbon Tax* and co-author of *Ocean and Coastal Resources Law*.

Capitalism and the Environment

A PROPOSAL TO SAVE THE PLANET

SHI-LING HSU

Florida State University College of Law

CAMBRIDGE
UNIVERSITY PRESS

CAMBRIDGE
UNIVERSITY PRESS

University Printing House, Cambridge CB2 8BS, United Kingdom

One Liberty Plaza, 20th Floor, New York, NY 10006, USA

477 Williamstown Road, Port Melbourne, VIC 3207, Australia

314–321, 3rd Floor, Plot 3, Splendor Forum, Jasola District Centre,
New Delhi – 110025, India

103 Penang Road, #05–06/07, Visioncrest Commercial, Singapore 238467

Cambridge University Press is part of the University of Cambridge.

It furthers the University's mission by disseminating knowledge in the pursuit of
education, learning, and research at the highest international levels of excellence.

www.cambridge.org
Information on this title: www.cambridge.org/9781108474825
DOI: 10.1017/9781108681599

First published 2021

A catalogue record for this publication is available from the British Library.

Library of Congress Cataloging-in-Publication Data
NAMES: Hsu, Shi-Ling, author.
TITLE: Capitalism and the environment : a proposal to save the planet / Shi-Ling Hsu,
Florida State University College of Law.
DESCRIPTION: Cambridge, United Kingdom ; New York, NY : Cambridge University Press,
2021. | Includes index.
IDENTIFIERS: LCCN 2021024552 (print) | LCCN 2021024553 (ebook) | ISBN 9781108474825
(hardback) | ISBN 9781108465526 (paperback) | ISBN 9781108681599 (ebook)
SUBJECTS: LCSH: Capitalism – Environmental aspects. | Sustainable development. |
Environmental policy.
CLASSIFICATION: LCC HD75.6 .H78 2021 (print) | LCC HD75.6 (ebook) | DDC 338.9/27–dc23
LC record available at https://lccn.loc.gov/2021024552
LC ebook record available at https://lccn.loc.gov/2021024553

ISBN 978-1-108-47482-5 Hardback
ISBN 978-1-108-46552-6 Paperback

Contents

Figures

Tables

Preface

The science of climate change is still inherently uncertain, but it seems safe to say that in recent decades, the news almost always seems to be *worse* than what climate scientists previously believed likely. Despite being villainized by Republican politicians as being "alarmist" (and being threatened with bodily harm), climate scientists seem to be erring consistently on the side of not being alarmist enough. Ice shelves that were projected to destabilize in decades are now showing signs of earlier destabilization, tropical cyclones are more strange, powerful, and destructive, wildfires and beetle infestations are more destructive and uncontrollable, and strange things are occurring in oceans that are either more ominous than previously thought, or completely unexpected. The world may be at risk of losing most of its coral reefs, not in the coming century, but in coming decades, perhaps even the coming years.

This is not to blame climate scientists. The nature of science is to only assert a positive finding after rigorous testing and peer review, and a near-certain rejection of the status quo. Science is fundamentally conservative in its methodology. That is as it should be.

What is problematic, however, is that *some* technologies, unfettered by the conservative methods of scientific research, have raced ahead of scientific inquiry as to its effects. Insofar as science is the way in which humankind understands its effect on the environment upon which it depends for everything, it is losing a race to determine what human society looks like, and how it affects the global environment. Technology is not itself the problem, but rather the mass deployment of some potentially harmful technologies with insufficient regard to their environmental effects. Some fast-developing technologies do not, as a first-order estimate, seem to have large environmental consequences. The technologies of the big five technology giants are an example. Other technologies are decidedly not neutral or benign, and some of those have developed despite warning signs that they are environmentally harmful. For example, it is mind-boggling that oil companies have developed the technology to construct a floating factory the size of thirty football fields, and extend from it a tube that drops down into 10,000 feet of ocean water, penetrates a geologic shell, and extracts oil. In Northern Alberta, Canada, oil companies dredge up enormous chunks of land, denuded of trees and other life, and heat up the chunks in enormous chambers in order to leach out bitumen. And the cost of these miraculous technologies is startlingly low. In Alberta, mature oil companies can distill this crude oil from Earthen chunks at the cost of just $8 per barrel, while in Saudi Arabia, extracting oil from its oil fields is less than $3 per barrel. How did we learn such technological heroics?

Belatedly, humankind is coming to grips with the human and ecological costs of an industrial, fossil fuel-centered modern society. A realization is growing that human society has been insufficiently attentive to the effects that civilization has had on the planet that it inhabits, and depends upon, for everything. A clear majority of people, even in the United States, a hotbed for climate-deniers, believe that climate change is real, is a serious problem, and warrants strong government and international action. California wildfires have burned out of control in three of the last four years, killing hundreds and scorching millions of acres, forestland greater than the size of New Jersey in 2020 alone. The call in the United States for a vast, expensive "Green New Deal" highlights the environmental angst that has developed in many quarters of the United States. Worldwide, the sudden superstardom of a Swedish teenager, Greta Thunberg, has galvanized people. Caring about climate change and the environment, and seeing the problem in terms of the planet we bequeath to the coming generations, has become a globally common concern.

At the same time that humankind is waking up to the darkening of its prospects of life on Earth, it is wrapped in economic turmoil. Even before the COVID crisis, economic inequality had been gaining attention worldwide. Thomas Piketty's 2015 publication of his *Capital in the Twenty-first Century* exploded in popularity, surprising even Piketty and his publishers. Readers were concerned enough with inequality to be willing to work their way through 788 pages fully stocked with data. Scholarly criticism has dulled his message a bit, but the underlying theme is clearly intact: capitalism must be constrained. And the stakes are great: even in stable, social democratic countries, a new, xenophobic, often violent populism has emerged, threatening a world order that just decades ago seemed comfortably committed to classic liberalism. Capitalism is on trial. The United States is also a hotbed of hostility to socialism, but now is also home to a younger generation of people that feel at ease with socialism. Bernie Sanders ran two spirited presidential campaigns railing against the excesses of capitalism. He actually promised a socialist state, and got quite far with that platform.

It does not take much imagination to connect the two currents. Populist writers conflate capitalism with greed and excess, and point to the profit motive as the driver of countless environmental insults and tragedies. Everywhere you look, it seems, a greedy corporation acts with wanton disregard for the environmental conse- quences, and worse still, distorts government and public policy to protect its little (perhaps not so little) economic fiefdom. For decades, oil companies such as ExxonMobil funded misinformation campaigns, carried out by zealots, intent on foiling government action on climate change. They continue. Organizations such as the Competitive Enterprise Institute, the Heartland Institute, and the Heritage Foundation, continue to push for environmental deregulation, and continue to try and cast doubt on the science of climate change and the economics of climate policy. Behind the campaign to stall climate policy activists see the corrupting influence of the profit motive, and capitalism at its worst.

That is the wrong way to think about capitalism. Capitalism is a system of economic governance, a way of achieving a coordination of resources. Capitalism is extremely efficient at coordinating resources, and if the capitalist enterprise happens to impose uncounted costs upon the rest of society, then things can unravel quickly. But capitalism is still directed by *political choices*, which determine the direction that private firms take in their quest for profits and capital. That capitalist societies have produced an inordinate amount of pollution, that firms have been able to distort government policy through these misinformation organizations is a *political* failure, not a flaw with capitalism. Capitalism should never have been considered, as it is still considered in too many quarters, a self-governing state of existence. Capitalism has always required a direction. The political failure to provide one has set capitalism off on a course, too exuberantly bounding in the wrong direction.

That capitalism is blamed for a global environment careening towards collapse is a serious mistake on two fronts. First, it deflects blame away from where it squarely belongs: on the political classes that have allowed capitalism to metastasize into fossil fuel oligarchies controlling a political fiefdom. If the fault lies with capitalism, so the illusion goes, then replacing it with something like socialism will fix everything. That mistake naively forgets the kind of corruption that occurs under socialist governments, necessarily authoritarian. A socialist economic order will be worse for the environment, not better. Second, the mistaken impulse to abolish capitalism spurns the means by which humankind can right itself in its relationship with the global environment. Fixing industrial societies that are too dependent upon fossil fuels and unsustainable farming practices will require an *injection* of capitalism, not a rejection. Economies and societies do not change easily. One of the few forces capable of making profound change in a short period of time is capitalism. In the United States and elsewhere, that change can be costly: Amazon and Walmart have hollowed out many communities and retail industries, and changed the way people interact with each other. But capitalism is also hollowing out the coal industry. Both of those transformations are socially wrenching, creating dislocations that must be urgently addressed. But reducing coal use is something that *had* to happen, and after decades of weak successes in regulating the many effects of coal extraction and combustion, it was finally the capitalist transformation of natural gas extraction that brought about a much-needed decline in coal use. Capitalism is the engine of change, but it does not steer it. Political choices steer it, and this book is a call to make a different set of political choices. Humankind must harness capitalism, not quash it.

Mistaken thinking about capitalism is understandable, because it is abetted by incumbent industries that have captured too secure of a foothold in the political classes. The two administrators of the U.S. Environmental Protection Agency under the Trump Administration were, respectively, an Oklahoma Attorney General that championed the oil, gas, and coal industries (with their unwavering financial support), and a coal lobbyist and lawyer. So, too, Interior Secretary David Bernhardt, who was a lobbyist for the coal industry before his public position. In President George W. Bush and Vice President Dick Cheney, the Executive Branch was led by two individuals who had made their personal fortunes in the energy industry. These people did not preside over a capitalism that would have been recognizable to Adam Smith or Joseph Schumpeter. These people were the beneficiaries of an energy oligarchy, and once in political office, the guardians of energy interests.

And yet, these were individuals who wrapped themselves up in the flag of capitalism, propounding the specious claim that they were paragons of capitalism. Unfortunately, their political supporters believed them, and unfortunately so did the opposing side of environmentalists, activists, and most Democrats. What so many people missed was that far from being capitalists, they were actually oligarchs sliding towards socialism. Energy industries have enjoyed subsidies and privileges unavailable to other industries. One stands out: the insulation from environmental laws that would internalize the costs they impose on society. While difficult to price, those unpriced costs may turn out to be among the most expensive suffered in the history of all humankind. Continuing that slide would bring about more socialist environmental catastrophes, such as Chernobyl, the Three Gorges Dam, and the hollowing out of the Aral Sea. That is the stuff of socialism, and ultimately how socialism costs and corrupts.

This book is a call for two disparate but vitally important groups to find common cause: environmentalists and capitalists. Both must reject ideological dogmas that have divided them. Environmentalists must reject the calls from populist calls to burn down the whole "system" and install a socialist system, supposedly responsive to environmental needs. That has never happened at any significant scale in the history of humankind, and never will. For their part, capitalists must recognize how far capitalist economies have slid from true capitalism, an economic governance that is meant to minimize costs. Capitalist economies in flagging democracies have minimized costs to private firms, not to society. The tragedy is that the private gains have been far smaller than the public costs. A true capitalism would account for and internalize the social and environmental costs, and eliminate this perverse accounting.

Both of these assertions are difficult to accept. For environmentalists, the paradigm that conflates capitalism with environmental harm is a politically convenient one. As long as capitalism is considered the problem, the difficult job of repairing broken politics can be deferred. It is not just removing corrupt and captured politicians. Longstanding legal rules and institutions that have contributed to the broken politics must be reformed. There are many in the environmentalist and activist groups, and many Democratic politicians and political operatives that benefit from these rules and institutions. They will have to go.

On the other side, an enormous number of jobs depend upon the economic status quo. Capitalism is predicated on failure, as a disciplining mechanism, and that mechanism has been severely robbed of its effectiveness. Capitalism has been too breezily invoked to explain how some companies rise to spectacular profitability, and somehow conveniently neutered when those same companies face difficulty due to a changing legal or economic landscape. Getting industries and their people to face failure is excruciating. Some plan for alleviating hardship must accompany a harder, truer, more genuine capitalism. But change must come.

Ultimately, this book makes a populist call. While some capitalist titans have begun to accept the need for certain policy changes (such as climate policy), in order for the programs in this book to become law, a push must come from a much broader group of people. These people must recognize that what we have in most capitalist countries is not so much capitalism but an uneasy and unsustainable bargain to continue to do things a certain way. That is the antithesis of Schumpeter's capitalism. What I hope this book does is create the discussion space needed for some much-delayed, much-needed recognition of all that has gone wrong with both environmentalism and capitalism, and a bracing and honest reevaluation of how these two movements might work in concert to save the future of human civilization.

Acknowledgments

Writing this book in the midst of the COVID crisis certainly *felt* like I was doing this alone, but that was never the case. Not even close. To begin with, this book is the product of a long, meandering, and not altogether purposeful journey inspired by my primary Ph.D. advisor, Jim Wilen, now Professor Emeritus at the University of California at Davis's Agricultural and Resource Economics Department. He may be chagrined that I've strayed so far from the fisheries economics work for which he was so justly famous, but he was always proud of his students, whatever they did, as long as they did it well. I hope this book meets his standards. Indeed, this book is *not* what he and his colleagues at U.C. Davis trained me to do, which is to undertake rigorous economic inquiry and testing. But while this book is not in that style, my hope is that those that happen to find themselves reading this book will readily recognize Jim's influence, and that of his colleagues, in my arguments in this book.

Along the way, I have workshopped many papers leading up this book, benefiting from the counsel and advice of countless friends and colleagues. Among those, I wish to specifically acknowledge the help from events at the Pritzker School of Law at Northwestern University, the Maurer School of Law at Indiana University, the Wake Forest University School of Law, and meetings of the Midwestern Law and Economics Association, the American Law and Economics Association, and the Society for Environmental Law and Economics. I wish especially, however, to acknowledge my colleagues that participated in a workshop at the James E. Rogers College of Law at the University of Arizona, organized and moderated by my friend and colleague, Justin Pidot. It was after that workshop that I made a sharp turn to a new thesis.

I was supported by so many in the research and writing of this book. I benefited at various stages from comments from and conversations with Roberta Mann, Peter Grossman, Steve Johnson, Dan Cole, Jonathan Nash, Shahar Dilbary, Eyal Chich, Patrick Westhoff, Katrina Kuh, Geoffrey Hodgson, and Marc Hafstead. I wish to single out Bruce Huber, who alone among my reviewers read the entire thing, front to back, and helped me with several important reorientations. Three anonymous reviewers of my book proposal helped me sharpen my focus in writing the book.

In addition to the generous institutional support of the Florida State University College of Law, I have been greatly aided throughout my years here by an outstanding professional library staff, which has always done first-rate work, and by a team led by Margaret Clark, which especially rose to the occasion in helping me complete this book. And I am indebted to Matt Gallaway at Cambridge University Press for his encouragement, responsiveness, and counsel, and Cameron Daddis for her shepherding this book through the production process. The sometimes meandering nature of my journey to completion of this book necessitated much advice from Matt and the Cambridge editorial staff.

My parents were alive at the completion of my first book but sadly are not for this one. I dedicate this book to their memory, because they were among the truest capitalists I have ever known. Although my father was an academic and my mother a math teacher, they were true capitalists in that they sought out and embraced both hardship and opportunity, finding their way in a world completely foreign to them, earning every single inch they ever gained in any endeavor.

On the other side of the generational divide, I am inspired every day to try and do better by my children, Katharine and Allen, and my wife, Deborah, who are my bedrock. During the COVID crisis, the four of us holed up together, always together (!) at home, for months and months and months. And months. But despite all that we missed out on life outside, I would never trade these past months for anything at all. Thank you for being my family.

1

Introduction

Just a little more than 150 years after the publication of *Das Kapital*,[1] by the eponymous Karl Marx, capitalism finds itself under scrutiny again. For a time the failures of Marxism, as a political ideology, and the failures of socialism, as a means of economic organization, were so globally apparent that there seemed no longer to be anything to argue about. Inequality has now rekindled the old debate over capitalism versus alternative forms of government or economic organization.

Differences in degree are masked by a simple capitalism-versus-socialism dichotomy. Nevertheless, this book takes up this debate on these simplified terms, and with respect to only one question, but one of existential importance to humankind: How will human civilization right its horribly, tragically errant relationship with the planet it inhabits? Climate change, water pollution by nutrients, plastics, and hydrocarbons, the vast transformation of large landscapes, and the assault of industrial chemicals about which we know virtually nothing, head up a long list of ways in which human civilization faces colossal upheaval, a comeuppance of a longstanding disregard for the environmental consequences of human activity. Earth itself will support some lifeforms indefinitely, but the range of climatic and environmental conditions in which humans can thrive is limited. Humankind is now threatening the planet's ability to support humankind. What will save us from ourselves? For better or for worse, it will be capitalism that saves us.

That may seem like a strange assertion to some. Activists, scholars, researchers, interested citizens, and maybe even politicians that have been concerned with environmental issues may be surprised, and some chagrined, to hear such a thing, given how much damage capitalist economies have already done to the global environment. Not only that, some prominent capitalists continue to get in the way of environmental regulation and reform. It seems Pollyannaish to suggest that capitalism can turn around and start doing the opposite of what it's been doing for well over a century.

But that simplistic view misses the wide varieties of ways in which capitalism works and the infinite number of goals that capitalists pursue (it is not just profit).

Capitalism is not a monolith. Capitalism can exist in authoritarian states such as China, in libertarian states such as the United States, and in social democratic states such as the Scandinavian countries. In this variety of governments, cultures, and ideologies, capitalism has clearly held sway as the preferred method of economic governance, even as it faces different limits in different countries. In this hour of global environmental crisis, capitalism is the only way to quickly enough marshal the human, financial, and material resources necessary to right the direction of a huge, ponderous ship: a global economy powered by fossil fuels and trillions of dollars of polluting capital. If there is something that can fix this broken form of capitalism, it is capitalism.

Capitalism, like socialism, is difficult to define and frequently misunderstood. By "capitalism" I mean a form of economic governance with decentralized decision-making through prices, explicit or implicit, which govern a system in which not only is there free trading in markets, but free movement of factors of production. Money, labor, and other useful inputs (including environmental ones) are all factors of production, and capitalism requires that the owners of these factors of production be free to deploy them in whatever venture they choose. There are limits, of course. Slavery is forbidden, so there is no price on human bondage. But capitalism often means that the most profitable venture finds itself with the most useful factors of production, and competitors fall away, even fail. This is an oversimplification, and I undertake a lengthier discussion in Chapter 2.

Importantly, capitalism is not the absence of law or government, nor even a widely held illusion that government is "neutral" with respect to values, and that it can simply "call balls and strikes" like an impartial umpire in a baseball game. Capitalism embodies bundles of values that vary from country to country. This book suggests only elevating one: protection and restoration of the global environment. It is a far-reaching value because humankind has fouled its own nest in so many ways in so many countries and cultures. But it is a momentous one, because the whole of humankind is now at risk of descending into greatly diminished, and possibly some post-apocalyptic, existence. Whatever diverse meanings people may place on "capitalism" and on "human civilization," it is now a clear and present danger that the global environment may deteriorate enough to make both of these things difficult to sustain in a recognizable form. That dark future may be nearer than we would like to believe.

The way that capitalism is practiced must change, of course. It has been profitable to externalize environmental harms onto the planet and the rest of society. That is not only a human and planetary tragedy, but it is an anathema to capitalism. At a minimum, a healthy capitalist economy would count and value the vast forms of ecosystem services provided to many productive, profit-making enterprises. Clean air and water are not only vital to a healthy and productive population of human workers, but also as inputs to many industrial processes. But a healthy capitalism would go well beyond that, and place protection of the global environment at the *center* of industrial and commercial activity, where it belongs. Just as capitalism wrought momentous changes that have transformed society, it can be redirected to transform it again, but with the new goal of protecting and restoring the global environment.

This book suggests ways in which capitalism can be shunted away from its currently unsustainable (ecologically *and* economically) collision course with the global environment, and how capitalism can be harnessed to help solve the environmental crises facing humankind. Some parts of capitalism are already hard at work solving some of the environmental market failures that other parts of capitalism have created. Saving humankind and many other species will require that these restorative forms of capitalism be allowed to thrive. But more than that is required. Capitalist society must not only beat a hasty retreat from its destructive aspects, but also allow some new forms of capitalism to emerge, develop, and mature.

The necessary transformation of capitalism will be profound, but not necessarily jarring for everybody. In fact, it is already well underway. Driving electric cars or hybrid-electric cars, drawing electricity from a solar rooftop, and using energy- and water-efficient appliances is already routine for many, and would represent just a minor change for most consumers. Overall consumption patterns need not change dramatically.

It is on the production side that change is afoot. Given what we now know about impacts on human and nonhuman life, some methods of industry and commerce are now clearly inferior to alternatives. The *way* that energy and goods are produced must clearly change. Change is of course difficult, but the nature of capitalism is that progress comes through competition and change. Joseph Schumpeter thought that "creative destruction" brought about by healthy competition was the core feature of capitalism.[2] Businesses and industries *must* come and go. One example of an industry that has become anachronistic is coal mining. Coal combustion can now be replaced by a variety of alternative energy sources, and in fact has been in many places. In the United States and elsewhere, low natural gas prices have outcompeted coal as a fuel of choice for electricity generation. While it is important to acknowledge the economic and emotional toll of change for coal workers, it is also worth keeping it in context. With the development of the internet and the advent of travel websites, about 50,000 travel agents in the United States went out of business from 2000 to 2016.[3] That is also about the same number of workers in the coal mining industry who are at risk.[4] In healthy capitalist economies, the only constant is change.

There has been considerable discussion at times in the United States and other countries of a "Green New Deal" to address not only climate change, but a variety of related social ills, such as inequality, health care, and education. Almost all countries must absolutely do better on all of these issues, but it does not necessarily follow that they must all be addressed together, even if there are significant linkages. This book argues that transformative change need not cost extremely large amounts of money, nor need it involve a dizzying number of legal changes, provided it retains a laser-like focus on protecting and restoring the global environment. Most of what is needed to address climate change and the other critical environmental problems is readily available in a familiar policy toolbox. It is just that none of these have been explicitly put forth as ways to redress environmental harms within the rubric of capitalism. As it happens, the Green New Deal has been vague enough that different political candidates have been able to endorse the idea while putting a unique stamp upon it. My view is that profound change does not require the scale of change and expenditure that seems to be suggested by Green New Deal proponents.

1.1 MEETING THE ANTHROPOCENE

Some scientists have argued that in terms of Earth's history, it has entered a new geological epoch: the Anthropocene. Following the Holocene, a period of about 12,000 years beginning with the end of the Ice Age, the Anthropocene would be that period in which human activity began to have a significant impact on the Earth's ecosystems. The International Union of Geological Sciences, which declares these epochs, charged a working group with a preliminary decision and recommendation as to whether to declare this new epoch. In 2019, the Anthropocene Working Group voted overwhelmingly in favor of declaring that the Anthropocene should be treated as a "formal chrono-stratigraphic unit," or epoch. The recommendation would date the beginning of the Anthropocene to about the mid-twentieth century, when the advent of the nuclear age and the time in which many signals – "geological proxy signals," to the Working Group – indicate that the Earth has begun to change. The Working Group described these geological signals of human activity:

> Phenomena associated with the Anthropocene include: an order-of-magnitude increase in erosion and sediment transport associated with urbanization and agriculture; marked and abrupt anthropogenic perturbations of the cycles of elements such as carbon, nitrogen, phosphorus and various metals together with new chemical compounds; environmental changes generated by these perturbations, including global warming, sea-level rise, ocean acidification and spreading oceanic "dead zones"; rapid changes in the biosphere both on land and in the sea, as a result of habitat loss, predation, explosion of domestic animal populations and species invasions; and the proliferation and global dispersion of many new "minerals" and "rocks" including concrete, fly ash and plastics, and the myriad "technofossils" produced from these and other materials.[5]

This is a to-do list, and it is a daunting one. It is even a bit understated, as the threat of climate change is not described in its actual nightmarish detail: the last time that atmospheric carbon dioxide concentrations were this high – more than 400 parts per million – was 3 to 5 million years ago,[6] the temperature was approximately 5 to 7 degrees Fahrenheit warmer, and sea levels were between 16 and 130 feet higher than today.[7] And yet, the news always seems to be getting *worse*: ice shelfs are melting more quickly than expected,[8] coral reefs are dying off more quickly and dramatically than expected,[9] and wildfires have burned more ferociously and longer than expected.[10] And climate change is not the only threat, perhaps not even the most immediate one. Millions of people worldwide die annually of air pollution.[11] Humankind is not so much at a crossroads as it is at a precipice.

There is no doubt that the Anthropocene has the fingerprints of capitalism all over it. But to try to *rein in* capitalism so that it does less of what it currently does is not enough. The world's extractive, destructive, fossil fuel-based economy strives *against* restraints imposed by environmental law. It must somehow be made to strive *for* good environmental outcomes. Capitalism has undergone dramatic transformations in the past. Never has it been more important that it do so again.

Nor is there anything capable of changing capitalism's direction other than capitalism itself. Moral arguments are clearly necessary to change broad, worldwide attitudes toward environmental stewardship. But that cannot be the basis for industrial transformation, as is evident from decades of bickering over environmental priorities, locally, nationally, and globally. Some propose socialism, or something akin to it. But the environmental record of socialist countries is clearly worse than that of capitalist countries. Nothing short of an authoritarian state, and a harshly punitive one at that, could actually direct everybody in the right direction. Even then, the history of corruption, illegal markets, and bureaucratic fecklessness in authoritarian states does not bode well if the mission is to change direction quickly.

1.2 ONLY CAPITALISM CAN SAVE HUMANKIND FROM ITSELF

In 1833, the United States had only 380 miles of railroad tracks, most of it local, with no sense that trains could run on anything more than a dedicated line running from one place to another.[12] There was no network. Alfred Chandler's account of railroad expansion highlights what was new about the railroad venture: railroad tycoons, using joint stock corporations, began to undertake complex managerial tasks, like harmonizing the design of railroad tracks, keeping track of production and delivery of goods, agricultural commodities, and consumers, all in a variety of places throughout a very large area. The amount of money needed to create these business enterprises, to enter into production and delivery agreements, and to build the railroad tracks themselves was extremely large for that time. There was not even enough money that could be raised from all of the beneficiaries: farmers, merchants, and manufacturers that would be connected by a rail network. Unable to raise enough money in the United States, the railroad companies sought investment from European investors.[13] Once funded, the railroad enterprises became these institutions unto themselves, said to "take on a life of their own."[14] Investment in building railroad tracks and cars was massive for the time: $700 million between 1850 and 1860 alone.[15] By 1860, 30,000 miles of track had been laid.[16] By 1881, at

Promontory Summit in Utah, the West and East Coasts of a newly enlarged and post–Civil War country had been connected by rail. By 1890 railroad companies were the largest business enterprises in the world, employing more workers and handling more funds than the largest American governmental or military organizations.[17]

It is hard to overstate the significance of the railroads to development of the United States. Mid-nineteenth century railroad construction represents one of the earliest large-scale construction projects not undertaken by a government. Railroads connected an entire nation, and a large one at that, fomenting the rapid economic development that followed. As Alfred Chandler chronicled,

> The new sources of energy, and new speed and regularity of transportation and communication caused entrepreneurs to integrate and subdivide their business activities and to hire salary managers to monitor and coordinate the flow of goods to their enlarged enterprises.[18]

Railroad investment even ushered in a new era in finance. The amount of trading in railroad stocks and bonds made the New York Stock Exchange one of the largest and perhaps the most sophisticated capital market in the world.[19]

That is not to celebrate it all. Much of the hard labor was performed by Chinese immigrants treated like slaves, and the resulting massive, haphazard, indiscriminate development of the American West was predicated on the largest displacement and disenfranchisement of aboriginal populations carried out by any human society, ever. But it is also important to notice the railroad example as evidence of the ability of human society to dramatically remake itself. Capitalism *can* transform itself from a resource-consuming to a resource-restoring juggernaut. In addition to a very large amount of investment and capitalist energy, it will require direction.

A more modern example of the transformative impact of capitalism is the fairly dramatic – by the standards of the electricity generation industry – change in fuel sources for electricity generation in the United States. Decades of regulatory efforts produced some modest reductions in the use of coal for generating electricity. What sustained regulatory efforts could not do, however, a distinctly capitalist enterprise did. The advent of hydraulic fracturing, or "fracking," the cracking of geologic formations to gather small and disparate bubbles of natural gas, sent natural gas prices plummeting, and relegated coal to a fossil fuel of second choice. The story of how fracking became a scale operation by many atomistic natural gas companies is a complex one, weaving together narratives of technology, property rights and energy economics,[20] but one thing is for sure: the development of unconventional natural gas sources was an intensely capitalist enterprise. As in the railroad business, that is not to say that this story is an entirely uplifting one; natural gas has forced coal production to the margins, but must very soon give way to renewable, fossil-free sources of energy. Fracking also uses and spoils large amounts of water, and has been implicated in cases of drinking water contamination.[21]

Finally, of course, under a global capitalist system, technology has transformed telecommunications, consumer electronics, retail, and even politics; again, not necessarily for the better. Electronic gadgets, the product of a worldwide production chain, do things unimaginable just a few years ago. Online retail dominated by Amazon has brought almost everything to doorsteps. Along with its competitor Walmart, the two have together transformed retail and lowered prices, even as they have wiped out entire towns and the civic life within. Social media has profoundly changed the way people relate to each other. While it has served as a social conduit and fundraising tool, it has also spread dark and shadowy misinformation broadly and dangerously. While it has been a tool for democracy movements such as the Arab Spring, it has also facilitated Russian interference with American elections.

It is easy to find fault with how capitalism has imposed tremendous social and environmental costs. In each case and in countless other examples of capitalism run wild, enormous benefits were realized and also enormous costs suffered. But these examples illustrate how powerful and transformative capitalism can be, not just the resulting damages. If it is argued that capitalist economies produce greater social and environmental costs than those under say, socialist economies – a dubious claim – it is because only capitalist economies have been truly transformative. Only under a capitalist system could the vast Western United States be connected and settled, could the plodding electricity generation sector change its energy source, and could electronics have taken hold of so many lifestyle choices. There is no evidence that socialist economies are capable of such transformation, though in fairness that is due in part to the paucity of sustained examples of a socialist economy.

Capitalism is a form of economic governance that embraces the decentralization of information, rather than trying to conquer it, as a socialist system must. Capitalism is a means of achieving hyper-coordination of resources, ideas, and human initiative. It is that hyper-coordination of disparate factors of production that makes capitalism so powerful and potentially disruptive. A free flow of factors of production means that they can be withdrawn from some industry or some geographic region. There is nothing about capitalism that requires such large social and environmental damages, or ignorance of these damages. The large social and environmental costs suffered under capitalist systems have been failures of government, not failures of capitalism. Capitalism has been pointed in the wrong direction, and has bounded off too exuberantly in that wrong direction.

Energy companies are a case in point. The advent of hydraulic fracturing, or fracking, has been a mixed blessing. On the one hand, it has and will continue to push out the use of coal as an electricity generation fuel and dramatically reduce carbon dioxide emissions and other pollutants. On the other hand, fracking has produced a variety of other environmental costs, and given the increasingly dire findings about climate change, natural gas cannot stay long at the apex of the energy pyramid. But it has been transformative in a way that is hard to envision in a socialist economy. For those that imagine that the social and environmental costs of energy production would be better managed under something other than capitalism, the track records of Saudi Aramco, the Chinese oil giants, and many state-owned energy companies are not very reassuring.

Winston Churchill said that "Democracy is the worst form of government, except for all the others that have been tried from time to time."[22] He has been misquoted at times as having said that *capitalism* is the worst economic system, except for all the others. That seems accurate as well. There is something fundamental about capitalism, in all its forms, that creates a tendency to produce both wealth and transformation. The environmental crises that are now upon humankind require large changes in a relatively short time, and nothing appears quite capable of that other than capitalism.

1.3 FIXING CAPITALISM: TAXING BADS

Fixing capitalism, at least in the United States, will require capital investment to be driven by genuine market principles, *including* an accurate accounting of the external environmental costs. If polluters are not required to pay for their costs of pollution, then they will enjoy a competitive advantage over other firms and other industries, attracting more and better financing and more and better workers. Ignoring pollution is not "liberty." It is anarchy, and a gross misallocation of resources. The point of capitalism is to allocate factors of production to their most productive uses. A functional capitalism is one that would send price signals to divert factors of production away from polluting firms and toward firms that can make the same products with less pollution.

In the United States, pollution regulation has been accomplished mostly by the Congressional enactment of large, complex environmental statutes, to be carried out by the U.S. Environmental Protection Agency (EPA). The EPA has historically gone about its job mostly by issuing regulations to proscribe pollution, which have evolved over time. Once quite specific and prescriptive, pejoratively (and not entirely fairly) dubbed "command-and-control" regulation, they suffered from a propensity to micromanage production processes to reduce pollution. While having the advantage of certainty and ease of enforcement, this micromanagement caused polluting firms to eschew or entirely overlook more effective and cheaper pollution reduction methods. That is not the EPA's fault: its regulatory mandate under statutes such as the Clean Air Act and the Clean Water Act restrict its discretion as to how to reduce pollution. Then and now, Congress and some environmental advocacy organizations have exhibited some inclinations toward this micromanagement, sometimes with ironically negative environmental consequences. In a widely cited book, Bruce Ackerman and William Hassler document how environmental groups and coal interests conspired to convince naïve members of Congress to enact a requirement that new coal-fired power plants install sulfur dioxide pollution-reducing "scrubber" technology, an end-of-pipe piece of equipment.[23] This convenient deal simultaneously gave the coal industry a lifeline and the environmental groups a superficial "win" in supposedly reducing emissions (unclear). The problem is that of all of the different ways to reduce sulfur dioxide, scrubbers were among the least efficient. Everybody got a win, except for electricity consumers and the environment.

The lesson is that preventing environmental harm must be less prescriptive and more outcome-focused. For its part, the EPA, operating on the front lines of environmental regulation and having no desire to micromanage, seems to have had some sense of this, and has actually been quite innovative in introducing flexibility into its regulations while remaining consistent with its statutory mandates. Specific and prescriptive technology standards have mostly given way to performance standards, which only mandate a certain *rate* of pollution, not the method itself.

But the evolution of how environmental harms are reduced must press deeper into the capitalist realm to unleash entrepreneurial energies. Laws to reduce environmental harms must target the harms directly, not the processes that produce the harm. Unleashing entrepreneurial energies requires maximizing the options available to reduce pollution. A firm seeking to reduce its pollution might tinker with a polluting process, replace the entire process, or it might dispense with the product altogether in favor of a new way to meet consumer demand. It might even redefine consumer demand by creating new markets. A pollution reduction scheme must throw open all of these options for pollution reduction. A government regulation might leave open some of these options, but insofar as they are predicated on any specific process, product, or method, they can never be truly neutral.

Moving forward, a capitalism-friendly environmental legal regime would directly *tax* environmental harm on a per-unit basis, so that polluters would always face a marginal cost of polluting, and constantly have an incentive to try to reduce it. Environmental law should avoid, as much as possible, prescribing *how* harm is reduced. A scheme of environmental taxation would focus on the outcome – the proper role of government – while leaving methodology to the polluter, which possesses not only the intimate knowledge of its production processes, but its entire array of options. Faced with a price signal on environmental harm, a private firm may alter its production process, substitute products, or even leave the product market altogether. These would be complex and multilayered decisions that would be very difficult for a government agency to navigate. Grappling with alternatives and wrestling them into a tractable menu of options is what private, capitalist firms do. In the interests of reducing costs and increasing profits, firms search for more effective ways of meeting market demand. As long as firms face a marginal cost of polluting, they will hunt for new ways to reduce their pollution tax bills. In fact, this is one of the principal strengths of capitalism: its capacity to induce innovation.

What a system of environmental taxation would do is align the profit-making incentives and incentives to innovate with environmental objectives.

Not every environmental harm can be taxed, of course. Some pollutants, such as mercury, lead, or asbestos, are so harmful that outright bans are more appropriate. And many acts of pollution are difficult to detect, so that taxation would be fruitless. Moreover, in many cases, industries might benefit from government agencies simply setting certain standards in the interests of coordination, so that scale economies might be developed in certain pollution reduction methods. For example, the regulation of chlorine emissions from pulp and paper mills is difficult to detect, but what is known is that certain methods reduce emissions to a very small, if still slightly malodorous level. Industry and the EPA seem to have made peace in terms of the amount of industry expense needed to install this equipment, and the amount of public harm suffered as a result of it. Some arrangements or regulation might be best left alone.

Environmental taxation is nothing new. It is not even news that environmental taxation can feed a healthy capitalist economy – over the past thirty years, Sweden has both reduced its environmental impacts and prospered economically. What is new is the urgency of marshaling capitalist energies in the cause of reducing humankind's massive footprint. The Swedish experience – it is too mature to be labeled an experiment – must be upgraded, scaled up, and globalized. First and foremost, a carbon tax must be instituted to impose a price on greenhouse gas emissions, mostly but not exclusively on fossil fuels. Carbon taxation (and other carbon prices, such as cap-and-trading programs that require tradable permits to emit) have already demonstrated a capacity to unleash new entrepreneurial energies for figuring out how to do almost everything while emitting less. But a carbon tax, still in need of expansion, is just a template for other environmental taxes.

Much environmental policymaking has focused, and continues to focus, on subsidizing what is viewed as being a positive environmental outcome. Politically, that is a much easier task than imposing a tax on what is known to be negative environmental outcome. But as it happens, subsidization perversely moves away from the relative strength of government, and activates the relative weaknesses of both government and the private sector. It is politically difficult, but much more effective, efficient, and principled for government bodies to exercise its relative strengths: identifying harms and threats to the public. The United States Environmental Protection Agency, probably the most important information-gathering and environmental regulatory agency in the world, has been adept at identifying environmental "bads," pollution problems that pose threats to human health or the environment. Much-maligned and often fighting rearguard actions against politicians with anti-environmental agendas, the EPA has done an admirable (if imperfect) job of identifying and regulating numerous air, water, and land pollutants. It is after all, the job of government to identify public harms and protect the public from them, because it would never be in the interest of any single person or firm to undertake the needed investigation. That is not to say that government must actually be small, or passive. In terms of environmental harm, there are an awful lot of market failures to correct.

On the flipside, Congress, federal agencies, or any governmental bodies have rarely sported an enviable record of affirmatively doing good deeds. In some instances, the effort may be worthwhile, as it is in the provision of public housing, even as it has been beset with failures. But in the environmental field, the government record on public projects has been spotty, at best. Environmental transgressions are too numerous to even begin to list, but just a few examples might suffice to reinforce the point. Dam building, levee-constructions, and power plants leap to mind. And yet, governments are constantly being asked to subsidize or otherwise support what seem like "good" projects with "good" outcomes. What are we to make of those proposals?

There is a saying, the attribution of which is difficult to trace, that goes something like "governments are bad at picking winners, and losers are good at picking governments."[24] Government can and must provide public goods, such as defense, education, roads, police and fire protection, parks, other things that would be undersupplied if left to private initiatives only. But too often private industrialists, unable to make a profit in a competitive market, come seeking the government's help, and too often, they are granted help. This is a time-tested theory of government's vulnerability to "rent-seeking," and a very large body of literature[25] has been validated by countless dubious government initiatives to support one industry or another.

Fundamentally, there is a critical difference between government taking action to prevent bad things from happening, like pollution and crime, and government taking action to try and affirmatively make good things happen, like subsidizing a specific industry, firm, or process. A system of environmental taxation creates a division of labor that is more appropriate for the strengths and weaknesses of government and of the private sector. Government agencies are effective at recognizing public harm – that is their charge – and within their ranks are tens of thousands of career employees that have been trained for that specific task. Agencies can and should set environmental objectives that clearly focus on public health and environmental protection. How best to achieve those objectives should be left up to the private sector.

EPA's efforts to be more flexible in its regulation is limited by its statutory mandates. At least in the United States, any shift from regulation to taxation would likely require legislation amending the existing Clean Air Act and Clean Water Act, and other statutes charging EPA with pollution regulation. That is a heavy lift. Between 1990 and 2016, Congress enacted no significant environmental legislation whatsoever. Eventually, however, even lawmakers that are skeptical of the environmental risks must recognize that capitalism itself is at stake. Saving capitalism and repairing the global environment requires a new division of labor, one that places responsibility for setting environmental objectives with government, and responsibility for reaching those objectives with capitalists.

This book should be distinguished from calls by some right-wing advocacy groups to reduce or dispense with environmental regulation or pollution deterrence altogether. It is one thing to say that *some* environmental regulation should be replaced with environmental taxation, it is wholly another to say that it should be replaced with nothing. These groups are wholly ideological, demonstrating an aversion to not just government, but also science, economics, and facts. Even some principled and credible advocates of reduced environmental regulation, self-labeled as "free market environmentalists," are sometimes prone to overreach, arguing that environmental regulation is excessive and out of control. Some of these points are well-made, but my view is most of these sorts of claims tend to be exaggerations, sometimes by orders of magnitude. A cost-benefit analysis on the U.S. Clean Air Act from 1990 to 2020 carried out by the EPA found that the benefits exceed the costs by thirty to one.[26] This book acknowledges that environmental regulation can be improved. Indeed, it argues that it *must* be improved, alongside a transformation of capitalist enterprise. But the goal is to draw attention, resources, and energy to the cause of environmental protection and restoration. That stands in stark contrast to the call by the antienvironmental zealots, who would just as soon any discussion of environmental problems disappear entirely.

It may seem a bit ironic to some that a legal regime most faithful to small government principles, and most consistent with capitalism, is one in which environmental taxes are prominent. Is that not government interference? Some might argue that by controlling environmental taxes, government can control the economy just as they might with onerous regulations. But taxation is not the same thing as control. Unless one is in favor of dispensing with government altogether – which appears to be an objective of antienvironmental anarchists – the choice is not between taxation and liberty, it is a choice among different means of constraining liberty: taxation or regulation. Capitalism has *always* required coercive rules and institutions in order to function.[27] Some regulation or other coercion has always been necessary, and a truly libertarian position would posit a taxation state supplanting much (but not nearly all) of a regulatory state. To be sure, an environmental taxation scheme must have a transparent, science-based, and economic-based analysis supporting a tax level. That much is required of an environmental taxation scheme. But that is an easier task than arriving at and explaining the complicated regulations that have characterized environmental law.

1.4 FIXING CAPITALISM: GENERATING ENVIRONMENTAL KNOWLEDGE

While small government principles would call for being careful with taxpayer money, they would not call for complete abstention of government spending. No one argues that government should abstain from providing public goods, which are things that are "nonexcludable" and "nonrival" in consumption.[28] Nonexcludable goods are goods that by their nature would benefit everyone, so that no one could possibly be excluded from enjoying them. Hence, the United States spends quite liberally for a national defense, a public good that, having protected one citizen from foreign invasion, necessarily protects others from foreign invasion also. Nonrival goods are goods that are not depleted by consumption of one individual. So, the protection of one citizen from foreign invasion leaves undiminished the protection of another. Public goods supplied by federal, state, and local governments also include networks for transportation, water and sewage, energy transmission, and a system of police and courts.

Education is not purely a public good, because knowledge obtained by one student is something that can redound to her private benefit, without necessarily benefiting others. But insofar as education is inextricably bound with knowledge generally, it is still supplied by government, because knowledge itself is a public good. Human knowledge is nonexcludable in that once in the public realm, it becomes a free resource for everyone, and is nonrival in that one person's possession of knowledge does not reduce its value for another person. In fact, some knowledge may be said to have *positive network externalities*, in which the more people are in possession of a piece of knowledge, the more valuable that knowledge becomes.

Fixing capitalism will require the increased generation of a certain kind of knowledge, one that has received grossly insufficient emphasis, and quite possibly the most important of all: what I will call "environmental knowledge," the knowledge of how the human and nonhuman life systems react to the many disruptions caused by large-scale human activity. Probably most importantly, environmental knowledge must include continued and expanded study of the mechanisms and effects of climate change. Environmental knowledge must delve into a broad and deep variety of living systems, sometimes in places that seem remote or disconnected from humankind. It was only relatively recently that people have begun to appreciate how important coral reefs are to ocean life, occupying less than 1 percent of the ocean floor but housing over 25 percent of all marine species.[29]

Capitalism has embarked on this collision with the natural and human environment, and humankind has scarcely any idea of how that happened. Worse still, environmental insults not only portend gargantuan future costs – possibly apocalyptic consequences, in the case of climate change – but are already visiting massive costs upon humankind. Those costs are imposed in ways that are poorly understood. How many cases of cancer are attributable to glyphosphates, perfluoroalkyl and polyfluoroalkyl substances (PFAS), bisphenols, and just plain old benzene, a common gasoline component? It is still hard to say, in part because affected industries have been effective in blocking or obfuscating health research.

The ongoing Harvard Six Cities study dating back to the 1980s, has firmly established a link between fine particulate matter ($PM_{2.5}$) pollution and a variety of adverse health outcomes, most prominently premature death. $PM_{2.5}$ air pollution causes about 100,000 premature deaths annually in the United States,[30] millions worldwide.[31] It took decades of careful epidemiological research by hundreds of individuals, at dozens of top research institutions, and then a bit of advocacy to make $PM_{2.5}$ air pollution part of environmental regulation. But this long, ongoing research on $PM_{2.5}$, pertains to only one pollutant and one human health outcome, and raises the troubling question: *What else don't we know?* The effects of $PM_{2.5}$ on life expectancy can be studied because life expectancy is a metric that can be measured, the statistical effects of pollution measured against it. There are many, many other ways in which pollution harms people and the environment, very few of which have a measurable, objective metric. Air pollution is also a driver of asthma, but how does one measure those costs? Lost work productivity? Lost time playing outdoors with other children? The pecuniary and lost time costs of doctor's visits? What other health effects are there, and what sacrifices have we unwittingly made to cope with them? We now know, only after the phase-out of leaded gasoline, that an entire generation of Americans born before 1980 suffered a loss of more than two IQ points due to lead pollution.[32] What will we find out tomorrow?

Fixing capitalism requires a more informed decision-making environment, one that is supported by a much, much larger storehouse of environmental knowledge. 150 years into the industrial revolution is too late to undertake a comprehensive study of how human activities impact the environment. But better too little too late, than not at all, ever. Studying the impacts of human activities on humans and the rest of the Earth is perhaps the purest public good of all, and cannot be left to market forces.

Can we afford it? The more appropriate question is, "can we afford *not* to study the effects of pollution?" Just confining the inquiry to the effects of pollution on GDP – a narrow and deeply flawed metric – pollution was estimated to total $4.6 *trillion* per year, about 6 percent of global output, at least before the COVID-19 crisis.[33] Ignoring that magnitude of cost is scandalous.

Putting aside spending for environmental research for the moment, let us just consider federal U.S. funding for health. The budget for the National Institutes for Health (NIH) was in the $30 to $40 billion range for most of the decade from 2010 to 2020.[34] What have we gotten for that money? One of the thousands of funded studies, those pertaining to fine particulate matter air pollution described above, compelled air pollution regulations that are believed to have reduced the number of premature deaths from 123,700 to 58,600 per year, a difference of about 65,000.[35] As a very rough estimate, if the standard (though contested) price tag of a statistical life, $9.3 million[36] were applied to that piece of knowledge alone – translated grudgingly into environmental policy – then it was worth over $600 billion, *per year.*

This is not an isolated example of the benefits of health research. The list of medical advances funded or partially funded by NIH, some for cancer, heart disease, stroke, high blood pressure, drug addiction, contagious diseases, viral and bacterial disease, is far too long to list. Economists Kevin Murphy and Robert Topel have estimated that the value of added longevity just from medical and public health research in the United States has produced the equivalent of $3.2 *trillion* of benefit, *every year since* 1970.[37] And these are all figures that are focused on human mortality and human health. What do we know about health impacts that decrease productivity, human happiness, and the welfare of other species upon which we depend? Next to nothing, in the grand scheme of things. A much more efficient capitalism requires a massive infusion of research funds, to begin to chip away at the deficit in environmental knowledge, accumulated over decades and decades of doing before thinking.

There are many reasons to expand environmental knowledge, but there is one prosaic but absolutely vital use of that knowledge: the inclusion of environmental costs in economic accounting. Accounting for environmental harms has been an ongoing project for decades, but recent research using more detailed models has done a better job of attribution of harm, and forms the basis for a much better method of evaluating the total worth of economic activity, subtracting the environmental harm from the attributable GDP. Recent research only scratches the surface, however, and a more complete accounting of environmental harms is badly needed, which necessitates more knowledge of how economic activity creates harm.

1.5 FIXING CAPITALISM: LOOKING BEFORE LEAPING

Part of what has caused some capitalist economies to rot into oligarchy is the capital itself metastasizing into something other than just a factor of production. Capital has, in oligarchic economies, become the locus of wealth and power, and has itself become the raison d'être of business enterprise. Capital has, in some cases, assumed a life of its own, and inevitably, its social and environmental costs have been swept under the rug. With that in mind, it is important to revisit the legal and economic environment for capital investments. Even with environmental taxes to reduce environmental harm, and even with a much richer storehouse of environmental knowledge, more is needed. The very act of capital investing must be more sober and deliberate because once formed, capital has a tendency to create its own political economy to protect itself. It will take some time before environmental knowledge catches up to the current base of human activity. But *some* dampers on *some* capital investing are needed, even as it potentially impedes the capitalist fix of capitalism.

Capital investment is a commitment, often an expensive, long-term proposition. The problem arises when firms that own capital undertake efforts to protect their capital from regulation, competition, or any change in its legal or economic environment. The problem is particularly pronounced for capital that is found to impose environmental harms. The nature of environmental information is such that it is uncovered incrementally, as scientists gradually narrow the bounds of uncertainty. This information can be threatening, and because this kind of information is discovered incrementally, there is an opportunity for threatened capital owners to control the flow of that information and to change legal rules to either protect their investments or to stanch the flow of adverse information altogether. Some industries have developed a standard playbook for protecting their large, expensive, and valuable capital investments from adverse information: (1) suppress it, (2) ignore it, (3) downplay it, and (4) attack it and attack the scientists that produced it.[38] Even if this obfuscation strategy is only partially successful, it may still buy the firm time to continue operations. Troublingly, these types of strategies have been more successful than one suspects their practitioners even expected them to be. In fact, some industries and ideological interest groups have lately begun to attack scientific research generally,[39] reckoning that environmental law is an ideological war, and that depriving regulators of the weapon of information is fair game.

It is not as if this chain of events is inevitable once a capital investment is made. But it has occurred often enough to warrant raising some yellow flags for certain capital investments. The nature of capitalism as currently practiced, at least in some industries, is to maximize the differential between revenues and costs. Where does one go looking to minimize costs? Where costs are unpriced. Where is that? If environmental harm is not the largest category of unpriced costs, it is very near the top of the list. It is hard to compare different kinds of harm and damage, but remember that we have only yet scratched the surface when it comes to environmental knowledge. What we don't yet know may hurt us very much in the future, or may already be hurting us in ways that we don't yet even comprehend.

The problem with capital "stickiness" – the propensity for capital to be long-lived, persisting through events and discoveries that should render them obsolete – is more serious still. Over the past four decades, the capital-labor ratio, traditionally assumed to be constant, has ticked up gradually but significantly.[40] This central stylized fact of macroeconomics has thus given way to a new reality that capital is starting to get the better of labor, accounting for a greater share of returns vis-à-vis labor than historically the case.[41] This results in more capital vis-à-vis labor, and presents problems because all other things being equal, a larger capital stock creates a larger incentive for defending it, and insulating it from changes in its legal and economic environment. Capital creates its own political economy, and a larger stock of capital sharpens that political economy.

Capitalist economies have been operating under the notion that capital investments are strictly private actions with only private consequences. This is a mistake. The problem with this notion is that it ignores how, once created, capital takes on a life and importance all its own. By the time external, latent harms are discovered, it is too late: the political economy of displacing capital (or even inconveniencing capital owners) is locked in. It is critically important to try and take some stock of the external effects – the *externalities* of capital expenditures *before* they are made. Thus, as the third and final element of a proposed transformation of capitalism, this book proposes a suite of measures, all building upon existing laws and regulations, to slow down certain capital investments, which this book discusses in detail in Chapter 8.

1.6 HOW DOES CAPITALISM SAVE US?

The call in this book for a "transformation" of capitalism, with profound consequences for wealth, health, and the global environment might sound like a fantasy.
While this book is not a "hail Mary," I concede that my package of proposals is a very
big lift. Incumbent industries operate with the ruthless efficiency of assassins in
mashing down almost any policy effort that even comes close to jeopardizing their
modus operandi.

But at some point, every industry, even highly polluting industries, comes to
a reckoning. Even within a profit-maximizing, shareholder-primacy framework,
companies can and do consider the long-term sustainability of their business
model, periodically revising its endgame and its methods for getting there. Many
oil and gas companies, including ExxonMobil and many Canadian oil sands
companies, have long supported a carbon tax, though not strongly enough to the
point at which they were willing to coerce politicians the way they do on other, more
dear issues. Although a handful of capitalist robber barons makes headlines for their
flamboyance, I suspect that the caricature of corporate leaders as narrowly greedy,
avaricious capitalists is *mostly* faulty. It is simply too tempting to focus on the most
egregious ones. I suspect there is an emerging shared recognition of the environmental threats confronting humankind. Walmart pledged in 2010 to reduce its
carbon footprint by twenty million metric tons by 2015, which it did with an extra
20 percent to spare. Its more recent, more ambitious pledge is to reduce emissions in
its supply chain by a billion tons by 2030.[42] Why do that? Was there a clamor from
Walmart shoppers or its employees? Almost certainly not. There are certainly
considerations of profit-making, marketing and employee retention. But it seems
implausible to believe that there was absolutely no sense of social responsibility
present. The prospect of environmental catastrophe and the immediate and intermediate costs of environmental harm are becoming so prominent that even capitalist titans are warming to the notion of change within capitalism.

What would a transformed capitalism look like? That is not an abstract question,
because some jurisdictions have already moved forward with less pollution-intensive
economies, with no detectable economic loss. If anything, those economies with
smaller carbon and pollution footprints are doing *better* than their dirtier counterparts, suggesting there may be potentially significant co-benefits to greening an
economy.

In 1985, Sweden introduced an environmental tax on emissions of nitrogen oxides,
commonly abbreviated NOx, on electricity generation firms, of 40 Swedish kroner, or
about $5 U.S., per kilogram of NOx emissions. Emissions declined about 23 percent
over a thirteen-year period for those facilities.[43] That is not earthshaking, but not at all
bad, especially compared with a 6.6 percent decline in emissions from U.S. power
plants.[44] One thing that made the Swedish program effective was that the NOx tax
proceeds were gathered up and redistributed to the emitters on a per-unit-electricity

basis, thus rewarding those that were able to reduce their emissions. Under this plan, firm managers recruited and rewarded line workers to help find ways to combust more efficiently and reduce NOx emissions. In pure economic terms, this tax-and-rebate scheme amounts to an output subsidy, which is inefficient because it has the effect of encouraging the more efficient NOx-reducers to produce more energy; too much so, because the money could well have been better spent on say, ways to conserve electricity. That said, opposing such a scheme might be allowing the perfect to be the enemy of the good. What the Swedish NOx tax-and-rebate scheme demonstrates is the potential for recruiting those with the most intimate knowledge of industrial workings to the cause of reducing pollution.

Sweden also first instituted a carbon tax to address climate change in 1991. Sweden's carbon tax regime has spawned so many low-carbon and non-carbon technologies that it has almost single-handedly demonstrated a prosperous, low-carbon future. At the time this book was written, Sweden had the world's highest carbon tax, approximately $130 U.S., and has prospered spectacularly in spite of it, and perhaps in part because of it. From the inception of its carbon tax until 2017, emissions fell by 26 percent in absolute terms, its GDP grew by over 70 percent, in real dollars. Of course, that in itself does not prove that taxing carbon makes a country prosperous. But a closer look at Sweden's example suggests that there may be economic co-benefits to pursuing a less carbon-intensive path. Recent research suggests so much, finding that carbon taxation has a modest but significantly positive effect on GDP growth and employment.[45] Sweden's carbon tax has, in particular, spurred a development of a new fuel source, "bioenergy," which is derived from organic waste materials, gathered mostly from timber and agricultural operations. In just thirty years, bioenergy has almost completely pushed out fuel oil as the predominant source of building heating. Sweden's carbon tax has also reduced transportations emissions significantly. It is difficult to be precise, because Sweden also levies an energy tax and its value-added-tax, which have the effect of reducing CO_2 emissions. But credibly good efforts at attribution place the figure between 6 percent and 10 percent.[46]

What else might be done? How else might capitalist energies be channeled to repair a broken relationship between humankind and the environment? What must happen in the future under the guise of capitalist enterprise?

For one thing, a carbon tax must be put into place, as soon as possible, everywhere possible. Among many crises, climate change is the one with the most existential implications. The fact that fossil fuel emissions are so ubiquitous in human society is an obstacle but also an opportunity. The far-flung ways that energy consumption results in emissions also means that there are an almost uncountable number of ways to reduce greenhouse gas emissions. Ferreting out all of them is a job for capitalism, which has its advantages in coordinating disparate pieces of information and organizing markets through prices. In energy, a carbon tax could induce the replacement of fossil fuels, the organization of renewable energy sources, the development of energy storage technology, the decentralization of energy distribution, and efficiency increases in everything that uses energy. In transportation, a carbon tax would unleash a wider variety of innovations beyond lighter vehicles, reaching into other transportation modes, and possibly reaching into innovative work arrangements and lifestyles.

For another thing, capitalism can help reverse some of the damage done by emissions of greenhouse gases. It has become clear that not only must humankind reduce its emissions of greenhouse gases, it must undertake what is referred to as "negative emissions," or "carbon removal," the active capture and sequestration of carbon dioxide from the ambient air. Ambient carbon dioxide is taken up in huge quantities, by trees, plants, other greenery (such as algae), and a variety of other biogeochemical process, just not quickly enough to offset humankind's emissions. The fact that carbon dioxide can be absorbed in so many ways gives rise to numerous possibilities for innovation and biomimicry – the artificial recreation of biological processes that can take up carbon dioxide at the much higher rates needed. Incentivizing this kind of innovation would be one way of aligning private interests with compelling public ones.

Capitalism can also dramatically reduce, and eventually eliminate, emissions resulting from the generation of electricity. A highly centralized, hub-and-spokes model of electricity generation, transmission, and distribution has dominated the retail electricity industry for over a century. Scale economies and the need for electricity to be always available have justified a reliable but inflexible industry. It turns out that generating and transmitting large amounts of electricity is physically inefficient, and the possibility for efficiency gains and the elimination of fossil-based fuel sources have been obvious for a long time. Investor-owned utilities had been extremely effective in locking out competition, but now, technological advances in rooftop solar energy and information technologies pose a real competitive threat. A more efficient and lower-emitting electricity system would still need some source of backup electricity, but could conceivably be focused on local generation on rooftops, an exciting prospect but an existential threat to electricity utility companies. Therein lies the possibility for reform, and an unleashing of capitalist innovation: the divesting of electricity utility companies of their privileged status, and for many, a truly competitive market for retail electricity.

As a final example, capitalism can reduce the carbon and pollution footprint of livestock farming, by providing meat substitutes. It already has. Spurred by a consumer push for more sustainable forms of food protein, several companies have already developed plant-based meat substitutes that have drawn very positive reviews. Cattle, in particular, have a huge footprint in several ways. Cattle are the largest category of livestock, which now represent 60 percent of all of the biomass of all terrestrial mammals on earth, as compared with just 4 percent for all wild mammals.[47] Being able to provide a caloric and protein substitute for beef would take a big bite out of numerous environmental externalities of raising cattle, such as water pollution and range degradation, but more importantly, eliminate the carbon footprint of one of the most carbon-intensive foods. Cows emit enteric methane, a by-product of their digestive process, which is a powerful greenhouse gas, which makes a pound of beef about eight times as harmful, climate change-wise, than a pound of chicken.[48] The livestock industry seems to have some awareness of this problem, as some of the largest livestock companies have invested in these meat alternative companies.

The many extant ideas floating around barely scratch the surface of what might be possible. A large reason for that is the historically low priority and funding that humankind has assigned to study of the global environment, and how it interacts with human activity and welfare, an omission that must be corrected. Another large reason that environmental innovation lags is that industries have found ways to suppress them. Rooftop solar has been vigorously opposed by electric utilities that may lose sales of kilowatt-hours to residential consumers.

1.7 SOCIALISM IS NOT THE ANSWER

Could a socialist state lead the way in repairing humankind's fractured relationship with the environment? As one should suspect, "socialism" has taken on a wide variety of meanings in a variety of contexts over the centuries. For purposes of comparison, what I mean by "socialism" has a core policy implication: a decisive movement *away* from private property ownership of capital assets, governing an entire country. Smaller forms of socialism, such as for individual business enterprises, may be feasible, even in a capitalist economy. But that kind of "small socialism" would be incapable of the kind of transformation required to pull humankind back from the precipice. Reorienting an economy away from unnecessarily polluting industries is complicated; *prices* are necessary to move factors of production to different industries. Socialism governed by central planning, lacking prices, cannot do that.

Not all critics of modern capitalism would turn to socialism. While Schumpeter believed capitalism to be unsustainable in the long run, he was at least as critical of socialism. James Gustave "Gus" Speth, a longtime prominent environmental advocate and the author of a trilogy of books on environmentalism, was dismissive, citing examples of environmental catastrophe under socialist regimes. Bruce Scott laments the power that capitalist entities have seized, but advocates for better rules to constrain capitalist excess. Thomas Piketty would impose a wealth tax to alleviate inequality.

For others, however, the story is attractively simple: there is a flawed system (capitalism), identifiable villains (capitalists), and a solution (something like socialism, though they are often fuzzy on the details). Their answer is to blow up capitalism to save the environment. But the evidence tying capitalism to environmental destruction is too thin, the counterexamples too vexing, and the changeover plan too vague. Naomi Klein, in her book *This Changes Everything: Capitalism vs. The Climate*, proposes to abolish capitalism, but in favor of what? Magdoff and Foster, in their book *What Every Environmentalist Needs to Know About Capitalism*, write that "[i]t is precisely because ecological destruction is built into the inner nature and logic of our present system of production and distribution that it is so difficult to end."

The "abolish capitalism" critics make two major mistakes: (1) that environmental destruction has occurred in capitalist systems means that it must be *caused* by capitalism; and (2) countries with socialist economies are somehow different from capitalist ones, in that there is no growth imperative for them.

With respect to the first mistake, there simply has not been very much socialism in history for it to have caused as much trouble as capitalist countries. Just about *all* of the economic growth occurring in the history of humankind has occurred under capitalist systems, so of course those have caused most of the environmental destruction. The little bit of socialism that human history has seen thus far has plenty to answer for in terms of environmental destruction. The former Soviet Union is a fertile source of shame. The Chernobyl nuclear power plant was a poor investment, badly carried out, with a predictably catastrophic environmental outcome. The Soviet Union also heavily polluted the largest and deepest freshwater lake in the world, Lake Baikal, by erecting pulp and paper mills on its shores, and inefficient ones at that. It also caused the dramatic shrinking of the Aral Sea, to about one-fifth its original size, into a patchwork of smaller lakes and deserts, by diverting the rivers feeding the Aral Sea, in the name of self-sufficiency in cotton production. Sure enough, the wasting of the Aral Sea and cotton production has outlasted *glasnost.*

Soviet-era Poland is one of the few Eastern bloc countries to have made significant attempts to legislate environmental protection, and even tolerated a fair amount of environmental protest and dissent within its authoritarian regime.[49] But by the time that the Solidarity government took over in 1989, sweeping away Soviet-era socialism, Poland had become one of the most polluted countries in the world. Soil tests in Poland's industrial region near Krakow showed levels of lead and cadmium that were higher than that *ever* recorded, *anywhere*, 200 times that considered safe by the Polish government. Sixty percent of the vegetables grown in the region were rendered unfit for human consumption. Katowice, a city forty miles west of Krakow, managed to belch out five times the amount of sulfur dioxide pollution than West Germany's Ruhr Valley, while producing far less. The result? A shocking *two-thirds* of all ten-year-old children suffered from a mental or physical disability caused by that pollution. Half of all river water in the entire country was unfit for industrial use, let alone human consumption.[50]

How and why? It turns out, even in a socialist country that placed at least some formal emphasis on environmental protection, party politics, and a bureaucratic hierarchy that placed a higher emphasis on industrial production led to nonenforcement of well-intentioned environmental laws.[51] The problem with socialist economies is that they must necessarily be governed by authoritarian regimes. How else is "central" planning to be carried out, except by a central government? Under authoritarianism, government is both the environmental regulator and the regulated party, so it is difficult for government to separate its regulatory functions from its ownership interests. Capital abolitionists misunderstand: removing a capitalist profit motive does not transform production entities into socially enlightened firms. The production of goods in socialist regimes are subjected to other pressures that also ignore or discount environmental harms. Nobody was particularly surprised in 2013 when 6,000 dead pigs were pulled out of the Huangpu River just upriver from Shanghai, the most populous city in the world.[52]

With respect to the second mistake, it has been commonly observed that the current capitalist impulse to boost GDP by any means necessary is a tragically errant edict. That lament is not limited to the capital abolitionists. But the impulse to grow is not unique to countries with capitalist systems. Chinese communist leader Mao Tse-Tung was obsessed with growth, declaring once that industrialization could be made to occur in every backyard with homemade steel furnaces. It was Mao who put in motion a plan to dam the Three Gorges, which displaced nearly two million people in 1,500 cities and villages, and flooded rivers as much as 375 miles upstream.[53] Mao's vision of economic growth has been realized to a great extent: the People's Republic of China now has the second-largest economy in the world. It is an authoritarian state, albeit with enough tolerance for capitalism to have produced, in 2019, 324 billionaires, second-most in the world to the United States.[54] It is also the world's largest greenhouse gas emitter, emitting more CO_2 in 2017 than nine countries combined: the United States, Japan, Germany, the United Kingdom, France, Italy, Canada, South Korea, and Australia.[55] At the time that this book was being written, China was embarking upon the construction of more *new* coal-fired power plants *than the entire existing fleet of American coal-fired plants.*[56]

The impulse to grow is what caused the former Soviet Union and Soviet-era Eastern bloc countries to make their tragicomic mistakes. Growth for growth's sake is, in socialist and capitalist societies alike, a political goal. It is naïve to think that socialism does away with the political imperative for "growth." The failure of socialist systems to grow to the satisfaction of political leaders and their polity is why, for example, East Germany placed armed guards on the top of the Berlin Wall, why defection is such a sensitive topic for North Korea, and why escaping the former Soviet Union was a life-or-death proposition. Growth in socialist economies run by authoritarian regimes is a matter of political survival. The most egregious environmental insults emerging from China – greenhouse gas emissions and its historical intransigence to international cooperation, its three gigantic state-owned oil companies, and the Three Gorges Dam – are all clearly political organizations. It is the *politics* of growth in socialist regimes that have invariably emphasized production over environmental protection, as production has been the only metric by which socialist governments have tried to legitimate themselves.

Capitalism does not require environmental destruction, and does not even require "growth," except insofar as it strives for an efficient allocation of resources. Formally, neither does socialism. But the problem with socialism is that it tends to create institutional incentives to prioritize industrial productivity over environmental protection. The problem with capitalism has been that efficiency has not been widely defined to include the importance of the global environment. That is solvable. Once it is, then capitalism will reorder resources much more quickly than a socialist system would. Countries with capitalist economies have done a rotten job of controlling environmental harm, but it is implausible that countries with socialist economies have done or would do better.

It is difficult to prove a negative, and this book does not claim to do so, especially with the paucity of socialist experience. But it seems that capital abolitionists should explain some of these socialist tragicomedies before suggesting that it replace capitalism.

1.8 THE PLAN AND AIMS OF THIS BOOK

Broadly speaking, the aim of this book is to provide a path forward, and some hope. Among those that have been concerned about the deterioration of the environment, and in particular worried about the potentially apocalyptic consequences of climate change, this book makes the case that surprising progress can be made surprisingly quickly, by embracing capitalism. To repair humankind's relationship with the global environment, hope is not a sufficient condition, but it is a necessary one. And hope, in my view, is realistic. Capitalism does not, by its nature, necessarily destroy the global environment, but has only filled this dubious role because of the way that capitalist industry has haphazardly developed. Unfortunately, capitalism can also be path-dependent, so that correcting course can be quite difficult. That would explain the paucity and ineffectiveness of efforts to change course over the past century, but that need not be the future. Not only can capitalism be pointed in the right direction and, like a scent hound, retrained and cut loose, but it is possible that it could make political sense in the United States. No transformation of the scale needed will be easy, but it is possible.

This book proceeds as follows: Chapter 2 will provide a *very* brief synopsis of capitalism. I claim no special expertise in this area, only an attentive study of how it has developed into a system that has brought humankind to the brink of self-destruction. The key, as this book argues in Chapters 3 and 4, is that capital investment creates some path-dependency, and the resulting economy unfortunately reflects very little in the way of environmental considerations. In Chapter 5, this book makes the case that environmental taxation is the cornerstone of a catharsis of capitalism, both activating entrepreneurial energies and pointing them in the new direction of environmental protection and restoration. In Chapter 6, this book proposes five environmental taxes that will point capitalism in the right direction. These five taxes do not represent a comprehensive system of environmental taxes but represent a start, and they are low-hanging fruit, even if they do not seem that way politically. A new capitalism requires a new knowledge base, and in Chapter 7 this book makes the case for a refocus of government-funded research toward the environmental and Earth sciences, with a nod toward economics. The path-dependency of capital investment is a tricky problem, and in Chapter 8 this book proposes some measures to reduce that path dependency. Part of my proposal is to strengthen the National Environmental Policy Act. Chapter 9 concludes.

For the sake of concreteness, the package of proposals made in this book are introduced as proposals for domestic law in the United States. The political, social, and economic factors are analyzed in that context. Most of the factors, though, are portable, so that most of the analysis contained herein can apply to other countries as well. Effectual action must take place on a global scale, but given the difficulty with international agreement, this book works from the premise that unilateral action by a large country such as the United States is a necessary, but not sufficient condition for a comprehensive, global program to reform capitalism and save the global environment. Some domestic measures are proposed to improve the chances of international coordination, but a thorough discussion of international law is beyond the scope of this book. This book is limited to a prescription for domestic reform of capitalist economies, not a blueprint for global reform.

Notes

1. Karl Marx, Contribution to the Critique of Political Economy (1867).
2. Joseph Schumpeter, Capitalism, Socialism and Democracy 81–86 (1950).
3. Bourree Lam, *Who Uses a Travel Agent in This Day and Age?*, Atlantic (June 22, 2016), https://www.theatlantic.com/business/archive/2016/06/travel-agent/488282 [https://perma.cc/5694-LPMJ].
4. Nat'l Ass'n. State Energy Officials & the Energy Futures Initiative, The 2019 U.S. Energy & Employment Report 4 (2019).
5. Anthropocene Working Group, *Working Group on the "Anthropocene,"* Subcommission On Quaternary Stratigraphy, http://quaternary.stratigraphy.org/working-groups/anthropocene/ [https://perma.cc/3B9X-H8Z3].
6. Rebecca Lindsey, *Climate Change: Atmospheric Carbon Dioxide*, National Oceanic and Atmospheric Administration, Noaa: Climate.gov (Aug. 1, 2018), https://www.climate.gov/news-features/understanding-climate/climate-change-atmospheric-carbon-dioxide [https://perma.cc/KD8S-S94J] (showing 2017 level at 405 ppm).
7. *Graphic: Carbon Dioxide Hits New High*, NASA: Glob, Climate Change, Vital Signs of the Planet (Dec. 13, 2018), climate.nasa.gov/climate%5Fresources/7/graphic-carbon-dioxide-hits-new-high">https://climate.nasa.gov/climate_resources/7/graphic-carbon-dioxide-hits-new-high/ [https://perma.cc/8YER-D2P7].
8. *See, e.g.,* Pietro Milillo, et al., *Heterogeneous Retreat and Ice Melt of Thwaites Glacier, West Antarctica*, 5 Sci. Adv. 3443 (2019).
9. *See, e.g.,* Terry P. Hughes et al., *Global Warming Impairs Stock-Recruitment Dynamics of Corals*, 568 Nature 387 (2019).

10. Jennifer Marlon et al., *Wildfire Responses to Abrupt Climate Change in North America*, 106 PROC. NAT'L ACAD. SCI. 2519 (2009). *See also* A. Leroy Westerling & Benjamin P. Bryant, *Climate Change and Wildfire in California*, 87 CLIMATIC CHANGE S231, S231–S249 (2008).

11. *Burden of Disease from Ambient Air Pollution for 2016*, WHO (Apr. 2018), https://www .who.int/airpollution/data/AAP_BoD_results_May2018_final.pdf?ua=1 [https://perma.cc /7N7D-3YY6].

12. *Chronology of Railroading in America*, ASS'N OF AM. R.R., https://www.aar.org/data/chron ology-railroading-america [https://perma.cc/U9C8-ADJZ].

13. ALFRED D. CHANDLER, JR., THE VISIBLE HAND: THE MANAGERIAL REVOLUTION IN AMERICAN BUSINESS 91 (1977).

14. Werner Sombart, *Capitalism*, 3 ENCYCLOPEDIA SOC. SCIS 200 (1930).

15. CHANDLER, 90.

16. *Chronology of Railroading in America*, ASS'N OF AM. R.R., https://www.aar.org/data/chron ology-railroading-america [https://perma.cc/U9C8-ADJZ].

17. CHANDLER, 204.

18. *Id.*, 77.

19. *Id.*, 92.

20. Thomas W. Merrill, *Four Questions about Fracking*, 63 CASE W. RES. L. REV. 971, 976–81 (2013) (describing the recent history and factors that led to the state of natural gas companies in America).

21. EPA, HYDRAULIC FRACTURING FOR OIL AND GAS: IMPACTS FROM THE HYDRAULIC FRACTURING WATER CYCLE ON DRINKING WATER RESOURCES IN THE UNITED STATES EXECUTIVE SUMMARY, 22, 33, 37 (2016).

22. *The Worst Form of Government*, INT'L CHURCHILL SOC'Y, https://winstonchurchill.org /resources/quotes/the-worst-form-of-government [https://perma.cc/J4X4-J6WL] (quoting a speech from Winston Churchill given on Nov. 11, 1947).

23. BRUCE A. ACKERMAN & WILLIAM T. HASSLER, CLEAN COAL/DIRTY AIR: OR HOW THE CLEAN AIR ACT BECAME A MULTIBILLION-DOLLAR BAIL-OUT FOR HIGH SULFUR COAL PRODUCERS 56–58 (1981).

24. *See, e.g.*, Richard E. Baldwin & Frederic Robert-Nicoud, *Entry and Asymmetric Lobbying: Why Governments Pick Losers*, 5 J. EUR. ECON. ASS'N 1064 (2007).

25. MANCUR OLSON, THE LOGIC OF COLLECTIVE ACTION: PUBLIC GOODS AND THE THEORY OF GROUPS 152–54 (1965); George J. Stigler, *The Theory of Economic Regulation*, 2 BELL J. ECON. & MGMT. SCI. 3 (1971); *See generally* JAMES M. BUCHANAN & GORDON TULLOCK, THE CALCULUS OF CONSENT: LOGICAL FOUNDATIONS OF CONSTITUTIONAL DEMOCRACY (1962).

26. EPA OFF. OF AIR & RADIATION, THE BENEFITS AND COSTS OF THE CLEAN AIR ACT FROM 1990 TO 2020, at 7–3, 7–8 (2011), https://www.epa.gov/clean-air-act-overview/benefits-and-costs-clean-air-act-1990-2020-second-prospective-study [https://perma.cc/VTC6-KEL8].

27. BRUCE SCOTT, CAPITALISM: ITS ORIGINS AND EVOLUTION AS A SYSTEM OF GOVERNANCE 43–47 (2011).

28. *See, e.g.*, ROBERT CAMERON MITCHELL & RICHARD T. CARSON, USING SURVEYS TO VALUE PUBLIC GOODS 1–2 n.1 (1989).

29. *Coral reef ecosystems*, NOAA (Feb. 2019), https://www.noaa.gov/education/resource-collections/marine-life/coral-reef-ecosystems [https://perma.cc/JL7B-NGAW].

30. Andrew Goodkind et al., *Fine-scale Damage Estimate of Particulate Matter Air Pollution Reveal Opportunities for Location-specific Mitigation of Emissions*, 116 PROCEEDINGS OF THE NATIONAL ACADEMY OF SCIENCES 8775 (2019) (citing CDC, UNDERLYING CAUSE OF DEATH, 1999–2018 (2018)), https://wonder.cdc.gov/ucd-icd10.html).

31. *Burden of Disease from Ambient Air Pollution for 2016.*

32. Alan S. Kaufman, *The Possible Societal Impacts of the Decrease in U.S. Blood Lead Levels on Adult IQ*, 132 ENVTL. RES. 413 (2014).

33. Philip J. Landrigan, *The Lancet Commission on Pollution and Health*, 391 LANCET 462 (2017).

34. *Appropriations (Section 2)*, NAT'L INST. HEALTH ALMANAC (Mar. 3, 2020), https://www.nih.gov/about-nih/what-we-do/nih-almanac/appropriations-section-2 [https://perma.cc/M39Z-XSMV].

35. Yuqiang Zhang, et al, *Long-term Trends in the Ambient PM$_{2.5}$ and O$_3$-related Mortality Burdens in the United States Under Emissions Reductions from 1990 to 2010*, 18 Atmos. Chem. Phys. 15003, 15008 (2018).

36. EPA OFF. POL'Y, NAT'L CTR. ENVTL. ECON. FOR REVIEW BY THE EPA'S SCI. ADVISORY BD., ENVTL. ECON. ADVISORY COMM., VALUING MORTALITY RISK REDUCTIONS FOR POLICY: A META-ANALYTIC APPROACH 2 (Feb. 2016).

37. Kevin M. Murphy & Robert H. Topel, *The Value of Health and Longevity*, 114 J. POLIT. ECON. 871, 872 (2006).

38. *Attacks on Science*, UNION OF CONCERNED SCIENTISTS (Jan. 20, 2017), https://www.ucsusa.org/resources/attacks-on-science.

39. Shi-Ling Hsu, *Anti-Science Ideology*, 74 U. MIAMI L. REV. 405 (2021).

40. David Autor, David Dorn, Lawrence F. Katz, Christina Patterson & John Van Reenen, *The Fall of the Labor Share and the Rise of the Superstar Firms*, at 21–22, IZA DISCUSSION PAPER 10756 (2017); David Autor, David Dorn, Lawrence F. Katz, Christina Patterson & John Van Reenen, *Concentrating on the Fall of the Labor Share* (NBER Working Paper Series, Working Paper 23108, 2017), http://www.nber.org/papers/w23108.

41. *See, e.g.*, David Autor & Anna Salomons, *Does Productivity Growth Threaten Employment?* (Euro. Cent. Bank Forum on Central Banking, Working Paper, 2017), http://pinguet.free.fr/autorsalomons617.pdf [https://perma.cc/XRY4-DM44].

42. *Walmart Launches Project Gigaton to Reduce Emissions in Company's Supply Chain*, WALMART (Apr. 19, 2017), https://corporate.walmart.com/newsroom/2017/04/19/walmart-launches-project-gigaton-to-reduce-emissions-in-companys-supply-chain [https://perma.cc/JQ47-ZWA2].

43. *The Swedish Charge on Nitrogen Oxides – Cost-Effective Emission Reduction*, NATURVÅRDSVERKET (Mar. 2006), http://www.naturvardsverket.se/Documents/publikationer/620-8245-0.pdf?pid=3960 [https://perma.cc/4TKH-35WD].

44. *National Emissions Inventory Air Pollutant Emissions Trends Data, 1970–2019*, EPA (2019), https://www.epa.gov/air-emissions-inventories/air-pollutant-emissions-trends-data [https://perma.cc/TGQ5-JGYJ].

45. Gilbert Metcalf & James H. Stock, *Measuring the Macroeconomic Impact of Carbon Taxes*, 110 AM. ECON. ASS'N PAPERS & PROCEEDINGS 106 (May 2020).

46. Julius J. Andersson, *Carbon Taxes and CO$_2$ Emissions: Sweden as a Case Study*, 11 AM. ECON. J.: ECON. POL'Y 1 (2019).

47. Yinon M. Bar-On, Rob Phillips & Ron Miloa, *The Biomass Distribution on Earth*, 115 PNAS 6508 (2018), https://www.pnas.org/content/pnas/115/25/6506.full.pdf.

48. PIERRE GERBER ET AL., TACKLING CLIMATE CHANGE THROUGH LIVESTOCK – A GLOBAL ASSESSMENT OF EMISSIONS AND MITIGATION OPPORTUNITIES 24, 38 (2013).

49. Daniel H. Cole, *An Outline History of Environmental Law and Administration in Poland*, 18 HASTINGS INT'L. & COMP. L. REV. 297 (1995).

50. Daniel H. Cole, *Cleaning Up Krakow: Poland's Ecological Crisis and the Political Economy of International Monetary Assistance*, 2 COLO. J. INT'L ENVTL. L. & POL'Y 205 (1991).

51. DANIEL H. COLE, INSTITUTING ENVIRONMENTAL PROTECTION: FROM RED TO GREEN IN POLAND (1999).

52. *China Pulls Nearly 6,000 Dead Pigs from Shanghai River*, BBC (Mar. 13, 2013), https://www.bbc.com/news/world-asia-china-21766377 [https://perma.cc/J4VB-3L8G].

53. *Three Gorges Dam*, ENCYCLOPAEDIA BRITANNICA (last updated May 28, 2020), https://www.britannica.com/topic/Three-Gorges-Dam.

54. *World's Billionaires List: The Richest in 2020*, FORBES (last updated Mar. 18, 2020), https://www.forbes.com/billionaires/#7240717c251c [https://perma.cc/Z93X-FF3H].

55. *Each Country's Share of CO2 Emissions*, UNION OF CONCERNED SCIENTISTS (May 11, 2020), https://www.ucsusa.org/resources/each-countrys-share-co2-emissions [https://perma.cc/2BB5-Z2AS].

56. *Brown Elephants: A Glut of New Coal-Fired Power Stations Endangers China's Green Ambitions*, ECONOMIST (May 23, 2020), https://www.economist.com/china/2020/05/21/a-glut-of-new-coal-fired-power-stations-endangers-chinas-green-ambitions [https://perma.cc/9MYG-BFDJ].

2

How Capitalism Saves the Environment

What is it about capitalism that is uniquely capable of reordering society so quickly and profoundly that it can undertake the job of repairing humankind's relationship with the global environment? This chapter represents an attempt to contextualize this book in a very long and very old literature, drawing upon many of the greatest economic thinkers throughout history, and occurring in several disciplines. Against that backdrop, there is a specialized but considerable literature on the relationship between capitalism and the environment. Necessarily, I have omitted much work that is thoughtful and profound, and might shed light on the relationship between capitalism and the environment. And inevitably, my editorial choices reflect my own unique prioritizations of what is important to understand. This chapter provides some sense of where, in my view, this problem of environmentally destructive capitalism comes from. And again, given the complexities and differences in degree, it is worth taking with a grain of salt black-and-white distinctions between capitalism and socialism, including this book. I make that contrast to highlight what is important to understand about a relationship between capitalism and environmental policy.

2.1 A VERY BRIEF HISTORY OF CAPITALISM

Adam Smith's *An Inquiry into the Nature and Causes of the Wealth of Nations*[1] must certainly be a starting point, widely recognized as one of the most important books ever written, in all of history and in any subject. His articulation of markets and the division of labor, and his demonstration of how people acting in their self-interest can give rise to an economic order, serve as the underpinnings of capitalism. Karl Marx, ironically, was probably the first to attempt to study capitalism as a system, though he usually referred to it as a "capitalist mode of production." Of course, Marx focused on "class struggle" as a consequence of capitalism, and ultimately the source of its demise.[2] Sociologists such as Max Weber[3] and more contemporary scholars such as James Coleman[4] and Mark Granovetter[5] have contributed to understanding the effects of capitalism on social relations and institutions, and vice versa.

Karl Polanyi provided a more precise understanding of capitalism, the crux of the problem with capitalism, and the potential for coping with capitalism. Capitalism requires that factors of production – in Polanyi's time, labor, land, and money – must be freely bought and sold.[6] A central tenet of capitalism is that ventures must be allowed to succeed or fail. Failure can occur when labor, land, or money is withdrawn, and redeployed in a more worthy, successful venture. For Polanyi, capitalism's core was a "self-regulating market," which could only function under certain social circumstances. Necessarily, then, any society that accepts a self-regulating market will have to subordinate its social structure to the needs of the market.[7]

Despite the slight tautology, one does not need to be a socialist to see that global markets have, in fact, come to require things of societies that would otherwise not be supplied. Profit-seeking firms can convince, coerce, or tempt legislators to pass favorable laws. The age-old common law of nuisance protects against the "unreasonable interference with the use and enjoyment" of land. Livestock farmers were held liable for the odors, flies, and other disamenities suffered by their neighbors, until they were able to obtain passage of "Right-to-farm" laws, which change nuisance law to insulate livestock farmers from liability, unique only to farmers. Had Polanyi lived to the modern day, he might have been appalled at the power that global financial institutions have to repel regulation and move assets to countries willing to reduce regulation and taxation. And Polanyi might have looked askance at section 230 of the Communications Decency Act, which prevents social media firms from being held liable for content they publish for their users. It has protected social media firms from liability for publishing content aiding terrorist organizations,[8] child sex traffickers,[9] conspiracy theorists claiming that the Holocaust and school shootings never happened,[10] and other purveyors of odiously defamatory material. This is not an immunity enjoyed by print newspapers[11] and represents a significant carve-out from what common law tort law would have otherwise provided.[12] In Polanyi's story, instead of markets being "embedded" within society, society would become embedded in markets. Capitalism, in the form of dominant markets, would thus rip apart the social fabric of society, and even breed people of "poor character."[13] Polanyi even foresaw that the environment would be a casualty of markets, writing that "Nature would be reduced to its elements, neighborhoods in landscapes defiled, rivers polluted, military safety jeopardized, the power to produce food and raw materials destroyed."[14] But Polanyi also noticed that from time to time, society fought back, and tried to control the expansion of markets and preserve social arrangements (for better or for worse, it should be noted). This was Polanyi's "double movement," a response to the natural tendency of markets to supplant existing social arrangements:

> [T]he dynamics of modern century was governed by a double movement vital though such a countermovement was for the protection of society, in the last

analysis it was incompatible with the self-regulation of the market and thus with the market system itself.[15]

Polanyi was ahead of his time in recognizing the power and importance of social relations, possessing a deeper and more sophisticated understanding than Marx. Of course, in Polanyi's time social relations themselves were more sophisticated and powerful than in Marx's time. While Marx thought workers powerless against the onslaught of capitalism except for revolt, Polanyi believed that from time to time some pushback would be organized against capitalism's larger insults to social structures, families or communal groups. The labor movement was clearly one of them. And because many social structures depend upon environmental integrity, or a continuing supply of some natural resource, the environmental movement can also be seen to be a reaction to the excesses of capitalism.

Ultimately, however, Polanyi was skeptical of the ability of capitalist markets to sustain themselves, in view of its propensity to unravel everything else about society. Even if self-defeating, capitalism would ultimately overwhelm attempts by societies to protect their social structures. Polanyi, Marx, and Joseph Schumpeter all predicted the ultimate demise of capitalism. By becoming a remorseless master of just about every other system of human organization, they believed that capitalism would undermine the institutions and social structures upon which it rests, and then ultimately collapse upon the foundation rotted out by capitalism itself. Even Adam Smith lamented that the culmination of a productive division of labor would worsen the conditions of laborers, create a concomitant social decay, and that "[a]ll the nobler parts of the human character may be in great measure obliterated and extinguished in the great body of the people."[16]

Polanyi, Marx, and Schumpeter were joined by more modern economic thinkers that see a series of crises – the 2008 global financial crisis, climate change, and political polarization and radicalization, as evidence that indeed, nation-states have lost control of capitalism. Some of these modern pessimists, such as Gar Alperovitz,[17] Robert Heilbroner,[18] and Manfred Bienefeld,[19] conclude that capitalism has the inevitable tendency to spoil the global environment, a potentially more serious problem for humankind; institutions and social structures are eventually replaced, but there is no substitute for Earth.

If capitalism has its critics and skeptics, it has far more adherents. Indisputably, the world has grown exponentially wealthier and healthier – albeit very unevenly – and at the center of this wealth creation, almost unimaginable to Marx, is capitalism. Meanwhile, countries most closely aligned with the tenets of Marxism or (more broadly) socialism have mostly been considered failed states. Even in authoritarian countries such as China, the extent to which the economy has grown is attributable to its embrace of capitalism, in certain quarters. Comparisons between the two different types of economic systems often mislead, given the inherent complexities

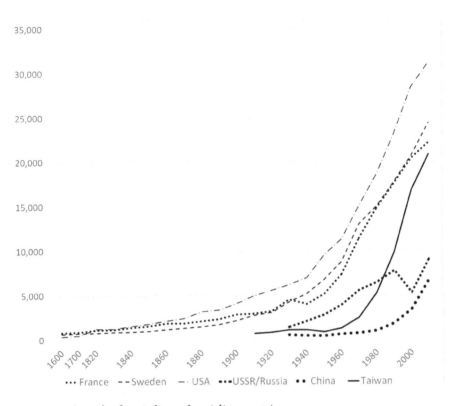

FIGURE 2.1 Growth of capitalist and socialist countries
Data source: Maddison (2010). GDP per capita in 1990 international dollars.

and differences in degree. But it so happens that few would dispute the implications of a graph such as that in Figure 2.1.

One could choose different countries and make different comparisons, and different points. But this comparison is common. And for those inclined to make it, Milton Friedman's *Capitalism and Freedom* has served as a beacon for free market advocacy. Adam Smith's own views about markets and what he then understood to be capitalism were complicated and sophisticated, as demonstrated by his other historically indispensable book, *The Theory of Moral Sentiments*. Friedman suffered no such ambivalence. His was a full-throated call for unfettered capitalism, unencumbered by ill-advised government interference. Whereas Marx, Polanyi, and other critics of capitalism see capitalism as coercive, Friedman sees capitalism a bulwark against coercive power wielded by government. For Friedman, capitalism is not just wealth-creating, but a "necessary condition for political freedom." Friedman saw government as the threat to freedom:

[H]ow can we keep the government we create from becoming a Frankenstein that will destroy the very freedom we establish it to protect? . . . Our minds tell us, and history confirms, that the great threat to freedom is the concentration of power. Government is necessary to preserve our freedom, it is an instrument through which we can exercise our freedom; yet by concentrating power in political hands it is also a threat to freedom.[20]

And whereas Polanyi and other critics of capitalism see capitalism breeding people "of poor character," Friedman sees a government as the corrupting influence on human nature, writing "Even though the man who wield this power initially be of goodwill and even though they be not corrupted by the power they exercise, the power will attract inform men of a different stamp."[21] Friedman's prescription for capitalism is unmistakable and unambiguous: government can only muck up markets, dirty up the cogs of free enterprise, and generally do mischief through coercion. Inherent in Friedman's view, shared by some of his Austrian colleagues propounding a similar view, is the sense that markets are a "natural" occurrence, forming spontaneously unless government got in the way. For Austrian scholars Ludwig von Mises and Friedrich A. Hayek, exchange is the natural propensity of humans, and the best that government could do to facilitate exchange is to enforce contracts, and little else.

The legacy of Friedman, von Mises, and Hayek have dimmed for a number of reasons. First, surging economic inequality worldwide has disillusioned many to the point of near revolt. In actuality, a much wider realization of Friedman's myopia has taken root: it is not just government that coerces, but all manner of private enterprise, operating under the guise of capitalism. Power has indeed concentrated but not always, as Friedman obsessed, in government. Not for the first time, industry holds immense power over not just economic life, but *social and political* life as well, perhaps even more than government. If anything, under-regulation seems to have left private firms and industries in control. Perhaps even more troubling is the thought that these powerful firms and industries are *not* in control, and are hurtling towards collapse, an unease exacerbated by the 2009 global financial crisis. Globally, vast majorities of populations polled believe that climate change is a serious risk and in need of government action, which is generally missing. A laissez-faire approach to antitrust law has held sway in the United States for over forty years, time and again causing the United States government to pull back from interfering with mergers that would reduce competition, and other anticompetitive practices. Now, even prominent economists at the University of Chicago – Friedman's home, and the capital of libertarian, small-government economics – have started to question the limits of government noninterventionism.[22] Friedman's warnings against government coercion have also been misinterpreted by some ideological groups to include environmental regulation, but climate change and a growing recognition of the importance of environment protection has rendered that species of demagoguery less viable.

Friedman and the Austrians have also lost standing because a more nuanced view of economic growth emerged following the rise and plateau of neoclassical economics, focusing on the institutions that make capitalism work. Countries in sub-Saharan Africa embracing capitalism have failed to thrive, and growth in Latin American countries has been tepid and sporadic, in comparison with Western European and Asian countries. Why? It turns out that government is needed to create the institutions needed for capitalism to thrive: trustworthy markets that move capital efficiently and free of corruption; financial institutions such as banks and their regulators with capacity and expertise in mobilizing resources for transacting; an infrastructure that can transport and support the movement of goods and people; and perhaps most importantly a legal system that protects property rights and enforces contracts, that is free from corruption. Whereas Friedman and the Austrians envisioned government as just a neutral referee enforcing contracts, a school of institutionalist scholars recognized institutions as unavoidably steering markets in one way or another. Up to this point, at least, capitalism has not generally been steered by its institutions towards a healthy relationship with the global environment.

This insight – that institutions matter for economic growth – was a major part of the field of institutional economics, which has now produced some Nobel Laureates of its own. What institutions, then, are needed for capitalism to thrive? In 1989, John Williamson, then a senior fellow at the Institute for International Economics (and once at the World Bank) circulated a survey of economists about what policies they thought would spur economic growth in Latin America, which became a ten-point list known as the "Washington Consensus."[23] They were fairly standard economic fare, and emphasized liberalization of trade and commerce, and a nod to anticorruption. Expanding upon that, Dani Rodrik proposed ten additional policies, and pointedly emphasized the need for better legal and political institutions, with some nod to poverty reduction.[24] In *Good Capitalism, Bad Capitalism, and the Economics of Growth and Prosperity*, Baumol, Litan, and Schramm try to narrow the list, focusing instead on the incentives produced by institutions to innovate and undertake wealth-creation.[25] Daron Acemoglu and James Robinson, in *Why Nations Fail* and in other works, have focused discussion on "extractive institutions," which are exploitive in nature and, not coincidentally, hinder economic growth.[26]

These and other scholars in this area have at least two commonalities. First, corruption is a pervasive concern among economists, for obvious reasons. Healthy capitalism – and healthy democracy, as well – require that resources flow to the most meritorious uses, and not those that benefit from a bribe for public officials. Second, almost all economists would agree that a robust and sound legal system should be in place to enforce contracts and protect private property rights. Recall how crucial it was for securing investors for American rail expansion that reasonable expectations of profit be honored, and that sovereign expropriation – the bogeyman of socialist societies – be out of the question.

Both of these sound reasonable in theory, but fail to grasp a key subtlety of legal rules and institutions. The mistake is an extension of Friedman's simplistic view that government should just be a neutral referee in case of contract dispute, "calling balls and strikes," as it were. The problem is that property rights can be *too protected*, which can itself be the source of undue government influence. In fact, the banner of property rights protection has been effectively used to ensconce incumbent business, at the expense of new entrants, which should certainly be a source of consternation to economists.

Lawmaking in general has emphatically sided with industry incumbents, often by slow-walking regulations. Friedman's fear of government coercion has been turned on its head, with property owners and capital owners using threats of litigation to intimidate governments from regulating land use or pollution. In institutional terms, government institutions have done an excellent job of protecting private property rights; too good in fact. The countervailing institutions concerned with environmental protection have failed to keep up.

There is still one more thing to say about the sin of oversimplification. A repudiation of Gross Domestic Product as the sole criteria for progress has been underway for decades. All the way back in 1972, William Nordhaus and James Tobin, two Nobel Laureates, said that "maximization of [GDP] is not a proper objective of policy. Economists all know that."[27] GDP remains the key metric for economic activity, in part because of the lack of alternatives. A substantial group of researchers, including prominent economists, have called for attention being paid to "happiness," or "subjective well-being."[28] Clearly, surveys can find credible measures of life satisfaction, happiness, and well-being, which can also manifest themselves in health metrics and economic performance. Surveys can and have highlighted happiness indices stagnating or even declining, even as GDP increases.[29] Apparently, more needs to be done before one of these indices becomes a staple of public policy and lawmaking. But the prominence of the literature casts a sidelong glance at the staple of Friedman's brand of libertarianism: that wealth creation leading to freedom is the prescription for good government. Friedman's belief that capitalism just inevitably created better people is increasingly implausible.

There is something critically important to salvage from Friedman's legacy. While government must adjust the objectives of capitalism, the means for achieving them must be as unfettered as possible. Governments must allow markets to work, without specifying how they work. Markets, acting through the mechanism of prices, have a way of ruthlessly and efficiently eliminating less important, less useful, less productive uses of resources. In a climate-changed future in which natural resources may be scarce, the power of markets to allocate them may be all-important to bear in mind. As a poke at her own profession's propensity to spin out mathematically elegant but unrealistic models, economist Maureen O'Hara once quipped, "we know markets work in practice, but we are not sure how they work in theory."[30] They work, which is important to keep in mind.

2.2 CAPITALISM AND THE ENVIRONMENT

Writers approaching the topic from the environmental or ecological perspective contribute some important insights about the relationship of capitalism and environment. One feature almost all writers in this genre share is the correct diagnosis that economic growth for its own sake, as measured by GDP and excluding an accounting of the environmental and natural resource harms, should *not* be the end goal of an economic society. As noted above, economists would agree.

James Gustave "Gus" Speth, the longtime prominent environmental advocate and advisor to President Carter, wrote a trilogy of books laying out his vision for a society in which environmental considerations and some other human needs are assigned higher priority, and in which economic growth ceases to be the sole measure of societal well-being. Speth acknowledges (as I do) that capitalism is here to stay, and acknowledges (as I do) that socialism can and has been horrible in terms of environmental protection. While Speth therefore proposes working within capitalist systems, his *manifesto* would include some fairly strong medicine in terms of curbing some of the worst impulses for corporations, including the revocation of corporate charters, rolling back the all-important limited liability protection for shareholders, and regulatory reform of corporate lobbying governance.[31] Justin Lewis, in *Beyond Consumer Capitalism*, is critical of capitalism for having fomented hyper-consumerist cultures which, turbocharged by an advertising industry that has manipulated entire societies into maximizing consumption, not only past the point of ecological sustainability, but in ways that are unaffordable, to both individuals and society at large. For both Speth and Lewis, and many other writers that follow Polanyi, Heilbroner, Bienefeld, and Alperovitz, capitalism must be subjugated to some higher human and ecological ends. None seem to view capitalism as playing any constructive role in terms of environmental repair or protection, realms in which, as Lewis puts it, "a capitalist ethos is widely regarded as capricious and inadequate."[32]

"Industrial ecology" is a field of research which emerged in the 1990s that seeks to find technical and economic opportunities within industry to reduce environmental harm. Rather than grudgingly accept capitalism as an unfortunate reality, industrial ecology purposefully works within capitalism, seeking the cooperation of industry in formulating not only different environmental solutions, but potentially different industrial processes. If Speth, Lewis, and other writers of that ilk see capitalists – corporations, in particular – as inherently capricious, industrial ecologists hope to harness the expertise of polluting corporations to help solve the technological problems of pollution:

[I]ndustrial ecology also positions corporate entities from service companies to manufacturing companies to mining corporations to giant agricultural operations as key players in the protection of the environment. The first generation view, which sees corporations as reprobates causes us to miss out on their potential for environmental leadership especially on the technological aspects of environmental problems by looking to industry for environmental benefit.[33]

This represented a clear conceptual break from what had been at the time a dominant paradigm of pollution control, which was adversarial in nature. Industrial ecology also sounded a call to reform pollution laws that addressed pollution piecemeal, one pollutant at a time, one media at a time, one industrial process at a time, by urging focus on industries and their environments as holistic systems, so that all of the linkages (including pollution) can be addressed at once. A broader systems view would hopefully produce environmental policy that is less myopic, more focused on preservation of ecological systems, and preventing separate regulations from working at cross-purposes. For example, one area of industrial ecology would concern solid wastes, and would call for a more careful search of opportunities to recycle and reuse industrial wastes, as opposed to stringent and inflexible regulations governing the waste that might preclude productive and cost-saving reuse.

In their book, *Natural Capitalism*, Paul Hawken, Amory Lovins, and Hunter Lovins make many of these same points, and seek many of the same opportunities. Their focus is more explicitly on the contribution of natural systems to human wealth creation and well-being, a concept that has been dubbed "ecosystem services." Viewed that way, natural systems like wetlands that provide a variety of benefits to humans, such as flood control, water purification, wildlife habitat, and recreation, are capital, or "natural capital."[34]

Like industrial ecologists, natural capitalists such as Hawken, Lovins, and Lovins would install an accounting system so that firms take account of harm to natural systems caused by their production processes. The hope is that not only that polluting firms internalize environmental externalities, but that there exist some incentive for firms to restore, or repair, or, *invest* in natural capital. Like industrial ecologists, natural capitalists see a number of production processes that are both inefficient and environmentally harmful, and look for policies to reform those processes. Like industrial ecologists, they contemplate extensive tax reform, taxing some polluting harms (like carbon dioxide) and eliminating harmful expenditures, such as most agricultural subsidies. Like industrial ecologists, and unlike Speth, Lewis, Marx, Schumpeter, and Polanyi, they are hopeful about preserving both capitalism and the global environment. And importantly, like industrial ecologists, they find inspiration in the ways that natural systems produce ecosystem services and process waste, seeking to install production systems that mimic natural processes. Those natural restorative processes provide potentially important lessons for private, capitalist firms in the business of environmental restoration. This would require, as this book argues in Chapter 7, a much, much broader scientific knowledge base of how human activity affects the global environment.

My call in this book goes further than industrial ecologists and natural capitalists do. Not only do I believe that capitalism, and its profit-making corporate machines, are compatible with a more enlightened approach to environmental protection, I believe that it will be the central means by which the global environment is restored and protected. Capitalism is a powerful social force that will drive society in whatever direction it is pointed. But it has to be consciously pointed in the right direction.

2.3 ARE CAPITALISTS WILLING TO REFORM?

Polanyi seems to have been proven correct that capitalist firms, compelled to make profits in competitive markets, have supplanted many social structures, and profoundly influenced the development of people within them. But it is proving too much to say that capitalist firms are driven *only* by profits. It is true that the environment seems to be the most convenient dumping ground for external costs, causing Speth to pronounce corporations "externalizing machines." The built-in incentive to find ways to cut costs by fobbing them off on others is undeniable. But while corporations routinely greenwash and whitewash their behavior, it seems too simplistic to caricature all corporations in the era of capitalism driven solely, inexorably, by greed, and utterly indifferent to the disintegration of society and the global environment.

If there is an undeniable logic to the externalizing compulsion within capitalism, there is also much reason to expect responses pushing back. First, there is Polanyi's "double movement," efforts to protect societal structures from displacement by capitalism. Social structures are critical to most people, rivaling or surpassing economic opportunity in importance. Politically, at least in democracies, there apparently is at least as much purchase to be had by politicians promising to restore social structures, even by demagoguery or deceit, as there is in promising economic riches. The history of labor laws, environmental laws, and once upon a time antitrust laws, has vindicated Polanyi. Polanyi thought these responses would ultimately fall short, and capitalism would wind up cannibalizing both society and itself. But while all of these areas of regulation have regressed at some point, it is premature to declare defeat.

Second, it seems oversimplistic to assume that all capitalist titans are capriciously indifferent to a dark future of broken capitalism and a ruined environment. Corporate behavior may often seem to point in that direction, but a closer look is warranted. It is implausible that even the wealthiest capitalists imagine they can insulate themselves from massive crises that roil the masses. Some imagine that capitalist titans *think* they could build a moat around a castle of economic opulence and lock out the masses. This seems implausible in the environmental context. Nor does it seem likely that, even if capitalist titans think they *can* somehow construct a lifeboat for themselves, their family, and something like a community of their friends, this would seem a worthy endeavor, even to capitalists. The cognitive dissonance is just too great. The former Volvo and IKEA executive, and now a sustainability expert, Göran Carstedt, once said "People say that corporations must first and foremost make profits ... Of course they do! But that is like saying people must first and foremost breathe."[35]

As Donald Trump began the formal withdrawal of the United States from the Paris agreement, the 2015 United Nations Conference of Parties agreement that created an international framework for the reduction of greenhouse gases, the Chief Executive Officers of seventy-five large global corporations announced their support for the agreement, and their company's commitment to voluntarily contribute their share of emissions reductions. These firms included Apple, Google, Microsoft, Bank of America, Citigroup, Coca-Cola, PepsiCo, Unilever, Nestlé, Disney, and Goldman Sachs, heading a up a who's-who list of rapaciously greedy capitalists.

It is more plausible that capitalist firms, and the officers and directors therein, would *prefer* to pursue more sustainable paths of profit-making, but feel constrained by corporation laws and some hard-to-define business norms. To embark upon something less than a profit-maximization path would require the solution of two difficult problems: (i) inculcating a cultural change within the firm, and (ii) coordination with competitors and rivals. In addition to economic barriers, strongly held norms and emotions usually obstruct changes in operation. In that sense, Polanyi and the capitalism skeptics are right in that there is something inexorable about capitalism and about competitive global markets that compels a firm to make profits first and foremost.

In *The Rise and Decline of Nations*, Olson argued that special interest groups are to blame for unemployment, stagflation, and the ultimate economic decline of nations.[36] Countries with a stable political environment allow special interest groups to develop. These special interest groups exist *only* to engage in rent-seeking – the achievement of favorable government policy that secures above-normal wealth for members of the special interest group. Why else would members of special interest group pay dues, unless they expect the group to obtain benefits they could not obtain themselves as individuals?[37] Those special interest groups are the solution to the collective action problem on the industry side. Over time, if enough special interest groups secure enough above-normal wealth, then what is left over is below-normal wealth for everybody else. That, argues Olson, is the storyline of developed countries that seem to suddenly find themselves grappling with chronic economic underperformance.[38]

Olson modernizes the worry of Polanyi and Schumpeter by accurately describing the institutionalization of opposition to reform. While Olson's concern was economic reform, it is not hard to extrapolate to environmental reform. The problem is that firms that cause environmental problems are able to solve the coordination problem, while those on the environmental side are so diffuse and underresourced, they cannot.

Again, it is premature to declare defeat. The Polanyi scholar Fred Block argues that these policy conflicts are not just dry exercises in counting up dollar-weighted votes; ideology matters a great deal. Even those acolytes of Milton Friedman arguing for laissez-faire economic policies needed to invoke interests broader than just their own desire to profit. Winning policy conflicts for laissez-faire economic policies required that they invoke theories of self-regulating markets creating wealth for everyone.[39] And Friedman himself invoked *freedom* as a reason for resisting regulation, in *Capitalism and Freedom*. That found an especially ready audience in the United States.

But ideology can work against the Friedman movement, too, and is beginning to do so. Some go so far as to embrace self-declared socialists such as Bernie Sanders or Jeremy Corbyn. But even in what we might simplistically call the "capitalist" class, views on capitalism are extremely wide-ranging, as it must be given the many dimensions of capitalism and its effects. Fred Block identifies conditions in which policy change can occur, despite apparent political economic disadvantages. Tensions inevitably arise in coalitions, as Block observes, when members of a capitalist class are divided, as they are on the issue of climate change,[40] and indeed on many environmental issues generally. In those situations, charismatic leaders may emerge to seize an ideological initiative, as they most certainly can in the environmental realm. There must be hunger for environmental reform if Greta Thunberg, a Swedish teenager, can gain as wide an audience as she has. A growing majority in the United States – one of the most persistent bastions of climate denial – recognize that climate change was not a "hoax," but indeed a very serious problem. A majority of people in the United States and worldwide were willing to use the word "emergency" to describe climate change.[41]

Pessimism about the willingness of capitalist titans to embrace a more sustainable capitalism is understandable. Antienvironmental ideologues have taken Friedman's warning about government coercion to an extreme, and warped lawmaking to help incumbent firms maintain the ability to externalize social and environmental costs. In effect, antienvironmental ideologues have been more effective in solving their coordination problem, rallying firms around a platform of grievance. It might seem Pollyannaish to suppose that most capitalist titans are actually conflicted about the social and environmental effects of their enterprises, but it is at least worth remembering that the most outspoken are rarely the most representative. What is required is a way to solve the coordination problem from the environmental side. Potential leaders of that side have shown themselves often, but usually lack the sufficient critical mass, or the right platform on which to build support. This book aims to provide that platform.

In short, the circumstances have to be right, but an embrace of a new, environmentally focused capitalism is possible. It is no longer a given, but the embrace of a new capitalist focus is likely to eventually be followed by the political will to enshrine it in law. While the package of reforms proposed in this book do not represent a costless, Pareto Superior transformation of capitalism, they do represent familiar and fundamental pieces of a new, environmentally focused capitalism.

No less a capitalist icon than Margaret Thatcher pushed for British research to study climate change. In her 1990 dedication speech for the opening of the Hadley Centre for Climate Prediction and Research (a leading research institution on climate change), the Prime Minister spoke knowledgeably about the 1990 Intergovernmental Panel on Climate Change report, climatic history through the millennia, the migration of plant and animal life, rising sea levels, and the plight facing low-lying countries such as Bangladesh. An Oxford-trained chemist, it is striking how impassioned was the Iron Lady:

> Many of us have been worried for some time now about the accumulating evidence of damage to the global environment and the consequences for life on Earth and for future generations . . . we have an . . . agreed assessment from some three hundred of the world's leading scientists on what is happening to the world's climate . . . It is not something arcane or remote from everyday concerns . . . Governments and international organisations in every part of the world are going to have to sit up and take notice and respond . . . The changes which we are talking about now will occur at a faster rate than anything our natural world has known in the past. [M]ore than ever we are one world . . . The problems do not lie in the future – they are here and now – and it is our children and grandchildren, who are already growing up, who will be affected.[42]

But this Prime Minister would never let pass an opportunity to point out the merits of capitalism. She continued:

> [T]he private sector is constantly showing the way with its ingenuity and inventiveness . . . It shows what can be done by people struggling to remain competitive and by doing all the necessary research for that and having an excellent by-product in environmental benefits.[43]

Although 1990 was eons ago politically, a strong environmental sentiment by this ardent advocate of capitalism is worthy of a bit of notice. For all the criticism leveled at Mrs. Thatcher, she did not indulge in whims. This serious thought by one of the twentieth-century's leading lights of capitalism is one that will find its way to daylight again. At some point in the near to intermediate future, a sufficient mass of capitalists will join a sufficient mass of interest groups and government actors in agreement, that unless dramatic transformation of capitalism takes place, the global economy will collapse, and will take modern human civilization down with it.

2.4 THE FEATURES OF CAPITALISM

What exactly is capitalism? There is no widely agreed-upon formal definition, among economists or anybody else. There are, however, some common elements in many notions of capital. Geoffrey Hodgson, in *Conceptualizing Capitalism*, defines capitalism as consisting of six components:

1. A legal system supporting widespread individual rights and liberties to own, buy, and sell private property,
2. Widespread commodity exchange and markets involving money,
3. Widespread private ownership of the means of production by firms producing goods or services for sale in the pursuit of profit,
4. Much of production organized separately and apart from the home and family,
5. Widespread wage labor and employment contracts, and
6. A developed financial system with banking institutions, the widespread use of credit with property as collateral, and the selling of debt.[44]

One could quibble with this definition as being lengthier and therefore more restrictive than necessary. But Hodgson's treatment of capitalism synthesizes many different kinds of capitalism, and brings together commonalities across time, geography, and culture. His focus, like that of this book, are those features that make capitalism such a powerful economic and social force.

Capitalism is not just trading and markets, which have existed for thousands of years. Capitalism requires that factors of production must be freely bought and sold. The transformative power of capitalism stems from its capacity to connect otherwise far-flung actors with each other, amplifying trading, and increasing the potential for gains from trading. British grain markets in the middle of the eighteenth century had already ceased to be exclusively local, suggesting that already there were connections that extended well beyond a local market. It is this ability to extend the reach of both investors and entrepreneurs, as well as all factors of production.

Hodgson's definition is institutional in focus, because it requires some amount of *financial infrastructure* in order for capitalism to take root and thrive. In order for contracts and property to be protected by law over long distances and potentially very different people, legal rules and institutions must exist, and be robust enough to earn the trust of all parties to a venture. So critical is the development of those legal rules and institutions that it helped give rise to an entire subfield, institutional economics, which produced several of its own Nobel Laureates.

Central to Hodgson's thinking is the role of debt. Before the legal rules and institutions were developed to incur debt to finance large-scale enterprise, financing was almost exclusively obtained by saving up, or tapping into local sources. The ability to raise money is crucial to capitalism, and the development of banks and other lending institutions was crucial to launching enterprises that might otherwise have languished. And once debt became negotiable, it took on some aspects of a *price*, which could signal something about the merits of the project.

Prices, as the Austrian school of small-government economics argued, are the lifeblood of economics, as they reduce an unfathomable amount of complex information into a single number, representing the opportunity cost of a good or activity. But prices are not just expressions of value; they critically convey *information*, which would otherwise be impossible to transmit and process. Relevant information may reside in a variety of disparate, far-flung places. Friedrich Hayek, in his Nobel Laureate speech, summed up perhaps the central tenet of the Austrian school:

> Into the determination of these prices and wages there will enter the effects of particular information possessed by every one of the participants in the market process – a sum of facts which in their totality cannot be known to the scientific observer, or to any other single brain. It is indeed the source of the superiority of the market order, and the reason why, when it is not suppressed by the powers of government, it regularly displaces other types of order, that in the resulting allocation of resources more of the knowledge of particular facts will be utilized which exists only dispersed among uncounted persons, than any one person can possess.[45]

Hayek owes a debt to Karl Polanyi's brother, Michael, much a student of capitalism and socialism himself. Michael Polanyi developed the idea of *tacit* information, knowledge that is not recorded or even explicit. And yet, tacit information is crucial information, as certain unspoken norms fill many contractual gaps, many common expectations unspoken, simply because they are understood. Prices are important because they capture, better than any other information-gathering mechanism, these implicit, *tacit* pieces of information.

In an essay, *I, Pencil*, the role of prices is illustrated using the surprisingly complex production chain of an ordinary pencil. Back in 1958 when the essay was written by Leonard Read, a pencil consisted of wood harvested from a cedar tree in Oregon, but that act of logging had many antecedents, such as the logger, the chain saw and other logging gear, and materials used to make the chain saw and other gear. After felling a tree, the trucks, the fuel, and the drivers are needed to transport raw logs to a mill in California, which cuts them into the distinctive octagonal barrel shape, kiln-dried, bored with a hole to accommodate the graphite (by 1958 lead had been eliminated from pencils) shaft. Actually, the graphite is a mix of graphite, mined in Southeast Asia, and clay, which is mined in Mississippi. A tiny and thin slab of metal is cut, rolled and shaped to fit around the pencil shaft to hold the eraser, which is a rubber-like product that itself is composed of many ingredients.

At the end of a paean to a pencil, the reader is impressed that a previously unimaginable amount of industrial coordination is required to manufacture a simple pencil. The point of the exercise is to appreciate how that coordination is achieved through *prices*, each ingredient having a distinct market price which communicated to all potential users its scarcity. The price of graphite reflects the mining conditions, labor costs, transport costs, and the opportunity costs of using graphite for pencils; graphite is also used for brake linings, and other industrial uses as well. But the marvel of markets is that so many different ingredients can be purchased, obtained, and shipped, and all along the entire production chain, prices communicate to the pencil entrepreneur how scarce each ingredient is, or how difficult it is to obtain. The Hayekian/Polanyi point is this: prices are mechanisms by which an intractable amount of information is synthesized into a single number, enabling users to evaluate, by considering the prices, whether to go ahead with a pencil factory. Prices are the most awesome information network known to humankind, gathering unfathomable amounts of information and sending simple and stark signals to buyers about scarcity and opportunity costs. If cars become more important and car-buying increases and graphite becomes more valuable, then the cost of pencils increase, unless a production change can be made to substitute for lost graphite.

On this point of prices as information, the Austrians have surely routed the socialists, both in theory and in practice. No centrally planned economy has been successful in allocating resources efficiently for any breadth of resources for any length of time. As Thomas Piketty, no shill for capitalism, put it:

> People need to eat, dress, move about, and find housing, and these things require large numbers of workers in production units of various sizes, sometimes quite small, which can be organized only in a fairly decentralized way. Society depends on each person's knowledge and aspirations and sometimes requires small businesses funded with private capital and employing a handful of workers.[46]

Not only does socialism fail in its economic objective, it must inevitably fail in its political objective. As Albert Schäffle argued, any central authority, purporting to be acting on behalf of a collective, could only gather the disparate pieces of information through a centralization of power, which would run counter to the egalitarian purposes of a collective in the first place.[47]

Prices play another critical role, which give rise to another feature of capitalism: *competition*. Without competition and the risk of failure, there is no capitalism, only oligarchy or monopoly. And without competition, there is no incentive for innovation. Competition provides the impetus for capitalist firms to continuously innovate, out of fear that unless they do, rival firms may discover more efficient methods of production and be able to offer better goods at lower prices. Not only does capitalism offer the sharpest spur for innovation, but it offers the best incubator for innovation. The flipside of failure is success, and the profit motive which drives capitalism also drives innovation.

But none of this is possible without the financial infrastructure, which includes most critically, the legal rules and institutions that *form* a capitalist economy. Diverse legal rules and institutions can make capitalist economies work in different ways, some more profitable than others. But it is a mistake, as small-government advocates following Friedman and the Austrians have made, to think of laws only as necessarily *limiting* capitalism. *Laws and government are crucial to capitalism.* The vast markets accessed by capitalism depend upon a robust and reliable legal system that can enforce contracts and protect property rights, and is perceived, as John Commons argued, as reasonable, appropriate, and fair.[48] Moreover, that legitimacy must be strong enough to extend into other sovereign jurisdictions, if capitalism is to cross boundaries. The railroad expansion in the mid-nineteenth century United States was accomplished in large part because of foreign financing, which would not be forthcoming unless Americans were willing to subject themselves to laws governing foreign investors. To reiterate a theme from earlier in this chapter, laws represent complex and explicit choices that shape capitalism; but it is a fatal mistake to consider laws as obstacles to capitalism. The existence of laws and government are condition precedents to capitalism.

2.5 STATE CAPITALISM IS INFERIOR

From 1978 until 2020, the year that the COVID-19 virus derailed the global economy, the People's Republic of China grew an average of almost 10 percent a year, and produced over 300 billionaires. Over that period, more than 850 million Chinese people were lifted out of poverty.[49] In 2011, China surpassed Japan as the second-largest economy in the world. Former U.S. Treasury Secretary Henry Paulsen once remarked hopefully that a partnership between the United States and China to deploy renewable energy technologies could draw upon the strengths of both countries: the technological creativity of Americans and the amazing ability of Chinese industry to scale up production quickly.[50]

And yet China has remained an authoritarian state. China has clearly carved out a very special place for capitalism in its authoritarian state, but as its assault on civil liberties in Hong Kong demonstrates, it clearly remains committed to an authoritarian state, dependent upon centralized political control. The economic decentralization that is essential to capitalism does not necessarily lead to political freedoms. Moreover, the country's economic decentralization is partial, as it must be in an authoritarian regime. Its vast banking system remains under state control. Of the ninety-five Chinese companies on the 2014 Fortune 500 list, seventy-five were state-owned.[51] Rapid economic growth, and the fact that some people have been allowed to become fabulously wealthy, does not mean that the country has *fully* embraced capitalism.

The People's Republic of China is an example of what Geoffrey Hodgson calls "state capitalism," or what Baumol, Litan and Schramm call "state-guided capitalism," a capitalist economy with state control over some allocations of capital resources. This state control over some capital resources has generated meteoric economic growth, but that reflects the conscious and explicit political choice that

China has made, maintained for the last half century, that the country must undertake economic growth. There is clearly enough law for capitalism to thrive in certain quarters, and even attract a great deal of foreign investment. But that political choice was made by the Chinese Communist Party, more specifically the Politburo Standing Committee, and made in ignorance of many, many other political, social, and environmental consequences. The uncountably many environmental insults – thousands of dead pigs washing up ashore near the world's most populous city, the undrinkability of tap water, impenetrable smog in its cities, and China's pariah status as the world's largest greenhouse gas emitter – are signs of this ignorance. But not only is such massive degradation economically inefficient in itself, there is also good reason to believe that capitalism does not quite function as well in authoritarian China as it does in countries with more decentralized political control, more political freedoms, and more *democracy*. China, by embracing capitalism for certain limited purposes, is simply executing an economic growth plan more effectively than the Soviet Union and all of those failed twentieth-century authoritarian-socialist states.

Without a counterfactual of what China would have been in the absence of state control altogether, it is hard to say what it would have done, but there is good reason to suppose that China would be an even more prosperous, much more efficient, and certainly much cleaner society with a more complete embrace of capitalism. There is a reason that its GDP per capita, despite all that political emphasis on growth, lags behind capitalist counterparts, even neighboring South Korea. While China emits more greenhouse gases than ten of the largest greenhouse gas-emitting countries in the world, it had less than a third of the GDP of those combined countries.[52] With central political control over its vast banking system, capital investment inevitably gets funneled toward projects enjoying Party favor. No one would say that capital investment in the United States is perfect, but it is vastly more efficient than in China. Capital is quickly drying up for anything relating to coal in the United States, not only in anticipation of a global need to reduce greenhouse gas emissions, but also because coal has become uneconomic. Capitalism is less creative in China than it is in countries with greater political freedoms, and more complete forms of capitalism. Authoritarian states are simply and necessarily less creative. After all, there is a reason that China relies heavily on thievery of ideas and intellectual property for industrial growth.

How does this superiority of capitalism help save humankind from environmental catastrophe? The brand of capitalism proposed in this book is premised on the ability to detect, quantify, and price environmental harm. Even if that condition is not *fully* met, I argue that where and when it can be met, it should be implemented in the form of an environmental tax. If it cannot be met, reasonably close proxies might serve a sufficiently similar purpose. A capitalist approach that includes environmental taxes would not only be a more economical approach, but would offer better environmental results as well. If this condition can be met, even partially, the features of capitalism are likely to be more suited to environmental protection than alternative forms of economic or environmental governance. I offer three reasons why capitalism represents a better economic system than socialism or central planning, for purposes of restoring and protecting the environment: prices, innovation, and scale production.

2.6 CHOOSING CAPITALISM TO SAVE THE ENVIRONMENT: PRICES AS INFORMATION

First, the influence of a price is most important when environmental effects are felt far away. Ecological systems are complex and interconnected with other ecological systems, sometimes at a great distance. For example, nutrient pollution from the entire Mississippi River watershed has far exceeded the capacity of the river system to assimilate pollution so that every summer, a hyper-polluted "dead zone," within which there is almost no marine life, forms in the Gulf of Mexico near the mouth of the river. The cause of the dead zone, usually about the size of New Jersey, is pollution in the form of nitrogen and phosphorus from farms and sewage from the thirty-one states that drain into the Mississippi, so most of the pollution sources are thousands of miles away from the dead zone. Most municipalities and counties of any appreciable size are required under the Clean Water Act to treat their sewage before releasing it into waterways. Not so for farms. Over-application of fertilizer by farmers seeking an inexpensive way to boost yields is the leading culprit of nutrient pollution. But fertilizer runoff from farms – so-called "nonpoint source" pollution – is difficult to measure and, because of the political power of the agricultural industry, not monitored by the EPA. Some economic estimates of the dead zone exist, with caveats as to how much information they exclude, but even modest lower-bound estimates would surprise farmers and others that view the Mississippi River and its tributaries as a common dumping ground.

To be sure, a number of policy proposals exist, most of which have to do with curbing nonpoint source pollution from the predominantly farming region of the American Midwest. American farmers push back with the argument that the food they grow feeds Americans and increasingly, people all over the world. The United States is the world's largest food exporter. If farmers were required to reduce the amount of fertilizer applied to crops, or were otherwise required to reduce the amount of nonpoint source pollution running off of their farms, growing might be more costly, and the costs might be passed onto consumers. Would consumers tolerate price increases? Would countries receiving American agricultural exports tolerate price increases? As well, curtailment of domestic agricultural production might be replaced by imports, which contribute their own environmental problems by virtue of the need to transport them for long distances. And as it turns out, the production of fertilizer is very energy-intensive, and accounts for a fair amount of greenhouse gas emission. A wide variety of considerations, a daunting menu of information needs, environmental and economic, potentially factor into decisions about how to reduce nonpoint source pollution, and that information may come from all over the world. Sound like a familiar problem?

Two environmental taxes, both feasible (if both politically fraught), would simplify the problem if enacted: a fertilizer tax and a carbon tax. Both of these are treated in Chapter 6, but are worth a brief description here. As it turns out, both would raise the cost of applying fertilizer, as a carbon tax would increase the costs of the energy used to produce the fertilizer. Fertilizer is applied in many different ways by different farmers, so a translation from fertilizer to water pollution could be fraught with heterogeneity. But generally, if the cost of nutrient pollution could be estimated and converted into a flat per-pound tax, then a fertilizer tax could change farming decisions. As for carbon dioxide emissions, twice under the Obama Administration, an interagency group was convened to estimate the costs of climate change and convert it into a "social cost of carbon" that reflects the marginal damage from emitting a ton-equivalent of carbon dioxide. That figure is tailor-made for a carbon tax, which would then cover the wide, wide variety of energy consumed throughout the huge supply chain embodied in agricultural products, much longer than that of a pencil. A carbon tax would raise the costs of transporting agricultural products long distances, and might favor rail transportation over trucks. A carbon tax would raise the costs of anything energy-intensive, so that the use of tractors might have to be reevaluated, or tractors themselves might need to evolve. Tractor makers already are innovating, in the interests of saving farmers money, but might redouble their efforts were tractor emissions taxed.

With those two environmental taxes, the thousands, maybe millions of decisions about farming, land use, production, livestock, sewage treatment, land development, manufacturing, and others, could be simplified greatly. The smaller question of whether and how to farm would then be informed not only by market prices, but also these two environmental prices, which serve as a proxy for the environmental harm imposed by nutrient pollution and climate change. Faced with a marginal cost of applying fertilizer, farmers may be moved to consider ways in which they might alter planting to reduce fertilizer application. Differential transportation distances would be reflected in different carbon tax bills faced by transporters. Even the opaque footprint of fertilizer would be revealed, as fertilizer manufacturers would be forced to either absorb the carbon tax of energy used to produce it, or pass the cost to farmers. Farmers might, given the cost, figure out a way to apply less fertilizer, which could involve cover crops, or other crops. All of these environmental costs may or may not be passed onto consumers, who become the ultimate judges on whether these agricultural products are worth having, or whether alternatives might prevail. But consumers are not trying to gather and collate widely disparate and disorganized pieces of information. What was a complex balancing of a variety of factors is boiled down to one: price.

Some environmental advocates object to the pricing of environmental harm, on the grounds that they understate the true costs. That is undoubtably true more often than not. That objection makes the perfect the enemy of the good. It also overlooks the more important role of prices as information. A carbon tax serves as an illustration of this point. The "carbon footprint" of a product – the amount of carbon dioxide emissions resulting from production of the product, from raw materials to parts to assembly to finished product – is notoriously hard to determine, given the variety of materials and activities that go into a typical product. Fertilizer is one example: not the EPA, and not even the data-rich U.S. Department of Agriculture could tell you exactly how much energy went into the production of synthetic fertilizers.

This lack of good information about the carbon footprint of a product also hangs a dark cloud over one of the longest-running and most influential environmental, agricultural, and industrial programs in the United States: the ethanol mandate, which requires refiners to blend in a minimum amount of plant-based fuel into the nation's gasoline supply. With bipartisan support and bipartisan opposition, but with uniform support from farm states, the ethanol mandate has enjoyed some support from some environmental organizations on the grounds that these "biofuels" such as ethanol can substitute for petroleum, and reduce greenhouse gas emissions from transportation. Biofuels emit carbon dioxide when burned, but because they are derived from plants, they also sequester carbon dioxide in the plant growth stage. Some ethanol advocates have claimed that using corn-based ethanol to power motor vehicles may reduce carbon dioxide emissions by as much as 30 percent when compared with conventional gasoline. But this estimate, an aggressively optimistic one at that, only covers the combustion stage. If one considers the *life-cycle emissions* – the total net changes in carbon dioxide emissions attributable to producing ethanol, then its comparative advantages over gasoline become ambiguous or even turn into disadvantages. The comparison would depend on the farming and harvesting practices of growing biofeedstocks (including fertilizer usage!), and the production process of converting the biofeedstock into a refinable fuel. And it still says nothing of construction of the conversion plant itself. This is an enormously complicated determination, and accounting for the emissions of each stage is extremely difficult. The best guess is that the ethanol mandate is just another expensive agricultural subsidy.

Does the ethanol mandate result in lower greenhouse gas emissions? Without a carbon tax, it is impossible to know. Would Midwestern farmers be able and willing to reduce the amount of fertilizer they apply to their crops? Without some sort of a tax on nutrient pollution, it would be impossible to know; no farmer would spend the time to even explore alternative planting methods, crops, or even the business of farming altogether. Imperfect information is better than none, and a capitalist orientation centered upon the derivation of environmental taxes would generate much-needed information.

2.7 CHOOSING CAPITALISM TO SAVE THE ENVIRONMENT: INNOVATION

Frankly, humankind needs some technological breakthroughs akin to miracles to rescue the planet on which it depends. A second reason that capitalism is suited to the job of environmental restoration and protection is its propensity to spur innovation. Humankind does not currently have the technological capability to adequately repair harm already done to the environment, or to even monitor ongoing and future harms. It certainly does not have sufficient technological capability to deal with climate change. Humankind is ill-equipped to reduce its carbon footprint, adapt to unavoidable climatic changes, or reverse some of the emissions already extant in the biosphere. Innovation is an existential matter to humankind and, for that matter, most of the species currently in existence on the planet.

There are no magic bullets for innovation. By their nature, innovation is uncertain, and often unexpected. Many solutions are still unknown, perhaps not even dreamed of yet. Hawken et al. describe the experience of a plant operations manager at a Dow Chemical plant in Louisiana, who experimented with a contest among its line workers to suggest operational efficiencies. No tinkerers need apply: project proposals were required to provide a minimum return on investment of 50 percent. In the first year, he received twenty-seven suggestions that averaged a return of 173 percent. In the second year, he received thirty-two suggestions that averaged a return of 340 percent. Somehow, these not-so-little improvements had escaped the attention of management.[53] Like the Swedish line workers that found ways to reduce NOx emissions, Dow workers most intimate with plant operations were able to find an astounding number of operational improvements. Perhaps the most that could be said about the role of government in innovation is that the best that it can do is provide the incentives for innovation, but avoid interfering with development.

One example of unexpected innovation started in the automotive industry, and has now unexpectedly branched out into residential electricity generation and storage. More than a few financial analysts expressed surprise when the electric carmaker Tesla surpassed the *combined* value of Ford and General Motors in January 2020. That was such a shocking event because at the time Ford and GM were selling twenty-six times as many cars as Tesla. What gives? Financial analysts writing about the astronomical value of Tesla stock see electric vehicles as a growth industry – itself a good sign – and that Tesla had a unique head start on all of the other carmakers in the world. Tesla CEO Elon Musk is nothing if not an opportunistic capitalist, and despite his mercurial management of the company, he seems to have assured investors that his company is poised to make and sell many, many more electric vehicles.

Parenthetically, and potentially very relevant, Tesla acquired a rooftop solar company, Solar City, in 2016. What is the connection? Tesla and Solar City were two of the entities out there entertaining the idea that electric vehicles could serve a residential household as a *battery*, collecting and storing excess solar energy during the sunny day, for drawing down at night. If this idea remains nascent, the idea of storing excess solar energy has pulled Tesla into the energy storage business, as a supplement to its rooftop solar business. Combining electric vehicle technology and rooftop solar technology has the potential to reduce greenhouse gas emissions and save money in *two* realms, transportation and home electricity.

Perhaps even more importantly, Tesla's foray into residential electricity has actually enabled an even broader push, into the large-scale energy storage business. Energy stored in large batteries – another area where capitalist energies might colonize – is extremely useful in its ability to deliver electricity when demand unexpectedly surges. Energy storage is such an important technology because it can fix a chronic problem with renewable energy sources such as wind and solar: their intermittency. Storing excess electricity generated by renewable sources adds value to the renewable source, and represents a potentially low-cost, zero-carbon replacement for fossil fuel-fired power plants built to handle sporadic and unexpected peak demands. State regulators and electric utilities are scrambling to find alternative ways of delivering power during these peak demand times, without having to start up a fossil fuel-fired power plant.

Suffice it to say, electric vehicle dominance is far from assured for Tesla. In recent years, the behemoth automaker General Motors has jettisoned some of its costly capital assets to raise money to try and challenge Tesla for electric vehicle leadership. Whether the stodgy, century-old company, which had required federal subsidies in 2010 to survive, can reinvent itself, is an open question. But it is likely to play a role in ensuring that Tesla continues to innovate, and perhaps not just in the electric vehicle industry.

2.8 CHOOSING CAPITALISM TO SAVE THE ENVIRONMENT: LARGE-SCALE DEPLOYMENT

Finally, a third reason that capitalism is suited to the job of environmental restoration and protection is its ability to undertake and complete projects at very large scales. In keeping with a major thesis of this book, construction at very large scales should give us a little pause, because of the propensity of capital to metastasize into a source of political resistance to change. But some global problems, especially climate change, may require very large-scale enterprises.

For example, because greenhouse gas emissions may already have passed a threshold for catastrophic climate change, technology is almost certainly needed to chemically capture carbon dioxide from ambient air. But carbon dioxide is only about 0.15% of ambient air by molecular weight, and a tremendous amount of ambient air must be processed just to capture a small amount of carbon dioxide. This technology has often been referred to as "direct air capture," or "carbon removal." Given that inherent limitation, direct air capture technology must be deployed at vast scales in order to make any appreciable difference in greenhouse gas concentrations. There is certainly no guarantee that direct air capture will be a silver bullet. But if it is to be an effectual item on a menu of survival techniques, it will more assuredly be accomplished under the incentives of a capitalist economy.

Capitalism might also help with the looming crisis of climate change by helping to ensure the supply of vital life staples such as food, water, and other basic needs in future shortages caused by climate-change. In a climate-changed future, there is the distinct possibility that supplies of vital life staples may run short, possibly for long periods of time. Droughts are projected to last longer, with water supplies and growing conditions increasingly precarious. Capitalist enterprise could, first of all, provide the impetus to finally reform a dizzying multitude of price distortions that plague water supply and agriculture worldwide. Second, capitalist enterprise can undertake scale production of some emergent technologies that might alleviate shortages. Desalination technology can convert salty seawater into drinkable freshwater.[54] A number of environmental and economic issues need to be solved to deploy these technologies at large scales, but in a crisis, solutions will be more likely to present themselves.

A technology that is already being adopted to produce food is the modernized version of old-fashioned greenhouses. The tiny country of the Netherlands, with its 17 million people crowded onto 13,000 square miles, is the second largest food exporter in the world,[55] exporting fully three-quarters that of the United States in 2017.[56] The secret to Dutch agriculture is its climate-controlled, low-energy green-houses that project solar panel-powered artificial sunlight around the clock. Dutch greenhouses produce lettuce at ten times the yield[57] and tomatoes at fifteen times the yield outdoors in the United States[58] while using less than one-thirteenth the amount of water,[59] very little in the way of synthetic pesticides and, of course, very little fertilizer given its advanced composting techniques. Sustained shortages in a climate-changed future might require that a capitalist take hold of greenhouse growing and expand production to feed the masses that might otherwise revolt.

2.9 CHOOSE CAPITALISM

Clearly, the job in front of humankind is enormous, complex, and many-faceted. The best hope is to be able to identify certain human impacts that are clearly harmful to the global environment, and to disincentivize them. Getting back to notions of institutions in capitalism, what is crucial is aligning the right incentives with profit-making activity. What capitalism does so well – beyond human compre-hension – is coordinate activity and send broad signals about scarcity. Information about a wide variety of environmental phenomena is extremely difficult to collect and process. If a set of environmental taxes can help establish a network of environ-mental prices, then an unfathomably large and complex machinery will have been set in motion in the right direction.

Also, because of the need for new scientific solutions to this daunting list of problems, new science and technology is desperately needed. Capitalism is tried and true in terms of producing innovation. Again drawing upon the study of institutions, it is not so much that individuals need a profit-motive in order to tinker, but the prospect of profit-making has to be present in order for institutions, including corporations, to devote resources, attention, and energy towards the development of solutions to environmental problems. Corporations can and should demonstrate social responsibility by attempting to mitigate their impacts on the global environment, but a much more conscious push for new knowledge, new techniques, and new solutions are needed.

Finally, the scale of needed change is profound. Huge networks of infrastructure centered upon a fossil fuel-centered economy must somehow be replaced or adapted to new ways of generating, transmitting, consuming, and storing energy. A global system of feeding seven billion humans (and counting), unsustainable on its face, must be morphed into something else that can fill that huge role. About a billion and a half cars and trucks in the world must, over time, be swapped out for vehicles that must be dramatically different.

This is a daunting to-do list, but look a bit more carefully among the gloomy news. Elon Musk, a freewheeling, pot-smoking entrepreneur shows signs of breaking into not one, but two industries dominated by behemoths with political power. Thanks to California emissions standards, automobile manufacturers have developed cars that emit a fraction of what they did less than a generation ago. Hybrid electric vehicles have thoroughly penetrated an American market that powerful American politicians had tried to cordon off for American manufacturers only. At least two companies have developed meat substitutes that are now widely judged to be indistinguishable from meat, and have established product outposts in the ancient power centers of fast food, McDonald's and Burger King. The tiny country of the Netherlands, about half the size of West Virginia, exports almost as much food as the United States, able to ship fresh produce all the way to Africa. At bottom, all of these accomplishments and thousands more are and were capitalist in nature. While they collectively represent a trifle of what still needs to be accomplished, they were also undertaken without the correct incentives in place, and thus also represent the tremendous promise of capitalism.

Notes

1. ADAM SMITH, AN INQUIRY INTO THE NATURE AND CAUSES OF THE WEALTH OF NATIONS 736 (1776).
2. KARL MARX, CONTRIBUTION TO THE CRITIQUE OF POLITICAL ECONOMY (1867).
3. MAX WEBER, THE PROTESTANT ETHIC AND THE SPIRIT OF CAPITALISM (1905).
4. JAMES S. COLEMAN, FOUNDATIONS OF SOCIAL THEORY (1994).

5. Richard Swedberg & Mark Granovetter, *Introduction, in* THE SOCIOLOGY OF ECONOMIC LIFE (M. Granovetter ed., 2018).

6. KARL POLANYI, THE GREAT TRANSFORMATION: THE POLITICAL AND ECONOMIC ORIGINS OF OUR TIME 72 (1944).

7. KARL POLANYI, THE GREAT TRANSFORMATION: THE POLITICAL AND ECONOMIC ORIGINS OF OUR TIME 71 (1944).

8. Danielle Keats Citron & Benjamin Wittes, *The Internet Will Not Break: Denying Bad Samaritans Sec. 230 Immunity*, 86 FORDHAM L. REV. 401 (2017).

9. Mary Graw Leary, *The Indecency and Injustice of section 230 of the Communications Decency Act*, 41 HARV. J.L. & PUB. POL'Y 553 (2018). There is now an exception to section 230 that allows for liability in the case of child sex trafficking. 47 U.S.C. §230(e)(5).

10. Kate Starbird, *Examining the Alternative Media Ecosystem Through the Production of Alternative Narratives of Mass Shooting Events on Twitter*, PROCEEDINGS OF THE ELEVENTH INTERNATIONAL AAAI CONFERENCE ON WEB AND SOCIAL MEDIA, http://faculty.washington.edu/kstarbi/Alt_Narratives_ICWSM17-CameraReady.pdf.

11. Davis R. Sheridan, *Zeran v. AOL and the Effect of Section 230 of the Communications Decency Act upon Liability for Defamation on the Internet*, 61 ALB. L. REV. 147 (1997).

12. David S. Ardia, *Free Speech Savior or Shield For Scoundrels: An Empirical Study of Intermediary Immunity Under Section 230 of The Communications Decency Act*, 43 LOY. L.A. L. REV. 373 (2009).

13. KARL POLANYI, THE GREAT TRANSFORMATION: THE POLITICAL AND ECONOMIC ORIGINS OF OUR TIME 128 (1944).

14. KARL POLANYI, THE GREAT TRANSFORMATION: THE POLITICAL AND ECONOMIC ORIGINS OF OUR TIME 73 (1944).

15. KARL POLANYI, THE GREAT TRANSFORMATION: THE POLITICAL AND ECONOMIC ORIGINS OF OUR TIME 130 (1944).

16. ADAM SMITH, AN INQUIRY INTO THE NATURE AND CAUSES OF THE WEALTH OF NATIONS 736 (1776).

17. GAR ALPEROVITZ, AMERICA BEYOND CAPITALISM: RECLAIMING OUR WEALTH, OUR LIBERTY, AND OUR DEMOCRACY 215–16 (2005).

18. ROBERT HEILBRONER, 21stCENTURY CAPITALISM 161 (1993).

19. Manfred Bienfeld, *Suppressing the Double Movement to Secure the Dictatorship of Finance, in* READING KARL POLANYI FOR THE 21ST CENTURY: MARKET ECONOMY AS A POLITICAL PROJECT 18 (Ayşe Buğra & Kaan Ağartan eds., 2007).

20. MILTON FRIEDMAN, CAPITALISM AND FREEDOM 2 (1962).

21. MILTON FRIEDMAN, CAPITALISM AND FREEDOM 2 (1962).

22. Daisuke Wakabayashi, *A Challenge to Big Tech and Antitrust Thinking in a Surprising Place*, Sept. 16, 2019, N.Y. TIMES, at B1.

23. John Williamson, *The Washington Consensus as Policy Prescription for Development*, INST. INT'L ECON. (Jan. 13, 2004), https://www.piie.com/publications/papers/williamson0204.pdf.

24. Dani Rodrik, *Goodbye Washington Consensus, Hello Washington Confusion? A Review of the World Bank's Economic Growth in the 1990s: Learning from a Decade of Reform*, 44 J. ECON. LIT. 973 (2006).

25. WILLIAM J. BAUMOL, ROBERT E. LITAN & CARL J. SCHRAMM, GOOD CAPITALISM, BAD CAPITALISM, AND THE ECONOMICS OF GROWTH AND PROSPERITY (2009).

26. DARON ACEMOGLU & JAMES A. ROBINSON, WHY NATIONS FAIL: THE ORIGINS OF POWER, PROSPERITY AND POVERTY (2012).

27. William D. Nordhaus & James Tobin, *Is Growth Obsolete?*, in THE MEASUREMENT OF ECONOMIC AND SOCIAL PERFORMANCE 509–64 (M. Moss ed., 1973).

28. Matthew D. Adler, *Happiness Surveys and Public Policy: What's the Use?*, 62 DUKE L.J. 1509 (2013).

29. JAMES GUSTAVE SPETH, THE BRIDGE AT THE END OF THE WORLD: CAPITALISM, THE ENVIRONMENT, AND CROSSING FROM CRISIS TO SUSTAINABILITY 132 (2008).

30. Maureen O'Hara, *Making Market Microstructure Matter*, FIN. MGMT., 83 (Summer 1999).

31. JAMES GUSTAVE SPETH, THE BRIDGE AT THE END OF THE WORLD: CAPITALISM, THE ENVIRONMENT, AND CROSSING FROM CRISIS TO SUSTAINABILITY 177–80 (2008).

32. JUSTIN LEWIS, BEYOND CONSUMER CAPITALISM: MEDIA AND THE LIMITS TO IMAGINATION 156 (2014).

33. Charles W. Powers & Marian R. Chertow, *Industrial Ecology*, in THINKING ECOLOGICALLY: THE NEXT GENERATION OF ENVIRONMENTAL POLICY (M. R. Chertow & D.C. Esty eds., 1997).

34. PAUL HAWKEN, AMORY LOVINS, & HUNTER LOVINS, NATURAL CAPITALISM: CREATING THE NEXT INDUSTRIAL REVOLUTION (1999).

35. Göran Carstedt, *Presentation, Conversation on Leadership & Creating a Sustainable Future*, CTR. INTERACTIVE RESEARCH ON SUSTAINABILITY (Feb. 21, 2012).

36. MANCUR OLSON, THE RISE AND DECLINE OF NATIONS 181–237 (1982).

37. MANCUR OLSON, THE RISE AND DECLINE OF NATIONS 41–47 (1982).

38. See, e.g., *America's European Moment*, ECONOMIST 7 (Jan. 5, 2013) ("The reason behind this lamentable outcome is the outsize influence of narrow interest groups – which marks a second, unhappy parallel with Europe.").

39. Fred Block, *Polanyi's Double Movement and the Reconstruction of Critical Theory*, 28 PAPERS IN POLIT. ECON. 3 (2008).

40. Fred Block, *Polanyi's Double Movement and the Reconstruction of Critical Theory*, 28 PAPERS IN POLIT. ECON. 12 (2008).

41. QUINNIPIAC UNIV. POLL, MAJORITY OF VOTERS SAY CLIMATE CHANGE IS AN EMERGENCY QUINNIPIAC UNIVERSITY POLL FINDS; 72% SAY CONGRESS NEEDS TO ACT TO REDUCE GUN VIOLENCE 1 (Aug. 29, 2019), https://poll.qu.edu/national/release-detail?ReleaseID=3639; Alice Tidey, *Climate Change: Poll Finds a Majority Think It's an Emergency*, EURO NEWS (Sept. 20, 2019), https://www.euronews.com/2019/09/20/climate-change-poll-finds-a-majority-think-it-s-an-emergency.

42. Margaret Thatcher, *Speech opening Hadley Centre for Climate Prediction and Research* (May 25, 1990), https://www.margaretthatcher.org/document/108102.

43. Margaret Thatcher, *Speech opening Hadley Centre for Climate Prediction and Research* (May 25, 1990), https://www.margaretthatcher.org/document/108102.

44. GEOFFREY M. HODGSON, CONCEPTUALIZING CAPITALISM: INSTITUTIONS, EVOLUTION, FUTURE 259 (2015).

45. Friedrich von Hayek, *Prize Lecture: The Pretence of Knowledge*, NOBEL PRIZE (Dec. 11, 1974), https://www.nobelprize.org/prizes/economic-sciences/1974/hayek/lecture/.

46. THOMAS PIKETTY, CAPITAL AND IDEOLOGY 581 (2020).

47. ALBERT SCHÄFFLE, THE IMPOSSIBILITY OF SOCIAL DEMOCRACY: BEING A SUPPLEMENT TO THE QUINTESSENCE OF SOCIALISM (1892).

48. JOHN R. COMMONS, LEGAL FOUNDATIONS OF CAPITALISM (1924).

49. *The World Bank in China*, WORLD BANK, https://www.worldbank.org/en/country/china/overview.

50. Daniel Cusick, A *U.S. Clean-tech Enthusiast Helps China Plot its Energy Future*, CLIMATEWIRE (Oct. 29, 2015).

51. ABHIJIT BANERJEE & ESTHER DUFLO, GOOD ECONOMICS FOR HARD TIMES 185 (2019) (citing *Global 500 2014*, FORTUNE, https://fortune.com/global500/2014/).

52. WORLD BANK OPEN DATA, GDP (CURRENT US$), ALL COUNTRIES AND ECONOMIES (2020), https://data.worldbank.org/indicator/NY.GDP.MKTP.CD [https://perma.cc/C2AA-B562].

53. PAUL HAWKEN, AMORY LOVINS, & HUNTER LOVINS, NATURAL CAPITALISM: CREATING THE NEXT INDUSTRIAL REVOLUTION 245 (1999).

54. Nir Becker, *Water Pricing in Israel: Various Waters, Various Neighbors, in* WATER PRICING EXPERIENCES AND INNOVATIONS 181–99 (A. Dinar, V. Pochat & J. Albiac-Murillo, eds., 2015), https://link.springer.com/chapter/10.1007/978-3-319-16465-6_10.

55. Government of the Netherlands, *Agriculture and Horticulture*, https://www.government.nl /topics/agriculture/agriculture-and-horticulture.

56. The estimated value of U.S. Agricultural exports was $138,157 billion. U.S. Dep't of Agric., Foreign Agric. Serv., *Global Agriculture System*, https://apps.fas.usda.gov/gats/ (queried Feb. 10, 2019). With 9.1 million square kilometers in land, U.S. CENTRAL INTELLIGENCE AGENCY, THE WORLD FACTBOOK, NORTH AMERICA: THE UNITED STATES (2019), https://www.cia.gov /LIBRAR/publications/the-world-factbook/geos/us.html, the United States has about 220 times the land of the Netherlands. The Netherlands exported €92 billion, the equivalent of about $102 billion. Government of the Netherlands, *Agricultural Exports Worth Nearly €92 billion in 2017* (Jan. 19, 2018), https://tinyurl.com/yxlv8mfw.

57. *Dutch Greenhouses Have Revolutionized Modern Farming*, THE CIVIL ENGINEER (Feb. 6, 2018), https://tinyurl.com/y4bas39x.

58. Dutch Greenhouses, Blog: *How on Earth Have the Dutch Done it?* (Mar. 16, 2018), https:// dutchgreenhouses.com/blog/how-on-earth-have-the-dutch-done-it (showing Dutch tomato yield at 144,352 tons per square mile). Average tomato yield in the United States was 28,600 pounds per acre in 2015, U.S. DEP'T OF AGRIC., VEGETABLE 2016 SUMMARY 89 (2017), which translates into 9,152 tons per square mile.

59. Frank Viviano, *A Tiny Country Feeds the World: Agricultural Giant Holland is Changing the Way We Farm*, NAT'L GEOGRAPHIC 82 (Sept. 2017).

3

Capital Investments Create Their Own Political Economy

Capitalism is not the reason that humankind has so badly mistreated its environment. It is true that capitalism has taken a very wrong turn, and having gone down this route, it is difficult to change it. But there is nothing about capitalism preordaining it to produce environmental destruction. Capitalism has taken on a malignant form, but it has been steered by mistaken political choices, born of political failures, greed, tribalism, and that toxic cocktail of human arrogance mixed with abject ignorance.

In May 2020, during the COVID-19 crisis, which pummeled markets and industries of almost all types, fourteen Republican senators and two Republican congressmen wrote to the President, urging him to "use every administrative and regulatory tool at your disposal to prevent America's financial institutions from discriminating against America's energy sector . . . ."[1] Their complaint? Investment firms, most prominently the behemoth Blackrock, were considering divesting their holdings in fossil fuel energy stocks as gas, coal, and petroleum prices plummeted. Their prescription? That the President find a way to forbid investment firms from divesting their fossil fuel holdings.

That is a shocking ask, for the White House to dictate investments to private firms. That this gambit is unlikely to be successful does not seem sufficient consolation. Critics of capitalism might seize on this and blame capitalism for the naked greed displayed by the oil industry (and those Republican members of Congress, too, so unashamedly seeking political support), but miss the point: *this is not capitalism!* There is nothing more socialist than to have government dictate investments to private firms. How ironic that this request for government intervention came from the party that so vociferously denounces socialism.

Among those few Congressional Republican lawmakers that have entertained climate policy, some have favored federal subsidies to reduce emissions by attaching technology to the end of a smokestack of a coal-fired power plant to capture the carbon dioxide emissions and store them underground where they would remain, benign, for centuries. This technology is known as "carbon capture and storage."

It would be a neat solution that could offset a *part* of the environmental costs of burning coal to generate electricity (coal-fired electricity generation is also responsible for a variety of other forms of pollution, including fine particulate matter that kills tens of thousands of people annually in the United States, millions worldwide), except that over the two decades of pilot projects it has been too costly and ineffective. The technology has been so disappointing that the electricity generation firms with whom the federal government partnered – the firms that the subsidies were meant to help – have abandoned the effort, opting instead to focus on installing renewable energy sources.[2] This example might not be quite as comical as examples of communist investing under the old Soviet Union, except for the fact that it still, at the time of writing this book, seemed to form a central platform plank for Republican climate proposals. In 2020, speaking in support of a proposal to keep throwing good taxpayer money in after bad, Louisiana Republican Congressman Garret Graves inveighed, "[t]hose who identify fossil fuels as the enemy have misidentified what the enemy is. It's the emissions."[3] At least Congressman Graves is at least one of the few Congressional Republicans concerned about climate change. But he and his like-minded colleagues were mistaken: the enemy *is* the fossil fuel, and taxpayers pay for that folly. The Trump Administration spent more than $1 billion researching new coal plant designs that could minimize emissions,[4] despite the lack of *any* interest on the part of private utilities. Not a single coal-fired power plant has been planned for construction in the United States since 2017, and that plan was abandoned in 2020.[5] Again, this dismal waste of taxpayer money comes from the party that rails against the evils of socialism.

The Corporate Average Fuel Economy (CAFE) standards, born out of the oil crisis of the 1970s and the emergence of competition from upstart Japanese automakers, require every large manufacturer of passenger vehicles selling cars in the United States to have the average of all of their produced vehicles meet a certain standard in any given year. After impressive initial efficiency gains, Americans lapsed into complacency, and CAFE standards languished for two decades without increases. One reason for hiatus was a detour taken by President George W. Bush who, in his January 28, 2003 State of the Union address, announced that he would provide $1.2 billion in research and development funding for hydrogen fuel technology, so "America can lead the world in developing clean, hydrogen-powered automobiles."[6] Hydrogen fuel cell technology may yet prove to be a feasible vehicle technology, but when it was touted by President Bush in 2003, it had already suffered several decades of disappointments. Two American automakers, Ford and Chrysler, had invested in a Canadian start-up company to commercialize the technology, but without success. Was this truly a futuristic vision for automaking? It is hard to know, but it is worth noticing that at the time of President Bush's announcement, (i) American automakers were making large profits from selling large sport utility vehicles, a competitive advantage over Japanese imports that were weighted towards smaller vehicles, (ii) the hydrogen fuel cell initiative forestalled the increase of CAFE standards, which would reduce the advantage enjoyed by the American automakers, (iii) it was about twenty months before President Bush's hoped-for reelection, and (iv) the advantage conferred upon American automakers would yield disproportionate benefit in the important electoral state of Michigan, home of President Bush's Energy Secretary, Spencer Abraham. Government Corruption 1, Democracy 0.

While President Bush was trying to prop up American automakers, Japanese automakers were working on an alternative: hybrid vehicle technology. A tightening of CAFE standards would be to the advantage of Japanese automakers refining this technology. President Bush, however, had long been allied with American automakers in his skepticism about hybrid electric vehicle technology. During his 2000 Presidential campaign, then-candidate Bush mocked, of then-candidate Al Gore's proposed tax credits, "Let me ask you a question ... how many of you own hybrid electric-gasoline engine vehicles?"[7] The answer to that question, as every American driver knows, changed dramatically. California, which has been allowed by EPA to implement some of its own air pollution rules, sought to introduce regulations to encourage hybrid electric vehicle sales in the state, and was unsuccessfully sued by American automakers, with support from the Bush Administration, to stop it.[8]

Unfortunately for American automakers, capitalism had the last word. While the Bush Administration was busy denigrating hybrid electric vehicle technology,[9] Toyota and Honda were refining it. While GM and Chrysler averted bankruptcy in 2009 only because of government generosity (yet again – 2009 was the second time that federal taxpayers bailed out Chrysler), Toyota was making itself the world's largest automaker. Ironically, when the Ford Escape hybrid vehicle went on sale in the United States, it did so by licensing Toyota's hybrid electric vehicle technology.[10] As a final comeuppance, a rule allowing automakers to trade "credits" – for overcomplying with their manufacturer-specific CAFE standard – resulted in large payments being made from lagging American automakers to Japanese ones. Congress finally forced CAFE increases, with the Energy Independence and Security Act of 2007,[11] which mandated an increased new standard for 2008. Capitalism 1; Government Corruption 0.

It is not capitalism that is failing, but the elected officials and political institutions upon which capitalism relies to remain dynamic and robust. Elected political leaders have, consciously or unwittingly, conflated large corporations with capitalism, dynasticism for dynamism. That is not capitalism at all. When capital investments begin to have political, rather than economic objectives, the resulting economy is less dynamic, the ideas less forthcoming, the flow of goods, labor, capital and technology less free, and most importantly, the industries less efficient and less competitive. Ironically, a capitalist economy that has gone too far down the road to oligarchic rot may resemble socialism more than capitalism, as taxpayers fund the white elephants favored by oligarchic capitalists. And still more ironically, socialism very likely descends into authoritarianism after all, as it has too often in the past.

This book does not supply a solution to the most obvious problem: political failure. Democracy tolerates the free formation of groups, and is thus constantly allowing the propagation of groups that could threaten democracy itself. The Trump presidency is an example, as was Adolph Hitler's rise to power in a functional German democracy. Similarly, democracy will always allow groups to form that are a threat to capitalism as well. Capitalists are constantly attempting to manipulate democratic processes to insulate themselves from competition and ultimately become oligarchs. Political solutions to problems such as those exemplified by the stories above are elusive, and outside of this author's expertise. A huge literature exists elsewhere, and I do not attempt to recreate it.

While this book does not purport to solve the problem of how political institutions corrupt capitalism, it does offer a voice within American democracy, and within other democracies similarly afflicted. This book asserts that capitalism is compatible with environmental stewardship, but requires recognition of the political behavior that threatens both capitalism and the environment. It requires, for starters, calling out the political shenanigans of Republican politicians who falsely label their politicking as "capitalism." They are not. They are slides down the road to socialism and authoritarianism. There must be no more nonsense of taxpayer dollars spent to salvage capital that even their private investors are unwilling to spend, no more mucking with capital markets to prop up energy industries, and no more promises that government will solve problems by picking winners. Healthy democracies do not have these pathologies, and genuine capitalists do not need them.

Simultaneously saving capitalism and the global environment also requires identification of the political and economic forces that cause the relationships between lawmakers and polluting industries to metastasize into corruption. Elected officials and industrial titans can synergistically subvert both democracy and capitalism, each finding unique ways to advance private interests and foil public interests. It is extremely tricky, within the confines of a democratic commitment to the rule of law, to curb this behavior. The goal of this book is to identify specific legal rules and institutions that enable and even induce this behavior, and suggest some fixes. This chapter sets out an explanation for how, within capitalism, the ruinous decline begins, and subsequently becomes difficult to stop.

3.1 THE GDP OBSESSION

The growth imperative is not fundamental to capitalism. Nevertheless, political leaders in both capitalist and socialist economies rely on it for political legitimacy, which gives rise to a serious and more practical objection. Economic growth is measured by Gross Domestic Product (GDP), a measure that economists freely acknowledge is problematic. GDP only measures economic activity if there is some monetary exchange that is reported as revenue by some party. If a coal-fired power plant generates 1,000 megawatt-hours of electricity and in the meantime sickens 100 people, GDP would capture the sale of the electricity, *and* the medical expenses of the 100 sickened people. If the same power plant were powered by natural gas (or better still, a renewable source of energy such as wind or solar), it could produce the same electricity without the medical expenses, resulting in a lower GDP – an unambiguously better outcome, but with a lower GDP.

A list of all the shortcomings of GDP would be very long and beyond the scope of this book, but it is worth noting that some efforts have been made and continue to be made, in accounting for environmental harm. In the 1990s, the Bureau of Economic Affairs started work on a system of accounting for environmental damages, the "Integrated Economic and Environmental Satellite Accounts." If GDP measures only the upside of economic activity, part of the point of a supplemental accounting system is to measure the environmental downside. While attribution to specific sources continues to be a work in progress, such an environmental accounting would at least point suggestive fingers at some industries. No doubt hearing displeasure from industries that produce large environmental damages, Congress ordered the Bureau of Economic Affairs to stop work on that project.[12] A House report accompanying an omnibus appropriations bill contained the following explanation for prohibiting further work:

> The Committee is concerned about the Administration's initiative on "Green GDP" or "Integrated Environmental-Economic Accounting," which seeks to provide a measurement of the contribution of natural resources to the Nation's economy. The Committee recognizes that there may be value to the measurements proposed to be taken under this initiative, but has concerns as to whether the Department has adequately addressed the questions of appropriate methodology and proposed applications of the data in developing this initiative. The Committee expects the Department to suspend its work on this initiative until a more thorough analysis of the proposed methodology and applications of Green GDP can be undertaken by an independent entity. The Committee has included $400,000 under this account to allow the Department to enter into a contract to carry out this evaluation . . . and expects the Department to report back to the Committee.[13]

The $400,000 independent study called for by the law was carried out by a panel appointed by the National Research Council, chaired by William Nordhaus, a future Nobel laureate and future President of the American Economic Association. In Nordhaus, the National Research Council found an economist that would never be accused of being a tree hugger lacking in economic rigor. While Nordhaus has pushed boundaries on research topics, opened new lines of inquiry, and was an early proponent of a carbon tax, he has vehemently resisted conclusions that are not thoroughly grounded in empirical research. In an unsightly spat with British economist Sir Nicholas Stern, who called for a high carbon tax in his UK-government-commissioned review on climate change economics,[14] Nordhaus scolded Stern, criticizing his report as "essentially political in nature and [having] advocacy as its purpose."[15] Chaired by such an orthodox economist, the panel could not be accused of harboring a green agenda.

The panel's recommendations were nevertheless clear: Congress should authorize and fund the Bureau of Economic Affairs to continue work on developing natural-resource and environmental accounts, and *furthermore*, to develop accounts for "near-market" and "nonmarket" accounts.[16] Near-market impacts are those nearly accounted for by market transactions, such as recreation providing a partial measure of the value of clean water. Nonmarket impacts are those that are not reflected at all in market transactions, such as the value of biological diversity. The panel's report was issued in 1999, with those and other recommendations. It was never even mentioned again.

For heavily polluting industries, it would simply be better not to know how much harm is caused by their activities. It would be better for polluting firms that no such numbers exist at all. But this debacle is a clear political failure, not one rooted in capitalism. The mistake made by capitalism abolitionists is that because for-profit firms pressured Congress to halt Green GDP work, it must be capitalism that is responsible for the impetus to politically meddle. But if anything, dominant firms in centrally-planned economies are more powerful. Even state-owned firms in "state-guided capitalist" countries have more sway than their counterparts in capitalist countries.

The political shenanigans over something so seemingly mundane are truly unfortunate, because if economic measures such as GDP were more balanced with environmental indicators, they could shed light on economic "growth" in a very new sense. GDP, by capturing economic activity, is meant to act as a proxy for life quality. In this it fails, as many have noted, pointing out disparities between GDP and surveys of life satisfaction or life quality.[17] Among other problems, leisure time, which is surely valued by the busiest and richest individuals, is not counted at all. And ecosystem services are generally not reflected by a monetary transaction, there is no measure of how valuable they are, creating a skew towards pollution. But if environmental accounting was to be married with economic accounting, in a Green GDP, improvements in environmental quality would present a more complete picture of how an economy was serving human needs. If an industry managed to reduce its pollution footprint, a better economic-and-environmental measure would show "growth" in that industry, as it should.

GDP is a flawed metric for many, many reasons, not just environmental. Its continued skew towards pollution and away from environmental awareness is a pathology. But the problems with GDP are political. GDP is only a statistic, created in a time when no one knew any better. Efforts to reform it have run up against industries with a vested interest in continued environmental ignorance. There is nothing capitalist about such meddling. Nothing in the exercise of reforming GDP is remotely inconsistent with a capitalist model of economic governance. A more balanced measure would in fact be a tool for measuring how capitalist enterprise is truly serving human needs.

3.2 RIGIDITY AND PATH-DEPENDENCY IN CAPITAL INVESTMENT

There is another, more subtle way in which capitalism has taken a wrong turn. It implicates the way that capital investments have been made, and how it has directed what people learn in pursuit of a livelihood. The problem with capitalism is what capitalists are able to do politically to preserve their economic position.

It is banal to denounce large industries for political meddling. Of course they meddle. The political failure has been in failing to control that meddling. But what exactly do industries protect when they meddle? Profits? International oil giants could generate profits in a wide variety of businesses. What locks firms into their existing lines of business is their fixed, immutable capital, trillions of dollars in fossil fuel industries. Schumpeter believed that was in the nature of capitalism:

> That in the era of big business the maintenance of the value of existing investment – conservation of capital – becomes the chief aim of entrepreneurial activity and bids fair to put a stop to all cost-reducing improvement. Hence the capitalist order becomes incompatible with progress.[18]

Politics and democracy being what they are, once an expensive capital investment has been made, the owners will resist any changes to the economic or legal environment that threaten the value of that capital investment. About 7,500 offshore oil rigs dot the world's oceans,[19] about 1,500 of them active,[20] each constructed at an average cost of about $500 million.[21] Oil and gas firms do not readily surrender to regulation of that kind of money.

Possibly even more important than the physical capital are all of the jobs wrapped up in all of the massive physical capital. People are employed in those jobs because of their *human capital*, the formal and informal education and on-the-job training that enable people to perform skilled productive tasks.[22] Like physical capital, human capital can be a valuable asset, generating a stream of benefits (income). But human capital can be much more existentially important to an individual than physical capital is to a corporation. It is one thing for a large, multinational firm to lose the value of capital. It is another thing for a person to be out of a job. While firms can diversify, humans only have a few chances in a lifetime (if that) to build up a stock of knowledge that will earn them an income. Education and training are time-consuming and expensive. Once their knowledge becomes highly specialized, they become vulnerable to disruption. Indeed, in the face of threatened regulation, the firm becomes a vehicle for humans to protect the value of their own human capital. Firms will attempt to manipulate the law to their advantage, insulating their capital investments – physical and human – from change.

A central tenet of public choice theory is that concentrated industrial interests will generally prevail over public interests, which are more diffuse by their natures.[23] Industries negatively affected by regulation will spend much more time and effort in a legal contest that affects its interests intensely, than will public advocates for whom the stakes are much lower, and their funding much less concentrated. If pollution from small diesel engines such as leaf blowers are harmful to human health, tighter regulation may be warranted if it passes a cost-benefit test: if the total human health benefits of tighter pollution regulation are greater than the combined loss to manufacturers (for having to build more expensive leaf blowers) and to consumers (for having to pay more for them). But whereas such a regulation could pose an existential threat to leaf blower manufacturers, for everybody else benefiting from cleaner air it is just one of numerous worries about pollution, which itself is one of numerous other health and economic worries. An intensely interested base trumps a broad and diffuse public. This book asserts that at the heart of public choice theory is the interest sought to be protected by regulated industries: their physical and human capital.

The introduction of capital creates another dimension to public choice theory: the size and extent of capital investment. Owners of capital engage vigorously in the regulatory and legislative processes to protect their capital from changes in the legal or economic environment; the more expensive the capital, the more vigorous the defense. Owners of capital have a variety of options to try and protect the legal and economic environment for their capital. They may undertake a public campaign, as explained in Chapter 1. They may undertake a wide array of legal options, including challenging regulations at the agency level and in court. They may secure the cooperation of legislators, and they do so, much too frequently.

3.3 A SIMPLE MODEL

Consider a very simple stylized example of two types of investments: a low-capital-cost, low-profit investment, and a high-capital-cost, high-profit investment. The goal of any acquisition of any capital is to enjoy a stream of future profits, but along with a higher stream of future profits comes the risk that the future profits may not fully materialize (for example, due to regulation or competition). Absent risk, the long-term value of the high-capital-cost, high-profit-stream investment is greater. In this simple example, the only reason to choose a low-capital, low-profit strategy over high-capital, high-profit strategy is the avoidance of risk. Of course, this abstracts away from many other determinants of capital ownership, like access to capital and discounting, and abstracts away from many other attributes of capital ownership, like market power and signaling benefits or detriments (like prestige or scorn). But heuristically, it is reasonable to work from the simplifying assumptions that the only reason to take on more expensive capital and the attendant risk is to generate a larger stream of benefits.

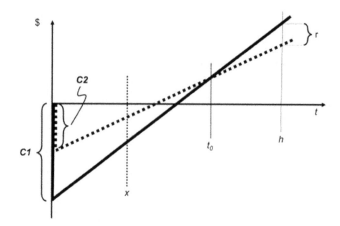

FIGURE 3.1 High-risk, high-payoff and low-risk, low-payoff investments

These two strategies are graphically depicted in Figure 3.1 above, of cumulative profitability over time. Two different firms make a capital investment at $t=0$ an initial investment cost, which instantly drives down profitability, but over time produces goods to generate a revenue stream that increases firm profitability, hopefully more than paying back the initial cost of capital. Consider two possible capital investments, an expensive high-volume machine costing C_1, and a lower-cost lower-volume machine costing the smaller amount C_2. Both machines produce goods that are sold over time, yielding a *cumulative* profitability, total firm revenues minus capital expenses, graphed as a linear function of time, the solid line for the expensive machine, the dotted line for the less expensive one. The expensive higher-volume machine can produce goods more quickly, so the rate at which it generates profits is greater than that of the less expensive one. The expected life of both machines is assumed to be h, at which time the more expensive machine will have generated a cumulative profit greater than the less expensive one by the amount r. This abstracts away from complications having to do with financing and discounting.

The risk faced by these firms is that at some time before h, some event x will occur that will render the capital investment obsolete and preclude any further sales of the product. A competing product or process could put the firm out of business, but so could an environmental regulation (or any other regulation) that prohibits further operation of the machines. If x occurs before the time t_0 the expensive machine will have been an inferior investment to the less expensive one. If the probability-weighted risk is greater for the expensive machine than it is for the less expensive one, then there may be some mix of expensive and less expensive investments, with risk-taking firms investing in the expensive machines, and the relatively risk-averse firms investing in the less expensive machines. In an equilibrium, the difference in expected cumulative profit r can be thought of as the relative risk premium for undertaking the expensive, and riskier investment.

Once the initial capital investments are made, however, how a firm views the obsolescence event x becomes very different. In the figures below, a regulatory change that renders the machines obsolete and valueless occurs at time x, and the losses for the high-capital, high-profits strategy and the low-capital, low-profits strategy are shown in Figures 3.2 and 3.3 below, respectively, as L_1 and L_2.

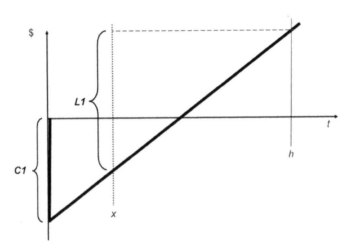

FIGURE 3.2 Loss incurred by high-risk investment

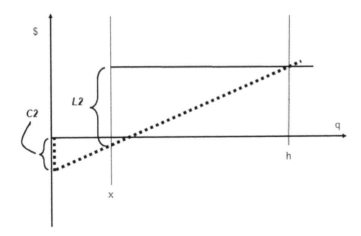

FIGURE 3.3 Loss incurred by low-risk investment

Obviously, the loss suffered by an unfavorable change in the legal or economic environment is greater in the high-capital, high-profits scenario; there is a larger stream of benefits to lose. All other things being equal, as long as the high-capital, high-profits strategy yields higher marginal profits (again, this is assumed, because in this simple model there would otherwise be no reason to expend higher amounts of capital), the loss L_1 will always be greater than the loss L_2.

Less obvious but more important, the decision environment becomes very different once the investment is made. Ex ante, the prospective investor can be expected to weigh the higher profits against the higher capital costs and also against the probability of the event x, multiplied by what the firm would spend in that event to preserve its rents and try and reverse the legal and economic implications of x. The firm could litigate against a regulation, or could seek legislative relief against the regulation or to lock out competition. But once the capital investment is made, the decision environment changes. If x occurs, the owner of capital could expend an amount of money up to the expected loss (L_1 or L_2), which could exceed the cost of the capital (C_1 or C_2). These collisions between the value of capital and some public policy can thus be expensive, more so than even the cost of capital.

A healthy economy would include a mixture of risk-taking and risk-averse firms. In case of a discovery of some latent harm, or the emergence of new competition, some fraction of firms would be able to better adapt to change. In the absence of a legal distortion, better adaptive capacity would be part of the advantage of taking on less risk. For those taking the risk of a high capital investment, however, obsolescence would be a very costly matter, and they might well find it in their interest to undertake *rent-preserving activities*, the ex post analog of rent-seeking, and the exercise of protecting existing rents.[24] Rent-preserving activities include lobbying or litigating, or prosecuting some public campaign to preserve its competitive position, which may be privately worthwhile but publicly costly. The problem is when some legal provision encourages the expensive, higher-cost investment, then the legal provision is effectively increasing the likelihood of a costly collision between the value of capital and some other public benefit, be it environmental quality, public safety, or competition.

The amount of effort spent resisting policy change can thus be very sensitive to initial decisions on capital investment. If a subsidy has the effect of bloating a capital stock by encouraging larger investments, it can have the effect of increasing the amount of costly rent-preserving activities. A small subsidy, or an obscure legal provision, can magnify differences in capital investment, and lead to a very different world in terms of capital stock, and in concomitantly, a different world of incentives to resist policy change. An overcapitalized industry will undertake more efforts to resist reform.

Such a simple model is not offered up as the singular explanation of why firms resist regulation or competition. That topic is far too large and complicated to be captured by any one theory, and by such a simple model. However, the model illustrates an overlooked dynamic: that capital investment is to some degree path-dependent, shaping subsequent activities in terms of how capital owners invest and what they do to preserve their rents. The effect of capital investments on subsequent rent-preserving activities may be larger than the capital itself, which is costly. Firms on the knife-edge of deciding whether to invest more or less, big or small, can be incentivized by relatively small subsidies to invest big, and once having gone big, they develop more elaborate defenses to protect their suboptimally large invest-ments. Subsidies have increased that probability that some collision will occur between a large capital investment and large environmental problem. Not only is that collision costly for all parties, but the larger the capital stock, the greater the likelihood that the environment will be the greater loser in that collision.

3.4 WHITHER, FLEXIBILITY?

This collision is not necessarily catastrophic if threatened capital were flexible enough to have uses other than those targeted by regulation. If, following a regulation that forbade or restricted a specific use of capital, that capital could be redeployed for some other profitable use, then the compulsion to defend that capital would be weaker. The troubling implication of this model is that a policy collision could be even more expensive than the cost of the capital itself. That prospect can be greatly reduced if the capital is not so vulnerable to complete loss due to regulation. Flexible capital is better.

This model, and this notion of capital flexibility, has some interesting implica-tions for human capital. Physical capital must certainly be operated by humans, even as that necessity is being reduced by advancements in artificial intelligence. Industries with physical capital threatened by regulation thus also employ a workforce that may also be threatened with the devaluation of their human capital. A threat of regulation is thus not only a threat to physical capital, but also to human capital. Indeed, because people have few opportunities in a lifetime to acquire human capital, the threat may be more existential to workers than it would be to corporations, which can diversify a capital base. If that is the case, then human capital is also important, perhaps a greater, possibly a *much* greater inducement for politically meddling to preserve an industry.

That need not be so if the human capital is flexible enough to garner another job for the people possessing it. If the nature of the education and training possessed by workers is such that they create opportunities in a number of different industries, then the threat of regulation is not quite so existential to those workers. Employees in mid-level management and higher often stand a reasonable chance of landing on their feet. Other employees with generalized technical skills may also find reem-ployment without too much trouble. Industries that employ workers with more generalized skills are less vulnerable to disruption by regulation.

Flexibility in human capital is unfortunately absent in a great many industries. Conspicuously, many industries that generate large or dangerous amounts of pollution and environmental harm seem especially to be saddled with workers that can only do one specific thing in the industry. Skills do not seem to be transferable to other jobs or other industries. Under those circumstances, the regulation that threatens the value of physical capital may well indeed be less compelling than the threat to human capital. And unfortunately, the regulation that poses such a great threat to these industries and workers often happen to be aimed at environmental protection.

The path-dependency of capital investment is no doubt complex. But the possibility that investment can lock itself in, and perhaps even beget more investment, is sobering. It implies that capital investments should be considered carefully in the context of their potential for harm, most importantly for harming the global environment.

3.5 A HEAD START FOR FOSSIL FUEL INVESTMENT

In 1913, Congress passed the first modern federal income tax in the United States,[25] and along with it, special tax treatment for oil, gas, and mining industries. Development of the oil, gas, and mining industries was a political and economic priority in those days, and Congress recognized that these industries had less physical capital, so it allowed some part of the reserves claimed by an extractive firm to be treated preferentially as capital for tax purposes. A certain percentage of the extracted oil, for example – once as high as 27.5 percent – was deductible against income, that is, tax-free. Additionally, oil and gas firms were (and still are) allowed to deduct *immediately*, not depreciate over a period of years, "intangible drilling costs," or "IDCs," including labor, fuel, power, materials, supplies, and other costs of drilling, such as site preparation and road grading.[26] Not only is this a subsidy because it allows oil and gas industries to deduct expenses that other industries cannot, but the immediate deduction, or "expensing," of such costs is a tax deferral that effectively hands cash to the oil or gas firm *early*, allowing it to put that cash to use.

Favorable tax rules and subsidies incentivized exploration and production, producing capital investment higher than private investment alone would have achieved.[27] But well past the point at which the oil and gas industries in the United States could be considered immature, and past the point at which firms were unable to diversify risks of failure, the subsidies persisted. The value of these subsidies to the oil and gas industries, along with a few others, have been substantial. One study estimated that from 1918 to 2009, oil and gas firms have received $447 billion in subsidies, measured in 2010 dollars, the equivalent of $4.85 billion per year.[28]

As much money as that is, it does not do justice to its effect on the oil and gas industries, and how it steered the American economy down a particular path. A subsidy need only *affect* capital decisions, not finance the entire capital investment. Thus, a $4.85 billion injection (it was greater in earlier years) would have induced capital investment far in excess of that amount. To see how much, it is worth examining some attempts to phase out these subsidies. Several times, the Obama Administration proposed the elimination, phase-out, or the delay of the deductibility of intangible drilling costs, which in 2010 amounted to about $1 billion per year.[29] In 2013, the American Petroleum Institute commissioned an economic analysis to see how a proposed delay in the deductibility of intangible drilling costs would affect production, jobs, and capital expenditures. According to the study, just the *delay* of IDC deductibility would have reduced capital expenditures by $44 billion in 2019, a 27 percent drop from the baseline case, and would have eliminated over 233,000 jobs. The effect of the approximately $1 billion per year was apparently – if the American Petroleum Institute is to be believed – to induce the additional investment of $44 billion.[30] If that is true and if that is representative of capital investments in oil and gas then the amount of induced investment over a century in the oil and gas extraction industry is many trillions of dollars. It is also worth remembering a number of induced downstream effects on capital investment, such as in refining and distribution, and in many other petroleum-fed industrial and chemical processes, some of which are subsidized as well.

This is not to minimize the value of oil and gas development in the United States, and elsewhere in the world. Low fossil fuel prices have generated enormous economic benefits throughout time and throughout the world. The pre-automobile, pre-gasoline world of horse manure in the streets is obviously one best left far behind. Rather, the point of highlighting the role of oil and gas subsidies is to appreciate how it created such a huge head start over all kinds of alternatives: alternative forms of energy creation, transportation, land development, and even alternative ways for people to interact with each other.

A head start in capital investment not only generates an advantage in market power, but also generates a head start in technological development. Capital investment in equipment usually generates improvements. Vis-à-vis competition, a head start in capital investment provides an advantage in opportunities to work on and improve production processes. The nature of human knowledge is such that it builds upon past knowledge. The first steam engine is commonly credited to Thomas Savery, who used steam energy to pump water upwards, but was shortly thereafter improved by Thomas Newcomen, who first captured the steam within a cylinder to improve condensation. James Watt improved it further, developing a separate condensing chamber and reducing the wasted steam. Watt patented the steam engine in 1769, and is still the most commonly used method in electricity generation plants, which use mostly fossil fuel combustion to heat water. Even with many efficiency improvements, modern plants still borrow from the basic concept of the Watt engine. It is also important to notice the interdependence of technology and human know-how. Modern steam plants, now powered by natural gas instead of coal, are much more efficient iterations of the original design, which generations of engineers had been improving all along. Every technological breakthrough is a pushing back of some frontier, which would not occur unless there were humans to not only discover, but put into practice new technology.

Fast forward to the twenty-first century. Globally, oil and gas extraction and production – not including the refining and distribution – was a $3.3 trillion industry in 2019, with about four million employees.[31] A century and half of experience has made the extraction of oil and gas one of the world's most technologically sophisticated industries. In Saudi Arabia, vast scale economies refined over decades of tinkering have driven the cost of oil production to under $3 US per barrel.[32] A 2016 study commissioned by the U.S. Energy Information Administration found that "upstream" drilling costs – largely IDCs – had fallen 25–30 percent from recent highs, and that "additional efficiencies in drilling rates, lateral lengths, proppant use, multi-well pads, and number of stages that will further drive down costs measured in terms of dollars per barrel of oil-equivalent ($/boe) by 7% to 22%."[33] It is indicative of an industry that has been relentless in reducing costs.

Oil giants have also pursued oil exploration into the seabeds of the world, operating at ocean depths of thousands of feet. Offshore oil and gas extraction technology began with platforms anchored to the ocean floor. Those platforms grew longer and longer "legs" until, pushing into deeper ocean waters, they jettisoned physical attachments to the seabed, and are now mostly floating, "mobile offshore drilling units," or "MODUs," huge factories sitting atop huge pontoons. Drilling is accomplished by extending a long, segmented tube, the "riser," down thousands of feet for drilling into bedrock and extracting the oil within. MODUs cost an average of about $500 million to build, and are specialized: some are designed specifically for *exploratory* drilling, only piercing the subsea oil aquifer, and preparing it for another MODU, specially designed for mass and long-term extraction of crude oil. Exploration has pushed into deeper and deeper waters: "deepwater" drilling technology enables drilling at depths of 10,000 or more, opening up vastly greater expanses of ocean to oil exploration, including the entire Gulf of Mexico.

Along with hyper-specialization of this large, expensive, and impressive physical capital, human capital has evolved to become highly specialized, and is critical to operation of oil rigs. Most jobs on offshore oil rigs require no education beyond high school, but require fairly extensive training through courses certified by a trade association, the International Well Control Forum. After completion, "drillers," "rig mechanics," "subsea engineers," "derrickmen," and "offshore roughnecks" are among the crew of 60–120 workers that can earn up to $150,000 for six months' work.[34] Water pressures are extremely high at great depths, and the pressure from oil reservoirs can be extremely high as well, so the training is very specific on how to manage the specialized equipment and the high pressures. As drilling proceeds downward, drill pipes must carry with it mud or other materials to equalize the increasing pressures to prevent a "blowout," the uncontrolled spurting of oil up the riser and into the well. Responsibility for choosing drilling procedures and materials and maintaining just the right amount of pressure lies with a crew of mostly subsea engineers who have become intimately familiar with the specialized equipment.

It is worth taking a step back and considering how much development went into not only building specialized offshore oil rigs, but also the variety of different jobs onboard a rig, from roughneck to chef. Different kinds of MODUs are the product of decades of development, the relentless push into deeper and deeper waters for more and more oil. The technology was developed by building upon the knowledge gained from building and operating older rigs, and all that offshore technology derived from simpler oil wells built for extraction on nice, solid, land. And along the way, many generations of workers learned the variety of skills needed to move, operate, manage, fix, and maintain a rig. But not much else.

3.6 A SLOW START FOR RENEWABLE ENERGY INVESTMENT

Given the size and longevity of fossil fuel subsidies, it is not hard to see how it swamped investment in renewable energy sources. Financing renewable energy investments was historically more difficult, and hiring workers was more difficult. Because physical and human capital are cumulative, intertwined, and synergistic, the head start for fossil fuels was decisive.

Fossil fuel's head start is not only in the sophistication of its physical capital, not only in the sophistication of its work force, but also in the staffing of the regulatory agencies that issue permits to drill. Only recently have these fossil fuel-centered agencies been asked to consider whether alternative energy sources might be available for use on the nation's ocean waters. The Bureau of Land Management (BLM) leases about 570 million acres for coal mining,[35] which account for about 40 percent of American coal production.[36] By comparison, the BLM leases about 276,000 acres for solar energy,[37] even in the sun-drenched states of Nevada, California, and Arizona. In the United States, the leasing of its ocean spaces has been so dominated by offshore oil leasing that the agency in charge of managing federal ocean spaces is the Bureau of Ocean Energy Management (BOEM). A sister agency, the Bureau of Safety and Environmental Enforcement, is in charge of monitoring and enforcing environmental and safety rules for offshore oil platforms. Its logo even sports an oil rig sitting on blue waters.

One alternative use of federal waters is offshore wind development. But the BOEM has moved extremely slowly in approving new leases, slow-walking proposals to serve even the electricity-starved Northeastern states. Some part of it is Donald Trump's superstition about wind – he has claimed that wind turbines cause cancer – and part of it perhaps his personal animus towards Northeastern states. But part of it is opposition from the fishing industry, and part of it stems from BOEM's lack of experience in permitting offshore wind farms. Having permitted thousands of offshore oil rigs, it lacked a permit template for wind farms. How would royalties be calculated, if there weren't barrels of oil to count? (Answer: kilowatt-hours generated.) How are the transmission lines permitted, if they are partially in federal and partially in state waters? While the leases for offshore oil rigs are extremely detailed and running into hundreds of pages, the lease for the first major offshore wind project, the ill-fated Cape Wind project, was a spare twelve pages, most of it a template adapted from oil leases.

Why should such a simple, limitless nonpolluting source of energy – wind – be so much less utilized than a fuel source that requires trillions of dollars of capital, millions of workers and contributes pollution and greenhouse gases that cause climate change? How is it that the entire world seems so committed to supplying energy the harder, dirtier, more dangerous way?

There is a bit of hard-earned wisdom among marathon runners, that at a certain late point in a 26.2-mile footrace, the only reason you keep running is because you were. Don't stop! It is somehow easier *not* to stop, but to just continue. This kind of path dependence explains how the world's fossil fuel-centered industrial economy simply carries on. As fossil fuel technology grew and improved, as scale economies locked in steam technology as the dominant method of generating electricity, and as millions of people became accustomed to generating, distributing, and selling electricity in this way, as governments became accustomed to regulating fossil fuel combustion, it became simpler not to change.

To be sure, wind and solar energy suffer from the drawback that they are intermittent: they do not generate energy when the wind is not blowing, or when the sun is not shining. Electricity cannot be available only intermittently. Electricity customers must be guaranteed power, whether they be individual households or power-hungry server farms, which traditionally required a certain amount of "baseload" power that can supply energy constantly, without interruption. Until recently, only fossil fuel plants – coal and natural gas – could meet that need. A system that was too dependent upon intermittent renewable energy sources could not provide that critical guarantee. Now, however, information and energy storage technologies have now penetrated the electricity sector, making it possible to store and distribute intermittent sources of electricity. It has become clear that there are now a variety of energy diversification strategies and technologies that should allow much greater penetration of renewable energy technologies. So why not indeed?

In hindsight, the problem of smoothing out intermittency of renewable energy should have been far less daunting than many problems solved by the fossil fuel industries. The technique of hydraulic fracturing involves the downward vertical drilling of a pipe, less than a meter in width, to depths of more than a mile, at which point drilling takes a ninety-degree turn, and proceeds horizontally for, in some cases, over six miles. From these L-shaped pipes water, with many chemical additives, is forced out through small holes in the pipe at extremely high pressures, fracturing the bedrock and causing many tiny bubbles of oil or gas to escape through that same pipe, where it is captured for future energy combustion. Hydraulic fracturing is credited with dramatically lowering the price of natural gas. But all that seems like a lot of trouble, compared to figuring out how to capture and store energy from windmills and solar cells.

Economists Daron Acemoglu and Phillipe Aghion, along with their colleagues, have written about the need to supplement a carbon tax with research and development subsidies for non-carbon energy sources.[38] Economists almost always approve of environmental taxes, and rarely approve of subsidies, on the grounds that subsidies are blunt and inefficient, and too often decay into government "picking winners and losers." But Acemoglu's and Aghion's intuition of subsidizing non-carbon energy sources is that the fossil fuel industries have such an enormous head start, that there would otherwise be no way for non-carbon industries to catch up. The mere size of the fossil fuel industries – about twelve million oil and gas jobs in the United States alone – guarantees that research and development will disproportionately take place in those industries, as compared with the puny opportunities (at least until recently) in the non-carbon industries. Moreover, research and development in those fossil fuel industries are so much richer and more advanced than that of their renewable energy competitors, building as they do upon a century and a half's worth of knowledge already acquired. It is no wonder that the playing field seems decisively tilted in favor of fossil fuel energy. Indeed, of the forty-six technologies identified by the International Energy Agency as being crucial for meeting the climate goals established by the 2015 Paris Agreement, most are languishing. Of the forty-six needed to keep global average temperatures from increasing by two degrees Celsius, only six were considered fully "on track" and sixteen were considered "off track entirely."[39]

3.7 AN EVEN SLOWER START FOR THE EARTH SCIENCES

In addition to fossil fuels enjoying a head start over their competition, the fossil fuel industries have also enjoyed an advantage in the government decision-making arena. All human decision, private or public, individual, group, or polity, inherently weighs advantages against disadvantages of action, set against the backdrop of alternatives, each with their own advantages and disadvantages. One of the reasons that so many capitalist enterprises have proven to be, on net, so harmful to the global environment is that momentous, expensive decisions have been made with incomplete information as to its environmental consequences. Government decision-making has long been premised on recognition of the concrete economic benefits of fossil fuel-centered industry, oblivious to alternatives and in ignorance of environmental consequences. Governments themselves have made ill-informed energy decisions that only seem comical well after the fact. Economic development has thus been skewed toward certain technologies and away from others, made in broad ignorance of environmental impacts. In a sense, the knowledge race is also between fossil fuels and ecological science. Broadly speaking, government decision-making depends on information about both, and there is much, much more of the former than the latter. Those with ecological training arguing against fossil fuels stand at a great disadvantage.

Despite a fairly long history of study of the Earth and its environment, it would not be until 1962 when Rachel Carson's *Silent Spring* would dramatically illustrate how human industrial activity could affect the environment by disrupting or altogether destroying ecological systems. Coupled with some unusual, attention-grabbing environmental mishaps,[40] *Silent Spring* is widely believed to have catalyzed the modern-day environmental movement. Supreme Court Justice William O. Douglas pronounced the book to be "the most important chronicle of this century for the human race."[41] Several federal U.S. environmental statutes followed,[42] including the 1970 passage of the National Environmental Policy Act.[43] The 1970s followed as the decade in which virtually all of the major federal environmental statutes of the United States were passed and signed into law. University departments of Earth Sciences, Environmental Sciences, and Geosciences began to explore more expansively the impacts of human activities impacting living organisms and systems.

But the development of these fields of study and institutions devoted to studying the Earth and its environment cannot compete with the money, time and people devoted to industrial pursuits, particularly the fossil fuel industries. At least the upstart renewable energy industries seeking to break into the club of fossil fuel-based energy incumbents have the capitalist profit motive driving them. But those who worry about and study the environmental effects of fossil fuels suffer from the lack of any financial incentive. They would be employed in universities, and generally depend on external funds to carry out their study. The argument made by Acemoglu, Aghion, and their colleagues applies conceptually to the juxtaposition between fossil fuel-related activities and study of the environmental effects of those activities. With its millions of jobs[44] and trillions of dollars of physical capital, the oil industry is a behemoth. Those studying the environmental effects of that industry are at an extreme disadvantage.

Federal grant funding in the United States for research expenditures in the area of "Environmental Sciences" represent about 7 percent of all fields, as compared with life sciences (mostly medical) at about 50 percent, engineering at about 19 percent, and physical sciences at 10 percent.[45] As I briefly mentioned in Chapter 1, and as I lay out in full in Chapter 7 of this book, I propose a dramatic increase in funding for researching in the Earth and Environmental Sciences, so that a better understanding of environmental damages can support a system of accounting for them. To better reduce humankind's footprint, it is important to be able to see and measure it.

3.8 DEEPWATER HORIZON

On April 22, 2010, Earth Day of all days, the Deepwater Horizon, an exploration MODU leased by oil giant BP, operating forty-three miles off the coast of Louisiana, exploded into flames. After burning for several days, the $560 million vessel sank, snapping the 5,000-foot-long riser and allowing oil to flow uncontrolled for eighty-seven days into the Gulf of Mexico. Eleven workers aboard were killed. About four million barrels of oil were spilled, seventeen times more than the next largest spill in history, the Exxon Valdez spill in Alaska. The amount of oil spilled was about one-five billionth of the amount of water in the entire Gulf of Mexico. BP ultimately reached settlement with the U.S. government and other parties for a total of about $25 billion.[46]

The series of mistakes that were made at different levels of responsibility are well-documented, and even dramatized reasonably accurately in a feature-length film. As an exploratory MODU, Deepwater Horizon's job was to drill into the oil reservoir and then seal it, leaving it for a production MODU to come along and commence long-term production of oil. Deepwater Horizon was actually the second vessel to attempt this at the site, a site that oil rig workers had called "the well from hell." The first, a MODU named *Marianas*, had tried and failed. By the time that Deepwater Horizon had arrived on the scene, the project was already $54 million behind schedule, and losing $1 million per day. BP sent representatives to the rig to make sure the project proceeded quickly. What the BP representatives did was preside over a series of notoriously reckless decisions, bypassing safety procedures and testing protocols, ultimately leading to the explosion and destruction of the Deepwater Horizon, and most deadly and the largest oil spill in history by more than an order of magnitude.

That the Deepwater Horizon explosion occurred was a legal and political failure. Environmental and safety regulations should have covered the possibility that offshore oil operators might cut corners. Most of the critical mistakes made by the BP supervisors and the crew onboard the Deepwater Horizon were avoidable mistakes that could have been the subject of regulation. Before an exploratory well is sealed with cement, a test is typically done on the soundness of the cement. The contractor charged with doing that for the well at the Macondo site, Halliburton, left without doing so. Before beginning to pull up the riser and abandon the well for a production rig, the crew performs a "negative pressure test," checking the pressure inside the riser to check for any pressure emanating from the well, that might suggest the well has not been sealed, and that more work needs to be done. The test was performed, failed, and BP ordered the crew of the Deepwater Horizon to proceed anyway. At multiple junctures, a regulation could have averted the catastrophe. But in the interests of "regulatory flexibility," these critical decisions were devolved to the regulated party. Occasionally, but not occasionally enough, a cascade of bad decisions leads to catastrophe.

Of course, the temptation is to point to the profit motive that supposedly drove the BP representatives to make such reckless decisions, endangering the workers, themselves, and the delicate marine environment. That a culture of greed and recklessness was responsible for the tragedy is beyond doubt. But that is not specific to capitalism. Given the history of firm behavior under socialist regimes, it is inevitable that an oil giant operating under a socialist regime would have been vulnerable to the same mistakes made by BP and other defendants.

The more relevant problem is the lack of attention and awareness of the possibility of harm from offshore oil exploration. Even a $25 billion settlement raises questions: how much ecological harm was done? Research still being performed ten years after the disaster cast doubt on conventional estimates of the spill's reach, suggesting that the toxicity of the spilled oil spread much further than originally believed.[47] Ten years after, a University of South Florida study of over 2,500 fish of 90 species failed to turn up a single fish that was free of crude oil.[48] Even after thirty years, the effects of the Exxon Valdez spill are still being felt, in the form of depleted fisheries and scarce wildlife.[49] What will ultimately be the effect of an environmental disaster seventeen times worse? What effect will it have on the five endangered species of sea turtles that migrate across the Gulf? On marine mammals? Fish stocks? How will we know?

3.9 A THOUGHT EXPERIMENT

Capitalism does *not* require the occasional oil catastrophe, nor does it require all 1,500 or so offshore oil rigs throughout the world. Healthy capitalism requires that energy be available and affordable, but does not require that it take the form of fossil fuels. The reason that renewable energies, for example, languished for so long is *because* of the vast amounts of capital devoted to fossil fuel extraction, transportation, and combustion. An entire infrastructure grew up, worldwide, around fossil fuels. Moreover, because human capital is wrapped up in these trillions of dollars of physical capital, and because human capital cumulates, human society became fully ensconced in a fossil fuel-centered global economy. It is difficult to change course, even when it can be demonstrated that an alternative system is economically, environmentally, and socially superior. Physical and human capital are difficult to swap out.

It is worth undertaking the thought experiment of how the world's capital stock might have been different if just some appropriate environmental warnings had been heeded. This is an exercise in speculation, of course. But it is worth remembering the example of how just a proposed delay in the deduction of intangible drilling costs would apparently have reduced capital investment by forty-four times the amount of the subsidy, if the American Petroleum Institute is to be believed. How might capitalism have taken a different path?

In 1976, Stephen Schneider and Lynne Mesirow published *The Genesis Strategy: Climate and Global Survival,* perhaps the earliest comprehensive work to raise the possibility that the buildup of atmospheric carbon dioxide could have negative consequences.[50] Schneider and fellow NASA scientist James Hansen would repeatedly warn Congress and other lawmakers that a very substantial risk lay in failing to contain emissions of carbon dioxide, and continuing investments in fossil fuel-centered technology. According to a *New York Times* feature by Nathaniel Rich, their warnings did not so much fall on deaf ears but founder on government and corporate indecision.[51]

But what if a carbon tax, which had been suggested by William Nordhaus, while he was a member of President Jimmy Carter's Council of Economic Advisors, and which had been openly and frequently discussed in federal government and policy circles, was actually adopted by the United States in 1980? Or what if fossil fuel subsidies had started to wind down? Or both? About a third of the United States stock of coal-fired power plants that were in operation in 2018 had not yet been built.[52] China and India, the first and third-largest emitters in 2020, were still decades away from building the vast majority of their coal-fired power plants. CO_2 emissions from China's coal-fired power plants more than tripled from 1.5 Gt in 2000 to 4.6 Gt in 2018.[53] In 1980, world oil production stood at about sixty billion barrels, about two-thirds the annual output of 2018.[54] A domestic carbon tax would not oblige any actions in countries such as China and India, but it would have seemed so innocuous to those countries back then, without the physical and human investments in coal-fired power plants. An American-led proposal back then would certainly have offered a better international negotiating platform, and stands in such stark contrast from current affairs.

But we don't have to imagine how things could have been different. As a natural experiment, we have Sweden. Other countries, prominently Scandinavian countries, have also imposed a carbon tax, though none quite as sweeping as Sweden's. Even Norway, which is rich in oil reserves, has a carbon tax. Granted, Sweden never had much in the way of fossil fuels, and it was partially out of necessity that it developed a very low-carbon economy. But it is an empirically verifiable assertion that its carbon tax dating back to 1990 changed its capital investments from that point.[55] There it is: a prosperous, capitalist, democratic country with a capital stock very different from that of the United States. Is it so fanciful to think that technological development and innovation might have been different with a carbon tax elsewhere?

Notes

1. Letter from Dan Sullivan, Don Young, & Liz Cheney, U.S. Senators, to Donald J. Trump, President (May 7, 2020), https://perma.cc/5GBW-4M57.

2. Kristi E. Swartz, *Southern Co. Suspends its $7.5B Next-generation Plant*, ENERGYWIRE, June 29, 2017.

3. Nick Sobczyk, *Republicans Take Heat from the "Retro" Crowd*, E&E NEWS (Feb. 13, 2020), https://www.eenews.net/stories/1063430425 [https://perma.cc/K943-XD4F].

4. Benjamin Storrow, *More Coal Has Retired Under Trump Than in Obama's Second Term*, E&E NEWS (June 22, 2020), https://www.eenews.net/stories/1063430425 [https://perma.cc /H5FG-4QBV].

5. Chance Swaim & Jonathan Shorman, *Kansas Energy Company Abandons Plans for $2.2 Billion Coal Power Plant*, WICHITA EAGLE (Jan. 15, 2020), https://www.kansas.com/news/ politics-government/article239319253.html.

6. The Presidency Project, *Address Before a Joint Session of the Congress and a State of the Union* (Jan. 28, 2003), http://www.presidency.ucsb.edu/ws/index.php?pid=29645 [https:// perma.cc/R8C6-BPRQ]</int_u>.

7. Frank Bruni, *The 2000 Campaign: The Texas Governor; Bush Ridicules Gore's Proposals for Tax Cuts*, N.Y. TIMES (Oct. 25, 2000), https://www.nytimes.com/2000/10/25/us/2000-campaign-texas-governor-bush-ridicules-gore-s-proposals-for-tax-cuts.html [https://perma .cc/84NR-ZMLP].

8. Danny Hakim, *Automakers Drop Suits on Air Rules*, N.Y. TIMES (Aug. 12, 2003), https://www .nytimes.com/2003/08/12/business/automakers-drop-suits-on-air-rules.html [https://perma.cc /VD43-T4RA].

9. Katharine Q. Seelye, *White House Joins Fight Against Electric Cars*, N.Y. TIMES (Oct. 10, 2002), https://www.nytimes.com/2002/10/10/us/white-house-joins-fight-against-electric-cars.html [https://perma.cc/7KU2-U6AU].

10. Todd Zaun, *Ford to Use Toyota's Hybrid Technology*, N.Y. TIMES (Mar. 10, 2004), http:// www.nytimes.com/2004/03/10/business/ford-to-use-toyota-s-hybrid-technology.html [https://perma.cc/558C-WV3G].

11. Energy Independence and Security Act of 2007, Pub. L. No. 110-140, 121 Stat. 1495 (2007).

12. The Committee intends that the Bureau fully fund the requested increase for modernizing and restructuring the Standard Industrial Classification code system (+ $2,400,000). Because of the importance of this effort to the ability of the Department to better identify and categorize the Nation's small and medium sized manufacturing base, the Committee feels that this initiative is of the highest priority. The Committee has not provided funds under this account for the "Green GDP" initiative. H.R. Rep. No. 103-552, at 63 (1994).

13. *Id.* at 64.

14. NICHOLAS STERN, STERN REVIEW ON THE ECONOMICS OF CLIMATE CHANGE (2007) [hereinafter STERN], https://webarchive.nationalarchives.gov.uk/20100407173719tf_/http://www .hm-treasury.gov.uk/sternreview_index.htm [https://perma.cc/J2AM-BPX6].

15. William D. Nordhaus, *A Review of the Stern Review on the Economics of Climate Change*, 45 J. ECON. PERSP. 686, 688 (2007).

16. NAT'L RSCH. COUNCIL, NATURE'S NUMBERS: EXPANDING THE NATIONAL ECONOMIC ACCOUNTS TO INCLUDE THE ENVIRONMENT 2–3 (WILLIAM D. NORDHAUS & EDWARD C. KOKKLENBERG eds., 1999).

17. *See, e.g.*, MARC FLEURBAEY & DIDIER BLANCHET, BEYOND GDP: MEASURING WELFARE AND ASSESSING SUSTAINABILITY (2013); JAMES GUSTAVE SPETH, THE BRIDGE AT THE END OF THE WORLD 132 (2008).

18. JOSEPH A. SCHUMPETER, CAPITALISM, SOCIALISM AND DEMOCRACY 96 (2013).

19. Lina Zeldovich, *The Afterlife of Old Offshore Oil Rigs*, Am. Soc'y Mechanical Engineers (Oct. 31, 2019), https://www.asme.org/topics-resources/content/the-afterlife-of-old-offshore-oil-rigs [https://perma.cc/535W-LNRK].

20. Sebastian Brixey-Williams, *Where Are the World's Oilrigs?*, World Econ. F. (Oct. 22, 2015), https://www.weforum.org/agenda/2015/10/where-are-the-worlds-oil-rigs/ [https://perma.cc/P578-UD3F]

21. Nick Lioudis, *How Do Average Costs Compare Among Various Oil Drilling Rigs?*, Investopedia (Feb. 11, 2020), https://www.investopedia.com/ask/answers/061115/how-do-average-costs-compare-different-types-oil-drilling-rigs.asp [https://perma.cc/YGT2-9NLP]; Mark J. Kaiser & Brian F. Snyder, *Reviewing Rig Construction Cost Factors*, Offshore (July 1, 2012), https://www.offshore-mag.com/business-briefs/equipment-engineering/article/16760123/reviewing-rig-construction-cost-factors [https://perma.cc/Q287-YZ37].

22. Gary S. Becker, Human Capital: A Theoretical and Empirical Analysis, with Special Reference to Education 30–54 (3d ed. 1993).

23. James M. Buchanan & Gordon Tullock, The Calculus of Consent: Logical Foundations of Constitutional Democracy (1962).

24. Mancur Olson, The Rise and Decline of Nations 41–47 (1982).

25. Revenue Act of 1861, ch. 45, 12 Stat. 292, 309.

26. 26 C.F.R. § 3.23(m)-16 (1936); 26 C.F.R. § 1.263(c) (2019).

27. *See, e.g.*, James C. Cox & Arthur W. Wright, *The Cost-effectiveness of Federal Tax Subsidies for Petroleum Reserves: Some Empirical Results and Their Implications*, in Studies in Energy Tax Policy 177, 188–89 (Gerard Brannon ed., 1975) (finding that special tax provisions induced the petroleum industry to maintain larger investments in proved reserves); Walter J. Mead, *The Performance of Government in Energy Regulations*, 69 Am. Econ. Rev. 352, 352 (1979) ("These tax subsidies [percentage depletion allowance and expensing of intangible drilling costs] led to increased capital flows into exploration.").

28. Nancy Pfund & Ben Healey, *What Would Jefferson Do? The Historical Role of Federal Subsidies in Shaping America's Energy Future*, at 29 (Sept. 2011), http://i.bnet.com/blogs/dbl_energy_subsidies_paper.pdf [https://perma.cc/TN3V-YTDB].

29. U.S. Dep't Energy, Energy Info. Admin., *Direct Financial Interventions and Subsidies in Energy in Fiscal Year 2010*, at 18 (Table 6) (July 2011), https://www.eia.gov/analysis/requests/subsidy/archive/2010/pdf/subsidy.pdf [https://perma.cc/TN3V-YTDB].

30. Wood Mackenzie Consulting, Impacts of Delaying IDC Deductibility (2014-2025), prepared for American Petroleum Institute (July 2013), https://www.api.org/~/media/Files/Policy/Taxes/13-July/API-US-IDC-Delay-Impacts-Release-7-11-13.pdf [https://perma.cc/ZKV6-6EVW].

31. *What Percentage of the Global Economy Is the Oil and Gas Drilling Sector?*, Investopedia (Feb. 15, 2020), https://www.investopedia.com/ask/answers/030915/what-percentage-global-economy-comprised-oil-gas-drilling-sector.asp [https://perma.cc/4VYP-47KK].

32. *The Oil Price War Is a Nightmare for U.S. Shale Producers*, Aljazeera (Mar. 9, 2020), https://www.aljazeera.com/ajimpact/oil-price-war-nightmare-shale-producers-200309173245129.html[https://perma.cc/N7SV-SC45]

33. U.S. Dep't Energy, U.S. Energy Info. Admin., Trends in U.S. Oil and Natural Gas Upstream Costs 1 (2016).

34. *See, e.g.*, Claire Calkin, *Offshore Oil Rig Jobs Can Be Tough, But Very Rewarding* (June 29, 2017), https://www.experience.com/alumnus/article?channel_id=energy_utilities&source_page=additional_articles&article_id=article_1128902416846 [https://perma.cc

/HG2X-LEAA]; UCAS Progress, *Offshore Drilling Worker,* https://www.ucas.com/ucas/after-gcses/find-career-ideas/explore-jobs/job-profile/offshore-drilling-worker [https://perma.cc/6UCL-8YGA]; Offshore Technology, *The 10 Most Lucrative Offshore Platform Jobs* (July 18, 2020), https://www.offshore-technology.com/features/featurethe-10-most-lucrative-offshore-platform-jobs-4521413/ [https://perma.cc/PXR8-YJLJ]; Diamond Offshore, *Offshore Drilling Basics* http://www.diamondoffshore.com/offshore-drilling-basics [https://perma.cc/544C-T3WJ].

35. U.S. Bur. Land Mgmt., *Coal,* https://www.blm.gov/programs/energy-and-minerals/coal [https://perma.cc/X3NN-B3Q5].

36. U.S. ENERGY INFO. ADMIN., SALES OF FOSSIL FUELS PRODUCED ON FEDERAL AND INDIAN LANDS, FY 2003 THROUGH FY 2014 (Table 1) (July 2015), https://www.eia.gov/analysis/requests/federallands/pdf/table1.pdf [https://perma.cc/2L3Q-FTDH].

37. KARL CATES ET AL., INST. ENERGY ECON. & FIN. ANALYSIS, FEDERAL LAND AGENCY LAGS ON SOLAR DEVELOPMENT APPROVALS ACROSS SOUTHWEST U.S. (2020), https://ieefa.org/wp-content/uploads/2020/06/Federal-Land-Agency-Lags-on-Solar-Development-Approvals-Across-SW-US_June-2020.pdf [https://perma.cc/5ZPU-F7TS].

38. Phillipe Aghion, David Hemous & Reinhilde Veugelers, *No Green Growth Without Innovation,* BRUEGEL POL'Y BRIEF (Nov. 2009), https://www.bruegel.org/wp-content/uploads/imported/publications/pb_climatervpa_231109_01.pdf [https://perma.cc/MPT3-2K4D]; Daron Acemoglu, Philllipe Aghion, Leonardo Bursztyn & David Hemous, *The Environment and Directed Technical Change,* 102 AM. ECON. REV. 131 (2012).

39. Miranda Wilson & Carlos Anchondo, *Not on Track: 35% of Energy Technologies Lag GHG Goals,* ENERGYWIRE, June 10, 2020.

40. Lorraine Boissoneault, *The Cuyahoga River Caught Fire at least a Dozen Times, but No One Cared Until 1969,* SMITHSONIAN MAG. (June 19, 2019), https://www.smithsonianmag.com/history/cuyahoga-river-caught-fire-least-dozen-times-no-one-cared-until-1969-180972444 [https://perma.cc/TS3N-N6VH]; Christine Mai-Duc, *The 1969 Santa Barbara Oil Spill That Changed Oil and Gas Exploration Forever,* L.A. TIMES (May 20, 2015), https://www.latimes.com/local/lanow/la-me-ln-santa-barbara-oil-spill-1969-20150520-htmlstory.html [https://perma.cc/V6AZ-PB7Y].

41. MD. COMM'N WOMEN, *Maryland Women's Hall of Fame: Rachel Carson (1907–1964)* (1985), https://tinyurl.com/y8z52prb.

42. Clean Air Act of 1970, Pub. L. No. 88-206, 77 Stat. 392 (1970) (codified as amended at 42 U.S.C. §§ 7401–7671q (2012)); Clean Water Act of 1972, Pub. L. No. 92-500, 86 Stat. 816 (codified as amended at 33 U.S.C. §§1251–1388 (2012)).

43. National Environmental Policy Act, 42 U.S.C. §§ 4331–70(h) (1970).

44. Energy API, *How Many Jobs Has the Oil and Natural Gas Industry Created?,* https://www.api.org/oil-and-natural-gas/energy-primers/hydraulic-fracturing/how-many-jobs-has-the-oil-and-natural-gas-industry-created [https://perma.cc/G7Q6-NRKR]; U.S. Bur. Ocean Energy Mgmt., *Offshore Oil and Gas Economic Contributions,* https://www.boem.gov/sites/default/files/oil-and-gas-energy-program/Leasing/Five-Year-Program/2019-2024/DPP/NP-Economic-Benefits.pdf [https://perma.cc/8JXA-6KVA].

45. Nat'l Sci. Found., *National Center for Science and Engineering Statistics InfoBrief,* NSF17-316 (Mar. 2017), https://www.nsf.gov/statistics/2017/nsf17316/nsf17316.pdf [https://perma.cc/2FXL-EL3G].

46. Consent Decree Among Defendant BP Exploration & Production Inc. ("BPXP"), the United States of America, and the States of Alabama, Florida, Louisiana, Mississippi, and Texas at 1, In re Oil Spill by the Oil Rig "Deepwater Horizon" in the Gulf of Mex., on Apr. 20, 2010, No. 10-4536, MDL No. 2179 (E.D. La. Apr. 4, 2016); Consent Decree Between

the U.S. and MOEX Offshore 2007 LLC, In re Oil Spill, No. 10-MDL-2179 (E.D. La. Feb. 17, 2012); U.S. v. BP Exploration, No. 2:12-cr-00292 (E. Dist. La. Jan. 29, 2013); U.S. v. Transocean Deepwater, No. 2:13-cr-00001 (5th Cir. Feb. 14, 2013).

47. Igal Berenshtein et al., *Invisible Oil Beyond the Deepwater Horizon Sattelite Footprint*, 6 Sci. Adv. 1 (Feb. 12, 2020), https://advances.sciencemag.org/content/6/7/eaaw8863 [https://perma.cc/N8UY-GG4J].

48. Erin L. Pulster et al., *A First Comprehensive Baseline of Hydrocarbon Pollution in Gulf of Mexico Fishes*, 10 Sci. Rep. 6437 (Apr. 15, 2020), https://doi.org/10.1038/s41598-020-62944-6 [https://perma.cc/N8UY-GG4J].

49. Shamseer Mambra, *The Complete Story of the Exxon Valdez Oil Spill*, Marine Insight (Oct. 2, 2019), https://www.marineinsight.com/maritime-history/the-complete-story-of-the-exxon-valdez-oil-spill/ [https://perma.cc/S2WS-HN4U].

50. Stephen Schneider, Lynne Mesirow The Genesis Strategy: Climate and Global Survival (1976).

51. Nathaniel Rich, *Losing Earth: The Decade We Almost Stopped Climate Change*, N.Y. Times (Aug. 1, 2018), https://www.nytimes.com/interactive/2018/08/01/magazine/climate-change-losing-earth.html [https://perma.cc/HCM2-A97M].

52. U.S. Energy Info. Admin., *Most coal plants in the United States were built before 1990*, Today in Energy (Apr. 17, 2017), https://www.eia.gov/todayinenergy/detail.php?id=30812 [https://perma.cc/FAQ7-ZH3N].

53. Int'l Energy Agency, CO2 Emission from Coal-fired Power Plants in China by Age of Plant, 2000–2018, https://www.iea.org/data-and-statistics/charts/co2-emissions-from-coal-fired-power-plants-in-china-by-age-of-plant-2000-2018.

54. Int'l Energy Agency, World Oil Production by Region, 1971–1980, https://www.iea.org/data-and-statistics/charts/world-oil-production-by-region-1971-2018.

55. Julius J. Anderson, *Carbon Taxes and CO₂ Emissions: Sweden as a Case Study*, 11 Am. Econ. J. 1 (2019).

4

Bloated Capital

How Capitalism Went Awry

While it would be impractical to try and regulate capital investment, it is still surprising that there is so little to deter risky investments. It is still easy to invest in capital equipment that produces harmful effects or products. The reasoning would seem to be the notion that capital investments are purely private decisions. We leave it to the private investor to consider the private benefits. As to the potential for public harm, a dual system of ex post and ex ante disincentives are supposed to send a signal to prospective investors. Ex post, liability could be costly, and could serve as a deterrent for engaging in potentially harmful behavior, by investing in harmful capital. Ex ante, a regulatory state is supposed to intercept the most dangerous industrial practices, and should disincentivize the capital investments that enable them. These dual disincentives have been insufficient in stemming the investment in harmful capital.

For capital that actually produces a harm, or a product that is harmful, liability serves as an ex post remedy. It is also hoped that the presence of that potential liability sends an ex ante signal to capital investors to beware. But litigation is a rarely satisfactory ex post resolution, and a weak ex ante signal for deterring risky capital investments. Litigation only takes place after a harm has occurred, the burdens of proof are often prohibitive, and the costs of litigation are a huge barrier for the vast majority of plaintiffs. Even state attorney generals that might bring an action on behalf of their citizenry find themselves outgunned by expensive legal teams representing defendants. Moreover, if there is a delay in identifying or detecting harm (as there often is in tort litigation or environmental litigation), a great deal of capital investment may already have been made by the time a lawsuit is brought. Pharmaceutical companies began marketing opioids as a safe, nonaddictive pain reliever in the late 1990s, and hundreds of thousands of people have died from opioid overdoses since.[1] And whether justified or not, a substantial buildup of expectations may have developed. If trouble is afoot, those with something to lose will circle the wagons. Recent litigation strongly suggests that pharmaceutical executives *knew*, beforehand, about the dangers of opioid addiction, but took measures to downplay risks,[2] not unlike the decades-long campaign by oil giants to downplay the risks of climate change.[3] By the time that litigation becomes a plausible avenue of redress, it is already too late.

Clearly, it is important for investors to take some stock of the externalities of capital investments *before* they are made. There happens to be a second, more proactive check: regulations and regulatory agencies, often with mandates to prevent certain known injuries before they occur. Environmental, land use, safety, consumer product, food and drug, health, workplace, financial, securities, and a variety of other regulations are meant to complement litigation as a pre-harm remedy. Ideally, subject-area expertise resident in administrative agencies enable the prospective identification of harm, before too much capital investment has taken place. U.S. environmental law includes an extensive permitting regime whereby a variety of conditions may be imposed to limit air and water pollution, which must be satisfied before commencement of operation. Sophisticated investors can be expected to be familiar with the regulatory regimes for polluting capital, anticipate problems with the permitting process and withhold investment if the problems are too serious. Local building codes usually require a certificate of occupancy, which must meet a variety of safety and building regulations before it can be occupied. In general, the goal of this administrative state is to identify threats to the public and promulgate regulations to prevent those harms from occurring.

The aspiration is that the combination of post-harm remedies (litigation) and preventative measures (regulation) will serve as the counterbalance against the private and public benefits of capital at the investment stage. But the regulatory process is imperfect at intercepting these harmful outcomes, and litigation is too weak of a disincentive to affect capital investments. Sometimes harms are truly latent, science only emerging and solidifying decades after much has been invested. The mortality caused by fine particulate matter from coal combustion is a body of research that was decades in the making. If unanticipated harmful side effects of pharmaceuticals are detected after years of development, clinical testing, and manufacturing, the temptation to downplay or discount evidence of harm can be overwhelming. Other times, the harms are known to manufacturers, but hidden from regulators, or the information is shaded in ways that are self-serving. Fossil fuel industries had decades of exalted tax treatment before the specter of climate change presented itself, by which time they all had become, worldwide, a network of sprawling social and economic institutions. The industry had become too big to fail, being the repository of a tremendous amount of inertia and formidable political and social defenses. And certainly, enough ink has been spilled over the duplicity of the tobacco industry which, incidentally, supplied the fossil fuel industries with a playbook, and even some of the same consultants in an effort to deceive the public.[4]

Again, it is not as if sustainable capitalism can be achieved through a capital investment police, making ex ante judgments about the appropriateness of individual investments. Something more modest will help: a recognition of the biases embedded in legal rules and institutions that tend to create path dependency in capital investment. Perhaps inevitably in democracies, those with substantial capital, who therefore have significant stakes in the protection of that capital, will have outsized influence of laws and regulations that affect the value of that capital. But apart from strengthening democratic institutions, legal rules and institutions can simply *stop reinforcing* that path dependency. Beyond the clear-eyed recognition of rent-seeking and rent-preserving activities by capital owners, reform can be achieved by recognizing the systematization of these biases, and implementing appropriate legal doctrine and government policy to counter those biases. Ceasing longstanding subsidization of the oil, gas and coal industries is one example. What follows are two additional examples of this habit of throwing good money in after bad, only because the capital investments are familiar.

4.1 ELECTRIC UTILITY REGULATION

For most of the twentieth century, the electricity industry in the United States operated under a regulated utility model, in which firms were granted a monopoly over some defined service area, but agreed to be bound by certain terms of service, including regulated rates: customer rates and capital investments had to be approved by regulatory bodies, usually state-level public commissions. Regulated utility firms cannot refuse service to customers within a service area (except for nonpayment, of course). The model implied a "regulatory compact" between electricity utilities and the general public, whose interests were to be represented by the public commissions. The granting of a service-area monopoly was necessary, because of the nature of the business of providing electricity, which had once required very high capital expenditures, which was to be paid for over long periods of time in small payments from individual customers. Under such high-capital-cost circumstances, competition would be ruinous and counterproductive; hence the granting of a monopoly.

In a competitive market, firms trade off capital for labor in accordance with some model of profit maximation. In competition, inefficient capital investments lead to high prices, that might drive customers to competitors. That remedy is not available in a regulated monopoly. But in this regulated utility model, the public commission regulates prices, making some judgment as to whether the regulated utility is making decisions that do a reasonable job of keeping electricity rates low. For capital investments, utilities propose to their regulators a capital project, along with a request for permission to pass the cost of the capital project onto its customers. If the capital project is allowed by the public commission, the utility is permitted a specified rate of return on that capital project, as a proxy for what it might have earned in a nonregulated, market setting, incorporating that cost into the rates it charges its customers. Regulated electric utilities are thus permitted by their regulators to charge ratepayers in accordance with the general formula

$$R = O + B \cdot r$$

where R is the total allowed revenues (to be divided up among ratepayers), O is the allowed operating expenses, B is the company's "rate base," all those capital assets from which the company is permitted to earn a return, and r is the permitted rate of return.

Given this regulatory structure, it is in the company's interest to acquire more capital, and expand the rate base as much as possible in order to maximize their permitted revenues. This bias is commonly known as the "Averch-Johnson effect."[5] Although additions to the company's rate base are supposed to be "prudently incurred"[6] and "used and useful,"[7] the reality is that the company often has the upper hand in a ratemaking setting in which it seeks to justify its expenditures to the public commission.[8] Regulated utilities must reveal large amounts of business information that private firms would otherwise keep secret, but do not have to divulge the availability of alternatives. This deprives the public commission of context. And while regulated utilities must reveal some accounting of the total labor and capital costs in any given year, they do not have to reveal their own analysis of the marginal costs and marginal productivity of labor and capital.[9]

Courts and commissions hearing ratemaking cases do not commonly concern themselves with the Averch-Johnson effect. In *Limerick Nuclear Generating Station*,[10] the Pennsylvania Public Utility Commission addressed the question of whether a project may be included in the utility's rate base if the project was prudent at the time of commencement but had subsequently become unnecessary. The opinion, one of only a few that actually considered and discussed the Averch-Johnson effect, minimized its import:[11]

> This [Averch-Johnson] concept . . . maintains that the utilities will invariably seek to overbuild their systems. The financial disincentive of not allowing [construction works in progress] in the rate base is seen as counteracting this tendency . . . It is unlikely that these arguments will ever lead to a satisfactory resolution of whether CWIP is innately fair and equitable. It is far more important not to lose sight of the vital issue of how necessary future system expansion will be accomplished.[12]

The Commission's dismissal of the Averch-Johnson effect is revealing, as is its apparent acceptance that system expansion is necessary. Driven by past precedent and presented with familiar capital investments, public commissions seem to find it difficult to take a hard look at the true usefulness of new investments. Drawn into the weeds of specific capital decisions and lacking context, commissions find it hard to imagine how a competitive firm would behave.

The Averch-Johnson hypothesis has been criticized,[13] some have noted that not all of its implications have been borne out in practice,[14] and the effect has diminished as electricity deregulation has spread across the United States.[15] But empirical evidence for the Averch-Johnson effect has mostly borne it out.[16] The Averch-Johnson bias is one of several sources of regulatory inefficiency, and there is geographical and temporal variation on the vigilance of public commissions. But on the whole, most energy experts would say that in the era of regulated electricity provision, the regulatory commissions have oftentimes been unnecessarily lenient in their allowance of capital investments by electric utility firms.[17] One study found only a handful of cases – about one per decade from 1930 to 1980 – in which a state agency disallowed an investment because it deemed it not to have been "prudently incurred."[18]

The most obvious implication of this "capital stuffing" in the electricity industry is an inefficiently large capital base, higher costs than necessary, and thus unnecessarily high electricity rates paid by consumers. But the second, less obvious implication is that having bloated themselves with excessive capital, regulated utility firms find themselves more vulnerable to change. Any environmental law or regulation that will require a change in equipment or operations, or any economic change, such as competition or a worldwide pandemic, will now threaten a larger set of assets. Faced with a greater, more existential threat, firms will resist change more vigorously.

Both the vulnerability and the resistance to change were on display as vulnerable electric utilities tried to derail and then forestall the deregulation, or "restructuring," of their industry. The deregulation of natural gas introduced a fossil fuel that made it possible to generate electricity at lower cost and with less pollution, giving impetus to a push – long advocated by economists – to deregulate electricity provision generally.[19] The idea that electricity provision necessarily required a regulated monopoly came under challenge, as new, cheaper, and cleaner ways of generating electricity emerged. While transmission and distribution of electricity would still be regulated by a public commission, the generation of electricity by power plants would be thrown open to competition – from which regulated utilities had previously been insulated. Firms complained that they would be saddled with "stranded costs," large, expensive power plants that might be rendered obsolete by competition and liberalized energy markets.[20] These were almost exclusively coal-fired power plants, which cost much more money to build, and were therefore more vulnerable to changes in their legal or economic environment.

Regulated electric utilities were also likely concerned with the devaluation of the vast stock of human capital embedded in existing electricity systems. Granted, to the extent that workers in coal-fired power plants could also work in natural gas-fired power plants, the loss in jobs and human capital might be minimized. Workers and managers could still have been fearful of the rigors of competition, and if so, those fears were not unfounded: plants in states that deregulated electricity generation employed about 6 percent fewer employees after deregulation and, incidentally, enjoyed a 13 percent decrease in nonfuel operating expenses.[21] Market liberalization means loss of monopoly power, and incumbent electricity generation firms in states trending towards deregulation complained loudly about the costs of power plants that had not yet been recouped from ratepayers.[22]

There was some geographic variation, but regulated utilities in states with lenient public commissions – those in the Southeast and the lower Midwest – spent heavily to protect their capital by preventing their states from deregulating electricity provision.[23] As Richard Pierce put it,

> They were leading the quiet comfortable life of an ineffectively regulated monopolist and had no desire to be thrust into a new world in which they would actually have to compete to survive and prosper .... Those utilities became known in the trade as the "just say no" group.[24]

Electricity restructuring is a complex undertaking, and it might not be appropriate for every state, but there is no obvious reason that New Hampshire and New York should be deregulated, and Vermont not. There is no obvious reason, apart from the obstinance of Southeastern and Midwestern electricity generating companies, that they should persist in a regulated utility model, while electricity generation companies in Northeastern states compete. As of 2020, seventeen states and the District of Columbia were deregulated, and the remainder still operated under some form of a regulated monopoly model.[25]

It would be tricky to counteract a pro-utility bias in allowing capital investments to be included in the rate base. Electricity generation is regulated by the fifty public utility commissions of the individual states. Some are friendlier towards their regulated entities than others, so there is no one clear solution. It is not even obvious that there should be any capital investment reform at all. Most utilities are racing to replace their coal-fired power plants with plants powered by natural gas and renewable energy sources. Electric utilities in Florida have politically captured the state's Public Service Commission, obtaining extremely favorable rates of return on a regular basis. The largest electricity provider in Florida, Florida Power and Light, has enviable political power, but its parent corporation, NextEra, also has the nation's largest renewable energy capacity.

In the end, however, even utilities that are progressing towards lower greenhouse gas emissions must still be discouraged from making excessively large capital investments. That their investment choices are moving in the right direction environmentally is a positive development, but one that should be further incentivized by a carbon tax, not passivity on the part of regulatory commissions. The *way* that electricity generation companies move towards a more sustainable energy future – the capital investments that they make – should be governed by policy that is more wary of large capital investments. For example, while Florida Power and Light has dramatically increased its solar energy capacity – at great cost and at the loss of vast forests – it has eschewed the less capital-intensive strategy of encouraging customers to install solar panels on their residential, commercial, and industrial rooftops. Florida Power and Light has in fact vigorously contested any public initiatives to facilitate them, even floating a misleading ballot initiative to counteract an initiative promoting rooftop solar energy. Also neglected in the State of Florida are energy conservation and energy efficiency measures, which would be the least expensive and least capital-intensive measures of all. A fetishism of large, expensive, physical capital, even if directed towards renewable energy sources, misses important alternatives. What should be obvious now is that capitalism works best when the broadest array of options are available. Allowing regulated electric utilities to only focus on the most capital-intensive ones is a curtailment of capitalism.

This book suggests some general tax reforms and environmental reforms in Chapter 8 that might move regulated electric utilities away from their traditionally large capital investments. Fixing the regulatory capture of state utility commissions is beyond the scope of this book. And while regulated electric utilities are a prominent and problematic example of an undue focus on physical capital, it is only one example. It is possible that some relatively simple measures can alter the tax and accounting environment of large capital investments not only by regulated electric utilities, but by other capital-intensive industries.

4.2 FARMS

Like other industries, farming has become increasingly efficient since the early twentieth century, increasing productivity and reducing costs. Between 1948 and 2015, agricultural productivity grew at an average annual rate of 1.48 percent.[26] That is less than the 2 percent average annual growth from 1947 to 2019 for nonfarm businesses,[27] but that latter figure masks a great deal of variation. Taking into account weather variation, agricultural production has grown more steadily and farm technology has advanced more regularly. Tractors have replaced farm animals, and mechanized harvesting became the norm for most crops. Plant and animal breeding have produced higher crop yields and larger animals, as have chemical fertilizers and pesticides.

Much more so than other industries, however, agriculture in the United States has been heavily influenced by government subsidies. It seems to be a global truism that poor countries heavily dependent upon agriculture tend to tax farmers, while rich countries subsidize them. In that sense, the United States is not terribly different from other wealthy countries. In fact, in an increasingly integrated global market, subsidization is often justified on the grounds that domestic farmers need subsidies in order to compete. In the United States, agricultural exports have increased dramatically since the 1970s, but so have imports.[28] It is not straightforward to quantify the amount of subsidy, because there are so many forms of farm subsidies, including direct payments, price supports, insurance and disaster relief. Trade barriers are also an implicit subsidy, but does not require government expenditure, only higher consumer costs. In terms of government expenditures, the bulk of the 2018 Farm Bill was for food aid in the form of the Supplemental Nutrition Assistance Program, accounting for over 75 percent.[29]

Economists are generally critical of agricultural subsidization because they effect a transfer of wealth to farmers from just about everyone else for no reason grounded in economic efficiency.[30] Political scientists generally accept the inevitability of farm subsidies as a descriptive political matter.[31] Agricultural subsidies draw political support from legislators favoring food aid for the poor, and from those favoring some of the conservation programs. I will limit my normative comments about agricultural subsidization to its effects on capital investment.

Inevitably, some infusion of money must necessarily result in some capital investment. It is impossible to say how much, since the counterfactual of a subsidy-free sector is difficult to construct. However, we observe that among economic sectors, farming is a surprisingly capital-intensive one. For the amount of value that agriculture produces for the U.S. economy, farms spend quite a lot of money on capital investments. That is not just tractors and harvesters, but also seeds and plants.[32]

Inducements for capital expenditures need not occur on the front end, reducing the cost of capital. If a legal provision can insulate a capital investment from adverse changes in its legal or economic environment, then it has the same effect as subsidizing the expenditure on the front end. Consider Figure 4.1 below, first seen in the previous chapter.

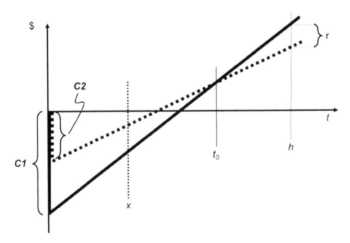

FIGURE 4.1 High-risk, high-payoff and low-risk, low-payoff investments

In that simple model, the only reason *not* to pursue the high-capital, high-profit strategy is the risk of some debilitating event x, such as an environmental regulation (or the emergence of superior competition), which would immediately halt production, and render the capital valueless. But if some favorable legal provision, even before capital investment, removed the risk of that event x then there would be no reason at all from refraining from the high-capital investment. All capital investments would be of the larger kind.

In the 1972 case *Spur Industries, Inc. v. Del E. Webb Development Co.*, the Supreme Court of Arizona predictably held that a property developer could successfully recover in nuisance against a nearby foul-smelling cattle feedlot.[33] From a jurisprudential point of view, it was not surprising that the plaintiff developer could force the cattle feedlot to move, despite actively expanding his retirement community towards the cattle feedlot, which had been operating for years prior to the expanding development. The old common law "coming to the nuisance" defense that would have protected the cattle feedlot as a matter of law, has long been declared, in most states, to be an incomplete defense to a nuisance claim.[34] In almost all states a coming-to-the-nuisance is one of several factors to be weighed by a court.

But the *Spur* ruling, despite the palliative measure of requiring the developer to pay the relocation costs of the cattle feedlot, triggered a backlash. Between 1976 and 1991, every single state and Puerto Rico passed or amended some form of a right-to-farm (RTF) law, legislation to resurrect the coming-to-the-nuisance defense to varying degrees. RTF laws thus reverse a trend towards diminishing the importance of the coming to the nuisance defense.[35] At least with respect to farms, nuisance lawsuits have become considerably more difficult to win.[36]

To widely varying degrees, RTF laws provide farms with a defense to nuisance claims brought by plaintiffs that migrate toward – or "come to" – any nuisance-creating farm. RTF laws commonly set out some definition of the agricultural operations that can raise the defense, a list of permitted operational changes that can be undertaken without losing the defense, and some time limit that serves as an effective statute of limitations on any claims of nuisance against a farm.[37] The stated purposes of RTF laws are to preserve agricultural lands and protect them against the encroaching sprawl of residential development. The preamble to Indiana's right-to-farm law reads as follows:

> The general assembly declares that it is the policy of the state to conserve, protect, and encourage the development and improvement of its agricultural products. The general assembly finds that when nonagricultural land uses extend into agricultural areas, agricultural operations often become the subject of nuisance suits. As a result, agricultural operations are sometimes forced to cease operations, and many persons may be discouraged from making investments in farm improvements. It is the purpose of this section to reduce the loss to the state of its agricultural resources by limiting the circumstances under which agricultural operations may be deemed to be a nuisance.[38]

Why indeed, should a cattle feedlot or hog farm that started out in the middle of nowhere have to continually worry about the approaching advance of property developers? It seemed not only unfair, but counterproductive to make them dance around the whim and caprice of developers. RTF laws seem to draw on a sentiment that business operations with settled expectations deserve some guarantee of legal continuity.

But that view is myopic, focusing too narrowly on just the farms. The perspective lost by zooming in on the farm is of that of surrounding land *uses*, not users. Even if there are, at the outset, no "others" in the vicinity of the farm, there is the latent cost of locking out other, possibly more productive uses if the farm is allowed to changelessly persist. If coming to the nuisance is expanded back into a more powerful insulation against litigation, then alternative land uses could conceivably never develop, and the area surrounding a noxious farm consigned to being an aesthetic dumping ground – if not forever, for an inefficiently long time. The opportunity costs, losses that reflect foregone opportunities, could be very large.

In 1970, when the *Spur* litigation commenced, the population of Phoenix was less than 600,000.[39] In 2018, Phoenix had grown to over 1.6 million, the fifth-most populous city in the United States. The metropolitan area has almost five million, eleventh-largest in the country. Where Spur Industries once lawfully operated its cattle feedlot, there are now approximately 300 single family homes, as part of residential subdivisions, with some county parks, golf courses, and an elementary school nearby. The retirement community built by the developer, Del Webb, has completed its march to the Spur property line. "Value" is a bit too subjective of a label to assign to either cattle feedlots or residential developments, but it would appear that the market has spoken, and that thumb has come down on the side of housing over cattle.

While the outcome of the *Spur* litigation may have been economically efficient, some RTF laws have gone considerably farther than just codifying *Spur*, and have put their own thumb on the scale down on the side of livestock. With literally millions of farms throughout the country, governed by fifty-one different RTF laws, there is no generalizing about the resulting land use effects. But there is little doubt that a strengthening of a coming to the nuisance defense for farms, specifically, makes it easier to raise livestock. All other things being equal, RTF laws increase the size, longevity, and obnoxiousness of farms. Not only do RTF laws privilege farms over other land uses, but they privilege more *intensive* farms over smaller, less intensive unobnoxious ones.

In *Parker v. Obert's Legacy Dairy*, an Indiana court heard a nuisance claim brought by an owner of a small farm against a neighbor, a dairy farm that grew from 100 to 760 dairy cows in a single year.[40] The difference between the two farms is that defendant's farm was large enough to be a nuisance due to the amount of manure and odor it produced, while plaintiff's was not.[41] Most serious nuisance lawsuits are filed against large livestock operations, often referred to as "concentrated animal feeding operations," or "CAFOs,"[42] because of the odors they generate.[43] The odors from hog CAFOs are particularly strong, as hog manure odors consist of over 300 discrete compounds, a handful of them harmful to human health.[44] Even in milder cases where odors may not cause health problems, they can still inhibit outdoor activity.[45] The prevailing evidence suggests that CAFOs cause significant devaluation of neighboring residential properties.[46] Not only does the ubiquitous odor of hog CAFOs cause houses for sale to show poorly every single day of the year, but air pollutants pose significant health risks for neighboring residents.[47]

And yet, the defendant CAFO in *Parker v. Obert's Legacy Dairy* prevailed. The defendant was deemed to be covered by the Indiana RTF law. The RTF law only protects farms if there is no "significant change" in the type of operation, but a change in the ownership or size of the farm, even going from 100 to 760 dairy cows, is not considered "significant."[48] RTF laws thus privilege expansions, which are accomplished by capital intensifications, and has done so repeatedly in Indiana.[49]

But most troubling, the Indiana RTF not only induces capital intensification by protecting it, it also induces capital intensification by placing the vast majority of farms, which are small, at a disadvantage.[50] Despite the label, RTF laws are an implicit subsidy for large CAFOs and, as such, are an assault on small farms. In creating a legal right to farm, state legislatures have unwittingly helped create economic conditions that have made it extremely difficult for small farmers to exist. The result is a livestock sector that is overcapitalized – larger than optimal, and more inclined to engage in rent-preserving activities – than would otherwise be the case. RTF laws, at least when they resemble Indiana's, set up an artificial arms race among farms to grow.

Should large CAFOs enjoy a strong or absolute coming to the nuisance defense? Lockean concepts of property ownership, vesting property rights in those that have mixed their labor with the land,[51] lend an appeal to the defense of farmers in particular. And a first-in-time, first-in-right rule offers simplicity and predictability. A coming to the nuisance defense is a differentiation of right on the basis of priority. Allocating a property priority to first settlers is to choose a particular point in time – the establishment of a CAFO – as the time for a baseline condition. But that is an arbitrary choice. There is no reason to allow noxious land uses to continue just because they were there first. The first land use, which could have begun many years ago, says little about the best *current* land use. In a healthy economy, firms should rise and fall, and cycle in and out of dominance; firms dominating for generations is a recipe for economic stagnation. In a healthy land economy, land uses should not be fixed in perpetuity.

CAFOs, along with farms, enjoy another legal preference: the lack of enforce-ment of water pollution rules and standards.[52] Agriculture, both animal and crop, is responsible for most of the nutrient pollution that causes very serious degradations in water quality. Excess nitrogen and phosphorus from commercial fertilizer and animal manure leaves farms, enters waterways, and produces algae blooms that die off and deplete oxygen in waterbodies. It is not just freshwater that is polluted. Each year, an extremely oxygen-poor patch of water in the Northern Gulf of Mexico roughly the size of New Jersey forms, killing off aquatic life within the zone. It is difficult to monitor and measure nutrient pollution runoff from farms, so EPA simply doesn't. In the Clean Water Act, Congress mandated regulation of large livestock operations, known as "concentrated animal feeding operations," or CAFOs as "point sources," equating them with industrial outflow pipes, and sewage treatment outflows. The analogy is apt, as hog farms often store a slurry of hog manure in a lagoon. Breaches and floods, such as those occurring in North Carolina during Hurricane Florence in 2018, create a river of hog excrement leaching from the lagoons. But while the latter are subject to quantitative regulation, CAFOs are subject to "general permits," virtual permits that simply require CAFOs to abide by certain practices, which are themselves rarely enforced. One should be careful about labeling every legal leniency as a "subsidy," lest we obsess over the distributional consequences of everything. But so aberrant is the treatment accorded farms under the Clean Water Act that it is difficult to see it otherwise.

The Indiana court in *Shatto v. McNulty*, in dismissing a suit against a CAFO because of the RTF law, opined "We must observe that pork production generates odors which cannot be prevented, and so long as the human race consumes pork, someone must tolerate the smell."[53] The point is *not* that someone must tolerate the smell; of course someone has to, if pork is to be produced that way. The point is that in a healthy capitalist economy those that impose harms on others *pay* for that harm. If a CAFO can pay for that harm and still make a profit, then the harm is "worth it," at least from an economic standpoint. The Indiana judge also misses the point that unless the farm pays for that harm, it has no incentive to try and find ways to reduce that harm.

Like most other industries, agriculture has grown in productivity and capital intensity. Unlike most other industries, the agricultural industry enjoys the infusion of massive government subsidies and many legal privileges. The effect of these advantages has been not only to bloat an industry, but to bloat its capital stock. More so than other industries, the capital investments in these industries have led to the perpetuation of the subsidies and other legal distortions that result in an unnecessarily high level of air, water, and land pollution.

4.3 CAPITAL INTENSITY

A subsidy, whether ex ante as a direct payment or ex post as a legal protection from liability or regulation, results in additional capital expenditures. What does any firm do with such a windfall? If it is at all interested in growing or maintaining the business, it would invest. Protection from liability or regulation certainly removes a significant obstacle to capital investment. It would be unsurprising to see industries that are heavily subsidized near the top of a list of capital-intensive industries. That is in fact what we see.

My argument here is inferential. It is difficult to say, and I do not say, how much subsidization in what form, or what kind of legal protection leads to how much capital investment. The capital-labor tradeoffs are different firm-to-firm, industry-to-industry, and year-to-year, to say nothing of other corporate expenditures such as stock buybacks and dividends. Technologies are very different and evolve very differently, industry-to-industry. I do assert, however, that subsidization will have the effect of bloating capital stock, and that a bloated capital stock will cause policy mischief.

Table 4.1 below sets forth a list of most of the NAICS four-digit subsectors, ranked in descending order of capital intensity. Capital intensity is measured by capital expenditures from the year 2014, divided by value added from the

TABLE 4.1 *Capital intensity (2014 expenditures / value added)*

Pipeline transportation	1.185
Oil and gas extraction	0.824
Farms	0.515
Mining, except oil and gas	0.476
Rail transportation	0.459
Utilities	0.449
Water transportation	0.407
Other transportation equipment	0.304
Air transportation	0.195
Plastics and rubber products	0.182
Wood products	0.165
Other retail	0.153
Nonmetallic mineral products	0.151
Truck transportation	0.150
Forestry, fishing, and related activities	0.132
Hospitals	0.131
Waste management and remediation services	0.127
Chemical products	0.125
Food and beverage and tobacco products	0.124
Educational services	0.121
Miscellaneous manufacturing	0.120
Paper products	0.119
Primary metals	0.115
Other transportation and support activities	0.104
Textile mills and textile product mills	0.102
Computer and electronic products	0.100
Machinery	0.097

TABLE 4.1 *(continued)*

Warehousing and storage	0.083
Petroleum and coal products	0.083
Fabricated metal products	0.082
Accommodation	0.081
Printing and related support activities	0.079
Electrical equipment, appliances, and components	0.064
Other services, except government	0.057
Motor vehicles, bodies and trailers, and parts	0.056
Food services and drinking places	0.056
Construction	0.053
Furniture and related products	0.046
Apparel and leather and allied products	0.044
Wholesale trade	0.042
Transit and ground passenger transportation	0.041
Administrative and support services	0.037
Support activities for mining	0.012

same year. Capital expenditures are obtained from the 2015 Annual Capital Expenditures Survey (table 4b, revised for 2014), with the exception of farm capital expenditures, which are obtained from USDA Farm Production Expenditures, 2018 Summary, Farm Production Expenditures by Year, 2014–2018. Farm capital expenditures include (i) farm supplies and repairs, (ii) farm improvements and construction, (iii) tractors and self-propelled farm machinery, (iv) other farm machinery, (v) seeds and plants, (vi) trucks and autos, and (vii) miscellaneous capital expenses. Value added data was compiled by Tschofen, Azevedo, and Muller.[54]

While my argument is inferential, it is still surely worth noting that many of the most capital-intensive industries fall into one of three categories: (i) predicated upon a fossil fuel-centered economy, (ii) are natural resource-based, or (iii) farms. All of these categories enjoy subsidies and legal preferences. Again, subsidies need not be large, just large enough to affect decisions. It is my contention that subsidies have had a role in pushing many of the industries towards the top of this ranking of capital intensity.

Some more caveats are in order. Capital investment does not include investment in human capital. Industries will invest varying amounts in training, that is difficult to capture systematically. Regulations will also affect capital investments. Environmental regulations could well increase the amount of capital investment. I will argue later in this book that if an environmental harm can ethically and effectively be taxed, it should, because it might allow the polluter to find some other way of reducing pollution other than having to make a capital investment.

4.4 ENVIRONMENTAL DAMAGES

How much environmental harm we tolerate from which industries is obviously a highly political question. There may be strong reasons to tolerate a large amount of harm from an industry that is deemed to be important, such as national security for example. We may even subsidize or protect harmful industries if they are deemed to be of sufficient importance. Energy subsidies have been justified on the grounds that low energy prices create a great number of other knock-off economic benefits. These tradeoffs are in fact made, as the product of political processes, as they should be. But these political calculations have been made with very little regard for the environmental costs of these decisions. Environmental damages from these industries have been ignored because the accounting has long been missing, industries and beholden politicians having suppressed that information. Sometimes, the economic importance of some industries is exaggerated. On occasion, environmental damages are exaggerated. But much more often, a great deal of effort is made to deflate environmental damages, hide them from view, or engage in a wide range of unsavory behaviors to essentially wage a campaign against unfavorable or embarrassing information.

It is a profound failing of human society, and may ultimately turn out to be the most consequential one, to have acted mostly in ignorance of the environmental effects of its actions. The omissions from environmental knowledge are not gaps; rather, the bits of environmental knowledge humans collectively possess are islands in a sea of ignorance. Hence, this book proposes to build up humankind's stock in environmental knowledge, a part of this book's proposal that is set out in more detail in Chapter 7. This privation of environmental knowledge, actively abetted by certain industry and antienvironmental groups, is part of why it is difficult to assess environmental damages across industries.

Studies of environmental damages across industries are thus rare. Had Congress not terminated the line of work at the Bureau of Economic Affairs for a "Green GDP," the effort might not be so difficult, especially given continued advances in computing power and information gathering. Economists studying the economic effects of environmental harm often use complex models known as "integrated assessment models," which combine economic modeling with environmental damages, accounting for environmental harm that reduces economic productivity. For example, air pollution can damage crop production, degrade structural materials such as steel and stone, and water pollution can reduce recreational values.

One group of economists has compared damages across industries for the most economically concrete source of environmental harm: premature mortality from fine particulate matter, $PM_{2.5}$. Of all air pollutants, fine particulate matter has been the most studied, the outgrowth of the now decades-long Harvard Six Cities study tracking long-term health outcomes and their relationship to $PM_{2.5}$ pollution levels.[55] $PM_{2.5}$ pollution causes many adverse health effects, but premature mortality is the easiest to measure, because well-studied dose-response relationships offer a linkage from pollution to death, and also because premature mortality is considered the costliest. $PM_{2.5}$ is also convenient to study because other air pollutants ammonia (NH_3), sulfur dioxide (SO_2), oxides of nitrogen (NOx), and volatile organic compounds (VOCs) cause a variety of harms, but their most deadly harm (as far as is currently known, an important caveat) is as a precursor of $PM_{2.5}$. Focusing *only* on premature mortality, Tschofen, Azevedo, and Muller find that damages from premature deaths caused by $PM_{2.5}$ have improved over time, but remain high: $790 billion in 2014, in 2018 dollars.[56]

The Tschofen et al. study, like several predecessor studies, used models to not just determine aggregate damages, but to attribute damages to *specific industries*. Utilizing spatial data and source-specific emissions data, this series of studies was able to tie pollution concentrations to actual emissions data. Industries were broken down into forty-seven subsectors delineated by four-digit North American Industry Classification System codes. This classification also allows for a comparison with each subsector's economic value, which the researchers measured using their economic value added, a Bureau of Labor Statistics figure of the value of goods and services produced, minus costs (inputs, employees, taxes less subsidies, and gross operating surplus).[57] Thus each subsector was tagged with a measure of what Tschofen et al. called "Gross Environmental Damages," and "value added," and a ratio, GED/VA, that represents, roughly speaking, harm per unit of value.

Conceptually, a GED/VA ratio greater than one suggests that the subsector is producing more harm than value. That is a more useful measure than just damages alone, because it provides some sense of whether it is "worth it" or not to tolerate the pollution, from the economic standpoint. The authors rush to say that they do not propose "shutting down" industries having a GED/VA ratio greater than one; just that pollution regulation might be more cost-beneficial in some industries than others. Consistent with the pro-capitalist theme in this book, if all industries were made to pay for their external environmental costs, the industries that are more valuable vis-à-vis their damages would emerge as being more viable.

It is worth reproducing Table 1 from the Tschofen et al. article, below, to give the reader a sense of the industries that emit the most $PM_{2.5}$ or $PM_{2.5}$ precursors. Several observations are in order. First, while the authors had good reason to limit their study to premature deaths from $PM_{2.5}$, it is quite obvious that environmental damages are broader and greater than the figures derived from this important study. There are manifestly many, many health effects of pollution that harm but do not kill. And there are many, many other sources of pollution. Toxic chemicals are not counted at all. Drawing only upon just that research that has been rigorously tested and peer-reviewed, and only upon studies that are able to analytically model premature deaths, the total costs of pollution harms would indeed be dominated by the figures

Excerpt of Table 1 from Tschofen et al. (2019)

Industry group (2014)	GED/VA
Animal production and aquaculture	2.00
Waste management and remediation services	0.87
Water transportation	0.78
Crop production	0.72
Electric power generation, transmission and distribution	0.63
Truck transportation	0.56
Rail transportation	0.35
Nonmetallic mineral products	0.28
Transit and ground passenger transportation	0.28
Iron and steel mills manufacturing from purchased steel	0.23

derived by Tschofen et al., and from previous studies. But research on environmental harm and damages is in its infancy. It is not even quite a fetus, let alone a body of research. What else don't we know?

There is also no accounting for greenhouse gas emissions in this analysis. Emissions of carbon dioxide and other greenhouse gases are well-inventoried for point sources, but are difficult to impute for other industries, such as wholesale trade, computer and electronic products, and food services and drinking places. Were there a method of imputing greenhouse gas emissions, several of the fossil fuel-intensive industries above would surely have a higher ratio. A side analysis done in an earlier and similar study in 2011, by Muller, Mendelson, and Nordhaus, found dramatically different results when greenhouse gas damages were included, using a very conservative figure for greenhouse gas damages.[58]

There are also a myriad of other harms. Even if the authors' working assumption that premature mortality due to $PM_{2.5}$ swamps other human health harms were accurate (they do not make this claim), there are other categories of harm about which very little is known, such as harm to other biota. It is worth interpreting GED carefully.

Another omission – and again, with valid research reasons – is water pollution. The harms of water pollution are more varied, and also less thoroughly researched. It may surprise some that agriculture fares so badly in this analysis. The reason for the high ratios in animal and crop production is the very high emissions of ammonia, especially due to animal manure, that converts into $PM_{2.5}$. But in addition to that, agriculture contributes disproportionately to water pollution. Were that included in the analysis, agriculture would fare even worse.

And finally, there are certain industries in the list of forty-seven subsectors that lie upstream or downstream of each other. For example, parts of oil and gas extraction, petroleum and coal products, and truck transportation are all predicated on an internal combustion engine. Without oil extraction, there would be no petroleum refining and no truck transportation, so arguably, damages all along a production chain should be aggregated and imputed to the original extraction of oil.

4.5 CAPITAL EXPENDITURES, ENVIRONMENTAL DAMAGES, AND VALUE ADDED

It should be no surprise that industries enjoying subsidies or extraordinary legal preferences should be more capital intensive. What else does one do with free or easy money but invest in more capital? And why not invest in capital equipment, if there is no legal risk? It should also be unsurprising that some industries impose far more environmental damages than others. Is there any correlation between capital intensity and environmental damages?

That is a complicated question that I do not attempt here to answer analytically. But again, I think it worthwhile to note some correlations. A thesis of this book is that capital investments have made some industries less flexible, less nimble, and inclined to battle any attempts to diminish the value of their capital through regulation, or any other attempt (including pollution taxation) to internalize the harms they impose. That would include attempts to fend off environmental regulation. It is quite possible that capital intensity uniquely affects the environment. Of all of the rent-preserving activities, fighting against environmental regulation is certainly prominent.

Combining the data from Tschofen et al. with data on capital expenditures from those industries, gives us some sense of whether capital intensive industries are the most polluting ones (at least in terms of $PM_{2.5}$). The results are shown in Figure 4.2 below, with the bubble size indicating the size of capital expenditures for the year 2014 (the last year of the Tschofen et al. study), in 2018 dollars. To make the graph readable, Figure 4.2 omits about half of the industries studied, all of which were bunched in an area of low value added, and lower damages.

The two largest polluters, in absolute terms, stand out clearly: farms and utilities (which include electricity generation). They also happen to be two industries that have been very capital intensive, and/or heavily subsidized. A third, the oil and gas extraction industry, is the most capital intensive, but not apparently very harmful in terms of deaths from $PM_{2.5}$. But that would look quite different if downstream pollution and the social cost of carbon were added. Oil and gas makes fossil-fueled transportation possible, so it would not be irrational to bunch together oil and gas extraction, pipeline transportation, truck transportation and water transportation. $PM_{2.5}$ pollution from ordinary passenger vehicles could be much greater, but is not

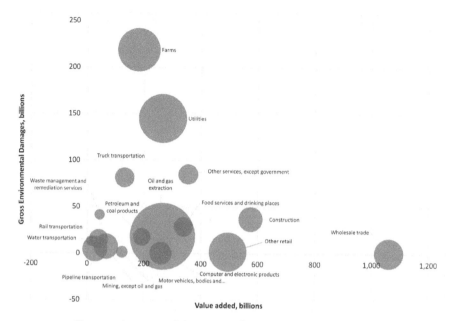

FIGURE 4.2 Gross environmental damages, value added, and capital expenditures
Data courtesy of Nicholas Muller, from U.S. Census Bureau,[59] and from U.S. Dept. of
Agriculture.[60]

classified in Tschofen et al., or by the Census Bureau. A caveat is nevertheless in
order about oil and gas extraction: capital investments from year-to-year are volatile.
For example, while capital investments in this area were high in 2014 – more than
$200 billion – they were less than half that just two years later, in 2016, at $85 billion.

This graph too, is inferential. I have not carried out a rigorous econometric study
to demonstrate a linkage between net environmental harmfulness (the GED/VA
ratio calculated by Tschofen et al.) and capital expenditures. This is not that kind of
book. But inferential as it is, this information raises some questions that should have
been asked before: what is society getting for its capital investments? Just a quick
glance at Figure 4.2 suggests that at least in the United States, it might be worth
investing in less pollution, not more.

Although data reporting platforms for the air pollutants studied by Tschofen
et al. differ from those for greenhouse gases, and therefore are excluded from the
Tschofen et al. estimates of gross environmental damage, it is still possible to
impute *some* climate damages to *some* of the industrial subsectors. Drawing from
the U.S. Greenhouse Gas Inventory,[61] I conservatively imputed greenhouse gas
emissions in 2014 (to correspond to the Tshofen et al. data) to several subsectors,
and adopting a "social cost of carbon" of $50 per ton (an estimate of the marginal
damages caused by emissions of one ton of carbon dioxide emissions, and

described in Chapter 6), added climate damages to the figures from Tschofen et al. The added amounts should not be considered estimates of the climate damages of these subsectors, because they are under-inclusive. The total amounts are shown in the third column of Table 4.2 below. Nor should these figures be viewed comparatively, among these subsectors or with subsectors not listed here, because of the underinclusiveness of the data. Table 4.2 is presented below solely to provide the reader of a sense of how climate damages can affect an overall estimate of the total pollution damages. The climate damages added on also do not include the emission of greenhouse gas precursors. The footnotes denote the tables in the U.S. Greenhouse Gas Inventory from which the greenhouse gas emissions were derived.

It is worth repeating that even if one were to accurately and systematically add climate damages to the figures from Tschofen et al., there would still be numerous sources of uncounted damages. Just to take one example, if the total $25 billion settlement for the Deepwater Horizon tragedy were included in 2014 (the settlement was in 2014), it would double damages from the oil and gas extraction sector.

TABLE 4.2 *Gross environmental damages*

	GED (millions $ 2018)	GED+SCC (millions $ 2018)
Air transportation[a]	242	8,110
Computer and electronic products[b]	158	407
Farms[c]	218,616	250,263
Oil and gas extraction[d]	18,247	27,104
Pipeline transportation[e]	4,582	6,631
Rail transportation[f]	15,302	17,689
Truck transportation[g]	81,360	102,290
Utilities[h]	145,034	252,508
Waste management and remediation services[i]	41,379	48,430
Water transportation[j]	13,054	14,572

Gross Environmental Damages data courtesy of Nicholas Muller, from U.S. Census Bureauand from U.S. Dept. of Agriculture.
[a] Inventory of U.S. Greenhouse Gas Emissions, table 2–13.
[b] table 2–6.
[c] table 2–7.
[d] tables 3–37, 3–39, 3–41, 3–57, 3–59, 3–61.
[e] table 2–13.
[f] table 2–13.
[g] table 2–13.
[h] table 2–11.
[i] table 2–9.
[j] table 2–13.

It is also worth noting again that in this data, oil and gas extraction appears environmentally benign, but would not if downstream effects were added. If the damages from oil and gas extraction were added in with air, truck, pipeline and water transportation, the total would be over $150 billion. That does not even include emissions from ordinary passenger vehicles. Goodkind et al., estimated the total *non-carbon* damages of light gas vehicles as $94 billion in 2011 US dollars.[62] CO_2 emissions from light duty vehicles has been over one billion tons per year recently,[63] so if the social cost of carbon of $50 per ton were multiplied to emissions, that would add an additional $50 in damages. That would clearly make upstream and downstream oil and gas production and consumption by far the most damaging activity. Of course, this does not take into consideration the value of transportation, so it would be inappropriate to compare that with industrial categories. But a price tag of about $300 billion per year ought to raise questions about whether transportation could be less polluting, and less fossil fuel-intensive.

Finally, not reflected in this data (but discussed in Tschofen et al.), damages from the utility sector continue to decline, due to the constant decline of the use of coal and increase in the use of renewable energy sources for electricity generation. In 2019, for the first time since 1885, more electricity was generated from renewable sources than from coal combustion.[64] Damages both in terms of $PM_{2.5}$ pollution and greenhouse gas emissions will likely continue to decline.

At the risk of being repetitive, these figures and more generally this chapter are not proffered as *proof* of the failures of capitalism (and in this case, specifically American capitalism). Capitalism is malfunctioning, but this book is just part of a collage of evidence that the environmental harm is far higher than need be: hundreds of billions of dollars, and still an underestimate of the total harm, known and unknown. Water pollution damages, a vastly underexplored area of economic science, is not included. Although economists have a typology of types of damages suffered through the pollution of water resources, only a few have been extensively researched, and those that do leave the policy analyst with a haunting feeling that much has been excluded. Some of the most rigorous and robust work on water pollution damages has to do with the loss of recreational value of a polluted waterbody. Like the ongoing study of $PM_{2.5}$ as an air pollutant, studying recreational damages is empirically satisfying because the pollution indicators and the outcomes are measurable: concentration of pollutants and algal blooms can be measured, and so can the decline in tourist dollars spent. However, given the numerous other values of water far more important than recreation, it is clear that recreational water uses are just a tip of the iceberg of water pollution damages.

The more specific question that is raised is this: Could money be invested in different, less polluting forms of capital? The answer is manifestly yes. Like Tshofen et al. and Muller et al., I rush to disclaim that none of this is a call to shut down any industry. But consistent with the most basic precepts of capitalism, it is a call for industries to pay for the harms they impose. Those harms are large, and some have already embarked upon a realignment to much less harmful modes of production by changing capital investments. The electricity utility industry is one example, having started the ponderous switch from a coal-dominated industry to a gas-dominated one, and hopefully very soon one dominated by renewable non-carbon sources of energy. Farms can well do the same. What is lacking is the incentive for these industries to reduce their environmental harms.

Notes

1. NIH, Nat'l Institute on Drug Abuse, Opioid Overdose Crisis, https://www.drugabuse.gov/drugs-abuse/opioids/opioid-overdose-crisis [https://perma.cc/Z32D-UBH7].
2. Art Van Zee, *The Promotion and Marketing of OxyContin: Commercial Triumph, Public Health Tragedy*, 99 AM. J. PUBLIC HEALTH 221–27 (2009), https://www.ncbi.nlm.nih.gov/pmc/articles/PMC2622774/ [https://perma.cc/2AGG-T2FZ].
3. NAOMI ORESKES & ERIK M. CONWAY, MERCHANTS OF DOUBT: HOW A HANDFUL OF SCIENTISTS OBSCURED THE TRUTH ON ISSUES FROM TOBACCO SMOKE TO CLIMATE CHANGE (2011).
4. Benjamin Hulac, *Tobacco and Oil Industries Used Same Researchers to Sway Public*, SCI. AM. (July 20, 2016), https://www.scientificamerican.com/article/tobacco-and-oil-industries-used-same-researchers-to-sway-public1/ [https://perma.cc/D98E-Y7M7].
5. Harvey Averch & Leland L. Johnson, *Behavior of the Firm under Regulatory Constraint*, 52 AM. ECON. REV. 1052, 1053 (1962).
6. Duquesne Light Co. v. Barasch, 488 U.S. 299, 309 (1989) (citing Missouri *ex rel.* Southwestern Bell Telephone Co. v. Pub. Serv. Comm'n, 262 U.S. 276, 291 (1923) (Brandeis, J. dissenting)); Pa. Pub. Util. Comm'n v. Philadelphia Electric Co., 31 P.U. R.4th 15, 15 (Pa. PUC 1980); FPC v. Hope Natural Gas Co., 320 U.S. 591, 600 (1944); Richard A. Posner, *Natural Monopoly and Its Regulation*, 21 STAN. L. REV. 548 (1969).
7. *Duquesne Light Co.*, 488 U.S. at 302.
8. In *In Re Limerick Nuclear Generating Station*, the Pennsylvania Utilities Commission, in evaluating expert testimony on a variety of technical and economic matters, wrote: "In performing our analysis, we are cognizant of the fact that many of the calculations and figures presented in the context of this proceeding are somewhat speculative. Although no one can perfectly see the future, we are convinced that those estimates represent more than educated guesswork on the part of the witnesses." Docket No. I-80100341, 48 P.U.R. 4th 190. at 3 (Pa. P.U.C. May 7,1982).
9. Paul Joskow & Richard Schmalensee, *Incentive Regulation for Electric Utilities*, 4 YALE J. REG. 1 (1986).
10. *In Re Limerick Nuclear Generating Station*, 48 P.U.R.4th at 190.
11. *In Re Limerick Nuclear Generating Station*, 48 P.U.R.4th at 211. ("Averch-Johnson phenomenon. This concept, developed in the early 1960s, maintains that the utilities will invariably seek to overbuild their systems. The financial disincentive of not allowing CWIP in the rate base is seen as counteracting this tendency ... The Averch-Johnson phenomenon is no longer applicable. Even if it did apply in the early 1960s, there is little current credibility to the A-J phenomenon given the current depressed financial condition of the industry.").
12. *In Re Limerick Nuclear Generating Station*, 48 P.U.R.4th at 212.

13. Paul L. Joskow, *Inflation and Environmental Concern: Structural Change in the Process of Public Utility Price Regulation*, 17 J. L. & ECON. 291 (1974).

14. William J. Baumol & Alvin K. Klevorick, *Input Choices and Rate-of-return Regulation: An Overview of the Discussion*, 1 BELL J. ECON. & MGMT. SCI. 162 (1970).

15. Donald F. Vitaliano & Gregory P. Stella, *A Frontier Approach to Testing the Averch-Johnson Hypothesis*, 16 INT'L J. ECON. BUS. 347 (2009).

16. *See, e.g.*, Leon Courville, *Regulation and Efficiency in the Electric Utility Industry*, 5 BELL J. ECON. & MGMT. SCI. 53 (1974); H. Craig Peterson, *An Empirical Test of Regulatory Effects*, 6 BELL J. ECON. & MGMT. SCI. 111 (1975); Robert M. Spann, *Rate of Return Regulation and Efficiency in Production: An Empirical Test of the Averch-Johnson Thesis*, 5 BELL J. ECON. & MGMT. SCI. 38 (1974); Paul M. Hayashi & John M. Trapani, *Rate of Return Regulation and the Regulated Firm's Choice of Capital-Labor Ratio: Further Empirical Evidence on the Averch-Johnson Model*, 42 SO. ECON. J. 384 (1976); Scott E. Atkinson & Robert Halvorsen, *A Test of Relative and Absolute Price Efficiency in Regulated Utilities*, 62 REV. ECON. STAT. 81 (1980); Donald F. Vitaliano & Gregory P. Stella, *A Frontier Approach to Testing the Averch-Johnson Hypothesis*, 16 INT'L J. ECON. BUS. 347 (2009). *But see* William J. Boyes, *An Empirical Examination of the Averch-Johnson Effect*, 14 ECON. INQUIRY 25 (1976).

17. Richard J. Pierce, *The Regulatory Treatment of Mistakes in Retrospect: Canceled Plants and Excess Capacity*, 132 U. PA. L. REV. 497, 511–15 (1984).

18. Richard J. Pierce, *Public Utility Regulatory Takings: Should the Judiciary Attempt to Police the Political Institutions?*, 77 GEO. L.J. 2031, 2050 (1989).

19. *See, e.g.*, Severin Borenstein & James Bushnell, *Electricity Restructuring: Deregulation or Reregulation?*, 23 REGULATION 46 (2000).

20. Eric Hirst & Lester Baxter, *How Stranded Will Electric Utilities Be?*, PUB. UTIL. FORTNIGHTLY, Feb. 15, 1995, at 30.

21. Kira R. Fabrizio, Nancy L. Rose & Catherine D. Wolfram, *Does Competition Reduce Costs? Assessing the Impact of Regulatory Restructuring on U.S. Electric Generation Efficiency*, 97 AM. ECON. REV.1250, 1266–69 (Tables 4 & 5).

22. Timothy J. Brennan & James Boyd, *Stranded Costs, Takings, and the Law and Economics of Implicit Contracts*, 11 J. REG. ECON. 41, 42 (1997).

23. Richard J. Pierce, *Completing the Process of Restructuring the Electricity Market*, 40 WAKE FOREST L. REV. 451 (2005).

24. Richard J. Pierce, *Completing the Process of Restructuring the Electricity Market*, 40 WAKE FOREST L. REV. 451, 460 (2005).

25. *US Energy Deregulation Map*, DEREGULATEDENERGY.COM, https://deregulatedenergy .com/us-energy-deregulation-map/ [https://perma.cc/8WKU-S9SE].

26. SUN LING WANG, RICHARD NEHRING & ROBERTO MOSHEIM, U.S. DEP'T OF AGRIC., AGRICULTURAL PRODUCTIVITY GROWTH IN THE UNITED STATES: 1948–2015 (2018).

27. U.S. Bur. Lab. Stats., *Nonfarm Business Sector Labor Productivity Grew 1.9 Percent in 2019*, THE ECON. DAILY (Mar. 12, 2020), https://www.bls.gov/opub/ted/2020/nonfarm-business-sector-labor-productivity-grew-1-point-9-percent-in-2019.htm [https://perma.cc /DZ7Y-Z483].

28. U.S. Dep't Agric., *Ag and Food Statistics: Charting the Essentials, Agricultural Trade*, https://www.ers.usda.gov/data-products/ag-and-food-statistics-charting-the-essentials/agri cultural-trade/ [https://perma.cc/5277-TTK6].

29. John Newton, Congressional Budget Office Updates Farm Bill Math, FB.ORG (Apr. 12, 2018), https://www.fb.org/market-intel/congressional-budget-office-updates-farm-bill-math [https://perma.cc/VR8L-PAKT]; CONG. BUDGET OFF., SUPPLEMENTAL NUTRITION

ASSISTANCE PROGRAM—CBO's APRIL 2018 BASELINE, https://www.cbo.gov/system/files/ 2018-06/51312-2018-04-snap.pdf [https://perma.cc/HR2E-PR6N].

30. Daniel A. Sumner, *Agricultural Subsidy Programs*, ENCYCLOPEDIA ECON. & HISTORY (no date), https://www.econlib.org/library/Enc/AgriculturalSubsidyPrograms.html [https://perma.cc/KYN8-8XYN]; Julian M. Alston & Jennifer S. James, *The Incidence of Agricultural Policy*, in 2 HANDBOOK OF AGRICULTURAL ECONOMICS. 1689–1749 (Bruce L. Gardner & Gordon C. Rausser, eds. 2002).

31. *See, e.g.*, Cameron G. Thies & Schuyler Porche, *The Political Economy of Agricultural Protection*, 69 J. POL. 116 (2007).

32. U.S. DEP'T AGRIC., FARM PRODUCTION EXPENDITURES 2018 SUMMARY, https://www .nass.usda.gov/Publications/Todays_Reports/reports/fpex0819.pdf [https://perma.cc /D38J-Y5UY].

33. 494 P.2d 700, 707–08 (Ariz. 1972).

34. *See, e.g.*, Jacques v. Pioneer Plastics, Inc., 676 A.2d 504, 508 (Me. 1996); Mark v. Oregon *ex rel.* Dep't of Fish & Wildlife, 84 P.3d 155, 163 (Or. Ct. App. 2004).

35. Neil D. Hamilton, *Right-to-Farm Laws Reconsidered: Ten Reasons Why Legislative Efforts to Resolve Agricultural Nuisances May be Ineffective*, 3 DRAKE J. AGRIC. L. 103, 103–04 (1998).

36. *See* Jacqueline P. Hand, *Right-to-Farm Laws: Breaking New Ground in the Preservation of Farmland*, 45 U. PITT. L. REV. 289, 305 (1984).

37. *See, e.g.*, Shi-Ling Hsu, *Scale Economies, Scale Externalities: Hog Farming and the Changing American Agricultural Industry*, 94 OR. L. REV. 23 (2015).

38. *E.g.*, IND. CODE § 32-30-6-9(b) (2015); N.C. GEN. STAT. § 106-700 (2015) (with nearly identical language).

39. *Phoenix, Arizona Population History*, BIGGESTUSCITIES.COM, https://www .biggestuscities.com/city/phoenix-arizona [https://perma.cc/2MEY-92K8].

40. 988 N.E.2d 319, 320–21 (Ind. Ct. App. 2013). The court granted summary judgment for the larger dairy farm, finding that Indiana's right-to-farm law "insulate[d] the Obert's expansion of their dairy farm from nuisance suits under these circumstances." *Id.* at 325.

41. 988 N.E.2d at 320.

42. *See, e.g.*, Initial Case Management Order, *In re* NC Swine Farm Nuisance Litig., No. 5:15-CV-13-BR (E.D.N.C. Jan. 9, 2015). Murphy-Brown LLC, the defendant in this mass litigation, is a hog producer for Smithfield Foods. *Welcome to Smithfield's Hog Production Division*, MURPHY BROWN LLC, http://www.murphybrownllc.com [https://web .archive.org/web/20151031125906/http://www.murphybrownllc.com/] (archived Oct. 31, 2015).

43. *E.g.*, Shatto v. McNulty, 509 N.E.2d 897, 900 (Ind. Ct. App. 1987); Weinhold v. Wolff, 555 N.W.2d 454, 459 (Iowa 1996) (odor preventing neighbors from sleeping); Flansburgh v. Coffey, 370 N.W.2d 127, 130 (Neb. 1985) (odor causing watering eyes and breathing problems); JULIAN CONRAD JUERGENSMEYER & THOMAS E. ROBERTS, LAND USE PLANNING AND DEVELOPMENT REGULATION LAW § 13:3 (3d ed. 2013); Harrison M. Pittman, *Validity, Construction, and Application of Right-to-Farm Acts*, 8 A.L.R.6th 465 (2005); J. Patrick Wheeler, *Livestock Odor & Nuisance Actions vs. "Right-to-Farm" Laws: Report by Defendant Farmer's Attorney*, 68 N.D. L. REV. 459, 460–63 (1992) (summarizing a wide variety of cases of nuisance lawsuits involving odors from hog farms); Tomislav Vukina et al., *Swine Odor Nuisance: Voluntary Negotiation, Litigation, and Regulation: North Carolina's Experience*, 11 CHOICES, First Quarter 1996, at 26 ("The strongest public opposition has focused on offensive odors released from hog barns and manure-collecting lagoons of these large hog operations.").

44. Susan S. Schiffman et al., *Quantification of Odors and Odorants from Swine Operations in North Carolina*, 108 AGRIC. & FOREST METEOROLOGY 213, 236–38 (2001).
45. *Flansburgh*, 370 N.W.2d at 130 ("They can no longer have backyard cookouts, and their grandchildren cannot play outside.").
46. Joseph A. Herriges et al., *Living With Hogs in Iowa: The Impact of Livestock Facilities on Rural Residential Property Values*, 81 LAND ECON. 530 (2005); Jungik Kim et al., *Economic Impact and Public Costs of Confined Animal Feeding Operations at the Parcel Level of Craven County, North Carolina*, 27 AGRIC. & HUM. VALUES 29, 39–41 (2010); Katherine Milla et al., *Evaluating the Effect of Proximity to Hog Farms on Residential Property Values: A GIS-Based Hedonic Price Model Approach*, 17 URB. & REGIONAL INFO. SYS. ASS'N J. 27, 30–31 (2005); Raymond B. Palmquist et al., *Hog Operations, Environmental Effects, and Residential Property Values*, 73 LAND ECON. 114, 121 tbl.3 (1997).
47. K. M. Thu, *Public Health Concerns for Neighbors of Large-Scale Swine Production Operations*, 8 J. AGRIC. SAFETY & HEALTH 175, 178 (2002).
48. IND. CODE § 32-20-6-9(d)(1)(B).
49. *E.g.*, Dalzell v. Country View Family Farms, 517 F. App'x 518, 519 (7th Cir. 2013); *Obert's Legacy Dairy*, 988 N.E.2d at 324–25; Lindsey v. DeGroot, 898 N.E.2d 1251, 1257 (Ind. Ct. App. 2009); Laux v. Chopin Land Assocs., Inc., 550 N.E.2d 100, 103 (Ind. Ct. App. 1990); Shatto v. McNulty, 509 N.E.2d 897, 900 (Ind. Ct. App. 1987).
50S *See generally, e.g.*, Miguel A. Altieri, *Small Farms as a Planetary Ecological Asset: Five Key Reasons Why We Should Support the Revitalization of Small Farms in the Global South* (TWN ENVIR. & DEV. SERIES, NO. 72008), http://twn.my/title/end/pdf/endo7.pdf [https://perma.cc/32Z9-RASS]; Gerard D'Souza & John Ikerd, *Small Farms and Sustainable Development: Is Small More Sustainable?*, 28 J. AGRIC. & APPLIED ECON. 73, 73–78 (1996).
51. Leigh Raymond & Sally K. Fairfax, *The "Shift to Privatization" in Land Conservation: A Cautionary Essay*, 42 NAT. RESOURCES J. 599, 606 (2002) ("Property arises, *in* Locke's familiar allegory, through labor: someone removes something from the state of nature, making it her property, by mixing her sweat with it.").
52. N. William Hines, *CAFOs and U.S. Law*, __ IOWA L.REV. __ (2020).
53. 509 N.E.2d 897, 900 (Ind. Ct. App. 1987).
54. Peter Tschofen, Inês L. Azevedo, & Nicholas Z. Muller, *Fine Particulate Matter Damages and Value-added in the US Economy*, 116 PNAS 19857 (2019), https://www.pnas.org/content/116/40/19857 [https://perma.cc/8UC2-GDQR].
55. Francine Laden et al., *Reduction in Fine Particulate Air Pollution and Mortality: Extended Follow-up of the Harvard Six Cities Study*, 173 AM. J. RESPIR. & CRIT. CARE MED. 667, 668–69 (2006) (finding that for every 10 $\mu g/m^3$ increase in fine-particulate matter pollution resulted in an increase in premature deaths to be on the order of 3 percent higher (Table 1)); Johanna Lepeule et al., *Chronic Exposure to Fine Particles and Mortality: an Extended Follow-up of the Harvard Six Cities Study from 1974 to 2009*, 120 ENVTL. HEALTH PERSP. 965 (2012); C. Arden Pope III et al., *Lung Cancer, Cardiopulmonary Mortality, and Long-term Exposure to Fine Particulate Air Pollution*, 287 JAMA 1132 (2002). Recent studies have estimated that fine particulate matter pollution cause over two million premature deaths annually, Raquel A. Silva et al., *Global Premature Mortality Due to Anthropogenic Outdoor Air Pollution and the Contribution of Past Climate Change*, 8 ENV. RES. LETTER 8 034005 (2013).
56. Peter Tschofen, Inês L. Azevedo & Nicholas Z. Muller, *Fine Particulate Matter Damages and Value-added in the US Economy*, 116 PNAS 19857 (2019), https://www.pnas.org/content/116/40/19857 [https://perma.cc/8UC2-GDQR].

57. Lucy P. Eldridge & Jennifer Price, *Measuring Quarterly Labor Productivity by Industry*, MONTHLY LAB. REV., June 2016, https://www.bls.gov/opub/mlr/2016/article/measuring-quarterly-labor-productivity-by-industry.htm [https://perma.cc/DGF2-NCWC].

58. Nicholas Z. Muller, Robert Mendelson, & William Nordhaus, *Environmental Accounting for Pollution in the United States Economy*, 101 AM. ECON. REV. 1649 (2012).

59. U.S. CENSUS BUREAU, ANNUAL CAPITAL EXPENDITURES: 2015, Table 4b (2016).

60. U.S. DEP'T AGRIC., FARM PRODUCTION EXPENDITURES, 2018 SUMMARY, FARM PRODUCTION EXPENDITURES BY YEAR – UNITED STATES: 2014–2018 (2019).

61. U.S. ENVTL. PROT. AGENCY, INVENTORY OF U.S. GREENHOUSE GAS EMISSIONS AND SINKS, 1990–2018 (2020).

62. Andrew L. Goodkind et al., *Fine-Scale Damage Estimates of Particulate Matter Air Pollution Reveal Missed Opportunities for Location-Specific Mitigation of Emissions*, 116 PNAS 8775, Table S2, Appendix (2019).

63. U.S. ENVTL. PROT. AGENCY, INVENTORY OF U.S. GREENHOUSE GAS EMISSIONS AND SINKS, 1990–2018, at 3-28 (Table 3-13) (2020).

64. U.S. Dep't Energy, Energy Info. Admin., *U.S. Renewable Energy Consumption Surpasses Coal for the First Time in 130 years*, EIA.GOV (May 28, 2020), https://www.eia.gov/todayinenergy/detail.php?id=43895# [https://perma.cc/QSQ3-B2C2].

5

The Case for Environmental Taxation

The cornerstone of this book's proposal is a system of environmental taxes, which will serve as price signals for polluting activities. This part of the proposal is so central because prices are the cornerstone of a healthy market economy; without prices, there is no market. With inaccurate prices, markets will function, but they will misallocate resources. That describes how the entire world, including even Sweden, functions: the value of the global environment is almost never accurately priced into day-to-day activities. An environmental tax, if set at the correct level, would reflect the cost of some harm inflicted upon the environment, and therefore act as an appropriate *price* for that harm. An environmental tax would typically be levied upon some small but measurable unit of pollution: a ton of carbon dioxide, a ton of sulfur dioxide, or a pound of nitrogen oxides.

The case for environmental taxation is well-rehearsed. Readers familiar with the suite of arguments could skim the next several pages, keeping mind that I have added specific case examples to help illustrate the theoretical and empirical findings. It is also necessary to acknowledge that despite near-unanimous endorsement of environmental taxes by economists, lawmakers rarely enact them. A populist sentiment against taxation is widespread, and especially violent in the United States. Environmental taxation is a pig in need of much lipstick. I will address this difficulty at the end of this chapter.

Environmental taxation, being an unpopular policy to begin with, will be crucial to establish legitimacy. Not only must the science of the environmental harms be understood with reasonable certainty – as is already the case with these five proposed environmental taxes – but setting the tax at an accepted level must be the product of a rigorous process backed not only by science and economics, but input from stakeholders, most notably affected industries. The Interagency Working Group on the Social Cost of Carbon is an admirable example, bringing in as it did so many people from so many agencies, as well as public input. At the very least, a federal tax-setting process in the United States should follow the rigorous federal administrative rulemaking process. Of course, rigorous science and economics and lawful, patient process will not remove opposition; but may reduce its intensity. In any case, it is what healthy democracies do.

5.1 A SHORT PRIMER

Environmental taxes are per-unit pollution taxes first conceptualized by English economist Arthur Cecil Pigou, and had a distinct orientation towards welfare economics and economic efficiency.[1] The idea is simply to make polluters pay for the costs they impose upon everybody else, and therefore reevaluate their production decisions in light of those costs. A "Pigouvian" tax would induce the polluter to make a socially optimal decision, instead of one that is privately optimal but socially suboptimal.[2]

Consider a widget factory that emits air pollution. In the absence of a mechanism in which such external costs, or *externalities*, are accounted for, one would expect the factory to produce too many widgets, and emit too much pollution. "Too much" in this sense means that the extra widgets produced by the factory were less valuable than the extra pollution was harmful. Economic efficiency would dictate that externalities be accounted for somehow, that the factory take into account the pollution it emitted – that is, pay for the harm it caused – in which case it would choose to produce fewer widgets, or perhaps none at all. Environmental taxes are sometimes referred to as Pigouvian taxes, even if they are not strictly calibrated to the marginal social harm, as Pigou would have it. They are the method generally preferred by economists for internalizing externalities, so that production decisions are more efficient, taking into account the harm they cause.

Externalities abound and there is more harm to go around than there should be. That is to say, there are many human activities for which the harm caused is greater than the value of the activities themselves. We know this analytically, through cost-benefit analyses. We also know this intuitively, as some activities seem so trivial when compared to their harm. Over 4,500 people in the United States died in 2018 due to people texting while driving a motor vehicle.[3] Using the standard value of a statistical life of $9.3 million, that amounts to a total cost of over $41 billion. That is just the cost of fatalities and does not include the many, many more nonfatal injuries from the remainder of the 1.5 million additional texting-and-driving-caused car crashes. If the reader will indulge me for making a nonempirical assertion, my guess is that the value gained by texting and driving nationwide is something less than the $41 billion (actually much more, if it included nonfatal injuries) of net harm it causes.

To take a more rigorous example, fine particulate matter ($PM_{2.5}$) air pollution is believed to account for at least 70,000 premature deaths per year,[4] and probably more like 100,000.[5] These figures are uncertain, but as the subject of continuing rigorous study, they have been fairly consistent. Again, applying a standard (but contested) value of a statistical life of $9.3 million[6] to those numbers, that would imply an *annual* cost of $651 to $930 billion in terms of lost lives. That is a remarkable figure, roughly 3 to 5 percent of the United States GDP, at least before the coronavirus crisis. And it does not count nonfatal health costs, productivity lost to illness, and a variety of hedonic costs, such as recreation, that easily run into the billions of dollars. It also excludes consideration of the possible contribution of $PM_{2.5}$ pollution to increased mortality from the COVID-19 virus[7] that, at the time that I am writing this book, is killing thousands of people daily.

Some proxy prices for pollution and other environmental harms exist in the form of environmental, natural resource, and land use laws and regulations. They impose costs on firms and people that engage in harmful activity and, it must be said, occasionally more than is warranted. Necessarily, the nature of such regulation is that it is meant to apply broadly and uniformly. As such, it treats different situations as the same. Born in an industrial era in which many of the most polluting industries in the United States were fairly uniform in their production methods, much pollution regulation has been predicated on the notion that the EPA, as regulator, could mandate *better* production methods or pollution control measures that would reduce harm.

In this, those first-generation laws were wildly successful: a cost-benefit analysis of the Clean Air Act estimated the annual benefits of cleaner air from 1970 to 1990 at about $22 trillion (within a range from $6 trillion to $50 trillion) and the costs of complying at about $523 billion, less than one-fortieth of the mean estimate.[8] While these first-generation laws can be clumsy and rigid, it is hard not to admire how much better off Americans have been made by this first stab at pollution reduction. The dramatic cost-benefit ratio also suggests that there is much, much more low-hanging fruit to be harvested in terms of protecting human lives and health. To see why, consider the following illustration in Figures 5.1 through 5.3.

In a paradigmatic polluting factory making widgets, the factory could reduce its emitted pollution drawing from a menu of different pollution reduction measures, including operational changes, equipment or input substitutions, and perhaps larger changes such as the purchase and installation of expensive pollution control equipment. If the factory were required to reduce its pollution by a small amount, it would choose the least expensive measure first. If the factory is required to further reduce its pollution, it will have to undertake more expensive measures, and as it is required to *still* further reduce its pollution so that its emissions are extremely small, it must finally undertake the most expensive and heroic measures. This menu of options can be represented by a declining cost curve, with the *marginal*, incremental cost lower at higher levels of pollution, and the costs higher when, moving towards the left, it has exhausted all of the cheaper measures and must undertake the heroic ones. The cost of any individual measure, say, effecting an incremental reduction in pollution from P_0 to P_1 as shown by Figure 5.1 below, is represented by the hatched area under the marginal cost curve.

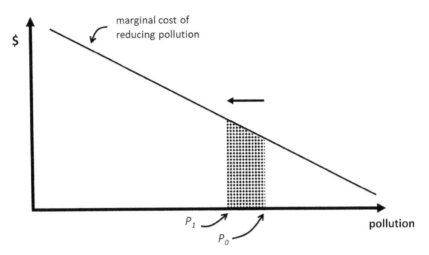

FIGURE 5.1 Marginal costs of pollution

Counterbalanced against the cost of any individual measure is the benefit in terms of lower pollution. This could include, to the extent they could be monetized or somehow accounted for in a cost-benefit analysis, health benefits, a reduction of deaths from pollution, and many other increases in welfare from reductions in pollution. But for the benefit side, the increment in welfare moves in the opposite way of marginal costs: when pollution levels are very low – when the environment is very clean – the incremental benefit of further lowering pollution is small. When pollution levels are high – when the environment is very dirty – the incremental benefit if reducing pollution is very valuable. This can be represented by an *increasing* marginal benefit curve, rising in value as pollution increases. The benefit of any individual improvement, say, from P_0 to P_1 as shown by Figure 5.2 below, is represented by the hatched area under the marginal benefit curve.

Putting together the benefits and the costs of any incremental change in pollution, Figures 5.1 and 5.2 can be combined into Figure 5.3, to represent both the benefit and the cost of a single pollution reduction measure, from P_0 to P_1.

If one were to map the aforementioned Clean Air Act cost-benefit analysis that found a greater than forty-to-one benefit to cost ratio on to a graph of this sort, it would require drawing a figure in which the benefit rhombus was more than forty times as large as cost rhombus. Figure 5.3 doesn't quite do justice to that analysis, but it does suffice to illustrate that quite likely, there is more low-hanging fruit to be picked in terms of further improvements in air quality.

A Pigouvian tax, however, would obviate the need to do at least half of the analysis: the cost side. A Pigouvian tax meant to perfectly internalize the environmental costs of a polluting activity would be exactly mapped out by the marginal benefit curve. In theory, the level of the Pigouvian tax would depend upon the level of pollution.

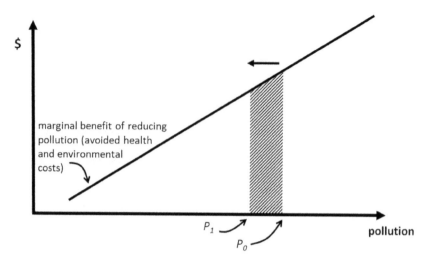

FIGURE 5.2 Marginal benefits of pollution

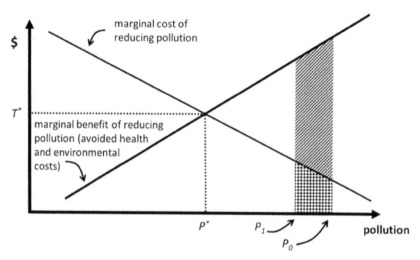

FIGURE 5.3 Combined marginal costs and benefits of pollution

A perfect Pigouvian tax would be set at the level T^*, the point at which the polluter would undertake pollution reduction to the point P^* at which any further pollution reductions (i.e., moving further to the left) would be more costly than the tax itself. The goal would be to set the tax at the level so that amount of pollution is just right, at the intersection of the marginal cost (of reducing pollution) curve and the marginal benefit (of reducing pollution) curve, where the marginal cost and the marginal benefit are both T^*, and the amount of pollution is P^*.

In reality, a Pigouvian tax would be set approximately at current levels of pollution, and the benefits estimated by estimating the *total* health costs caused by pollution by the current level of pollution. If a $PM_{2.5}$ tax were to be imposed, the total costs – most prominently the costs of those premature deaths – would be divided by current levels of $PM_{2.5}$ pollution. If $PM_{2.5}$ pollution could be monitored and measured and traced to their sources, an emitter of $PM_{2.5}$ could be made to pay for the costs of its contribution to the problem. There would be no need to estimate the marginal costs of reducing pollution, because a Pigouvian tax only purports to represent the harms resulting from pollution. If the environmental tax accurately represents the marginal social cost, then only businesses producing more value (as measured by their profits) than harm (as measured by the tax) will survive. An important advantage of an environmental tax is that it is a self-executing cost-benefit exercise. Avoiding one half of the controversial exercise of a cost-benefit analysis is an important advantage over regulating, and debating whether it is "worth it" or not.

The Clean Air Act regulates hundreds of air pollutants, so it is not so simple of a matter; some are air pollutants under-regulated and some are probably over-regulated. As a general matter, harm is probably underestimated because it is unlikely that we recognize or understand all of the ways in which human activity affects the environment. There are almost certainly many more cases of under-regulation than there is over-regulation. Suffice it to say, there is more work left to be done.

5.2 ADDITIONAL BENEFITS OF ENVIRONMENTAL TAXATION

At bottom, "too much pollution" is a misallocation of resources, including capital. Money is still spent mining, transporting, and burning coal, investor dollars are still financing those activities, when they could be directed toward the combustion of natural gas as a fuel source or, better still, renewable energy sources such as wind or solar. Using natural gas, the same amount of electricity could be generated while producing far less pollution. The result of having failed to assign a price to the pollution from coal combustion was more pollution for the same amount of electricity. An environmental, or Pigouvian tax in the form of a carbon tax, or a fine particulate matter tax, or a sulfur dioxide tax, would induce a more efficient allocation of resources.

These harms are borne by humankind in terms of premature deaths, illness, lost productivity due to illness, lost productivity due to the degradation of ecosystem services caused by pollution, and a large variety of adjustments that human society must make when environmental conditions change. When a tropical cyclone is stronger than it would be without the warmer waters caused by climate change, it can shut down entire regions and disrupt international commerce as it closes major ports and airport hubs. The costs of those increasingly frequent climatic disruptions routinely run into the tens and hundreds of millions of dollars, and now increasingly often, the tens of billions. In addition, there is the cost of the *risk* assumed of disruption, including the insurance that would otherwise be unnecessary. Indeed, the costs of climate change in a single unfortunate year could be so large that some insurers and reinsurers could be at risk of default. Many ethicists and economists would add that humans also place an altruistic value on the existence and well-being of living systems and creatures even if they have no discernible effect on human welfare. I strongly agree with that sentiment, but the case for environmental capitalism can be made even while omitting consideration of those altruistic concerns.

In addition to reallocating resources more efficiently, Pigou's concept has a second, related, pro-capitalism effect as well: if polluters must pay for every unit of pollution they emit, they have incentives to find new ways to reduce pollution. Not only might a Pigouvian tax induce the manufacturer to cut back on production of widgets, but if widgets are truly valuable, manufacturers might try to find new ways to reduce pollution from making widgets as well. Pigouvian taxes have this secret property of aligning economic incentives with environmental objectives. Once there is money to be saved in reducing pollution, entrepreneurial spirits will begin searching for new and better technologies, attracting investors along the way.

Economists have clearly and convincingly demonstrated the price effects of environmental taxation. The empirical evidence is robust. But empirically showing that environmental taxes stimulate innovation is more difficult. For one thing, innovation is difficult to measure. Research and development expenditures and patents are proxies for innovation, but imperfect ones. Some studies infer innovation from measurable improvements, such as for motor vehicle technology, but that technique is also vulnerable to omitted or confounding explanatory factors. In the end, innovation is difficult to quantify, and thus difficult to link to environmental policy.

As a theoretical matter, economists generally pronounce environmental taxation to be a more effective policy for stimulating innovation, though not always for all types of innovations. There are situations in which regulations might, for example, induce firms coordinate research and development in such a way that they in effect work together to improve technologies. Also, some regulations are effective in inducing polluting firms to find cheaper or more efficient ways to reach a regulatory goal, such as efficiency of removing a pollutant. But those types of regulatory goals are never quite as direct, and therefore not quite as effective, as one that focuses on the environmental outcome itself. By focusing on the environmental outcome, an environmental tax leaves open the maximum number of possibilities for reducing the pollutant. Environmental taxation, provided it truly represents a harm and provided the taxation level roughly approximates the harm, is always a closer proxy for the harm than any regulatory goal. Equipment could be extremely efficient in scrubbing out pollutants from an emissions stream, but if the plant operates continuously at a high capacity, then the absolute amount of emitted pollutants could still be very high. And from an innovation viewpoint, by leaving open the full panoply of options for reducing pollution, environmental taxation maximizes the different ways in which innovation can occur. This not only increases the raw probabilities but also introduces the possibilities of combining innovations from different processes and even different industries.

It is worth considering innovation on its own, and distinguishing it from less dramatic reactions to price. For purposes of this book, "behavioral change," or "price effects" could usefully be considered changes that do not involve changes in equipment or, capital, or other changes that occur along margins, such as substitution or conservation. See Figure 5.4 below.

With a Pigouvian tax at T^*, polluting at the level P_o would cost the polluter a total pollution tax bill of P_oT^*. The polluter would reduce the amount of her pollution to P^* because in so doing, she would reduce her pollution tax bill by the rectangle $[P_o\text{-}P^*]T^*$, and it would only cost her an amount represented by the shaded area under the marginal cost of reducing pollution curve between P_o and P^*. That would save her the amount shown by the hatched triangle above the marginal cost curve and between P_o and P^*. In this figure, she could accomplish this by reducing the number of widgets produced, but could also undertake a number of other adjustments, like installing pollution control equipment. Her total pollution tax bill would be lowered to P^*T^*.

Rather than reduce production, the firm could figure out a way to reduce pollution, change the production process, or even change the product. The firm could innovate. "Innovations" are movements of the margins themselves, possibly

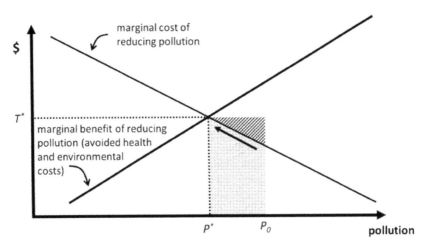

FIGURE 5.4 Marginal cost and benefit of pollution reduction

involving changes in equipment or capital, or entirely new arrangements. If innovations actually shift the marginal pollution abatement cost curves for a large number of producers or consumers, the potential exists for larger, more profound changes in environmental outcomes. See Figure 5.5 below.

By finding a new way to reduce pollution, the polluter has shifted her marginal cost of polluting curve downward, rather than sliding back along its marginal-cost-of-reducing-pollution curve. This shift enables the polluter to undertake a larger reduction in pollution, to P_1, and reducing its total pollution tax bill to P_1T^*. That would represent an even greater savings than the mere reduction in production shown in Figure 5.2, and might justify the research efforts needed to generate such an innovation. In fact, in this graph the pollution abatement would actually be excessive, and an innovation of such impact would warrant a lowering of the pollution tax rate.

Innovation is truly the secret ingredient to large advances in science, technology and medicine. The bulk of twentieth century economic growth in the United States is unexplained by economic models. Economists call that residual "total factor productivity," and most believe that innovation is the largest part of that residual.[9]

An excellent review of research on environmental policy and innovation is undertaken by David Popp,[10] and it is not my goal to attempt to replicate or summarize it, but to offer a complementary analysis. Whether one views changes as mere behavioral or profound technical change, the details of these changes are worth studying. This book takes the decidedly unempirical tack of using examples to demonstrate the potential for environmental taxes to stimulate both behavioral changes and innovation. Empirical validation is more robust, but my goal is to make the linkages between environmental policy and outcomes more concrete. The

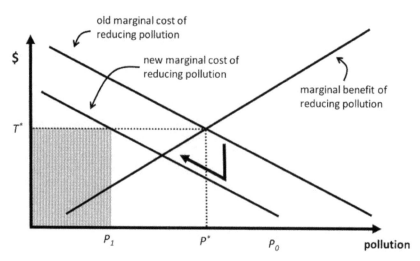

FIGURE 5.5 Effect of innovation on marginal costs and benefits of pollution reduction

changes and savings in these cases are clear and well-documented, and sufficiently linked to policy variations to be credible on their own. My hope is that the reader will find them compelling examples of the points I wish to make about capitalism and environmental taxation.

5.3 THE SULFUR DIOXIDE EMISSIONS "CAP-AND-TRADE" PROGRAM

"Market mechanisms" in environmental policy are policy tools that seek to use market activity and market forces, as opposed to regulatory requirements, to achieve environmental outcomes. These would include environmental taxes and their cousins, emissions "cap-and-trade" programs. Cap-and-trade programs do not tax emissions directly. Rather, cap-and-trade programs limit the overall amount of emissions and allow emitters to buy and sell permits to determine which firms will emit how much. Cap-and-trade programs are similar to environmental taxes in that they impose a *price* on a marginal unit of pollution. But whereas an environmental tax actually specifies that price, a cap-and-trade program specifies the total quantity of permits, and allows the price to emerge in the resulting market trading activity. In both cases the effect of a price stimulates the same kinds of behavior, due to the presence of a marginal cost of polluting. Cap-and-trade programs and Pigouvian taxes induce the same kinds of behavior but to different degrees, depending on the magnitude and stability of the price. Both are often proposed as substitutes for traditional forms of regulation, which in the case of coal-fired power plants includes requirements to install "scrubbers," the end-of-pipe technology to capture sulfur dioxide (SO_2). A review of the long-standing debate over the comparative strengths and weaknesses of these two instruments would not serve the purposes of this chapter. Rather, this description of the workings of the SO_2 emissions cap-and-trade program is offered to illustrate the entrepreneurial effects of having a marginal price on a quantity of pollution.

Any discussion on market mechanisms inevitably includes mention of the SO_2 cap-and-trade program under the 1990 Clean Air Act Amendments. Coal-fired power plants were given a limited number of permits to emit a quantity of SO_2, a pollutant unique to coal combustion, and were permitted to trade amongst each other. Under the program, some plants actually purchased from their peers more emissions permits, to be able to continue polluting business as usual. Others undertook ambitious pollution control measures, reducing pollution enough to generate an excess in permits, and selling them off, as they were no longer needed. The permit requirement introduced a new marginal cost of emitting SO_2, reflected in the trading price of permits. Faced for the first time with a marginal cost of emitting SO_2, a variety of firms – and not just electricity generation firms – found ways to make and save money. A variety of unforeseen abatement strategies emerged, previously thought infeasible.

For example, some electric utilities that used coal found new ways to use it. Coal mined in the Eastern and Midwestern United States tends to have high sulfur content, while coal mined in the West, much lower. Some, instead of installing scrubbers, switched from high-sulfur Eastern coal to low-sulfur Western coal. Those plants lowered their emissions enough to be able to cover the difference by buying a few extra emissions permits.[11] Previously, it had been thought that blending the two types of coal would lead to problems with the boilers used to generate steam. But it had never been tried. Why would anyone try it, and risk damaging an expensive asset? But with the new marginal price – the trading price of a permit – and tantalizingly, the potential permit savings, the experiment was undertaken, and succeeded.[12] SO_2 emissions were lowered without the installation of scrubbers.

Avoidance of the scrubber requirement was aided, surprisingly, by innovation in other industries. The deregulation of the rail industry in the 1980s created opportunities for shipping low-sulfur coal from Western states such as Wyoming all the way to Eastern power plants. Rail companies, liberated from regulation, were able to divert attention and resources towards more profitable ventures. As it happened, the potential for saving hundreds of millions of dollars in SO_2 permit costs was an economic boon that electricity generation companies were willing to share with the rail industry. Working with Western coal mines and Eastern utilities, helped with innovation by increasing the number of parallel tracks, and working with mines to speed and automate the loading and unloading of coal.[13] It bears repeating that this is an ingenious way of saving money, and an illustration of the power of capitalist impulses. It is not a heartwarming story environmentally, as the vast strip-mining of large swaths of Western states has left a large mark upon the landscape, and continues to impose other environmental costs, including climate change.

Electricity generation utilities found other ways to reduce emissions and avoid the scrubber requirement. Some of the larger utilities constructed natural gas-fired power plants, which were much smaller, much less expensive, and more nimble in terms of start-up and shutdown times. Rather than install scrubbers, some firms built natural gas-fired plants and shifted generation onto these newer, cleaner plants from their existing coal-fired plants, thereby reducing SO_2 emissions and permit purchases.[14] As a good capitalist firm would, firms with both coal-fired and gas-fired plants remained attentive to the tradeoffs of using one plant or the other, with the price of a permit now figuring prominently in that calculus. The permits also allowed firms flexibility in maintenance that had not been previously possible. Before the SO_2 cap-and-trade program, when maintenance or repairs were required of a power plant, regulations required it to shut down completely, and substitute an entire other redundant plant, that was itself subject to all of the normal regulatory requirements. Under the SO_2 emissions trading program, utilities could just temporarily run the substitute without the pollution controls, and simply pay for the extra emissions by buying a small number of permits.[15]

Finally, the newfound ways to reduce emissions lit a fire under the scrubber industry, which had previously enjoyed oligopolic conditions in a concentrated and expensive market. But faced now with competition and possible obsolescence, the scrubber industry suddenly found ways to reduce the costs of their product. Relieved of twenty-four-hour regulatory requirements and strict removal efficiency standards, scrubber manufacturers, working with electricity generation utilities, dispensed with much of the "gold-plating" that had previously been required by regulation, and redesigned scrubbers to cost less while still removing a worthwhile amount of SO_2 pollution.[16]

Finally, finally, as an example of just how entrepreneurial some firms could be, an engineer at an electricity generation utility, Baltimore Gas & Electric, noted that a byproduct of the scrubbing process was calcium carbonate, which happens to be the main mineral for the production of construction drywall. If the utility could take on a side business of producing drywall, it could defray the costs of buying, installing and operating the scrubber, and drastically reduce its disposal costs, which by the way also entailed fairly detailed regulations. As it turns out, producing drywall was simple enough for Baltimore Gas & Electric to make it worthwhile to engage in this side business.[17]

The SO_2 emissions trading program was not primarily successful because it reduced emissions, although it did. With cap-and-trade programs, the emissions quantity is defined by the cap, so the environmental outcome is defined by the program at the outset. Rather, the program was successful primarily in the economic sense because it provides an example of how a marginal price can launch a variety of emission-reducing innovations previously thought infeasible. Compliance cost estimates for the year 2000 (the beginning of a stringent phase of the program) are less than $800 million annually, compared with the hypothetical costs for a simple scrubber requirement, which were twice that amount,[18] and one-tenth the estimate made by the industry trade group, the Edison Electric Institute.[19]

The SO_2 cap-and-trade program was not exactly the same as an SO_2 tax, but it is the same in the sense that it introduced a marginal price on pollution. The marginal price is what makes an environmental tax work, and the SO_2 program had profound effects on the inner workings of not just coal-fired power plants, but also natural gas-fired power plants, railroads, the scrubber industry, and other firms. Switching environmental performance from the regulatory compliance division, probably staffed by lawyers, to elsewhere in the firm, had the effect of stimulating creativity in ideas to reduce pollution. That is not to sell short the creativity of compliance lawyers; innovation is likely a collaborative process. But market mechanisms introduce a different energy, converting the emissions reduction effort from a regulatory one to a profit-seeking one.

5.4 SWEDEN'S CARBON TAX

Sweden is a rough model for the kind of capitalism proposed in this book. While it still has some work to do in terms of lightening its human footprint on the Earth, it has much less to do than almost every other country. Sweden's carbon tax, introduced in 1991, is the highest in the world, and has played a prominent role in its extraordinary energy efficiency and its minimization of its carbon footprint. A carbon tax is levied on the emission of a ton of carbon dioxide, whether it be from burning coal, natural gas, petroleum, or waste. The carbon contents of fossil fuels are consistent and well-known, so determining the level of taxation is simple. Often, the tax can be collected at distribution points at which other taxes are already levied, such as the value-added tax, or other taxes on fossil fuels, making administration of the tax simple as well. Sweden does not have or produce any fossil fuels of its own, so the Swedish carbon tax is collected at one of about 300 import points where coal, natural gas, or petroleum products enter the country. Obviously, it is up to the owner of the fossil fuel how much of the carbon tax to try and pass onto the consumer.

Sweden's carbon tax has played a large part in baking energy efficiency and avoidance of fossil fuels into its economy. Lacking a fossil fuel industry of its own, Sweden does not suffer from heavy industry lobbying against climate policy as in the United States and Canada. Also, having no fossil fuels of its own, Swedes have demonstrated a willingness to sacrifice to secure its own sources of energy. Sweden has thus achieved a large measure of energy independence by relying on nuclear, bioenergy, hydro, and wind energy to meet its energy demand. Sweden's eight nuclear plants supply about 40 percent of the country's primary energy. Often the quest for energy independence is quixotic, yielding emotional or political satisfaction at the expense of economic security, in the rare instances it is achieved. But in Sweden's case, energy independence has yielded productivity and economic gains in well excess of what could have been predicted in 1991. Sweden has prospered economically, GDP per capital growing by 70 percent from 1991 to 2017. Correlation does not, of course, prove causation, but there is a growing body of research that Sweden's decarbonization has had some significantly positive economic side effects.[20] One economic cobenefit is its ability to dodge oil price volatility, aiding its transportation sector.

The most important development behind Sweden's decarbonization is its development of bioenergy derived from agricultural and household wastes. The adoption of bioenergy has played a role in reducing emissions from Sweden's concentrated industrial sector, but it has been central in dramatically reducing the country's emissions for building heating. Most of Sweden's cities and towns employ "district heating," a centralized source of heat production that recycles waste heat for the purpose of more heating. Until 1990, most district heating systems were fueled by imported fuel oil. With the advent of the carbon tax, entrepreneurs experimented with improving methods for deriving bioenergy from agricultural waste. A new end product was developed, wood pellets that feed boilers much the same way that fuel oil once did. District heating systems began switching over, cascading into a massive switchover and with it, the scale economies of manufacturing wood pellets as bioenergy. Along with the growth of the industry as well, come the continuing

refinements thereafter. For an illustration of just how rare fossil fuel heating is in
Sweden, see Figure 5.6 below.

Bioenergy has become a national technology, uniquely efficient in Sweden, and
accounting for almost 40 percent of all primary energy supply. The innovation
around bioenergy has not been limited to efficient ways to collect and burn organic
waste. Sweden industry has developed a "bio-methane" – a plant-derived version of
natural gas – that can be substituted for fossilized natural gas. If that can be produced
at scale, it could be exported to displace natural gas mined as a fossil fuel. If other
countries adopted a carbon tax as Sweden (and others) have, a biomass-based natural
gas would be an attractive alternative to fossil natural gas.

Lest the reader rush to anoint Swedish a holy state of climate action, it is worth
noting that Sweden did not subject its industrial sector the full amount of the carbon
tax until 2018. But even though Sweden applied a much lower carbon tax rate to
Swedish industry from 1996 to 2010, it still amounted to about $25 or $30 US per ton,
and at those levels of taxation industry still reduced fossil fuel usage. The progress
made under even modest levels of taxation bear witness to the power of pricing to
induce change. See Figure 5.7 below.

A country of less than ten million people is still a country with concentrated
industries. While there is an ever-present risk of oligopoly, it does not seem to have
materialized. What smallness does seem to have led to is rapid diffusion of innovation. The adoption by one brewery, Åbro, from fuel oil to bioenergy, led to other

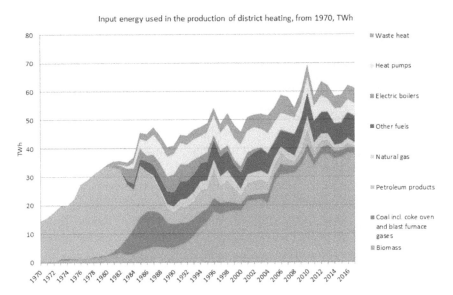

FIGURE 5.6 Input energy used in the production of district heating, from 1970, TWh
Source: Swedish Energy Agency and Statistics Sweden.[21]

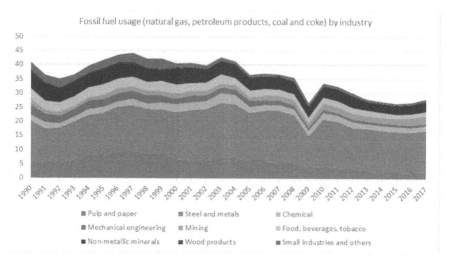

FIGURE 5.7 Fossil fuel usage (natural gas, petroleum products, coal and coke) by industry
Source: Swedish Energy Agency and Statistics Sweden.[22]

breweries also making the switch. The conversion of the country's largest dairy, Arla, to bioenergy, led to a switchover of most other dairies.

In general, life in prosperous and capitalist Sweden is much less carbon-intensive than in the United States. Swedes drive less than half the miles per year per person than Americans drive, despite having a much smaller population density than the United States (sixty-four people per square mile, as opposed to ninety-four in the United States). Is it a coincidence that they typically pay more than double for gasoline? Swedes spent an average of 1.97 percent of their income in 2016 on gasoline, while Americans spent 3.18 percent. Lest defensive Americans dismiss Swedes as just too strange and foreign for comparison, it is worth noticing that neighboring Canadians are very much like Americans, live in a *much* less dense country – eleven people per square mile, one-ninth that of the United States – and even Canadians drove 37 percent less than Americans – and paid about 37 percent more for gasoline in 2016.

Necessity in the form of a Swedish carbon tax has been the mother of invention in Swedish energy. Aided by a politics that is by design and by serendipity free of so much of the noxious pathologies of American politics, Swedes seem hardly inconvenienced at all by lifestyle changes, and sometimes profound industrial changes, that have reduced the impacts of their lives on the global environment. It is perhaps a secret weapon of capitalism that many changes take place quietly, contrasting with the loud ribbon-cutting "game-changers" often falsely touted by politicians.

5.5 WHY PEOPLE HATE ENVIRONMENTAL TAXES

The proposal in this book to enact a series of environmental taxes runs headlong into persistent, broad, and in the United States a particularly violent antipathy towards anything labeled a "tax." There is no escaping that this book leads with the policy instrument *most* unpopular as a means for protecting the global environment. That economists almost uniformly endorse the idea of Pigouvian taxation as a preferred means of reducing pollution seems to have very little influence. Environmental taxes seem to have this mystical repugnance, as if a magical spell had been cast upon all of humankind (except for economists), to recoil at the mention of the word "tax."

The problem with environmental taxation is aesthetic. If one were to design a policy instrument to be as unappealing as possible, one could scarcely do better than the simple, elegant unlikability of a Pigouvian tax. For one thing, the central point of a Pigouvian tax is to impose a cost on consumption. Who is against consumption? Consumption taxes such as sales taxes and excise taxes often meet with opposition because they are so salient, an insult repeated with every purchase of a taxed item. Deemphasized are considerations of the environmental objectives, or use of the tax revenues. Second, there is always the wish that government could affirmatively do positive things, as opposed to negative, punitive things. Even if that is misguided, it is widespread. Survey questions that hypothesize that the federal government "fund massive research projects to develop new clean energy technologies that can meet our needs without polluting"[23] or "[do] more to reduce the type of activities that cause climate change and sea level rise"[24] tend to poll very well. Finally, for those that consider themselves supporters of environmental initiatives, environmental taxation fails to place the onus of remediation on those perceived as the villains: fossil fuel companies and other big polluting corporations.

Unfortunately, not only do aesthetics matter, but they reinforce a certain amount of path-dependency in public opinion and policy. Elected officials depend greatly on public opinion polling, and public opinion surveys cannot provide that fuller, more candid explanation of proposed policies. What is too often presented to survey respondents are the oversimplified questions that highlight the downsides of environmental taxation, and the upsides of other instruments. Pollsters are not necessarily to blame: pollsters describe policies in the terms that are given to them by legislators and other policy analysts. For example, a 2019 poll conducted for the Democratic Party posed these choices:

Question A: Would you support or oppose a policy levying a new tax on carbon pollution to reduce pollution and protect the environment?

Question B: Would you support or oppose a policy providing for public investment in clean energy infrastructure and requiring carbon emissions reductions through regulation to reduce pollution and protect the environment?

Of the subgroup responding to question A, support for a carbon tax was 50 percent, 31 percent opposing, and 18 percent were unsure; of those responding to question B, support for "investment" and "regulation" was 59 percent, 25 percent opposing, and 15 percent were unsure. On the basis of this, the Democratic Party concluded that the public prefers "public investment in clean energy infrastructure and requiring carbon emissions reductions through regulation," to "levying a new tax on carbon."

Of course they do! The pollsters might as well have asked, "do you favor paying more for energy?" or "do you favor somebody else paying to invest in clean energy, and making polluters pay?" There is shockingly little awareness of the pollsters of just how loaded the terms "tax," "public investment," "clean energy," and "regulation" are. To state the obvious, nobody likes a tax, much less a new one. On the flipside, the phrases "clean energy" and "investment" connote positive action for a desirable goal. In the few seconds that a survey respondent is given to answer a question of that nature, there is barely enough time to grasp the question, let alone reach the second-order considerations of revenue, if they even go there at all. That is certainly *not* to say that I disfavor investment, only that there is a deep imbalance in the way those two options might be considered. There is a deep discounting of the revenues of carbon taxes, and of the fiscal costs of "investment."

Consider also a Stanford University poll conducted in 2010, shown in Table 5.1.

The answers to questions like these are not meaningful. One might as well ask, "do you favor having the government do something nice for the environment?" or "do you favor government making things more expensive?" Lost in these questions are any considerations of tradeoffs, hidden costs, or the possibility that, depending upon price elasticities, producers may pass costs down to consumers – or not. Lost in these questions are considerations of effectiveness, adjustments that can be made, or burdens on the Treasury.

Conversely, of course, survey respondents confronted with a question about an environmental tax do not think about the resulting revenues. In the time that it takes to answer a survey question, the respondent cannot or does not reach that higher level of inquiry. What will become of the revenues? Will this reduce consumption? Is this more cost-efficient than alternatives? Dunno. On to the next question.

TABLE 5.1 *Global Warming Poll, June 1–7, 2010, Stanford University*

Global Warming Poll, June 1–7, 2010, Stanford University:[25]	Strongly favor or somewhat favor	Somewhat oppose or strongly oppose
Give companies tax breaks to produce more electricity from water, wind, and solar power	84	15
Increase taxes on gasoline so people either drive less, or buy cars that use less gas	28	71
Increase taxes on electricity so people use less of it	22	78

And yet lawmakers rely upon the results of these surveys to guide their positions. John Podesta, the campaign chair for Hillary Clinton's failed presidential campaign, wrote in 2015: "we have done extensive polling on a carbon tax ... It all sucks."[26] Podesta has remained influential in steering climate policy in the Democratic Party, and while he and the Party have not disavowed carbon taxation, they have accepted as given the many illusory disadvantages of carbon taxation.[27] The path is circular: elected officials and the policy cognoscenti define the policy, and hand those definitions off to pollsters, who duly ask survey respondents the questions, reporting back to lawmakers about popularity. Unwittingly, perhaps, lawmakers and the cognoscenti reinforce the notion in voters' minds that environmental taxes hurt them, and other policies are cost-free.

At this point it is worth confronting a powerful political force that stands in opposition to almost all measures aimed at environmental protection or conservation, and especially anything that smacks of climate policy. A right-wing, antienvironmental movement has emerged, primarily but not solely in the United States, that has mobilized hostility towards environmental initiatives by framing environmentalism as a *cultural* issue. Some in the Republican Party, in particular, tap into a variety of grievances and channeled them into antienvironmentalism. Everything that protects the environment is fair game, without regard to any economic considerations whatsoever, and environmental taxes – in particular carbon taxes – serve as a convenient bogeyman, and evidence of malice aforethought on the part of environmentalists. Right-wing antienvironmentalists have astutely exploited the aesthetic shortcomings of a carbon tax and amplified them. Along the way, they have attached sympathetic interest groups as evidence that environmentalism hurts people – *real* people.

To be sure, right-wing antienvironmental zealots misrepresent much about science, economics, and law. But truthfully, environmental taxation raises some very important economic and social concerns, ones foreseen by critics of capitalism. The point of an increased emphasis on capitalism is the recognition that industries come and go, and jobs come and go. For the most part, in a healthy capitalist economy and a healthy democracy, they can be addressed in a humane manner. Even Schumpeter, who believed that creative destruction was part and parcel of capitalism, espoused an "orderly retreat" for industries moving into obsolescence, writing that "there is certainly no point in trying to conserve obsolescent industries indefinitely; but there is point in trying to avoid their coming down with a crash ... which may become a center of cumulative depressive effects."[28]

Managing dislocation from the vicissitudes of capitalism is one of the fundamental charges of government. Compensation for dislocation could be a palliative measure to ease transition, something that can be financed from the proceeds of environmental taxes. Many affluent capitalist countries have constructed extensive social safety nets to provide for basic needs of all citizens, so much the better in case of the obsolescence of some industries or skills. An extended discussion of the variety of different varieties of government and approaches of managing dislocation is beyond the scope of this part of the book. I wish only to make the simple point that environmental taxation generates proceeds from which dislocation compensation might be drawn. This is one of the most obvious and yet overlooked aspects of environmental taxation, one that is treated in following chapters.

Apart from addressing important distributional issues, there are steps that can be taken to address opposition to environmental taxes, which is a political mile wide and an intellectual inch deep. Environmental taxes seem to highlight the costs and downsides, while concealing the upsides and the benefits. Second- and higher-order economic effects are complex, and difficult to predict. In the absence of unambiguous information about these complex policy interactions, the median voter can be forgiven for throwing up her hands and just reacting. The goal of all policy, not just environmental policy, should be to present to the polity a fuller, more candid and more comprehensive explanation of all of the likely effects of policy.

One important step would be to conduct policy discussions with lengthier and more candid assessments of policy upsides and downsides, relative strengths and weaknesses, and relative costs and benefits. This is not a pipe dream. The Office of Information and Regulatory Affairs (OIRA), under the White House, conducts "regulatory impact assessments," or cost-benefit analyses, of any federal rule with significant impacts (more than $100 million, which almost every federal rule does). Cost-benefit analyses can be manipulated, but there are limits. The Congressional Budget and Impoundment Control Act of 1974[29] created the nonpartisan Congressional Budget Office (CBO), which estimates, or "scores," the costs of bills and resolutions approved by Congressional committees other than the appropriations committees. While CBO scoring only addresses the cost side, it still contributes to a fuller discussion of the economic impacts of proposed legislation.

Improvements in polling questions should surely be another simple step. Lawmakers can and should demand that public opinion polls provide meaningful results, not dumbed-down leading questions. One example of policy debiasing is this question, posed in 2019 by the Yale Program on Climate Change Communication, which has been polling on climate change for many years, and greatly refined its questions:

> **Require fossil fuel companies to pay a carbon tax** *How much do you support or oppose the following policies?* Require fossil fuel companies to pay a carbon tax and use the money to reduce other taxes (such as income tax) by an equal amount.

This question simultaneously fixed two biases against carbon taxation: that it would hurt the respondent, and that it failed to punish the villainy (fossil fuel companies). It still leaves unanalyzed the question of whether fossil fuel companies would pass the tax burden down to consumers. But given the propensity for survey respondents to reflexively oppose policies inimical to their self-interest, the deflection seems warranted. This carbon tax was either "somewhat supported" or "strongly supported" by 66 percent of respondents, achieving a majority in every single state. But even paired with the most positive possible revenue option (reducing income taxes) this carbon tax proposal still fared less well than "Fund more research into renewable energy sources, such as solar and wind power" (83 percent) and "Provide tax rebates for people who purchase energy-efficient vehicles or solar panels" (81 percent).[30]

At the risk of alienating respondents, pollsters could go a step further, and attempt a detailed engagement with the respondent. The following lengthy (for a poll) explanation and framing was conducted by *NBC News* and the *Wall Street Journal* in 2014:

> Now, as you may know, President Obama has directed the Environmental Protection Agency, known as the EPA for short, to set strict carbon dioxide emission limits on existing coal-fired power plants with a goal to reduce emissions significantly by the year 2030 ... When it comes to the new limits on carbon dioxide emissions being set by the Obama administration and the EPA, which comes closer to your point of view?
>
> Supporters say action is needed because coal plants are a major source of carbon pollution. These reductions will mean cleaner air and reduce the health care costs associated with asthma and respiratory diseases by billions of dollars. Significantly lowering carbon pollution is the critical step in addressing climate change and the natural disasters and property damage it causes. These reductions will help create a new generation of clean energy and jobs.
>
> Opponents say coal plant carbon emissions have already dropped over the last decade and this action will mean fewer jobs. The compliance costs for electric companies will be three times more expensive than any current EPA regulation, which means higher prices. Consumers and businesses will both end up paying more for electricity. These regulations will mean only a small change to the global climate as carbon emissions in China, India, and other developing countries will continue to rise.[31]

While I have some quibbles with the description of the effects, this question is much more nuanced and sophisticated in its attempt to present some of the better arguments of both sides. In so doing, it advances discussion by making both supporters and opponents hear arguments to which they might not otherwise be exposed. More is not necessarily always better, but it is important to convey the reality that policies are complicated, and have numerous unexpected effects.

5.6 RALLYING BEHIND ENVIRONMENTAL TAXATION

The Canadian province of British Columbia enacted a carbon tax in 2008 that started out in 2008 at $10 CAD per ton of CO_2-eq emissions, and ramped up to the rate of $30 CAD per ton.[32] It applies to twenty classes of fossil fuels and other specified combustibles,[33] but excludes fuels exported from British Columbia and fuels for interjurisdictional marine use and aviation.[34] Gasoline for motor vehicles is the largest source of greenhouse gas emissions for the province, and $30 CAD per ton of CO_2-eq translates roughly into 8 cents CAD per liter, or 30 cents CAD per gallon.

The tax was meant to be "revenue neutral," to gain the support of business interests in the province, and so was packaged with reductions in the marginal income tax rates of the lowest two tax brackets, as well as reductions in the corporate income tax rate.[35] The tax also included provisions for additional "adjustment measures"[36] to ensure that the province took in less money in carbon tax revenues than it spent under the law. The adjustment measures have actually been a blight on an otherwise well-designed carbon tax, at times just a form of political pork. Without any restrictions, adjustment measures money has been dispensed at the political whim of the provincial premier, money simply being given away to greenhouse growers, the broader provincial agricultural industry, and the motion picture industry.

Political opposition to the carbon tax was virulent at first. Notably, it was enacted by a governing party in British Columbia that was the more conservative of the two. In the provincial election following enactment, the opposition (and further left) party, the New Democratic Party campaigned to "axe the tax," and failed. The New Democratic Party later reversed its position and agitated for an *increase* in the carbon tax. It followed public sentiment: public opinion on the carbon tax swung from 55 percent opposing when it was announced, to 65 percent in favor four years later.[37]

The reason that the carbon tax is no longer controversial is that adjustment to the carbon tax has been uneventful, probably surprisingly so to British Columbians. Administration of the tax proved simple, even for a province half again larger than Texas, and with a sixth of its population: the cost of carbon tax revenue collection and administration has been modest: an estimated \$1.4 to \$1.8 CAD million annually, mostly for the hiring of 18 staff associated with the program.[38] But most significantly British Columbians have adjusted with much lower consumption of fossil fuels, a greater dip than would have been predicted by economic models. Gasoline sales were estimated to decline by 11–17 percent per capita by one study,[39] and 7 percent in another study.[40] British Columbians drove less, but also purchased more fuel-efficient vehicles.[41] There is also some evidence that natural gas consumption declined about 15 percent in response to the carbon tax.[42] Overall, emissions are estimated to have declined 5–15 percent due to the carbon tax,[43] which is quite substantial because British Columbia is a province with very little fossil fuel-generated electricity, more than 90 percent of it being generated by hydropower. The emissions reductions were thus accomplished with little help from the low-hanging fruit of emissions reductions from electricity generation. There is no evidence that British Columbia has suffered any negative economic impacts from the carbon tax.[44]

In the end, British Columbians seem to have concluded that opposition to the carbon tax was much ado about nothing. It is apparently one thing to be presented with a survey question asking you how you feel about spending more money on gasoline, and another to adjust to it, the latter surprisingly easy. Part of what public opinion polling, egged on by entrepreneurial politicians, has done is to *reinforce* misconceptions about environmental taxation. These misperceptions have been instrumental in suppressing environmental taxation.

5.7 A PUBLIC CHOICE PROBLEM

Not all opposition to environmental taxation is irrational. On the contrary, public choice theory offers a hyper-rational, and possibly a more powerful explanation of opposition to environmental taxes. As noted in Chapter 3, public choice theory posits that the public policy sphere is driven by private interests: the private interests of the regulated entities and other interest groups, and private interests of lawmakers as well, which would include elected officials and also regulatory agencies and the employees that staff them.[45] In a legislative or a rulemaking process that represents significant policy reform, these efforts to resist reform are expended through lobbying efforts,[46] strategic promises of campaign finance support,[47] and perhaps more tantalizing, remunerative future employment.[48] Public elected officials are thus able to serve their private interests by aiding or *resisting* changes in law, such as environmental taxes.

Public choice theory explains economic distortions when legislation or regulation affects a concentrated industry on the one hand, and a diffuse general public on the other hand. When legislation or regulation is confined to one issue, an affected industry can coordinate action to either obtain a favorable law or to defeat an unfavorable law, much better than a diffuse general public of many individuals. Also, a concentrated industry may have much at stake (as it often does in environmental law) and would be willing to spend considerable resources for its desired outcome, whereas that single issue is likely to be one of many for a distracted general public (as it often is in environmental law). In environmental policy, environmental organizations have helped to solve the coordination problem on the general public side, but remained vastly under-resourced when compared with industry trade groups.

Environmental taxation actually offers a particularly stark example of public choice theory at work.[49] As is often the case in environmental law, the environmental benefits are diffuse. Whether the burden of an environmental tax is borne by the industry or its consumers depends upon supply and demand elasticity, but in any case, an affected industry will contract. No industry wants its product markets disrupted by taxation. Compensation, perhaps fed by environmental tax revenues, offers some remedy, but it should still be expected that private firms will resist such intrusions.

At some point, however, crisis creates the impetus for change. If environmental crisis threatens capitalism, it becomes exceedingly difficult to justify to industrial peers intransigent opposition to any regulation of any sort. At bottom, if environmental crisis threatens business broadly and seriously enough – and climate change certainly does, at least – then the public choice problem can fall away. Broad acceptance of the package of proposals in this book require acceptance of only three propositions: (i) that capitalism is malfunctioning badly enough that it threatens the future viability of human civilization, at least as it is currently recognized, and (ii) it is only within the framework of capitalism that currently harmful industrial practices can be brought to heel, and (iii) environmental taxation is the best way to reorient capitalism. I hasten to repeat that I do not propose to discard existing regulations. But replacement of *some* of them with environmental taxes is necessary to recruiting a much broader and deeper workforce to the vital task of finding ways to reduce the human footprint on the global environment. I elaborate on these three propositions below.

First, success for this proposal is predicated on widespread agreement that the world is in a state of environmental crisis, and while capitalism itself is not to blame, the *way* that capitalism has taken root is to blame. Capitalism is malfunctioning, and hurtling down a catastrophic path foreseen by Polanyi, Marx, and Schumpeter, among others. But what these great thinkers did not foresee is actually worse: that of all the things capitalism destroys that it depends upon, the global environment is the most critical. This is not a matter of academic conjecture. If capitalist industries destroy the systems that provide vital ecosystem services to industry, and destroy the capacity to provide food, water, and energy to people, capitalism will die, along with billions of people.

Second, I already elaborated in Chapter 2 on the need to harness capitalism, not replace it with socialism. It seems worth briefly repeating that it is capitalism, and not socialism, that can transform industrial society more quickly. Change never comes easily to any society, but it has fared better in capitalist societies than socialist ones. This book contains several examples of upstart firms breaking through against incumbent ones, despite some legal and political obstacles, including Tesla, alternative meat products, and Toyota's hybrid-electric vehicle *coup* against entrenched American automakers. While not impossible in socialist regimes, the list of successful upstarts seem much shorter.

Third, and finally, environmental taxation is the most capitalism-friendly way to proceed with reform. It seems like such an uninspiring idea around which to rally. But if one accepts the proposition that environmental outcome *must* change (see proposition i), then just a quick review of the alternatives reveals it to be the least intrusive, and most efficient policy tool. Environmental taxation can be quite extensive, and can initiate profound changes while preserving existing legal and political institutions, and most social institutions. Granted, environmental taxation moves the goalposts. But importantly, it keeps the same rules of the game. Alternative policies either fail to achieve the environmental outcomes or require large dismantling of legal and political institutions. Capitalism is a hyper-coordination of resources, ideas, and human initiative, and what has been missing from capitalism thus far is a means of coordinating human activity with its impacts on the global environment. It is a big job, with human activities having so many impacts on many different parts of the global environment. Prices have done a flawed but remarkable job of coordinating markets generally. Environmental taxation represents that extension of pricing into the environmental realm.

From time to time, some large corporations have supported environmental taxes publicly, if not necessarily enthusiastically. Even ExxonMobil, along with other oil and gas concerns, have long supported carbon taxation,[50] as have electricity generation utilities[51] and automakers.[52] Automakers have long supported gasoline taxes over vehicle fuel efficiency standards.[53] Public choice theory aside, industries have been willing to support environmental taxes if the alternative is prescriptive regulation. It is not even so much that the regulations would be more stringent. Often, firms view regulation (rightly or wrongly) as introducing uncertainty in a way that is less manageable and less predictable than a Pigouvian tax.

The nature of capitalism is to innovate in search of new profits. The space for innovation is so much smaller in a regulatory realm than it is in an environmental taxation scheme (or cap-and-trade programs). Keeping with the spirit of capitalism, then, environmental taxation minimizes the government interference by limiting its role to that of determining the environmental end goal. That is the most important job, but it is separable from the job of determining *how* that goal is achieved. That is the capitalist job, best left decentralized in the many private firms to figure out.

Notes

1. ARTHUR CECIL PIGOU, THE ECONOMICS OF WELFARE 131–35 (1928).
2. WILLIAM J. BAUMOL & WALLACE E. OATES, THE THEORY OF ENVIRONMENTAL POLICY 21–23 (1988) (defining taxes that reflect the extent of negative externality as "Pigouvian" taxes).
3. Taylor Covington, *Texting and Driving Statistics*, ZEBRA (May 26, 2020), https://www.thezebra.com/texting-and-driving-statistics/#statistics.
4. *U.S. Air Pollution Deaths Nearly Halved Over Two Decades*, YALEENVIRONMENT360 (Oct. 19, 2018), https://e360.yale.edu/digest/us-air-pollution-deaths-nearly-halved-over-two-decades.
5. Andrew Goodkind et al., *Fine-scale Damage Estimate of Particulate Matter Air Pollution Reveal Opportunities for Location-specific Mitigation of Emissions*, 116 PROCEEDINGS OF THE NAT'L ACAD. SCIS. 8775 (2019) (citing CDC, UNDERLYING CAUSE OF DEATH, 1999–2018 (2018), https://wonder.cdc.gov/ucd-icd10.html).
6. *See, e.g.*, Joseph E. Aldy, *Birds of a Feather: Estimating the Value of Statistical Life From Dual-Earner Families*, 58 J. RISK & UNCERTAINTY 187 (2019) ("For example, the Environmental Protection Agency uses a VSL of $8.8 million and the Department of Transportation uses a VSL of $9.6 million in their regulatory impact analyses . . .").
7. Xiao Wu et al., *Exposure to Air Pollution and COVID-19 Mortality in the United State: A Nationwide Cross-Sectional Study*, medRxiv (forthcoming 2020) (manuscript at 14–18), https://doi.org/10.1101/2020.04.05.20054502.

8. U.S. ENVTL. PROT. AGENCY, BENEFITS AND COSTS OF THE CLEAN AIR ACT, 1970 TO 1990 53 (Oct. 1997), https://www.epa.gov/sites/production/files/2015-06/documents/contsetc.pdf [https://perma.cc/J5AA-Y3EX].

9. *See, e.g.*, ABHIJIT BANERJEE & ESTHER DUFLO, GOOD ECONOMICS FOR HARD TIMES 148 (2020).

10. David Popp, *Environmental Policy and Innovation: A Decade of Research* (CESifo, Working Paper No. 7544, 2019), https://www.econstor.eu/bitstream/10419/198904/1/cesifo1_wp7544.pdf.

11. Curtis Carlson et al., *SO2 Control by Electric Utilities: What are the Gains From Trade?*, 108 J. POLIT. ECON. 1292, 1318 (2000).

12. *See* A. DENNY ELLERMAN, MARKETS FOR CLEAN AIR: THE U.S. ACID RAIN PROGRAM 167 (2000).

13. *See, e.g.*, Byron Swift, *How Environmental Laws Work: An Analysis of the Utility Sector's Response to Regulation of Nitrogen Oxides and Sulfur Dioxide Under the Clean Air Act*, 14 TULANE ENVTL. L.J. 312 (2001).

14. A. DENNY ELLERMAN, MARKETS FOR CLEAN AIR: THE U.S. ACID RAIN PROGRAM 167 (2000).

15. Curtis Carlson et al., *SO2 Control by Electric Utilities: What are the Gains From Trade?* 108 J. POLIT. ECON. 1292, 1318 (2000).

16. Curtis Carlson et al., *SO2 Control by Electric Utilities: What are the Gains From Trade?* 108 J. POLIT. ECON.1292, 1318 (2000).

17. Byron Swift, *How Environmental Laws Work: An Analysis of the Utility Sector's Response to Regulation of Nitrogen Oxides and Sulfur Dioxide Under the Clean Air Act*, 14 TULANE ENVTL. L.J. 312 (2001).

18. Curtis Carlson, et al., *SO2 Control by Electric Utilities: What are the Gains From Trade?* 108 J. POLIT. ECON. 1292, 1318 (2000).

19 U.S. ENVTL. PROT. AGENCY, PROGRESS REPORT ON THE EPA ACID RAIN PROGRAM 4 (1999), https://www.epa.gov/sites/production/files/2015-08/documents/1999report.pdf [https://perma.cc/KP8Z-QRYK].

20. Gilbert Metcalf & James H. Stock, *Measuring the Macroeconomic Impact of Carbon Taxes*, 110 AM. ECON. ASS'N PAPERS & PROCEEDINGS 106 (May 2020).

21. Swedish Energy Agency, Energy in Sweden 2017, Input Energy Used in the Production of District Heating, from 1970, https://www.districtenergy.org/viewdocument/energy-in-sweden-2017 [https://perma.cc/SMG5-DAJR].

22. Swedish Energy Agency, Energy in Sweden 2017, Table 4.4 Use of Fossil Fuels (natural gas, petroleum products, coal and coke) by industry, from 1990, https://www.districtenergy.org/viewdocument/energy-in-sweden-2017 [https://perma.cc/SMG5-DAJR].

23. NATHAN CUMMINGS FOUNDATION, GLOBAL WARMING SURVEY 3 (Aug. 2007).

24. Monmouth University, *Climate Concerns Increase; Most Republicans Now Acknowledge Change* (Nov. 29, 2018), https://www.monmouth.edu/polling-institute/reports/monmouthpoll_us_112918 [https://perma.cc/5V86-NDDE].

25. *Global Warming Poll*, Stanford University (June 9, 2010), https://woodsinstitute.stanford.edu/system/files/publications/Global-Warming-Survey-Selected-Results-June2010.pdf [https://perma.cc/J4WS-LMWG].

26. Patrick Gleason, *For First Time in Six Years a Carbon Tax Won't be on the Ballot, but Politicians Supporting One Will*, FORBES (Sept. 29, 2020), www.forbes.com/sites/patrickgleason/2020/09/29/for-first-time-in-six-years-a-carbon-tax-wont-be-on-the-ballot-but-politicians-supporting-one-will/#4340d2f41fb4.

27. *Id.* Podesta was more recently quoted as saying "the [climate] community has largely moved into a different framework." Amy Harder, *Joe Biden Unlikely to Push Carbon Tax as a Part of Climate Change Plan*, AXIOS (Aug. 20, 2020), https://www.axios.com/joe-biden-carbon-tax-climate-change-plan-e8d522a8-5015-45fc-8164-3ec5c8a0d8a3.html.

28. JOSEPH SCHUMPETER, CAPITALISM, SOCIALISM AND DEMOCRACY 90 (1950).
29. 2 U.S.C. §§601–661.
30. Jennifer Marlon et al., *Yale Climate Opinion Maps 2019*, YALE PROGRAM ON CLIMATE CHANGE COMMUNICATION (Sep. 17, 2019), https://climatecommunication.yale.edu/visual izations-data/ycom-us/ [https://perma.cc/XE3F-ZZTY].
31. Patrick O'Connor, *Poll Shows Erosion in President's Support*, WALL ST. J. (June 18, 2014), https://www.wsj.com/articles/poll-shows-erosion-in-presidents-support-1403064301 [https://perma.cc/884V-RKUL].
32. Carbon Tax Act, S.B.C., sched. 1 (2008) (Can.).
33. Carbon Tax Act, S.B.C., sched. 2 (2008) (Can.).
34. Carbon Tax Act, S.B.C., §10 (2008) (Can.).
35. KATHRYN HARRISON, THE POLITICAL ECONOMY OF BRITISH COLUMBIA'S CARBON TAX 3 (Organisation for Economic Co-operation and Development, OECD Environment Working Papers No. 63, 2013), https://tinyurl.com/y7yhnq5h.
36. Carbon Tax Act, S.B.C., §2 (2008) (Can.).
37. KATHRYN HARRISON, THE POLITICAL ECONOMY OF BRITISH COLUMBIA'S CARBON TAX 14 (Figure 1) (Organisation for Economic Co-operation and Development, OECD Environment Working Papers No. 63, 2013), https://tinyurl.com/y7yhnq5h.
38. E-mail Communication From Hugh Hughson, Manager, Fuel & Carbon Tax, B.C. Ministry of Finance, to Hilary Kennedy, Senior Economic Advisor, Climate Action Secretariat, B.C. Ministry of Environment (July 11, 2013) (Re: Request on the Administrative Cost of the British Columbia Carbon Tax) (email on file with author).
39. Nic Rivers & Brandon Schaefele, *Carbon Tax Salience and Gasoline Demand*, 74 J. ENVTL. ECON. & MGMT. 23 (2015).
40. Brian Murray & Nicholas Rivers, *British Columbia's Revenue-neutral Carbon Tax: A Review of the Latest "Grand Experiment" in Environmental Policy*, 86 Energy Pol'y 674 (2015), (citing Jean-Thomas Bernard, Grant Guenther & Maral Kichian, *Price and Carbon Tax Effects on Gasoline and Diesel Demand*, draft manuscript (2014), https://tinyurl.com/y7e8ug7e).
41. Werner Antweiler & Sumeet Gulati, *Frugal Cars or Frugal Drivers?*, https://papers .ssrn.com/sol3/papers.cfm?abstract_id=2778868 (2016).
42. Brian Murray & Nicholas Rivers, *British Columbia's Revenue-neutral Carbon Tax: A Review of the Latest "Grand Experiment" in Environmental Policy*, 86 *Energy Pol'y* 674 (2015), (citing Sumeet Gulati & Zahra Gholami, *Case Study on the Effectiveness of Carbon Pricing Estimating the Impact of Carbon Tax on Natural Gas Demand*, unpublished master's thesis (2014), https://open.library.ubc.ca/cIRcle/collections/ubctheses/24/items/1.0166938).
43. Brian Murray & Nicholas Rivers, *British Columbia's Revenue-neutral Carbon Tax: A Review of the Latest "Grand Experiment" in Environmental Policy*, 86 ENERGY POL'Y 674 (2015).
44. GILBERT E. METCALF, A CONCEPTUAL FRAMEWORK FOR MEASURING THE EFFECTIVENESS OF GREEN FISCAL REFORMS, GREEN GROWTH KNOWLEDGE PLATFORM (GGKP) THIRD ANNUAL CONFERENCE: FISCAL POLICIES AND THE GREEN ECONOMY TRANSITION: GENERATING KNOWLEDGE – CREATING IMPACT 42 (2015).
45. WILLIAM NISKANEN, BUREAUCRACY AND REPRESENTATIVE GOVERNMENT 2–3 (1971).
46. *See, e.g.*, Jagdish N. Bhagwati, *Directly Unproductive, Profit-seeking (DUP) Activities*, 90 J. POLIT. ECON. 988, 988 (1982); Anne O. Krueger, *The Political Economy of the Rent-Seeking Society*, 64 AM. ECON. REV. 291, 292 (1974).

47. *See, e.g.*, Jonathan R. Macey, *Public Choice: The Theory of the Firm and the Theory of Market Exchange*, 74 CORNELL L. REV. 43, 53 (1988).

48. William C. Mitchell & Michael C. Munger, *Economic Models of Interest Groups: An Introductory Survey*, AM. J. POL. SCI. 512, 520 (1991).

49. Daniel Farber & Philip Frickey, *The Jurisprudence of Public Choice*, 65 TEX. L. REV. 873, 878 (1987).

50. Pete Trelenberg, *A Broad Carbon Tax Coalition*, ENERGY FACTOR BY EXXONMOBIL (June 21, 2017), https://energyfactor.exxonmobil.com/perspectives/broad-carbon-tax-coalition [https://perma.cc/728X-VRC8].

51. Rhys Gerholdt, *Leading U.S. Businesses Call on Congress to Enact a Market-Based Approach to Climate Change*, WORLD RESOURCES INST. (May 15, 2019), https://www.wri.org/news/2019/05/release-leading-us-businesses-call-congress-enact-market-based-approach-climate-change [https://perma.cc/NU2X-A3EC] ("We have long-supported carbon pricing as the fastest, most economical way to both reduce emissions and encourage investment in new and existing clean power sources … ").

52. Climate Leadership Council, *Founding Member Statements*, https://clcouncil.org/statements [https://perma.cc/D5T2-F768] ("General Motors … acknowledged long ago that climate change is real and that lowering emissions is both a social imperative and an economic opportunity.").

53. Danny Hakim, *A Fuel-Saving Proposal From Your Automaker: Tax the Gas*, N.Y. TIMES (Apr. 18, 2004).

6

What Should Be Taxed?

There is much work to be done. This chapter sets out a list of five proposed environmental taxes. This is by no means a comprehensive list of worthwhile environmental taxes. What else don't we know? These are five of the most important externalities to price. Some of these taxes have multiple effects. In fact, some of the effects overlap across different taxes. Some account can be made for overlap, so as not to double tax the same harmful activity, except of course for multiple harms. Each tax is described briefly, along with some discussion of the harms and the implementation and enforcement issues. Each proposed tax is worthy of a book-length discussion, but my purpose here is to introduce the need for the tax, and to lay out a roadmap for implementation, hoping the reader will forgive the omissions necessitated by considerations of space.

For the sake of concreteness, these environmental taxes are proposed as domestic legislation in the United States. The general prescription is the same for every country: a Pigouvian tax, or at least a per-unit of harm tax. Still, an attempt to reform capitalism and reorient it to operate in a more sustainable manner must involve global cooperation, so a proposal for domestic legislation is incomplete. I thus include some modest measures aimed at furthering international cooperation.

Environmental taxes are unpopular in part because of an inattention to the revenues collected. A Pigouvian tax is meant to internalize costs, and Pigou's writings did not address uses of tax revenues. But to ignore the fact that environmental taxes bring in revenues is to ignore one entire side of a policy. It would be incomplete to discuss these environmental taxes without a discussion of how to use the revenues. Since some environmental taxes will cause some industries to shrink, using tax revenues to compensate for dislocation might be a prominent option.

All of the environmental taxes proposed below are feasible. In some cases, an *accurate* measure of the emissions or environmental harm is technologically impossible at the present. Moreover, the administrative infrastructure for monitoring (if it were technologically possible) and collecting environmental taxes requires development. In those cases, I propose a tax on a proxy of the environmental harm, as a temporary substitute. As these proxy environmental taxes are imperfect, their goal is not so much to strike a Pigouvian balance between cost and benefit, but to give an initial boost to some of the ways in which some capitalist energies might be recruited to reduce these harms. Because the technology or administrative infrastructure for accurate monitoring is lacking, tax levels should be set at a low level, well below what is likely to be amount of social harm, so as to minimize distortions. For example, for lack of a way of accurately monitoring the emission of fine particulate matter air pollution ($PM_{2.5}$), I propose a tax on just the six largest sources of $PM_{2.5}$ or its precursors. Until a monitoring technology is developed that can detect emissions of $PM_{2.5}$ or major precursors at their individual sources, it would be unwise and unfair to tax those six sources too heavily. What I propose, however, is to dedicate some of the proceeds of these proxy environmental taxes to the development of the requisite technology and tax collection infrastructure, in the interests of eventually developing a more comprehensive and accurate system of detecting and taxing pollution. To some, it may sound Orwellian to develop what seems to be an intrusive system of pollution detection. But that reaction is the product of an anachronistic expectation of being able to pollute and to take for free. That mentality must go. Fortunately, once capitalist energies for reducing pollution and saving money are engaged, the expectation of being able to pollute with impunity will be displaced by the expectation of making money.

6.1 CARBON DIOXIDE EMISSIONS

By far the most important environmental tax to enact would be a carbon tax. Of all of the threats to humankind arising from environmental degradation, climate change is the most sweeping and the most serious. While a carbon tax is likely not sufficient by itself to adequately mitigate climate change, it is the most important and most efficient step. A carbon tax is easily administrable and enforceable in almost all countries, even those with relatively poor government infrastructure. There are ways to extend a carbon tax to cover emissions of other greenhouse gases, as well, that would improve effectiveness. And at the risk of sounding repetitive, there are many important regulations that are needed to supplement and complement a carbon tax, such as regulations that should (but don't) govern the burning off, or "flaring" of excess natural gas from oil wells, and regulations that should govern (but don't) fugitive emissions, most prominently the escape of methane from oil and gas operations.

Carbon taxation *could* replace some other regulations, such as the federal CAFE fuel efficiency standards that have been the source of so much legal and political wrangling, including President George W. Bush's interventions on hydrogen fuel cell technology. Automakers have in fact long supported replacing fuel efficiency standards with a gas tax or a carbon tax. A federal carbon tax would resolve disputes about whether the State of California can impose its own fuel efficiency standards.

The Trump Administration has sought to preclude California's attempts to require automakers to comply with a fuel efficiency standard more stringent than that proposed by the Trump Administration. Under a federal carbon tax scheme, any individual state could impose an additional carbon tax to further discourage fuel consumption. That may not seem quite as forceful as setting its own standards because it leaves motorists free to buy fuel-inefficient cars. But that is just an illusion, because a stiff enough additional state carbon tax could exactly replicate the disincentives posed by fuel efficiency standards.

A carbon tax, briefly described in the above section on Sweden's carbon tax, is levied primarily on fossil fuels – coal, natural gas, and petroleum – although it could cover combustion of some other materials resulting in the emissions of CO_2. CO_2 is only one of six recognized greenhouse gases contributing to climate change, though it is the most important one. Emissions of methane is also very important, increasingly so as scientists worry that huge stores of methane that have been stored for millennia under frozen ground in the far North may be unleashed by warming, caused by climate change itself. This is an example of one of several very worrisome positive feedbacks of climate change, in which failure to arrest climate change could lead to more and more climate change, quite likely catastrophic.

In terms of measurement and enforcement, CO_2 emissions can be very easily and uncontroversially measured, because the carbon content of almost every fossil fuel is well-known. A paper trail is initiated with every bit of fossil fuel extracted anywhere in the world. The same cannot be said of emissions of other greenhouse gases. It would be critical, however, to at least get a start with a carbon tax.

Following Pigou's prescription, a carbon tax should ideally be set at the level of marginal harm caused by emission of an extra unit – a ton of CO_2. What is that price? That is an exorbitantly complicated question, best simplified by approximating all forecasted damages, and modeling how they change with an increment of emissions, over a range of emissions levels. Complex models, known as "integrated assessment models," combine models of climatic changes with the economic effects of those changes. Over decades, these models have been developed and extensively and repeatedly refined, and generate increasingly better estimates of *some* of the economic effects of climate change: agricultural productivity, recreation, human health, property damages from flood risk, and the loss of ecosystem services (such as destruction of wetlands and thus increased flooding). These models project the amount of economic damage that would result from an incremental amount of CO_2 emissions. It is important to note that although integrated assessment models have been refined and refined and refined, they still miss potentially huge climate damages. Damages from tropical cyclones are still hard to estimate even though it is now well-accepted that the strength (though not number) of tropical cyclones will be greater in the future. Hurricane Sandy in 2012 cost the New York-New Jersey region about $50 billion,[1] and the trio of Hurricanes Harvey, Irma, and Maria cost a total of $265 billion.[2] Given the uncertainties, those are not costs that are easily captured in integrated assessment models. Harder still are estimates of how many lives will be lost (147 to Sandy, 68 to Harvey, 65 to Maria, 47 to Irma).

This estimated marginal damage from a ton of CO_2 emissions has been dubbed the "social cost of carbon." The Obama Administration convened an interagency effort to review and synthesize all of the models and develop some estimates for the social cost of carbon, bearing in mind the huge numbers of assumptions that have to be made to derive such an estimate.[3] In a 2016 revision,[4] the working group estimated the social cost of carbon for the year 2020 would be $52 per ton, in 2020 dollars. The social cost of carbon ranged from $15 to $78 per ton, depending on the assumed discount rate.

Because energy is embedded in almost every good produced, a carbon tax fulfills better than any other environmental tax its mission of conveying information through a vast network of prices. Agricultural products, for example, have a surprisingly large energy footprint, including the transportation of inputs (including fertilizer) and of harvested product and the energy for planting and harvesting. The footprint of an Apple iPhone is similarly complicated, with its complicated and sprawling supply chain. Driving emits CO_2. Building heating and cooling causes emissions of CO_2 if the electricity is generated by burning fossil fuels. The number of decisions that are made by weekly, daily, hourly, in every single minute, by almost every person, firm, or government, in ignorance of its climate impacts, is mind-boggling.

Part of what makes climate change such an intractable problem is the vast, sprawling collection of small bits of information about climate impacts, unsusceptible of aggregation, *unless it is priced*. What is so important about a carbon tax is that it collects and aggregates that information, and transmits it in the form of a price. Friedrich Hayek and Milton Friedman would have been in awe. An Apple iPhone embeds a great deal of energy at different stages of development, production and distribution. If CO_2 emissions were taxed, we would know how much. The online retailing giant Amazon faces intense criticism over its carbon footprint, having drivers deliver individual packages to doorsteps. But does it actually result in more emissions? That is not clear. Its 2018 emissions from its operations and deliveries were estimated to be 44.4 million metric tons of CO_2.[5] But what is the carbon footprint of individual shoppers visiting individual stores, sometimes searching for just the right item? One study estimated that online shopping is 17 percent more carbon-efficient than traditional, in-person retailing.[6] That is not the end of the story. People lament Amazon's destruction of retailing – which I share – but in terms of CO_2 emissions, the effect is unclear. The point is that a carbon tax would help steer commerce, electronic or not, towards less carbon-intensive methods of matching supply and demand.

Because fossil fuels are so deeply woven into the American economy, calculating the emissions reduction from a carbon tax is not as simple as taking a price elasticity and multiplying it by the price. There are many, many fossil fuel prices in many different contexts. Again, fairly complex models are required to project the effects of a carbon tax on fossil fuel use.

With carbon taxation, it would be inappropriate to ignore the second step of putting the carbon tax proceeds to work. Money is collected from fossil fuel producers; what is done with it? The tax has done its primary job of reducing emissions, which creates a benefit. But the revenues can be put to work, creating a second benefit. Unsurprisingly, the size of the revenue benefit depends on what is done with them.[7] This too, requires modeling, and is actually added into the models of emissions reductions. Ask a bit more of the economists constructing these models, and they will feed these results back into the first part, measure how different economic sectors react, and so on, until some equilibrium is reached with respect to the overall effect. These models commonly used to simulate the effects of climate policies, "computational general equilibrium" models, are massive models incorporating dozens of sectors, household and firm behavior, exports and imports, and resulting prices, quantities, incomes, and capital expenditures.

One authoritative cost-benefit analysis by Goulder and Hafstead[8] analyzes a hypothetical U.S. carbon tax starting at $20/ton in 2019, and increasing by 4 percent per year, adjusting for inflation. They consider four options for carbon tax revenues: (i) providing lump-sum rebates to individual households, (ii) reducing individual income taxes, (iii) reducing payroll taxes, and (iv) reducing corporate income taxes. They analyze the present value of the stream of costs and benefits of the carbon tax, extending out into the indefinite future and find the following (among many other things):

- that in terms of economic growth, reducing corporate income taxes is the most beneficial and providing lump sum rebates is the least beneficial;
- that in terms of reducing inequality, providing lump sum rebates is the most beneficial and reducing corporate income taxes is the least beneficial;
- taking the economically least beneficial option of providing lump-sum rebates to households, the benefits of reducing CO_2 emissions (using the social cost of carbon) exceeds the costs by 70 percent;
- still taking the economically least beneficial option of lump-sum rebates, the co-benefits in terms of reduced emissions of other pollutants, the benefits are four times that of the costs.

It is important to note that these figures underestimate the benefits and overestimate the costs. The authors are rigorous practitioners of economics, but that precludes quantification of some costs and benefits (which the authors duly note). In fact, the costs of climate policy are generally overestimated, and the benefits generally underestimated. I list five reasons, but there are more.

First, integrated assessment models, as sophisticated and complex as they are, do not generally account for positive feedback effects, such as warming leading to melting tundra leading to more methane emissions leading to more warming.

Another positive feedback effect is of melting polar ice, which makes the Earth less reflective, causing it to absorb more heat, causing more polar ice to melt. There are others, and they all point to greater climate damages and thus larger benefits from reducing emissions and trying to avoid more warming.

Second, even the most sophisticated modeling efforts underestimate innovation and its impacts, because it is so hard to predict. And yet, innovation accounts for the lion's share of welfare leaps throughout human history. To take one of many examples, the cost of wind and solar energy has been plummeting, and as those costs fall, so does the welfare cost of carbon taxation.

Third, with one exception, integrated assessment models do not cumulate economic growth; the problem with that omission is that lost economic growth in one year due to climate effects – say, for example Hurricane Sandy, or an extreme snowstorm that grounds many commercial airline flights for days – is lost productivity that is not simply made up when business resumes. The failure to conduct business is lost income which is no longer there to invest in productive activity next year, and so on.

Fourth, the social cost of carbon is too low, because it excludes many, many climate effects that are still too difficult to measure. For example, the loss of biological diversity is not modeled in integrated assessment models. The effects of ocean acidification and the bleaching of coral reefs, which house over a quarter of the ocean's species, is not modeled.

Fifth, nonclimate environmental benefits are undercounted. Goulder and Hafstead, more comprehensive than most, count the benefits of local air pollution reduction, such as fine particulate matter and SO_2. Fine particulate matter, in particular, is known with certainty to be harmful, as decades of research has demonstrated a link between fine particulate matter pollution and premature deaths. But Goulder and Hafstead still do not count, because they are still too speculative to estimate, other pollution benefits of a smaller reliance on coal combustion, such as the harm from the mining and transportation, water pollution, and land pollution from the deposit of "coal ash," the residue from coal combustion. All of these harms, and many others, would also be reduced by a carbon tax.

What does this tell us about carbon taxation? Even if a researcher takes only the most careful, most conservative, most concretely-grounded information, carbon taxation generates far, far more in benefits than costs. From a societal standpoint, a carbon tax is a no-brainer if there ever was one. In fact, what the plethora of underestimation issues and co-benefits of emissions reduction suggests is that an efficient carbon tax should really be set *higher* – considerably higher – than the social cost of carbon of $52 in 2020 dollars.

These analyses do *not* tell us what to do about the distributional effects of carbon taxation. There are two vulnerable groups of particular concern: (i) poor consumers for whom an increase in energy prices could be proportionately much worse than for affluent consumers, and (ii) dislocation suffered by coal workers and the places where they live. With respect to the former, opponents of carbon taxation argue that carbon taxes are *regressive* – that they disproportionately hurt poor people. Energy costs for heating and electricity comprise, at least in fossil-fuel heavy regions, a larger chunk of a poor household's budget than an affluent one, so increases in energy costs will require larger sacrifices. As the United States (and other nations) move away from coal as a fuel source, this becomes true of a smaller and smaller part of the country. Also, some carbon tax revenues can be used to rebate consumers, on a lump sum basis. A much-discussed "fee-and-dividend" carbon tax proposal involves the collection of *all* carbon tax revenues for redistribution on a flat, lump-sum-per-household basis. The effect of returning, in lump sum payments, all carbon tax revenues is to only partially compensate rich households for their large carbon footprints, and to *over*compensate poor households, making them *better off* than they would be without the fee-and-dividend proposal.[9] Canada has adopted such an approach, not only redistributing all carbon tax proceeds, but being careful to return proceeds back to the provinces from whence they were collected.[10]

Finding a way to compensate those losing jobs because of the decline of coal mining is more difficult, although it is economically achievable. A good number of those in communities dependent on the coal industry would benefit from a fee-and-dividend program. But some would not, and the fee-and-dividend would not make whole those losing their jobs. There were, as of 2020, slightly more than 50,000 people employed in the coal mining industry.[11] Adding in other people in coal-dependent communities still produces a manageable number. Possibly, some carbon tax revenues should be devoted to retraining workers or providing other relief. Since a fee-and-dividend program would actually overcompensate poor households,[12] it would be possible to earmark some carbon tax revenues towards coal industry relief. Perhaps, those living in coal-dependent regions might qualify for a super-dividend. Part of the creative, and highly political part of climate policy moving forward will be to find ways of compensating those suffering economic loss due to carbon taxation or other climate policies. Carbon taxes certainly generate a huge amount of revenues and surplus, and there is enough to compensate even an entire industry, at least economically.

A persistent concern about carbon taxation as a domestic policy pertains to its effects on the competitiveness of domestic industries vis-à-vis global competitors from countries that might not adopt a carbon tax, or any other climate policy. Energy being a key input for several important global industries, such as steel, aluminum, chemicals, and cement, an increase in the cost of energy might reduce global market share for American manufacturers. There are several responses to this problem. I offer three, one overlooked, one hopeful, and one uncertain. None are a complete response but together are more than sufficiently choate to justify moving ahead with enacting a carbon tax.

First, it has become broadly recognized (at least outside of Congress and the antienvironmental extremists close to some members of Congress) that reducing emissions of carbon dioxide also simultaneously reduces the ambient air concentration of fine particulate matter, or $PM_{2.5}$, which causes millions of premature deaths each year worldwide.[13] A single country reducing emissions of carbon dioxide would thus generate large *local* benefits, regardless of what other countries do.[14]

Second, it is worth taking hopeful notice of the nature of a carbon tax, and how it compares with obligations under other international agreements. Whereas other environmental agreements have foundered because of the incentives to shirk, a carbon tax is an obligation that would generate an important benefit for countries joining in agreement: the revenues themselves. The availability of a pool of money, possibly substantial, may create the political space that some otherwise reluctant countries might be able to use to form supportive coalitions. Moreover, an agreement to tax is much more like those of other binding, successful international agreements, in that compliance is made obvious by the existence of the tax and a collection infrastructure (though perhaps tricky to detect faulty, *imperfect* compliance). A carbon tax forms a much more coherent subject matter for international agreement than, say cap-and-trade concepts such as that under the flawed Kyoto Protocol.[15]

Third, shirking on climate policy might be fixed by the uncertain but probably legally permissible idea of levying a border tax adjustment on goods imported from competing manufacturers. Under the terms of the General Agreement on Tariffs and Trade (GATT), which governs trading between countries and sets out the rules under which tariffs can be imposed, countries may seek to equalize certain – not all – tax burdens suffered by domestic parties but not foreign competitors. While there is some disagreement, the weight of international trade opinion is that a border tax adjustment to equalize a carbon tax burden would *probably* be permissible under the GATT.[16] Were the United States to adopt a carbon tax, it would likely be allowed under international trade law to levy an import tax on carbon-intensive goods, like steel and chemicals, provided that these manufacturers in the United States *actually* bear some burden of carbon taxation. It is possible that they don't, if they derive some significant amount of electricity from renewable sources. While most international trade experts seem to agree that such a provision could be drafted to withstand scrutiny by the World Trade Organization, it remains an untested proposition. Were such a provision to be litigated and upheld, it would significantly reduce the competitive advantage that would be enjoyed by countries refusing to tax carbon, and possibly induce them to reconsider.

Of all of the environmental crises discussed in this book, climate change is the one posing the greatest risk to humankind and, for that matter, to millions of other species. A carbon tax is not by itself sufficient to arrest climate change, but represents the strongest step to harness capitalism and redirect entrepreneurial energies in a restorative direction, and away from destructive tendencies.

6.2 RUMINANTS

Ruminants are ungulate mammals that digest food by regurgitating food to be chewed again, and by fermenting it in their stomachs through microbial processes. This process, "enteric fermentation," is very efficient in extracting nutrients from plant materials, but produces methane, a greenhouse gas less long-lived than CO_2 but many times more powerful in trapping heat. Ruminants raised for meat and for milk include cattle, buffalo, sheep, and goats. Cattle make up by far the largest category of ruminants. By weight, there is fourteen times as much cattle as there are all wild mammals on Earth.[17] This section proposes a head tax on all ruminants, not just cattle, but deriving the tax for just cattle is illustrative. It is also most pressing to reduce the amount of cattle raising in the world, as cattle pose the most immediate threat to the environment.

Raising cattle for beef and for dairy creates many externalities: the greenhouse gas emissions from all that is required to raise cattle, and the greenhouse gas emissions from the cattle themselves; damage to range from cattle grazing; water pollution from cattle manure; water consumption for the cattle themselves (much more than required for other foods); and all of the externalities from producing the cattle feed. However, it is sufficient to focus just on the carbon footprint of cattle, which also happens to be readily susceptible of calculation. Although dairy and beef cattle are slightly different, it is sufficient to treat all cattle alike in terms of carbon footprint.

The United Nations Food and Agriculture Organization (FAO) reported in 2019 that global greenhouse gas emissions from cattle totaled 4.6 gigatons of CO_2-equivalent, about the same as the emissions of the entire United States. Of this, 2.9 gigatons was for beef production, and 1.4 for milk,[18] and the remainder for some small, miscellaneous uses of cattle. Because most cattle are given a specific feed, which itself must be grown, processed and transported, the supply chain and carbon footprint is longer than one might expect. The FAO report estimates the resulting emissions of CO_2, methane, and nitrous oxides, occurring at one or more stages of beef production. For most cattle farmers in the world, the largest category of emissions is enteric fermentation. But for Latin American cattle farmers, the largest category is deforestation, in which trees are burned (not even cut down for productive use) to make way for cattle, and for soy grown for cattle feed.[19]

Recommendations for reducing the carbon footprint for cattle farming usually focus on what cattle farmers can do better, such as improving manure management, which emits both methane and nitrous oxides, and is responsible for about 25 percent of CO_2-equivalent emissions globally.[20] As it happens, cattle farming in sub-Saharan Africa and South and Southeast Asia has a much higher carbon footprint, mostly due to low productivity. Smaller, less healthy cattle produce less meat at slaughter, so more enterically fermenting cattle are required to produce the same amount of beef. The FAO recommends improving breeding and animal health interventions to allow herd sizes to shrink.[21] Many organizations, including the FAO, also recommend manure management to help with the recycling of nutrients.[22] Of course, calls to reduce deforestation in South American countries have been made for decades, and occasionally heeded.

All of these recommendations are well and good. But as long as capitalism provides an incentive to maximize profits and externalize costs, cattle farmers will strive to make cattle as large as possible, and largely ignore environmental harms imposed on others, perhaps hundreds of miles away. At least in North America, the incentives to maximize profit are partially aligned with minimizing greenhouse gases, insofar as productivity is concerned. Not so much with cattle farming.

What is needed is an equalized playing field for cattle and other foods. Many U.S. states and Canadian provinces already collect a small head tax, but only to raise funds to maintain systems and infrastructure for the cattle industry, not to account for environmental externalities. If a head tax on cattle could be large enough to at least internalize the greenhouse gas emissions specific to enteric fermentation and manure management, then more efficient choices would be made with respect to food production and, eventually food consumption. The choice of protein should be made taking into account the externalities of each food. It is worth starting with cattle because the gap between external and internalized costs is so enormous, more so than with any other food.

North American cattle ranchers produced about 13 million tons, "carcass weight," of beef, with a footprint of about 29 kg CO_2-equivalent per kg of beef.[23] Almost all of this is specific to cattle ranching itself; very little is for transportation of finished beef product, which would be required of any food.[24] If we were to assume, however, enactment of the carbon tax proposed in the previous part of this section, the carbon footprint falls to about 22 kg CO_2-equivalent per kg of beef. Cattle are of widely varying sizes when sold for slaughter, but to take an average beef animal in the United States producing about 240 kg of beef,[25] an average carbon footprint would be about 5.8 tons.[26] Applying the social cost of carbon, a head tax imposed at slaughter would amount to about $280. Of course, a great deal of variation exists with respect to emissions of beef and dairy cattle, and such figures are only rough averages that mask a great deal of variation. It may be messy to try and develop a methodology for approximating emissions from a lifetime of enteric fermentation of different kinds cattle, but the effort is surely worthwhile, given its contribution to climate change and other environmental externalities.

Developing a methodology for estimating emissions for cattle is important for environmental reasons, but could also possibly work to the advantage of some cattle farmers, especially North American ones. Globally, beef is a highly competitive business. The United States exported 1.1 million metric tons of beef in 2016,[27] while also importing 1.3 million metric tons.[28] If say, the United States were to impose a head tax on its cattle farmers, they would suffer a competitive disadvantage vis-à-vis foreign cattle farmers. But if a reasonable methodology existed for estimating methane emissions from enteric fermentation, a head tax could actually be advantageous to some cattle farmers under international trade law.

The General Agreement on Tariffs and Trade, which sets out the rules under which tariffs can be imposed, generally forbids the imposition of import tariffs but contains exceptions, one of which provides as follows:

2. Nothing in this Article shall prevent any contracting party from imposing at any time on the importation of any product:
    (a) a charge equivalent to an internal tax imposed consistently with the provisions of paragraph 2 of Article III in respect of the like domestic product or in respect of an article from which the imported product has been manufactured or produced in whole or in part;[29]

The history and the jurisprudence of this provision are complicated. Suffice it to say, international trade law is rarely clear-cut, and confident conclusions are elusive, but this application of Article II:2(a) is about as straightforward as international trade law gets: an import tariff could be imposed upon beef imports, so long as it was designed to mimic the effect of the American head tax on cattle. Conversely, if beef is produced for export to a country lacking the same head tax on cattle, then the tax can be reduced or eliminated.

Here is where things get interesting, because North American cattle farmers are more efficient than counterparts in some other parts of the world. A cattle farmer that can produce beef with demonstrably less methane emissions than an international competitor may even enjoy a competitive advantage under international trade rules. For a domestic cattle farmer that can produce more beef per methane emissions, a head tax could conceivably be *smaller* than an import tariff on beef, provided it is considered a "like" product. The trick would be, of course, a sufficiently reliable and acceptable method of estimating methane emissions over the lifetime of a beef animal, given differing methods and conditions.

The FAO derives its global data from the Global Livestock Environmental Assessment Model, or "GLEAM," which compiles data on herds and practices from a wide variety of sources worldwide.[30] Data is not only region-specific, but country specific. On the basis of extensive data and models, the FAO is able to conclude that, for example, the carbon footprint of beef produced in Latin America is roughly 233 percent that of North American beef.[31] Critically, GLEAM utilizes actual *counts* of herds, sometimes by satellite imagery. This is important for purposes of calculating an import tariff, because beef imported from a high-footprint country could potentially be subject to a tariff that is higher than the effective rate paid by an American cattle farmer subjected to the head tax. In other words a head tax could be less burdensome to a domestic, efficient cattle farmer, than the tariff imposed upon a foreign, inefficient one.

International trade law provides a way to equalize the burden of a head tax, and possibly even provide an advantage to some cattle farmers. A head tax on cattle is not quite true to Pigouvian ideals like a carbon tax, because it would fail to capture all of the externalities of cattle raising. It could also be complicated to calibrate the head tax among different breeds and production methods. But even a rough head tax would be an important start in internalizing the climate costs of beef, and encouraging production favoring less methane emissions. While cattle farmers could be expected to oppose a head tax of the sort I propose here, the competitive advantage they might derive vis-à-vis their global competitors might soften their view. It could even provide a slight incentive for some cattle farmers to improve efficiency. Given the enormous impact of cattle as compared with other foods, a head tax is an essential step in accounting for the externalities of food production.

6.3 WATER CONSUMPTION

Water overconsumption and waste is not "pollution" in the conventional sense, but current practices in many parts of the world clearly constitute environmental degradation, and is very much part of how humankind is damaging the global environment, in some cases irrevocably. The amount of water within the Earth's biosphere does not change appreciably, but the distribution matters, and changes a great deal. This is especially true since humankind and all nonmarine species depend upon a scant 0.7 percent of the Earth's water that is available freshwater.[32] Climate change will reduce that figure because it will intensify hydrological cycles, increasing the number of droughts even as it increases severe rainfall and flooding, mostly depositing unusable water.[33] While assessing water scarcity is challenging because conditions are so heterogeneous, of the many studies of global water supply, none are sanguine. In addition to the billions of people already living under water stress, billions more will be added in a climate-changed future.[34] Humankind must adapt to water scarcity brought on by the growth of population and poor practices, but exacerbated by climate change.

The excessive consumption of water by humans at the expense of all other species on the planet is ethically indefensible. But even putting aside regards about other species, humankind will pay for its own improvidence; not in equal measure, because water has long been and will continue to be unjustly distributed. Indeed, one of the greatest dangers of climate change is the possibility that inequalities with respect to life staples like water could be so severe as to lead to mass unrest and international conflict. Water scholar Peter Gleick has expressed the opinion that the horrific situation in Syria was partially attributable to water shortage, exacerbating long-simmering conflicts.[35] Whether one agrees with Gleick or not about Syria, he is certainly correct about water often having been a source of international conflict in the past,[36] and the real prospect of it being so in a climate-changed future.

This section proposes moving towards a tax on water consumption, including groundwater consumption. This proposal builds upon, among others, the work of Professor Dave Owen,[37] in setting out some basic rationales for the taxation of water usage and articulates how and why water needs to be taxed, and why a more capitalist society would include a water tax.

It is not, at this moment in history, feasible nor even necessary to tax water consumption *everywhere*. First, water conditions are incredibly diverse, making water taxation in some places impractical. Second, monitoring and enforcement technologies and infrastructure are not yet sufficient to capture all water users. Water uses are currently too heterogeneous, too diffuse, and just too numerous to be able to monitor and tax. In fact, it is not yet possible to monitor the largest and most wasteful users of water, at least in the United States: agricultural users. What is needed is a menu of new technologies to monitor water uses down to the individual household and individual farm.

Taxing water would produce revenues for a taxing jurisdiction, and one productive use of those revenues would be to fund development of water monitoring technologies. Although such a technological push would amount to a public good, redounding to the benefit of a much broader population – unfairly, perhaps, from the point of view of the taxing jurisdiction – such a pairing of a water tax with a technological subsidy holds enormous potential for economic benefit. A water tax would generate large conservation benefits, drawing water away from wasteful uses and driving it to more valuable uses. But as the example of the country of Israel illustrates, local development of important water-saving technologies generate substantial, localized co-benefits: Israel has become an export juggernaut, sending abroad water, produce, and technology, a remarkable economic success story centering upon water, in one of the driest places in the world.[38]

A second beneficial use of revenues would be to buy out some wastefully utilized water rights. There is no way around untangling some of the most labyrinthine water laws. Water rights are sometimes among the most important property rights, while also some of the most wastefully used. Expenses and strategic behavior might be reduced by conducting a water rights buyback by auction. But there is no way around having to compensate the holders of some water rights, however anachronistic and wasteful. With climate change promising longer and more severe water shortages, the elimination of waste would be an enormous and critically necessary step towards resiliency.

This proposal for a water tax in this part is not Pigouvian. A Pigouvian tax at least has the ambition of taxing at a level that is equal to the external social costs of an activity. That would be extremely difficult to do in the case of water, because context matters so much. Even within the state of Oregon, for example, it is one thing to make a water withdrawal from the massive Columbia River, and another thing to make a groundwater withdrawal from the arid Eastern three-fifths of the state. Rather than pursue any Pigouvian ambitions, it would be more prudent to levy a modest tax on consumption just to begin the task of weeding out some of the most wasteful uses. Preparing for the impending climate-induced water crisis will certainly require a much, much more extensive imposition of some *price* on water consumption. The waste, particularly in the United States, is unfathomably inefficient, and represents lost opportunity, not only by the trillions of gallons, but of the discovery of ways to reduce consumption and waste. A water tax would generate many of the benefits of a Pigouvian tax. But contemplating some sort of an economic optimum is just too daunting at this point.

Water laws are generally complex, because of the nature of water and its uses. Again, heterogeneity is partially responsible for the complex and inconsistent doctrines governing water rights and contracts. But water law is especially patchwork and tortuous in the United States. Water law is closely tied to property law, both matters of state law in the United States. A key difference is that a water "right" is usufructuary – the right is to use of the water, not the water itself. States east of the 100th meridian generally adopted a *riparian* system of surface water rights, in which access to and rights to use water were tied to property ownership of land abutting surface water. In early days of settlement, conflicts among users of the same body of water were infrequent, and a vague common law notion of "reasonable use" sufficed as a general legal principle. Over time, the common law standard became less satisfactory, but because people had formed expectations about access to water, changing the standard was difficult. Reform has belatedly come to almost all states, with state statutes setting out how permits replace the previous riparian water rights, but with the "reasonable use" standard still a guiding principle governing permitting processes.

The historical account west of the 100th meridian contains similar themes, even though the legal doctrine and water availability are very different. West of the 100th meridian, climates can be very arid and water very scarce. As a result, in early days of settlement, water was governed by a system of *prior appropriation* as a basis for settling disputes over water uses. In the interests of developing the arid West, there was good reason not to limit usage to the very few parcels of land abutting water, and to reward the first to exploit the availability of water. At common law, the only limit to an appropriator's right to use water was that she make "beneficial use" of the water, and not waste it. Both of those concepts – beneficial use and waste – would undergo significant evolution.

Water laws in the United States are further complicated by the fact that groundwater usage is a completely different set of laws, and like the surface water laws described above, a matter of state law. State common laws governing groundwater usage vary even more than state surface water laws, though statutes are displacing or codifying the old case-based laws.[39] Increasing groundwater withdrawals are among the most troubling developments in terms of sustainability, and are extremely difficult to track and monitor. Long-standing warnings of unsustainable groundwater withdrawals from the Ogallala aquifer below the vitally important agricultural Midwestern United States, have been largely (though not completely) ignored.

A legacy of water waste has its roots in the westward expansion and early settlement years of the United States, in which a young but large country strove desperately for economic development. In those early days, it was capital, not water, that was the limiting ingredient for economic development, and water usage was rarely deemed to be anything but economically "beneficial," and rarely deemed to be "waste." Hence the case *Irwin v. Phillips*,[40] in which a California court held that it was beneficial and non-wasteful for a gold miner to use water for the purpose of hydraulically blasting entire mountainsides of rock into a slurry in order to find gold. An estimated one billion cubic meters of sediment were created, and miners used an estimated 10,000 tons of liquid mercury to extract gold, leading to contamination that still persists to this day.

These twin biases – in favor of development, and against the conservation of water – have been surprisingly persistent, even as environmental awareness has risen. Troublingly, these biases seem to have been institutionalized in the governance of water management districts and other water suppliers, making them harder to overcome.[41] The result has been a surprising persistence of some inexcusably wasteful water uses. It is as if water waste has become acculturated, resisting reason and logic.

Groundwater usage, as well, has followed this improvident boom-and-bust trajectory, both in law and in practice. For a time, extracting groundwater was essentially lawless, governed by a "rule of capture," or allowing every user entitled to take whatever she was able to. The notion of scarcity was nonexistent. Over time, states developed groundwater laws that were more conducive to conservation and sharing, which became important as users bumped up against the limits of groundwater extraction.

While some of the most wasteful practices have given way, some other wasteful habits refuse to die. California's agricultural sector has grown into the largest of all the states, producing about 13 percent in cash receipts of all agricultural products in the United States,[42] and even producing more dairy than the historical dairy powerhouse, Wisconsin.[43] But in the rush to claim water rights, California also developed industries in cotton, rice, alfalfa, and livestock – water-intensive uses ill-suited to arid environments. Some farmers in California's drought-plagued Central Valley still receive water under old contracts at the rate of $25 per acre-foot.[44] The idea that water unused is water wasted seems to have woven itself into some parts of Western culture. In 1984, a summer resort in Colorado drained a wetland and sued to establish a water right, on the theory that draining the wetland reduced evaporation losses.[45] Although the resort lost, it was still a shocking theory to propound, effectively assigning a negative value to wetlands. The City of Las Vegas, which carefully polices water waste, employs officers to issue citations in cases of violations.

One oblivious and angry homeowner, confronted by a city water officer about his lawn sprinkler, poked a finger into the officer's chest and exclaimed, "with all these new rules, you people are trying to turn this place into a desert!"[46]

Though these examples are not a fair representation of water usage everywhere, they do seem to suggest a notion persisting in some corners that using water is always better used than conserved. The bottled water industry serves as an example. There is no denying that the convenience of grabbing a water bottle is valuable for consumers. But it does not need to be *subsidized*, literally and figuratively. Until 2018, the Internal Revenue Code allowed corporations selling "electricity, natural gas, or *potable water*" to deduct a portion of expenses against gross receipts that would otherwise be nondeductible.[47] But more importantly, bottled water companies take water that would otherwise be for public consumption, most often extremely cheaply, put it inside a disposable plastic bottle, and sell it for healthy prices. The Florida bottled water company Zephyrhills, a subsidiary of the global water giant, Nestlé, holds permits to extract water from five springs watersheds within the state, which it bottles and markets.[48] In one of many typical water extraction permits held by Nestlé in Florida, Nestlé pays the Northwest Florida Water Management District a fee of $50 to extract 12 million gallons per month from a spring,[49] a value of about $76 million.[50] Apart from the colossal waste of energy and greenhouse gas emissions associated with the production of bottled water,[51] apart from the colossal waste of unrecycled plastic (less than 10 percent of all plastic water bottles are recycled),[52] just producing bottled water ironically wastes water – about three liters for every liter of bottled water.[53] The $50 permit fee does not even remotely pay for the administrative costs of permitting, let alone the opportunity costs of alternative uses such as domestic consumption, ecological services, recreation, and wildlife. Four labels: Arrowhead, Crystal Geyser, Aquafina, and Dasani, take either tap water or groundwater from water-poor California,[54] and did so even as California municipalities were asked to ration water during California's historic five-year drought.[55]

The need to change the way water is consumed is pressing and manifest. Billions of people worldwide face water shortages, and wealthy Californians still water hundreds of acres of green lawns, and did so in the state's historic drought.[56] An increment of rationality can be introduced into water provision by imposing a water tax. Not every place in the United States or the world faces a water shortage, so a water tax need not be uniform. Nonetheless, a price would provide an important signal, no matter where, as to the importance of this vital resource.

This proposal for a water tax is necessarily incomplete, because most jurisdictions lack capacity for effective monitoring of water usage and enforcement of violations. Because a water tax would rarely be comprehensive, it would be wise to avoid creating a large distortion by driving water users from monitored (and taxed) water uses to unmonitored (and untaxed) uses. The second part of this proposal is to dedicate some revenues from water taxes to fund the development of the technology and regulatory infrastructure needed to extend the water tax to cover *all* users, even agricultural ones. Some states such as Colorado have already made significant progress towards measuring water use.

As far as water monitoring technology goes, there is no flinching from the intrusive nature of such technology. Monitoring technology will no doubt strike some users accustomed to free reign as surveillance, which rouses concerns about privacy. But that, too, is a product of an unrealistic expectation of free use. Countries could follow the example of Israel, which passed a law in the 1950s that no water could flow into a home, business, or farm without first passing through an approved water meter.[57] That would be quite a dramatic move, politically, to mandate a monitoring device for water usage in the United States, an activity that is deemed in some American quarters as an important a right as property itself. But such a move would not be unprecedented. Federal monies (from water tax revenues, potentially) could be conditioned upon a water monitoring device mandate. That would actually follow the tradition of some parts of the Federal Water Pollution Control Act, which offer federal monies for water treatment subject to certain conditions. Despite the state law foundations of water law, such a comprehensive law would be well within the power of federal government to enact, and could solve the water use monitoring problem quickly.

The United States is not Israel, and the time for such a universal water metering requirement may not yet have arrived. But there is no shrinking from the need and the challenge of monitoring water usage. The need is especially pressing with respect to groundwater, which is suffering the greatest losses. While some ground-water withdrawal monitoring is in place, a comprehensive, tamper-proof system must be in place if a water consumption tax is ever to be imposed, and such a system will have to intrude on what many have previously taken for granted as their private domain.

Water is a life necessity, so a strong argument exists for a governmental role in ensuring that some minimum amount of water is available for every person within its jurisdiction. But that does not mean that water needs always to be *free*, much less grotesquely subsidized. It is not administratively trivial to distinguish between provision of a life-sustaining amount and provision for a wasteful use, but nor is it terribly difficult. Given the stakes, it is unjustifiable not to.

A push to tax water should be grounded in a call to incentivize capitalism with respect to water usage, conservation, and reclamation. A large reason that Americans are unsustainably accustomed to using and wasting huge amounts of water is because it is not adequately priced, and has thus failed to attract sufficient entrepreneurial energies. Most Americans are unaccustomed to the notion of thinking about water entrepreneurially because it has effectively been free; most fees paid for water are for delivery infrastructure and services, not for the water itself. How would Americans react if they were faced with cutting back on water consumption? Would Americans trust markets to allocate scarce water fairly, or efficiently? Most would instinctively answer "no."

Seth Siegel's *Let There Be Water: Israel's Solution for a Water-Starved World*,[58] is a compelling account of Israel, water scarcity, and above all in my view, capitalism. Israel is one of the driest countries in the world, with natural water supplies, groundwater and surface water, totaling about 1.8 billion cubic meters per year.[59] If that were divided equally among its 9 million residents, each would be allotted 200 cubic meters per year, or 0.55 cubic meters per person per day. That is not accounting for Israel needing industry and agriculture to thrive as a country, so actual consumption by Israelis is much, much less.

Water is nationalized in Israel, under the Israeli Water Authority (IWA), which owns every drop in the country, even rainfall.[60] Under such extreme situations of shortage, many might instinctively assume that the allocation of water is highly centralized. Water policy is centralized in the IWA, but allocation is almost completely accomplished by price-setting. Prices are set every six months based on expected water supply, and are generally quite high, eliminating shortages. From 2010 to 2019 typical Israeli households paid between $1.85 and $2.60 US per cubic meter of water, for the first 7 cubic meters per month, then much more after that.[61] Municipal corporations and industry pay less, and agriculture less still. Water users can buy reclaimed water and non-potable water at discounted rates.[62]

Israel's water rates are not, strictly speaking, taxes, but they are very high prices that function like an environmental tax. As in the case of Sweden, high prices induce profound behavioral changes and entrepreneurialism. Toilets use much less water than North American or European toilets. Showers are shorter. Wasting water is blasphemous in Israel. Israelis do not even waste wastewater, recycling over 85 percent of it. For some perspective, second place on the top recyclers list is Spain, which recycles about 20 percent of its wastewater.[63]

But beyond behavioral changes, the scarcity and high cost of water in Israel have spawned many water-saving innovations. This is the potentially greater upside of capitalism: its superior ability to cultivate ideas. Along with the behavioral changes that have made the most of its natural water supply, scarcity has driven Israeli inventors to not just make do, but *expand* its water resources. A land that British economists believed could hold a maximum of two million people,[64] is now home to a total of fourteen million people – nine million Israelis and a total of five million living in the Gaza Strip and the West Bank.

One of the ways that water supply has been expanded is through the mundane but vital job of leak detection. One company developed pipeline sensors that transmit information back to servers for analysis, looking for possible leaks. Artificial intelligence software develops a consumption profile for every water user, and when anomalous uses occur, alerts officials and the user. Contrast that with New York City, which has an underground tunnel that delivers fresh water from upstate New York, responsible for about half of the city's water supply. But it leaks, the City knows not where, to the tune of about thirty-five million gallons *per day*. New York City loses water to leakage in one day the equivalent of the *monthly* allotment of water for 19,000 Israeli households. Even sewer pipes in Israel are policed for leakage, by small GPS-guided robots.[65] In Israel, sewage still contains valuable water. Israel's largest water recycling system, handling almost 200 million cubic meters per year, a third of all Israeli wastewater, pumps wastewater into sandy dunes south of Tel Aviv, where it gradually seeps into an underground aquifer. The migration takes between six months to a year, and by the time the water reaches the aquifer, the water is clean enough to be used for anything except drinking.[66]

Israelis have also expanded their natural water supplies by more blunt technological means, constructing several desalination plants. Desalination is an expensive, energy intensive technology, but modern desalination technology pioneered by Israelis is more efficient and relies upon a process known as "reverse osmosis," which forces water through nylon membranes and removes the salt from seawater. The process was invented by an American who immigrated and settled in Israel to develop the technology. Israeli engineers eventually turned around to help the City of San Diego in building the first major desalination plant in the United States.[67]

Agriculture must be innovative in a dry country with few trading partners. Drip irrigation was developed in Israel, the watering of crops by slowly dripping water through a pipe with small holes. The regularity of water allows plants to take up the water more efficiently, not only saving water but increasing yield. Nutrients are also delivered in drip irrigation pipes, in measured amounts.[68] Drip irrigation stands in stark contrast to the American habit of heavily fertilizing, heavily applying pesticides, and heavily irrigating crops with inefficient sprinkler systems which lose large amounts of water to evaporation before it even hits the ground. Not only is this blunt American method wasteful, but the overapplication of water and heavy rains wash the excess fertilizer and pesticides into lakes, streams, aquifers, and eventually oceans. Drip irrigation not only saves water and increases yield, but reduces water pollution and the need for fertilizer. Agricultural innovation has also reached into the biosciences, as Israeli farmers have bred wheat with short stalks, and bred new varieties of produce that grow well in the salty, brackish water found beneath deserts.

To appreciate the effect of Israel's high prices, it might be useful to make an informal comparison with California. It is impossible to figure out a single price of water in California, which has incredibly complex water laws, and very challenging conditions for the actual sale and purchase of water. Here is an estimate: during 2014, four years into California's historic drought, water trading occurred more frequently, and prices seemed to center around a mean price of about $0.13 per cubic meter,[69] less than six percent of what Israeli households paid, and about a one-fifth to one-sixth of what Israeli farmers pay.[70] While Israel does not have the GDP per capita of powerhouse California, it requires barely a third the water to produce wealth than does California: 5.6 cubic meters of water to produce $1,000 of GDP, as compared to California, which requires 16.4 cubic meters.[71] While the comparison is informal, it does suggest that California could very easily generate wealth with less water. The state could sacrifice crops such as rice, alfalfa, and cotton, and give up livestock, all of which are better done in wetter climates.

If one could call it an advantage, Israelis have the advantage of *never* having taken water for granted. Americans, having gotten used to wasting water from times when water was abundant, now find it difficult to reform medieval water laws. Bad habits, sunk capital, and long-standing expectations based on outdated conditions and expectations have derailed attempts to reform water usage and pricing in the United States.

The United States does not need to replicate Israel's extreme scarcity to bring about some rationality, but nor must it waste water so prolifically that it rushes headlong into pointless deprivation. A water tax, beginning with most users at a modest rate, and gradually increasing as more users become covered by a comprehensive monitoring system, would vitally introduce a price for water. Because water is not scarce everywhere in the United States, a prudent approach might be to err on the side of low taxation, though there are precious few corners in the United States where species fish, wildlife, and plant life would not benefit from just a little more abstemious human consumption. Even American farmers could learn that the current tragedy of the commons of water usage could be fixed by pricing. Israeli farmers were furious when the Israeli Water Authority raised water rates, but eventually realized that if they were only willing to pay for water, they would be assured of supply. If that can work in one of the driest countries on Earth, it could work in the United States.

Perhaps most importantly, a water tax might stimulate water-saving innovation. It is more than a little ironic that it was a Southern Californian, Sidney Loeb,[72] who developed the reverse osmosis technology that revolutionized desalination so that Israel could export that technology to, of all places, Southern California. If only all the other water-saving technologies were similarly adopted by Americans! Unfortunately, with free water, there never seems to be the need.

6.4 NUTRIENT WATER POLLUTION

Modern crop farmers are perpetually having to replace nitrogen and phosphorus, farm nutrients lost to uptake by their crops which are harvested and transported off-farm.[73] On small, old-fashioned farms, nutrients could be replaced by the manure of a few farm animals. But modern agriculture, driven by economies of scale, has become industrial in scale and production, and has not only necessitated larger applications of fertilizer, but also physically separated crop and livestock production. With the vast majority of farm production focusing on either crops or livestock but not both, it has become difficult to match livestock manure with crop fertilizing needs. Fortunately for crop farmers, nitrogen fixation, while energy-intensive, has made the large-scale production of commercial fertilizer inexpensive.

Too inexpensive, in fact. Farmers apply excessive amounts of commercial fertilizer because the cost of wasted fertilizer is much lower than the value of the lost opportunity to boost crop yield. Farmers fail to take into account the runoff of excess nutrients being washed from their fields into waterways during heavy rains. About 50 percent of all commercial nitrogen fertilizer in the United States is applied to corn, mostly in the Midwest,[74] and about 50 percent of that is lost to the environment as pollution.[75] At the same time, where livestock manure is used as fertilizer, it too is often overapplied, because the scale of livestock farming has become so large and so geographically concentrated that the amount of manure available far exceeds local fertilizing needs.[76] The result in both cases is the same: overapplication of fertilizer that has produced excess runoff of nutrients into waterbodies, with negative consequences for water quality. It is not necessarily wanton disregard for the environment that leads to excess fertilizer application; nitrogen uptake by crops is uncertain and highly variable, dependent upon soil-plant-water relationships, temperature, precipitation, soil conditions, and other factors.[77] Moreover, competition can be keen: many corn farmers in the Upper Midwest use specialized seed corn under competitive contracts, in which they are rewarded based on yield, increasing the incentive to overapply nitrogen fertilizer.[78] Faced with uncertainty in a low-margin, risky business, farmers might be forgiven for erring on the side of production.

But the effects of fertilizer overapplication are harmful. Excess nutrient "loading" of waterbodies causes eutrophication, the excessive growth of algae, sometimes toxic to aquatic organisms and people. When the algae dies, the decomposition process produces extremely unpleasant odors and reduces the amount of oxygen in the affected waterbody, killing off almost all aquatic organisms in its vicinity. When occurring intensely in waterbodies, algal "blooms" cover the water surface with an unsightly blue or green coat and mostly preclude recreational activities within and near the waterbody. Property values near frequently eutrophic waterbodies are worth considerably less than comparable properties.[79]

Perhaps most spectacularly, every summer a part of the Gulf of Mexico about the size of New Jersey forms near the mouth of the Mississippi River, that is so oxygen-poor that there is very little marine life within that patch. The largest cause of this annually occurring hyper-polluted "dead zone" is excess nitrogen and phosphorus, exiting livestock farms and running off of the surface of farms from thirty-one states that lie within the Mississippi River watershed.[80] Over 70 percent of the nitrogen and over 80 percent of the phosphorus ultimately delivered to the Gulf of Mexico are from crops or pasture and range (for grazing).[81] By contrast, urban runoff, industrial sources, and wastewater treatment plants (which are subject to regulation under the Clean Water Act) account for relatively small amounts (9 percent and 12 percent of nitrogen and phosphorus, respectively).[82]

Out of about 1.1 million miles of rivers and streams in the United States that have been assessed by the EPA, just over half, 588,000 miles, are considered "impaired," which means that they fail a water quality standard designated by the individual states for their own waterbodies.[83] That is likely an understatement of how polluted rivers and streams are, because more than a third of the river-miles are designated for "agricultural" uses, so the standards set for those rivers and streams are extremely lenient.[84] Water pollution is by no means confined to eutrophication caused by agriculture, but it is the largest category, and affects the most waterbodies. And whereas most industrial sources of water pollution are regulated under the Clean Air Act, it would be euphemistic to say that nutrient loading from agriculture is regulated to any meaningful extent.

The problem of "nonpoint source pollution," the term for water pollution that does not come from an identifiable *point source* such as an outflow pipe, or a facility, has hardly gone unnoticed. The Clean Water Act includes an entire regulatory program, the Maximum Daily Loading, or "TMDL" program, aimed at treating waterbodies as a unit and mandating the creation of a plan specific to each "impaired" waterbody.[85] This waterbody-specific approach requires some fairly data-intensive gathering about the pollutants in each waterbody and the sources of that pollution, and setting some limit, or total maximum daily load, for each impaired waterbody. The relatively easy part is identifying the factories, facilities, wastewater treatment plants, pulp and paper mills, and buildings from which there is an identifiable discharge of a water pollutant. But while these identifiable point sources of water pollution are regulated (typically by technological mandates), nonpoint source pollution from crop farms and livestock operations are regulated only in the sense that farmers are required to maintain certain practices, usually referred to as "best management practices." That is, nonpoint source polluters such as farms are required to undertake best management practices and if they do, there is no further monitoring or inquiry as to their actual pollution or even whether they actually undertake the best management practices. All of the required recordkeeping and sampling is carried out by the farmer with no oversight from EPA or the state regulators. Nonpoint source pollution compliance is just a gigantic honor system with vague standards.

Technically, large livestock operations are considered point sources, because the Clean Water Act lists "concentrated animal feeding operations" or CAFOs, as a point source,[86] necessitating EPA to develop a set of regulations governing CAFOs. EPA has done so, but they still amount to so-called "best management practices." CAFOs are governed by a "general permit," which means that as long as CAFOs abide by a certain set of operating conditions, they are relieved of the requirement of applying for and securing an actual, facility-specific, location-specific permit. In other words, a general permit functions just like a regulation. EPA even defines by regulation how large an animal feeding operation must be to be considered "concentrated." So for example, CAFOs are required to keep records on manure, keep it a minimum distance from water resources, and to keep a "nutrient management plan" to try and minimize the runoff of manure into waterways.[87] A typical nutrient management plan regulation requires the CAFO to maintain a plan that includes a site map, a manure storage plan, a plan and schedule for how and when to apply manure to crops. But again, as in the case of crop farms, oversight over such a vast number of operations is infeasible, so there is no oversight.

All of these regulations are clearly the product of much thought and knowledge of livestock farming as well as crop farming. But there is no assurance that all of those practices actually reduce nutrient runoff to any appreciable extent. Because of the lack of enforcement, there is no assurance that farmers actually carry out stated best management practices. Even if farmers undertake a good-faith effort to implement best management practices, they might be implemented ineffectively. For example, a farmer may install a buffer strip between crops and a drainage ditch to filter runoff, but the effectiveness of the strip depends on the plant species and spacing between plants. Farmers may not know how to properly install a buffer strip, and in this regime, there is certainly no incentive for them to find out.[88] In the end, wherever this scheme is failing, it is clear that it is has been failing for the nearly half-century that the Clean Water Act has mandated that the waters of the United States be cleaned up. Water quality continues to be poor, and nutrient runoff from farms continues to be a problem.

Although EPA and the state regulatory agencies charged with carrying out regulation of nonpoint sources have clearly failed, it is worth appreciating that water pollution is much more complicated than air pollution. Whereas the sources and types of air pollution are limited, the types and sources of water pollution are more numerous and more diverse. Water can be polluted in so many different ways. An elevation of temperature is considered pollution, because aquatic organisms such as fish and wildlife can sicken and die. The common runoff of sediments, even without nutrients, constitutes water pollution. Almost every human-built structure and use contributes to water pollution. Some pollution emanates from so many different sources that they are necessarily considered nonpoint sources. Nonpoint source pollution adds the additional challenge of identifying a place or places through which pollution exits a farm and enters a waterway. Unlike the flue stack of a power plant, or the outflow pipe of a factory or sewage treatment plant, there is usually no single place where excess fertilizer from a farm passes from farm to waterbody.

The complications of regulating nonpoint source water pollution create a very unfavorable political economy. Faced with capacity and resource limitations in monitoring and enforcement, and faced with a politically powerful farm lobby, EPA and its state agency partners have had to rely on mostly voluntary measures such as best management practices to attempt to reduce nonpoint source pollution. Farmers clearly favor voluntary programs, but so do EPA and state regulators because they are easier to carry out and require little staffing. That leaves only environmental advocacy groups, which have relentlessly sued EPA to try and hold its feet to the fire. The history of EPA's attempts to implement the TMDL program stretched out over two litigious decades, during which period EPA lost almost all of the two dozen or so lawsuits brought against it by environmental organizations, before EPA and its state agency partners got down to the business of actually looking at individual water-bodies and attempting to set limits on pollution.[89] Even now, the TMDL process remains – as the Clean Water Act intended – a state-driven process. States issue a designated use for waterbodies within their borders, and states set the water quality standards for those waterbodies. States in which agriculture is an important industry have designated many waterbodies for "agricultural use," and set lenient water quality standards. Standards are not even necessarily numeric; under the Clean Water Act, states may issue standards that are *narrative*, meaning that they describe water quality, rather than measure it. Consider the following Wyoming water quality standard criteria:

> [A]ll Wyoming surface waters which have the natural water quality potential for use as an agricultural water supply shall be maintained at a quality which allows continued use of such waters for agricultural purposes. Degradation of such waters shall not be of such an extent to cause a measurable decrease in crop or livestock production.[90]

That's it. There is no mention of any nutrients. The only thing that can go wrong with a class 4 water is that it causes crop or livestock production to drop. There is, in other sections in the code, mention of floating, settleable and suspended solids, which could make it difficult to use the waterbody as either an agricultural water supply or a dump. Granted, almost all of Wyoming's waters designated for agricul-tural uses are ditches and canals, but those ditches and canals feed into rivers and streams that ultimately, drain into either the Gulf of Mexico via the Mississippi River or the Pacific Ocean.

Or consider this regulation of Arkansas, one of the states contributing a disproportionate amount of nutrient loading to the Mississippi River basin:

> Materials stimulating algal growth shall not be present in concentrations sufficient to cause objectionable algal densities or other nuisance aquatic vegetation or otherwise impair any designated use of the waterbody.[91]

This kind of vagueness invites backsliding. Moreover, the absence of a local algal bloom says little about nutrient loading; in a state such as Arkansas where water-flows tend to be high, nutrients can be carried off towards the Gulf of Mexico without there being any local effects. Overall, given the lack of progress thus far, it would be fair to say that the TMDL process remains a work in progress, after half a century.

With regulators wielding no sticks and having only the option to hand out carrots, proposals to engage farmers have had to be creative. In the spirit of market mechan-isms, trading programs analogous to the SO_2 trading program have been proposed, that might create a marginal price on the discharge of nutrients into waterbodies. The marginal cost of reducing nutrient loading from farms is generally thought to be lower than that of point sources, such as wastewater treatment plants.[92] A trading program might transfer money from a point source to a farm if the farm can somehow prove that it did something to reduce its nutrient loading.

Alternatively, if an "ambient" level water quality can be determined, then a program could be designed where that ambient level serves as a baseline. Instead of credit trading, farmers could be subsidized for lowering nutrient runoff below the ambient level and taxed if they exceed it.[93] Admirably, this is an idea that is approximately revenue neutral for participating farms, so it might be politically plausible. But it begs a question about how to monitor runoff at the farm level, so as to separate one farm's nutrient loading from that of surrounding farms. What is "ambient" could change with other farmers changing their behavior.

What these proposals attempt to do is to introduce a marginal price for excess runoff of nutrients. Farmers can ignore the effects of excess fertilizer application because the costs are entirely external to them. Under continuing pressures to increase yield, farmers err on the side of excess application. A marginal price would at least introduce the potential for the farmer to consider fertilizer application as a tradeoff against the benefits of reducing runoff, those being monies they might save or receive. But these programs would have to be voluntary for farmers, who are not meaningfully regulated, and could still carry on with business as usual. In a credit trading program, for example, farmers will only supply credits for reducing nutrient loading, never buy them, because they are never really called upon in a binding way to truly reduce their nutrient loading. Even when farmers can commit to some practices that go above and beyond "best management practices," there is still no guarantee that they actually reduce nutrient loading. And, in reality, while nutrient reduction credit trading programs are plentiful, actual trading and nutrient loading reduction is not.[94]

A central problem with nonpoint source pollution is the problem of monitoring. Best management practices mean little when they are not verified on-site, which would be very resource-intensive for regulators. Even where best management practices are diligently followed there is no monitoring of water quality or nutrient loading.

One straightforward, if unpopular way to avoid the monitoring problem, is to impose a simple tax on fertilizer. Fertilizer taxes are common, especially in Europe, but many were discontinued after the formation of the European Union, raising competitiveness concerns.[95] Most fertilizer taxes serve as a funding mechanism for some specific purpose, such as university research and agricultural extension programs or environmental research.[96] California imposes a small fertilizer tax, but exempts farmers, the primary target being gardeners and hobby farmers, and uses the tax proceeds to fund research and extension for the handling of fertilizers.[97] A fertilizer tax would be administratively feasible, as it can be easily imposed at the point of sale, or the point of manufacture. Indignant farmers complaining about the contribution from urban lawn-growers may be less angry at urban dwellers having to pay for their contributions to nutrient loading. Fertilizer taxes could also include fertilizer derived from animal manure, as that is industrially produced as well, in addition to that using nitrogen fixation processes. Excess nitrogen fertilizer application is also a prominent source of emissions of nitrous oxide (N_2O), a powerful greenhouse gas, though that complicated relationship also depends on other factors, including farming practices. That said, a fertilizer tax specific to nitrogen would also have a beneficial side effect of addressing climate change as well.

A fertilizer tax would be imperfect. A fertilizer tax could be easily applied to commercially produced, composted manure, but that is less of a problem than the application of raw animal manure as a disposal method. A head tax might be applied to livestock for an imputed lifetime of manure, but such a head tax would be a blunt instrument, failing to account for wide variations in manure production and disposal. However, without a head tax, the application of raw animal manure would perversely become more prevalent. A head tax, despite the imprecision, would be necessary.

A fertilizer tax, like other input taxes, is only a tax on a *proxy* for the ultimate harm caused by the input. Unlike a carbon tax, the link between the input and the ultimate harm is unclear. Were a fertilizer tax to be imposed on nitrogen or phosphorus content, it is unclear how much of that fertilizer would actually be lost to pollution, how much would serve to restore soils, and how much would be taken up by crops. The point of a pro-capitalism environmental tax would be to incentivize polluters to find ways to minimize the pollution without dictating their methods. While a fertilizer tax would encourage farmers to consider some pollution reduction methods, such as crop rotations, cover crops, and which crops to plant, it would not affect other potentially cost-saving and pollution-reducing decisions, such as the proper installation of buffer strips, improved fertilizer timing and efficiency to increase soil absorption, and higher uptake by crops. Finally, fertilizer taxes are of limited effectiveness. The empirical literature is limited, but what little there is suggests that a fertilizer tax would have to be very large in order to affect farmers' decisions in the United States.[98]

A better taxation option exists, but was not, at the time that this book was being written, technologically available. An environmental tax that would better track the environmental harm and would leave as many mitigation options open as possible would be a direct tax on the nutrient pollution itself, as it left a farm or facility and entered a waterbody. Waterbodies are highly diverse in terms of their pollution problems, fragility to disturbance, value as habitat, and their uses. Thus, as in the case of the proposed water tax, a fertilizer tax would not be a truly "Pigouvian" tax in the sense that a tax could not feasibly be tailored to the actual harm caused by nutrient loading, or any pollution. A tax could be *closer* to measuring actual harm if it could be based upon the amount of nutrient entering a waterbody, and attributable to a specific source. For point sources, that is relatively straightforward, as they are regulated anyway and the largest sources – mostly wastewater treatment plants – are subject to reporting requirements. But for nonpoint sources, some method of ascertaining nutrient pollution – most prominently from farms – must be available.

The technology to measure the amount of pollution attributable to a specific farm is, however, within reach. Satellite remote sensing technology has developed to the point that it can measure concentrations of nitrogen, phosphorus, as well as Chlorophyll-*a*, the product of nutrient loading and an indicator of eutrophication. The resolution of remote sensing technologies is as fine at 0.3 meters, or about 12 inches.[99] Remote sensing technology involves a tradeoff between spatial resolution and spectral resolution, so that unfortunately at very fine spatial resolutions, the ability to detect and measure concentrations is poor. However, as a *complement* to traditional water quality monitoring through human sampling and through data collection by physical monitors, placed in strategic locations, remote sensing technology can provide broader coverage than traditional methods alone.[100] It is already commonly used for the assessment of waterbodies under the TMDL program, and is already used for fine-grained analysis. Satellite measurements are often calibrated to on-the-ground monitors, so that spatial patterns detectable at broad scales by satellite imagery can be anchored to reliable on-the-ground measurements. As is the case with other technologies, remote sensing is advancing quickly. And still as yet to be determined is the potential of unmanned aerial vehicles, or drones, to carry out waterbody sensing at much, much lower altitudes, with potentially finer resolutions.

Some monitoring system to attribute nutrient loading to specific sources would require an interdisciplinary effort and the combination of several elements. In addition to remote sensing data and on-the-ground monitors, geographic information systems are required to identify ownership of land and facilities from which nutrient loading might emanate. Hydrogeological information might also be needed in order to determine flows that might identify the likely sources of nutrient loading. In short, the technological needs for being able to identify the source and quantity (roughly) of nutrient pollution require some further development, but are within reach.

As things stand with eutrophication, there is almost certainly more harm to go around than there would be costs of limiting it, or dramatically reducing it. Although many costs of a dead zone the size of New Jersey are difficult to measure, it is a shocking enough of a problem that the National Research Council has tried to address it on multiple occasions. The problem has been identified for decades, but because of the inability of regulators to improve upon the hopelessly ineffective "best management practices" regime, the problem has not only resisted improvement, but worsened. In 2000, the National Research Council issued a report on nutrient pollution, and recommended the development of a national strategy to improve coastal water quality by bringing under control nutrient loading, mostly by farms.[101] In 2009, the National Research Council again convened a group of experts and produced another report, this time focused more explicitly on the Gulf of Mexico dead zone.[102] While the size of the dead zone varies from year to year, the trend during these past few decades has been steadily upwards. Myriad expensive programs have been offered as carrots to farmers to reduce nutrient loading. The Environmental Quality Incentives Program, which has received annual appropriations of about $1.8 billion per year,[103] "provides financial and technical assistance to agricultural producers to address natural resource concerns and deliver environmental benefits such as improved water and air quality, conserved ground and surface water, increased soil health and reduced soil erosion and sedimentation, improved or created wildlife habitat, and mitigation against increasing weather volatility."[104] EQIP does this by subsidizing "conservation practices" that promote one or more of the program's objectives. Two other USDA programs the Agriculture Water Enhancement Program and the Cooperative Partnership Initiative, also provide funding and support for farming practices that improve environmental outcomes. The list goes on. And at least in terms of water quality, conditions are no better.

The best solution is the truly environmental tax: a tax on the discharge – from a wastewater treatment plant or from a farm – on nutrient pollution. The technology and platform for such an environmental tax need further development. But the persistence and the increasing seriousness of the eutrophication problems are such that the perfect should not preclude the good. While remote sensing technologies advance towards providing the kind of spatial and spectral resolution that can support a nutrient tax, a simple and broad fertilizer tax should be instituted. The two purposes of a fertilizer tax would be to introduce a modest price signal, and to provide funding to accelerate the development of remote sensing technology. Past studies suggest that price elasticities are lower in North America than in Europe, and they are low in any case, so it may be that the response would be much smaller than would be considered economically efficient. However, even a small price may introduce some measure of entrepreneurship in terms of reducing the amount of nutrients wastefully lost in the form of water pollution or as a greenhouse gas. The end goal should remain, if not a Pigouvian tax that perfectly prices the external harm of nutrient runoff, a reasonable balance between crop productivity and soil health, and the costs of excess fertilizer application.

6.5 FINE PARTICULATE MATTER POLLUTION

The current, incomplete, state of knowledge about environmental harm suggests that fine particulate matter ($PM_{2.5}$) air pollution is the most expensive environmental problem, a cost measured in terms of the value of human lives lost: four million worldwide, perhaps over 100,000 in the United States, annually. There are certainly nonfatal harms from $PM_{2.5}$ pollution as well, since obviously not every pollution-induced illness results in death. While the literature on nonfatal harm from $PM_{2.5}$ is not sufficiently developed to monetize, it certainly bears repeating that premature mortality is just one of many harms from air pollution. One study found that people respond more negatively in subjective well-being, or "happiness" surveys, when and where levels of coarse particulate matter (PM_{10}, not $PM_{2.5}$) is higher,[105] a finding confirmed by studies showing higher incidences of emergency room visits for depression when levels of four pollutants (including $PM_{2.5}$) were elevated.[106] Perhaps unsurprisingly, another study found statistically significant linkages between air pollution (six pollutants including $PM_{2.5}$) and levels of criminal behavior.[107] Students perform less well on tests during days in which air pollution levels are elevated.[108] While it may be difficult to monetize these and other harms, it raises a troubling question familiar to readers by now: what else don't we know?

Recent studies by Tschofen et al. and Goodkind et al. model the emission and migration of $PM_{2.5}$. However, $PM_{2.5}$ pollution is only truly measured at individual air pollution receptors sprinkled throughout the United States, not at specific sources. The estimates of $PM_{2.5}$ air pollution emitted by specific, individual sources are just that: estimates. When emissions of say, a pulp and paper mill are reported to the U.S. Environmental Protection Agency, the states that report them are instructed to identify the type of facility, how much pulp and paper was produced, and then very roughly speaking, instructed to multiply the amount of production by an "emission factor" that is deemed typical of pulp and paper mills of that type, to derive an estimate of how much $PM_{2.5}$ was emitted. There is no direct measurement of emissions at the pulp and paper mill itself. The mill could be more efficient or less efficient than average in terms of emitting $PM_{2.5}$ pollution, but the calculation is the same for all pulp and paper mills of a certain *type*. The result is a reasonable estimate of emissions from all pulp and paper mills, but not precise enough to form a basis for a $PM_{2.5}$ emission tax to be levied on individual mills. Without a way of discriminating among different facilities, there is no incentive for individual mills to find ways to reduce $PM_{2.5}$ pollution.

Perhaps an even greater problem is that $PM_{2.5}$ pollution is so complicated. $PM_{2.5}$ is just a term for very small airborne particles, which could take on a variety of chemical and physical forms. $PM_{2.5}$ pollution emanates from residential fireplaces, restaurants, and prescribed burns, construction, unpaved roads, diesel trucks, passenger vehicles, and scores of other types of sources.[109] The variety of forms $PM_{2.5}$ might take also create problems in terms of enforcement. Not only all that, but $PM_{2.5}$ has a number of pollution precursors, including ammonia (emanating from livestock waste), sulfur dioxide (emitted from coal-fired power plants), and oxides of nitrogen (created with almost any combustion process). Models of how precursor pollutants become $PM_{2.5}$ are quite sophisticated, but underscore the informational challenges in reducing $PM_{2.5}$ through taxation. Estimation of well-understood sources like power plants, pulp and paper mills, steel mills and cement is quite a challenge, and estimation of these disparate, "nonpoint" sources another challenge altogether.

What is needed are a vastly greater number of pollution sensors, coupled with even more sophisticated air pollution transport and chemical transformation models, so that the largest of the individual sources of $PM_{2.5}$ pollution or its precursors can be identified and taxed. Much as in the case of detecting nonpoint source pollution in waterways, a massive deployment of monitoring technology is critical. Unlike the remote sensing technology required to detect nutrient pollution emanating from farms, the technology for measuring PM2.5 air pollution is in full operation. The system measures ambient levels of $PM_{2.5}$ well enough to make critical compliance classifications under the Clean Air Act, but not well enough to attribute emissions to individual sources. For that, a large, orders-of-magnitude increase in the number of air pollution sensors, along with increased development of air pollution transport and chemical transformation models, are required. A combination of tools could work together to attribute individual sources with the emission of $PM_{2.5}$ pollution. That is a tall order, but 100,000 American deaths, every single year, seems to be a high price to pay for not deploying that technology.

It is also worth imposing a small $PM_{2.5}$ tax on just the largest contributors to $PM_{2.5}$ pollution. Again, while Tschofen et al. and Gookind et al. do not purport to precisely attribute $PM_{2.5}$ emissions to specific sources, they quite reasonably attribute emissions to industries. An environmental tax of $PM_{2.5}$ pollution would be primarily supported extensive, vastly scaled-up monitoring network, well-developed models of air pollutant emission and migration, and with a well-developed body of literature on the effects of $PM_{2.5}$ pollution on mortality. But it can also be complemented by an input tax on the largest sources of $PM_{2.5}$ pollution. Not only would a small input tax on anticipated $PM_{2.5}$ emissions complement an extensive $PM_{2.5}$ monitoring system, but the proceeds could fund the scale-up and deployment of the monitoring system.

Part of a table (Table S2) in the appendix to Goodkind et al. is reproduced here, to formulate the basis for an initial, small $PM_{2.5}$ tax. After these six sources of $PM_{2.5}$ pollution, the next most damaging source, nonroad diesel engines, drops off by $13 billion, making these top six activities a logical starting target for modest taxation. Of course, Goodkind and Tschofen are not necessarily the last word, but nor is it likely that their results, which are quite consistent, are very far off. Proceeds from a $PM_{2.5}$ tax should be used to develop the technology necessary to measure emissions of $PM_{2.5}$ and of $PM_{2.5}$ precursor pollutants, at their sources.

Excerpt from Table S2 in Goodkind et al. (2019)

	Damages, in 2011 billion USD
Coal-fired power plants	118.44
Passenger vehicles	94.10
Livestock waste	70.52
Diesel vehicles	58.11
Residential firewood burning	50.04
Prescribed burning	47.04

From Goodkind et al. (2019).

Each of these activities can be taxed on the basis of an input. Power plants using coal can be taxed on a per-ton of coal basis. Passenger vehicles and diesel trucks can be taxed at the fuel pump (though at different rates), livestock can be taxed per head of animal (though differently for different animals, as hog waste tends to be the most harmful), prescribed burns can be taxed by the acre, and a tax can be added onto purchased residential firewood. It may be possible to evade these taxes say, by having firewood cut and collected privately. But with a small tax, the incentive to evade taxation is diminished. Moreover, the more important long-term objective would be to fund a research effort to identify $PM_{2.5}$ pollution, or that of precursors, at their sources. The long-term goal would be to work towards a regime of $PM_{2.5}$ taxes that accurately reflect social harms. While taxing $PM_{2.5}$ would require a great deal of information and technological development, the death toll would suggest that the cost-benefit analysis of the effort would pass with flying colors.

6.6 A START

There is much work to be done, and these five proposed taxes represent a start. In terms of redressing environmental harms, it makes sense to address the most important ones, and the ones that would be inexpensive to correct. These five taxes are proposed with these criteria in mind, though many, many more could be suggested. And as more is learned about previously unknown environmental harms, more taxes will need to enter the policy sphere.

Quite clearly, these taxes impact the fossil fuel industries and the agricultural industry. This is not by design or animus. But along with a sense gained from decades of litigation and policy conflict with these industries, quantitative estimates have begun to emerge confirming that the lowest-hanging fruit and the most important changes must occur in these industries. Increased modeling sophistication and research attention have elevated suspicions to the status of economic fact, even if uncertainties still persist. A particularly benign outcome could be that these industries are moved, finally, to find their own solutions to the environmental problems they create.

And yet, environmental taxes are not and should not be indirect means of simply punishing industries for their pollution. Retribution is not an appropriate objective of environmental policy. Rather, environmental taxation is *just* a way of sending a price signal that spurs changes, hopefully some of them in the form of innovation. Environmental taxation is an inroad for capitalism to colonize areas of policy that had previously languished in intellectual torpor directed by inertia, arrogance, and political opportunism.

Notes

1. Eric S. Blake et al., Nat'l Oceanic & Atmospheric Admin., Tropical Cyclone Report, Hurricane Sandy, October 22–29, 2012 (2013) (in unadjusted dollars), http://www .nhc.noaa.gov/data/tcr/AL182012_Sandy.pdf [https://perma.cc/X4CQ-83YV].

2. Eric S. Blake & David A. Zelinsky, Nat'l Oceanic & Atmospheric Admin., Tropical Cyclone Report, Hurricane Harvey, August 17-September 1, 2017 at 9 (2018) ($125 billion in unadjusted dollars), https://www.nhc.noaa.gov/data/tcr/AL092017_Harvey.pdf [https:// perma.cc/DUA3-QNCN; Richard J. Pasch et al., Nat'l Oceanic & Atmospheric Admin., Tropical Cyclone Report, Hurricane Maria, September 16–30, 2017 (2019) ($90 billion in unadjusted dollars), https://www.nhc.noaa.gov/data/tcr/AL152017_Maria.pdf [https://perma .cc/R6D2-8MRP]; Richard J. Pasch et al., Nat'l Oceanic & Atmospheric Admin., Tropical Cyclone Report, Hurricane Irma, August 30-September 12, 2017 (2018) ($50 billion in unadjusted dollars), https://www.nhc.noaa.gov/data/tcr/AL112017_Irma.pdf [https://perma.cc/5P22-NWRX].

3. Interagency Working Group on Social Cost of Carbon, United States Government, Technical Support Document: Social Cost of Carbon for Regulatory Impact Analysis Under Executive Order 12866 (Feb. 2010), https://www.epa.gov/sites/production/files/ 2016-12/documents/scc_tsd_2010.pdf [https://perma.cc/G6E2-7SNY].

4. Interagency Working Group on Social Cost of Carbon, United States Government, Technical Update of the Social Cost of Carbon for Regulatory Impact Analysis Under Executive Order 12866 (Aug. 2016), https://www.epa.gov/sites/production/files/ 2016-12/documents/sc_co2_tsd_august_2016.pdf [https://perma.cc/4ML9-T839].

5. Amazon's Enterprise-Wide Carbon Footprint for the 2018 Fiscal Year, https:// d39w7f4ix9f5s9.cloudfront.net/26/7f/e1693ffc45db88d839a4734b46e7/amazon-2018-car bon-footprint.pdf. [https://perma.cc/8YHN-MSP9].

6. Felix Preston et al., *The Carbon Footprint of Retail: Ecommerce vs. Bricks & Mortar*, Generationim.com (Mar. 17, 2020), https://www.generationim.com/research-centre /insights/ecommerce-vs-bricks-mortar/ [https://perma.cc/FYE9-EFYB].

7. Marc Hafstead et al., *Macroeconomic Analysis of Federal Carbon Taxes*, RFF Pol'y Brief 16–06 (June 2016), https://media.rff.org/documents/RFF-PB-16-06_0.pdf [https://perma .cc/Q4CB-HEMF].

8. Lawrence Goulder & Marc Hafstead, Confronting the Climate Challenge (2018).

9. Shi-Ling Hsu, *A Complete Analysis of Carbon Taxation: Considering the Revenue Side*, 65 Buff. L. Rev. 857 (2017).

10. Greenhouse Gas Pollution Pricing Act, S.C. 2018, c. 12, s. 186 (Can.).

11. Nat'l Ass'n State Energy Officials & the Energy Futures Initiative, The 2019 U.S. Energy & Employment Report 4–5 (2019), https://www.usenergyjobs.org/2019-report [https://perma.cc/U3EX-7RM9].

12. Roberton C. Williams III et al., *The Initial Incidence of a Carbon Tax Across Income Groups*, 68 Nat'l. Tax J. 195 (2015); Lawrence H. Goulder et al.,*Impacts of a Carbon Tax Across US Household Income Groups: What are the Equity-Efficiency Tradeoffs?*, 175 J. Pub. Econ. 44–64 (2019).

13. World Health Org., Burden of Disease from Ambient Air Pollution for 2016 (2018) https://www.who.int/airpollution/data/AAP_BoD_results_May2018_final.pdf [https:// perma.cc/K5JW-RZFL]; Andrew Goodkind et al., *Fine-scale Damage Estimate of Particulate Matter Air Pollution Reveal Opportunities for Location-specific Mitigation of Emissions*, 116 PNAS 8775 (2019), (citing CDC, Nat'l Ctr. Health Statistics, *About*

Underlying Cause of Death, 1999–2018, https://wonder.cdc.gov/ucd-icd10.html [https://perma.cc/57NB-QHNW]).

14. Ian Parry, Chandara Veung, & Dirk Heine, *How Much Carbon Pricing is in Countries' Own Interests? The Critical Role of Co-Benefits* (IMF Working Paper 14/174 2014), https://www.imf.org/external/pubs/ft/wp/2014/wp14174.pdf [https://perma.cc/79WP-WCM8].

15. Scott Barrett, Environment and Statecraft: The Strategy of Environmental Treaty-Making 393–96 (2003).

16. Joost Pauwelyn, *Carbon Leakage Measures and Border Tax Adjustments Under WTO Law*, in Research Handbook on Environment, Health and the WTO (Geert Van Calster & Denise Prévost eds., 2012); Shi-Ling Hsu, The Case for a Carbon Tax: Getting Past Our Hangups to Effective Climate Policy (2011); Aaron Cosbey et al., A Guide for the Concerned: Guidance on the Elaboration and Implementation of Border Carbon Adjustment (2012).

17. Yinon M. Bar-On, Rob Phillips & Ron Milo, *The Biomass Distribution on Earth*, 115 PNAS 6506–11 (2018).

18. Pierre J. Gerber et al., Tackling Climate Change Through Livestock: A Global Assessment of Emissions and Mitigation Opportunities 23 (2013).

19. Pierre J. Gerber et al., Tackling Climate Change Through Livestock: A Global Assessment of Emissions and Mitigation Opportunities 69 (2013).

20. Pierre J. Gerber et al., Tackling Climate Change Through Livestock: A Global Assessment of Emissions and Mitigation Opportunities 77 (2013).

21. Pierre J. Gerber et al., Tackling Climate Change Through Livestock: A Global Assessment of Emissions and Mitigation Opportunities xiv (2013).

22. U.S. Dep't of Agric., Nat. Resources Conservation Serv., *Manure and Nutrient Management*, https://www.nrcs.usda.gov/wps/portal/nrcs/main/national/plantsanimals/mnm/ [https://perma.cc/S2ZV-C6W6].

23. Pierre J. Gerber et al., Tackling Climate Change Through Livestock: A Global Assessment of Emissions and Mitigation Opportunities 25 (fig. 8) (2013).

24. Pierre J. Gerber et al., Tackling Climate Change Through Livestock: A Global Assessment of Emissions and Mitigation Opportunities 25 (fig. 8) (2013).

25. The average hot carcass weight is 750 lbs and produces 527 lbs (240 kg) of beef. Ron Lemenager, *Amount of Freezer Beef Expected From a Carcass?*, Beef2live.com, https://beef2live.com/story-amount-freezer-beef-expected-carcass-0-111639 [https://perma.cc/NM2A-8YBV]; Rob Holland, Dwight Loveday, & Kevin Ferguson, How Much Meat to Expect From a Beef Carcass 7, https://extension.tennessee.edu/publications/Documents/PB1822.pdf [https://perma.cc/Z7QW-NQCM]. Dairy cows, which are also eventually slaughtered for meat, are somewhat smaller. *Growth Charts for Dairy Heifers*, Penn State Extension, https://extension.psu.edu/growth-charts-for-dairy-heifers [https://perma.cc/P9PY-6TC8].

26. 5280 kg = 5.8 short tons.

27. Daniel Maina Wambugu, *The World's Largest Exporters of Beef*, Worldatlas.com, https://www.worldatlas.com/articles/the-world-s-largest-exporters-of-beef.html [https://perma.cc/A5FW-5GGG].

28. U.S. Dep't Agric., *Meat and Livestock Annual Cumulative Year-to-date U.S. Trade*, https://www.ers.usda.gov/data-products/livestock-and-meat-international-trade-data/ [https://perma.cc/HU23-BKZW](3,057,176,000 lbs. = 1.38 million metric tons).

29. General Agreement on Tariffs and Trade, art. II, Oct. 30, 1947, 61 Stat. 5, 55 U.N.T.S. 187.

30. Pierre J. Gerber et al., Tackling Climate Change Through Livestock: A Global Assessment of Emissions and Mitigation Opportunities 5–7 (2013).

31. Pierre J. Gerber et al., Tackling Climate Change Through Livestock: A Global Assessment of Emissions and Mitigation Opportunities 25 (fig. 8) (2013).

32. U.S. Geological Survey, *How Much Water Is There on Earth?*, https://www.usgs.gov/special-topic/water-science-school/science/how-much-water-there-earth?qt-science_center_objects=0#qt-science_center_objects [https://perma.cc/EJB6-4BPW]. The sum of fresh groundwater, lakes, and rivers is 2,548,339 cubic miles.

33. Intergovernmental Panel on Climate Change, Global Warming of 1.5 °C 191–97 (2018).

34. Jacob Schewe, *Multimodal Assessment of Water Scarcity Under Climate Change*, 111 PNAS 3245 (2014).

35. Peter H. Gleick, *Water, Drought, Climate Change, and Conflict in Syria*, 6 Weather Climate & Soc'y 331 (2014).

36. Peter H. Gleick, *Water and Conflict: Fresh Water Resources and International Security*, 18 Int'l Security 79 (1993); Shira Yoffe, Aaron T. Wolf & Mark Giordano, *Conflict and Cooperation Over International Freshwater Resources: Indicators of Basins at Risk*, 39 J. Am. Water Res. Assoc. 1109 (2003); Hans P.W. Toset, Nils P. Gleditsch & Havard Hegre, *Shared Rivers and Interstate Conflict*, 19 Polit. Geo. 971 (2000).

37. Dave Owen, *Water and Taxes*, 50 U.C. Davis L. Rev. 1559 (2017).

38. Seth M. Siegel, Let There Be Water: Israel's Solution for a Water-Starved World (2015).

39. *See, e.g.,* Kevin L. Patrick & Kelly E. Archer, *A Comparison of State Groundwater Laws*, 30 Tulsa L.J. 123 (1994).

40. 5 Cal. 140 (1855).

41. *See, e.g.,* Marc Reisner, Cadillac Desert: The American West and Its Disappearing Water (1993).

42. Cal. Dep't Food & Agric., Agricultural Statistics Review, 2018–2019, at 2 (2019), https://www.cdfa.ca.gov/statistics/PDFs/2018-2019AgReportnass.pdf [https://perma.cc/F9Q7-3E53].

43. California Department of Food and Agriculture, Agricultural Statistics Review, 2018–2019 at 2 (2019), https://www.cdfa.ca.gov/statistics/PDFs/2018-2019AgReportnass.pdf [https://perma.cc/F9Q7-3E53].

44. Cal. Pub. Utils. Comm'n, What Will Be the Cost of Future Sources of Water for California? 4 (2016), https://tinyurl.com/y89djebm. [https://perma.cc/6NGV-PAMG].

45. R.J.A. Inc. v. Water Users Association, 690 P.2d 823 (Colo. 1984).

46. Rene Sanchez, *West Wages a New Sort of Turf Battle; Water Conservation Pushed as Desert Communities Struggle With Growth*, Wash. Post, May 16, 1999.

47. 26 C.F.R. §1.199–3 (2020).

48. Zephyrhills Water, https://www.zephyrhillswater.com/our-springs.

49. Northwest Florida Water Management District, Notice of Agency Action, Letter Modification of Individual Water Use Permit No. 2B-133–6638-4, November 19, 2018.

50. Assuming that a 24-pack of 16.9 fl oz. bottles are sold for $20.

51. *See, e.g.,* Peter H. Gleick & Heather S. Cooley, *Energy Implications of Bottled Water*, 4 Envt'l Res. Letters 014009, 2–5 (2009).

52. Trevor Nace, *Were Now At a Million Plastic Bottles Per Minute – 91% of Which Are Not Recycled*, Forbes, July 26, 2017, https://www.forbes.com/sites/trevornace/2017/07/26/million-plastic-bottles-minute-91-not-recycled [https://perma.cc/ZH5T-SLPT].

53. Peter H. Gleick, Bottled and Sold: The Story Behind Our Obsession with Bottled Water 94 (2010).
54. Julia Lurie, *Bottled Water Comes From the Most Drought-Ridden Places in the Country*, Mother Jones (Apr. 13, 2015), https://www.motherjones.com/environment/2014/08/bottled-water-california-drought/ [https://perma.cc/T8HF-2Q4C].
55. Alejandra Reyes-Velarde, *California Will Have Water Consumption Limits for the First Time After "Landmark" Legislation Passed*, L.A. Times (June 1, 2018), https://www.latimes.com/socal/glendale-news-press/news/tn-gnp-me-water-efficiency-bill-20180601-story.html [https://perma.cc/ALY7-MJ3A].
56. Ian Lovett, *Where Grass Is Greener, a Push to Share Drought's Burden*, N.Y. Times, Nov. 30, 2014, at A22.
57. Water Measurement Law, 5715–1955, 9 L.S.I. 85 (1955) (Isr.).
58. Siegel.
59. Israel Ministry of Foreign Affairs Israel's Chronic Water Problem, https://mfa.gov.il/MFA/IsraelExperience/AboutIsrael/Spotlight/Pages/Israel-s%20Chronic%20Water%20Problem.aspx [https://perma.cc/C9C9-C6EJ].
60. Water Law, 5719–1959, 13 L.S.I. 173 (1959) (Isr.).
61. Israeli Water Authority, *Water Rates*, http://www.water.gov.il/Hebrew/Rates/Pages/Rates.aspx [https://perma.cc/6RHW-NG6S].
62. Israeli Water Authority, *Water Tariffs*, http://www.water.gov.il/hebrew/pages/water-authority-info.aspx?P=print [https://perma.cc/8RFV-Y6BV].
63. Israel Recycles 90% of Its Wastewater, *Four Times More Than Any Other Country*, TheTower.org (Dec. 15, 2016), http://www.thetower.org/4305oc-israel-recycles-90-of-its-wastewater-four-times-more-than-any-other-country/ [https://perma.cc/C8P2-6VPS].
64. Seth M. Siegel, Let There Be Water: Israel's Solution for a Water-Starved World 21 (2015).
65. Seth M. Siegel, Let There Be Water: Israel's Solution for a Water-Starved World 49–50 (2015).
66. *Wastewater Treatment and Effluent Resuse*, Mekorot.co.il, https://www.mekorot.co.il/Eng/newsite/Solutions/WastewaterReclamation/Pages/default.aspx [https://perma.cc/S55M-UKTJ].
67. Seth M. Siegel, Let There Be Water: Israel's Solution for a Water-Starved World 119 (2015).
68. Seth M. Siegel, Let There Be Water: Israel's Solution for a Water-Starved World 59 (2015).
69. *Drought Intensity Highlights Importance of Spot Market Water Transfers in California*, Water Market Insider (Q2 2014), https://www.waterexchange.com/wp-content/uploads/2015/02/California_q2_2014.pdf [https://perma.cc/6ZDG-PDVQ] (mean price of $162/acre-foot = $0.13 cubic meter).
70. Gilad Fernandes, Israeli Water Authority, Economic Aspects in Water Management in Israel (2012), http://www.water.gov.il/Hebrew/ProfessionalInfoAndData/2012/10-Israel-Water-Sector-Economics-Policy-and-Tarrifs.pdf [https://perma.cc/Q8KB-CFUK].
71. The comparison is made for California in 2015 and Israel in 2016, because of data availability constraints. California's GDP in 2015 was $2.426, FRED Economic Data, Real Total Gross Domestic Product for California, https://fred.stlouisfed.org/series/CARGSP [https://perma.cc/7U8F-CVT7], while Israel's GDP for 2016 was $319 billion, World Bank Open Data, *GDP (current US$) – Israel*, https://data.worldbank.org/indicator/NY.GDP.MKTP.CD?locations=IL [https://perma.cc/7WZX-KGZW]. California had total water *withdrawals* of

28,800 million gallons per day, U.S. Geo. Surv., Estimated Use of Water in the United States in 2015 (2017), https://pubs.usgs.gov/circ/1441/circ1441.pdf [https://perma.cc/R56W-VFMM], which translates to 39.792 billion cubic meters for the entire year. Israel's total water consumption was 2346 million cubic meters for 2016, but subtracting its use of reclaimed water, 575 million cubic meters, Knesset Res. & Info. Ctr., Israeli Water Sector – Key Issues (2018), https://main.knesset.gov.il/EN/activity/mmm/mmmeng250218.pdf [https://perma.cc/6A4X-7U35], produces a total of 1,771 million cubic meters for the entire year.

72. *Sidney Loan – Preface*, Desalination Dir. Online, http://www.desline.com/sidney-loeb.php [https://perma.cc/LDC7-PTJH].

73. Fred Magdoff & Harold van Es, Building Soils for Better Crops (3d ed. online vers. 2012), https://www.sare.org/Learning-Center/Books/Building-Soils-for-Better-Crops-3rd-Edition/Text-Version/Nutrient-Cycles-and-Flows/Implications-of-Nutrient-Flow-Patterns [https://perma.cc/YF2T-TS96].

74. U.S. Dep't Agric., *Fertilizer Use and Price*, www.ers.usda.gov/data-products/fertilizer-use-and-price.aspx [https://perma.cc/K6GD-RMCJ].

75. Kenneth G. Cassman, Achim Dobermann, & Daniel T. Walter, *Agroecosystems, Nitrogen-Use Efficiency, and Nitrogen Management*, 31 Ambio 132, 132–40 (2002).

76. U.S. Dep't Agric., Nat.l Resource Conservation Serv., Animal Manure Management, RCA Issue Brief #7, December 1995, https://www.nrcs.usda.gov/wps/portal/nrcs/detail/national/technical/?cid=nrcs143_014211 [https://perma.cc/769K-J4WK].

77. Giovani Preza Fontes et al., *Combining Environmental Monitoring and Remote Sensing Technologies to Evaluate Cropping System Nitrogen Dynamics at the Field-Scale*, 3 Frontiers in Sustainable Food Systems 1 (2019).

78. Diana Stuart & Matthew Houser, *Producing Compliant Polluters: Seed Companies and Nitrogen Fertilizer Application in U.S. Corn Agriculture*, 83 Rural Sociology 857 (2018).

79. *See, e.g.*, David Wolf & H. Allen Klaiber, *Bloom and Bust: Toxic Algae's Impact on Nearby Property Values*, 135 Ecol. Econ. 209 (2017).

80. Nat'l Rsch. Council, Comm. on the Miss. River & the Clean Water Act, Scientific, Modeling, and Technical Aspects of Nutrient Pollution Load Allocations and Implementation, Nutrient Control Actions for Improving Water Quality 1 (2009).

81. U.S. Geo. Surv., *Sources of Nutrients Delivered to the Gulf of Mexico*, https://water.usgs.gov/nawqa/sparrow/gulf_findings/primary_sources.html [https://perma.cc/8MAX-HF43].

82. U.S. Geo. Surv., *Sources of Nutrients Delivered to the Gulf of Mexico*, https://water.usgs.gov/nawqa/sparrow/gulf_findings/primary_sources.html [https://perma.cc/8MAX-HF43].

83. U.S. Environmental Protection Agency, *National Summary of State Information*, https://ofmpub.epa.gov/waters10/attains_nation_cy.control#total_assessed_waters [https://perma.cc/ZDT2-E55F].

84. U.S. Environmental Protection Agency, *National Summary of State Information*, https://ofmpub.epa.gov/waters10/attains_nation_cy.control#total_assessed_waters [https://perma.cc/ZDT2-E55F] (375,900 miles assessed designated for agricultural, out of total 1,110,961 miles assessed).

85. 33 U.S.C. § 1313 et seq. (2020).

86. 33 U.S.C. §1362(14) (2020).

87. *See, e.g.*, 9 Va. Admin. Code § 25-31-130 (2020).

88. Brian M. Dowd, Daniel Press & Marc Los Huertos, *Agricultural Nonpoint Source Water Pollution Policy: the Case of the California Central Coast*, 128 AGRIC. ECOSYSTEMS & ENVT. 151, 157 (2008).

89. OLIVER A. HOUCK, THE CLEAN WATER ACT TMDL PROGRAM: LAW, POLICY AND IMPLEMENTATION (1999); Terence J. Centner *Nutrient Pollution from Land Applications of Manure: Discerning a Remedy for Pollution*, 21 STAN. L. & POL'Y REV. 213, 217 (2010).

90. 20-1 WYO. CODE R. § 20 (LexisNexis 2020).

91. Ark. Pollution Control & Ecol. Comm., Regulation No. 2 Regulation Establishing Water Quality Standards for Surface Waters of the State of Arkansas, Reg. 2.509 (2018).

92. Marc Ribaudo & John Talberth, *Encouraging Reductions in Nonpoint Source Pollution Through Point-nonpoint Trading: The Roles of Baseline Choice and Practice Subsidies*, 36 APPL. ECON. PERSP. & POL'Y 560 (2014).

93. Richard D. Horan, James S. Shortle & David G. Abler, *Point-nonpoint Trading in the Susquehanna River Basin*, 38 WATER RES. RSCH. 1050 (2002).

94. Dana L. K. Hoag et al., *Policy Utopias for Nutrient Credit Trading Programs with Nonpoint Sources*, 53 J. AM. WATER RES. ASSOC. 514 (2017).

95. Kathleen Segerson & Dan Walker, *Nutrient Pollution: An Economic Perspective*, 25 ESTUARIES 797 (2002).

96. Brian M. Dowd, Daniel Press & Marc Los Huertos, *Agricultural Nonpoint Source Water Pollution Policy: The Case of the California Central Coast*, 128 AGRIC. ECOSYSTEMS & ENVT. 151, 157 (2008).

97. CAL. CODE REGS. TIT. 18, § 1588 (2020), https://www.cdtfa.ca.gov/lawguides/vol1/sutr/1588 .html [https://perma.cc/2GU5-KA6U].

98. Kathleen Segerson & Dan Walker, *Nutrient Pollution: an Economic Perspective*, 25 ESTUARIES 797 (2002).

99. *Characterization of Satellite Remote Sensing Systems*, SATIMAGINGCORP.COM, https://www .satimagingcorp.com/services/resources/characterization-of-satellite-remote-sensing-sys tems/ [https://perma.cc/F27S-FQXC].

100. Ni-Bin Chang, Sanaz Imen & Benjamin Vannah, *Remote Sensing for Monitoring Surface Water Quality Status and Ecosystem State in Relation to the Nutrient Cycle: a 40-Year Perspective*, 45 CRIT. REV. ENVTL. SCI. & Tech. 101 (2015).

101. NAT'L RES. COUNCIL, CLEAN COASTAL WATERS: UNDERSTANDING AND REDUCING THE EFFECTS OF NUTRIENT POLLUTION (2000).

102. NAT'L RES. COUNCIL, NUTRIENT CONTROL ACTIVITIES FOR IMPROVING WATER QUALITY IN THE MISSISSIPPI RIVER BASIN AND NORTHERN GULF OF MEXICO (2009).

103. NAT'L RES. COUNCIL, NUTRIENT CONTROL ACTIVITIES FOR IMPROVING WATER QUALITY IN THE MISSISSIPPI RIVER BASIN AND NORTHERN GULF OF MEXICO 38 (2009).

104. U.S. Dep't Agric., *Environmental Quality Incentives Program*, https://www.nrcs.usda.gov /wps/portal/nrcs/main/national/programs/financial/eqip/ [https://perma.cc/H46M-XFKH].

105. Arik Levinson, *Valuing Public Goods Using Happiness Data: The Case of Air Quality*, 96 J. PUB. ECON. 869 (2012).

106. Mieczyslaw Szyszkowicz et al., *Air Pollution and Emergency Department Visits for Depression: A Multicity Case-Crossover Study*, 10 ENVTL. HEALTH INSIGHTS 155 (2016).

107. Jackson G. Lu et al., *Polluted Morality: Air Pollution Predicts Criminal Activity and Unethical Behavior*, 29 PSYCH. SCI. 340 (2018).

108. Sefi Roth, *Air Pollution, Educational Achievements, and Human Capital Formation*, IZA WORLD OF LABOR (Aug. 2017), https://wol.iza.org/uploads/articles/381/pdfs/air-pollution-

educational-achievements-and-human-capital-formation.pdf?v=1 [https://perma.cc
/W2NC-GLHV].

109. Andrew Goodkind et al., *Fine-scale Damage Estimate of Particulate Matter Air Pollution
     Reveal Opportunities for Location-specific Mitigation of Emissions*, 116 PNAS 8775,
     Appendix, Table S2 (2019).

7

Generating Environmental Knowledge

Human capital is a phrase coined by economists to describe education and training.[1] Generally speaking, the higher the level of education, the more valuable the human capital.[2] Indisputably, human capital is valuable, as it clearly and consistently increases human productivity.[3] So human capital is, like physical capital, something that generates a stream of benefits, in the form of higher earnings that would not be possible without it. While human capital is most easily conceived as formal schooling or on-the-job training,[4] there are clearly many other forms of human capital. Human capital may be the acquired knowledge of some facet of resource extraction, or some operational expertise connected to a specific industrial process. Like physical capital, human capital can be costly to acquire, not only because of direct costs, but because of the opportunity costs of time and of foregone income.[5]

Even before Theodore Schultz and Gary Becker would rightfully receive Nobel prizes for their work on human capital, it had been supposed by some adventuresome economists that "capital" might be useful, productive knowledge. Adam Smith supposed that capital would include the "acquisition of such talents, by the maintenance of the acquirer during his education, study, or apprenticeship, always costs a real expense, which is a capital fixed and realized, as it were, in his person."[6] The product of learning can be an asset for the individual that is akin to some physical asset: costly (perhaps time-consuming) to acquire and making future labor more productive – in a sense, complementary to labor.

This chapter makes the case that a transformation of capitalism *must* include government investment for the development of human capital. But not just any kind of human capital: government must make haste in building up a stock of environmental knowledge, the kind of knowledge that will be essential to guiding government decision-making and capitalist enterprise. Environmental knowledge is the knowledge of how human and nonhuman life systems react to disruptions caused by large-scale human activity.

This is not human capital in a narrow traditional sense, which is confined to knowledge that increases GDP. That is a flaw with the traditional, narrow notion of economic progress. Capital is complementary to labor, with the end goal of enhancing economic well-being. Human capital in the form of an engineering degree makes an individual more productive. It increases her income, in so doing increases her well-being, and increases GDP. But environmental knowledge also increases societal well-being, only in ways that are not systematically measured. Recall the Murphy and Topel study cited in Chapter 1, which found that medical and public health research has lengthened life expectancies and produced $3.2 trillion of benefit every year since 1970.[7] Measured narrowly, the only increase in GDP is the salary of the medical and health researchers, and the economic activity their salaries generate. But GDP does not capture that $3.2 trillion, a staggering omission.

While environmental knowledge is less tangibly tied to income, it is vitally connected to broader notions of economic well-being.[8] Take as an illustration the life-extending health benefits studied by Murphy and Topel. Not only does extending longevity enhance well-being by enabling people to work longer and contribute economically, but it allows them to live longer and enjoy things that have value, whether or not they are priced. Living longer enables people to see their children marry and produce grandchildren. These things have value, but are not included in GDP, except for the relatively trivial expenditures of paying for a wedding or toys for grandchildren. And the Murphy and Topel study doesn't capture the benefits of research that improve health and well-being in ways that do not necessarily extend life expectancy. As any parent with children with developmental disabilities, allergies, asthma, mental illness, and other chronic health conditions can attest: these health problems can severely reduce the contributions of the parent and the future contributions of the children.

So too, with environmental knowledge. The link between environmental quality and well-being is less concrete than it is with health, because the effects are indirect. Improved environmental quality with less pollution leads to improved health, with all of the well-being benefits just described. But those links have only been studied in fairly narrow contexts: mercury, lead, $PM_{2.5}$ air pollution, asbestos, polychlorinated biphenyls (PCBs), and a handful of other hazardous substances. Strong suspicions and early to middling research exists, about the harmfulness of a wide, wide variety of other substances, such as polyfluoroalkyl substances (PFAS), flame retardants, the pesticide chlorpyrifos and the herbicide Roundup. The health impacts of climate change have been modeled and quantified, but the uncertainty is off-putting to some. As such, even these known harms have been harder to study, even in the narrow conditions when the impetus and funding to study them has been present. What else don't we know?

Some substances, such as lead or PCBs are so clearly harmful that they are no longer in the stream of commerce. For other pollution problems, such as air pollution, the few cost-benefit analyses that have been performed show orders of magnitude greater benefits than costs. There is more low-hanging fruit to be harvested, that would lead to large improvements in health, and therefore large improvements in well-being. But that requires more environmental knowledge. Human capital in the form of environmental knowledge is needed to make that progress.

As in the case for environmental taxation, it is worth confronting political headwinds. Science itself has fallen under attack in recent years, and scientists have come under suspicion for claims that are perceived to infringe upon liberties, no matter how trivial. Wearing facial coverings to avoid infecting others with the COVID-19 virus became political. A proposal to spend taxpayer money to advance causes which will surely draw the ire and demagoguery of some politicians seems again to lead with the nose. But as in the case of environmental taxation, the right response is not to declare defeat, but to persist, and make the case in the context of a call to rejuvenate capitalism.

7.1 ENVIRONMENTAL KNOWLEDGE VERSUS INDUSTRIAL KNOWLEDGE

A smattering of industries actually employ environmental knowledge for profit-making, and therefore produce measurable economic activity captured by GDP. Environmental consulting is an example of how environmental knowledge becomes human capital that is tangible and even increases GDP. In a healthier capitalism better calibrated with the workings of Earth's ecological systems, new industries will emerge in addition to environmental consulting, to help humankind coexist with other life systems. But in general, environmental knowledge is not better linked to measurable economic indicators because environmental externalities are not priced very well.

Generally speaking, human capital is undersupplied. There is less investment in human capital than would be optimal, from a societal point of view. Estimates of the value of human capital bear this out: the value of human capital in the United States is in the neighborhood of eleven to sixteen times the value of physical capital.[9] Individuals have only limited opportunities in life to acquire human capital, so unlike firms, human capital diversification is very difficult, and consumes more time than people have. In general, knowledge – human capital for positive, productive purposes – is a *public good*. It is nonrival in consumption – one person's knowledge does not subtract from another person's knowledge – and in fact much of the time creates positive network externalities. Many forms of knowledge become more valuable as more people acquire it. Knowledge is also nonexcludable, unless it is kept secret: knowledge redounds to everybody's benefit (provided it is knowledge for a positive endeavor).

Environmental knowledge is doubly undersupplied. Like other knowledge, environmental knowledge is nonrival in consumption and nonexcludable, but it is also undersupplied because the global environment itself is a public good. The benefits of environmental knowledge redound to everyone's benefit, even those who deny it, like climate change deniers. Since the public benefits are typically much, much broader than the private benefits, environmental knowledge will be undersupplied even more than knowledge itself is undersupplied. Humankind needs *much* more environmental knowledge than it currently has.

Contrast environmental knowledge with the kind of knowledge obtained in industry. Human capital includes on-the-job training, and much of that kind of human capital is *not* undersupplied. On-the-job training and knowledge closely associated with a specific job demonstrably improves human productivity. If that were not the case, private firms would not invest in it so heavily. It just so happens that some of this human capital resides in industries that have had negative impacts on the global environment.

Consider the case of offshore oil drilling. It is quite humbling to consider that the oil and gas industry has figured out how to extract from deep seabeds, as much as 10,000 feet below sea level, at tremendous pressures and uncertain geologic conditions. Consider how much knowledge had been acquired so that they could develop such specialized jobs as "derrickman," or "subsea engineer," and that persons without any post-secondary training can operate such expensive, sophisticated machinery to undertake a task unthinkable just a few decades ago.

It is important to notice two things about this kind of specialized training: first, that the oil and gas industry is only investing in human capital for which it can reap *private* benefits: the added productivity of its workers. A private firm can save on labor costs by hiring fewer workers, and hopefully enable them to innovate on the job, improving operations and *further* improving worker productivity. There is no incentive, however, for a private firm to invest in knowledge that would benefit the broader public. In fact, it might be disadvantageous, in terms of providing competitors with knowledge they might not have acquired on their own. And there certainly is no advantage to invest in knowledge any broader than that.

The second thing to notice is that this kind of training is also very specialized, and therefore very vulnerable to obsolescence, should the industry suffer a shock or a downturn. This kind of human capital, the kind fostered by the oil and gas industry and others, is *inflexible*. Specialized training may not be transferable to another occupation or another industry, should the oil and gas industry suffer an economic or regulatory setback. Years after the deep recession-induced downturn in Canada's oil sands industry, the vast majority of the tens of thousands of laid-off workers had still not found permanent employment.[10] This kind of specialized training provides individual workers with some stake in how the firm performs, and writ large, how the industry fares. This kind of human capital sharpens the political economy of trying to regulate or tax an industry.

Now consider what is known about the effects of drilling and of oil spills. Is there any investigation before drilling about the benthic organisms at the seabed well site? (No); What will be the short-term or long-term ecological effects of the drilling? (Dunno, Dunno); What would happen if a spill occurred? (Dunno); Could Deepwater Horizon happen again? To the credit of the oil industry, a recent study suggested that even while the Trump Administration was loosening safety and environmental regulations, the industry was busily trying to reduce the chances that such a catastrophe could happen again.[11] The odds of a reoccurrence are certainly lower now, but the answer to the question is still "dunno."

It is easy to see why a race between industry and the environment for human capital would favor industry. The reason that human capital has accumulated so prodigiously in the oil and gas industry, for example, is because the industry invested in human capital for its workers. Recall that most offshore oil and gas workers, while generally not requiring post-secondary education, are required to undergo extensive training through courses offered by the International Well Control Forum, a global trade association. Industry invests in human capital when it can reap the benefits – when it trains its workers to work with the highly sophisticated and specialized equipment involved with something as complex as drilling for oil under 10,000 feet of water.

By contrast, just about all research concerning the Earth sciences are carried out by people with at the very least a bachelor's degree in a demanding field, and under the auspices of universities and nonprofit organizations, funded by government and a few charitable organizations. Apart from intellectual curiosity, and apart from purely local environmental problems, and apart from some cottage industries such as environmental consulting, there is no reason to absorb the time and expense of acquiring human capital for purposes of understanding the global environment. Those who study the environmental effects of industries must overcome an additional disincentive; the hostility from those industries, and from kindred antienvironmental extremists, who have issued death threats at climate scientists.[12]

Viewed from these two perspectives, one can see the massive advantage enjoyed by industry over environment. In a competition for money and talent, the industry side enjoys numerous large advantages. And human capital is cumulative – knowledge begets knowledge – so just a shove in the direction of oil and gas subsidies is enough to tilt the development of human capital for, apparently, over a century. This comparison also reveals why human capital makes the political economy of reform even more unfavorable. Human capital is more valuable to those that are specialized, even though it is more vulnerable. Any policy clash that pits one interest against the other will induce a stronger reaction from the side with fewer alternatives. Because industry will necessarily be fostering the development of only specialized, and nontransferable human capital, industry will marshal the stronger response. Add to that the advantage of numbers and money, and the outcome of a policy clash is clear.

For the sake of legitimacy, better environmental knowledge is needed to anchor environmental taxes in science and economics. Already, some fairly good science and economics have produced a social cost of carbon, even if it is clear that estimates are too low. But not only must better environmental knowledge support better estimates of the social cost of carbon, they must also support reasonable bases upon which to tax other environmental harms. Even if environmental taxes need not be strictly Pigouvian in the sense that they should reflect the marginal social cost of some activity, they must be anchored in science and in economics. Environmental taxation may never be an exact science, but it must never be pure religion.

Better and more environmental knowledge is also needed to support better public decision-making processes beyond environmental taxation. To take just one example, cost-benefit analysis is a critical tool for evaluating the net worth of projects, programs, and a variety of other public decisions, but it is biased by the paucity of environmental knowledge. On the one hand, the private economic costs of some environmental regulation are well-known, as regulated industries are only too eager to help with that side of the ledger, quite often happy for the opportunity to help formulate those numbers. On the other hand, the public environmental costs are often limited to those that are either measurable by use of some proxy, such as the value of a statistical life, or the value of water-based recreation. But what else don't we know? In many cases, there are known unknowns, such as the unknown health and environmental consequences of Gulf of Mexico fish having some crude oil in their systems, for some time period, as yet also unknown. In many other cases, there are many unknown unknowns, such as the impact of oil spills on benthic species that are poorly understood and for which there is little knowledge or data. Without better environmental knowledge, the implicit value for those environmental costs are zero, despite very strong suspicions to the contrary.

7.2 A GREEN NEW DEAL FOR KNOWLEDGE

What is badly needed is government investment in human capital, not physical capital, not even wind turbines and solar panels. The latter should be left to the private sector. At the present, hard renewable energy assets seem like good investments from a societal point of view, but so did oil, gas, and coal at one point. The best thing we can do for the global environment is study it, and to *tax* those activities that are environmentally harmful. Enough doing before thinking.

Investment in environmental knowledge must be science-driven, as much as possible. There have been few bodies more expert, more prestigious, or less politicized than the National Science Foundation (NSF), which already dispenses grant funding in the field of "Geosciences," which is further divided into Atmospheric and Geospace Sciences, Earth Sciences, Ocean Sciences, and Polar Programs. In addition, NSF formed a new advisory committee and funding category, Environmental Research and Education, following a task force recommendation in 2000. (Unlike Congress, NSF sometimes heeds the recommendations of the task forces it convenes.) And finally, within the large NSF category "Biological Sciences" there are two subcategories, Environmental Biology and Integrative Organismal Systems, that fund proposals sometimes pertaining to interactions between humans and the environment. That is most certainly not an exhaustive list of places where environmental knowledge research might be funded, not even within NSF. The National Aeronautics and Space Administration (NASA) is a particularly strong research institution, a world leader on climate science. The Department of Commerce, because it houses the National Oceanic and Atmospheric Administration (NOAA), is also critical, as it carries out and sponsors much research pertaining to the oceans. But as a starting point, the NSF is a ready, credible vehicle, an experienced gatekeeper for dispensation of money, and historically at least, insulated from politicization.

It would be a bit arbitrary to affirmatively propose a specific amount of new monies to be appropriated for grant funding aimed at developing environmental knowledge. But certain markers are worth noticing for context. First, existing funding is at the very least an order of magnitude too small. Second, of all sources of federal funding, NSF funding for the "Geosciences" was $1.4 billion.[13] Other sources boost total Geosciences funding up to about $4 to $5 billion per year,[14] but the American fraction of budget devoted to geoscience research is nearly the lowest among all OECD countries.[15] By contrast, the 2018 Farm Bill will cost $867 billion over ten years, and U.S. defense spending was $732 billion for 2019. This is not necessarily to suggest that dollars should be clawed away from these programs in favor of funding the development of environmental knowledge. But it does suggest that these proportions do not reflect a rational allocation of the risks facing the United States, or the rest of the world.

Second, I argued in Chapter 1 that funding for the National Institutes for Health, which has been in the neighborhood of $30 to $40 billion annually, has likely paid for itself by orders of magnitude. If one were to limit "environmental knowledge" to that which impacts humans directly through health, then another $30 to $40 billion would still be an outrageous bargain. But of course advancing environmental knowledge must be much, much broader than just finding out and understanding activities with direct health impacts. Capitalism has gotten itself into this mess by advancing technologies without understanding their impacts on complex systems on which humankind depends. Humankind's ignorance of how its activities affect the global environment upon which it depends for survival seems a larger vacuum than $30 to $40 billion per year can fill.

This book does not purport to set a research agenda for the acquisition of environmental knowledge. That should be a science-driven process led by a respected science body such as NSF. But to help make the case that environmental knowledge is so critically needed, I offer just a few examples of critical questions in desperate need of research. These examples are in some ways overlapping and nested, but all point to some pressing need of understanding.

7.3 CLIMATE MODELING

Climate models have been a bit overoptimistic[16] but generally quite accurate, given the mindboggling complexities of modeling something as large and diverse as the planet's climate. Running on powerful supercomputers, climate models break down the entire Earth biosphere into billions of three-dimensional cells, each representing a spatial block with a latitude, longitude, and altitude, and each with a set of biological, chemical, and physical properties. Embedded within these models are known climatic phenomena such as the El Niño-Southern Oscillation, during which the surface waters of the tropical Pacific Ocean either cool or warm by 1° to 3° C, with resulting changes in rainfall patterns. Also embedded are known patterns of ocean water circulation, including the Atlantic Thermohaline Circulation, which is responsible for making life in Northern Europe habitable by bringing warm tropical waters from the Caribbean up to the North Atlantic. With principles of biology, chemistry and physics, and with these known climatic phenomena governing how each cell changes, climate models introduce perturbations such as increased carbon dioxide concentrations, and see what happens to each model cell. To test models, climate modelers run their models over the past thousands of years, and check to see if the model results match up with actual observations in recent recorded climatic history. A model for future predictions ought to be able to predict the past accurately. But with numerous uncertainties in billions of cells, confidence intervals are still necessarily large. Climate modelers have generally erred on the side of avoiding alarmism.

If anything, climate model projections have been too conservative, as some dire events that had been thought to be low-probability events, such as the disintegration of major ice formations in Antarctica and Greenland, now appear likely. And no climate modeler dared predict that the twenty-year period from 2000 to 2019 would include nineteen of the hottest twenty years in recorded history. Increased instances of extreme heat, drought, flooding, and tropical cyclones have been consistent with climate model projections.

But uncertainty has also been fodder for antienvironmental extremists, sometimes backed by fossil fuel industries, attempting to prevent climate policy from forming. A climate denying group of populist politicians in the United States, Brazil, Australia, and other countries, have seized on uncertainty as a reason for inaction. While climate communications must meet a demagogic challenge, the underlying science must also be made more robust.

Uncertainty also continues to foil planners. Within these climate models, of particular importance is how the hydrological cycle will change with increased emissions and resulting increases in temperature. Warmer air holds more water, making precipitation less frequent but more abundant when it does rain or snow. Moreover, water vapor is a greenhouse gas itself, creating a positive feedback of temperature increases. But that is an oversimplified description, and numerous other factors affect how water cycles change. Yet this is of extreme importance throughout the world, as it has enormous implications for water supply, food supply, and the resilience of societies to withstand droughts and floods. Having just suffered through an historic drought, Californians are understandably worried about when the next drought will strike, and how long it will last. It is hard to say. Other governments of the world, some highly dependent upon agriculture, are similarly worried. Refinements to climate models may never be able to provide definitive answers to many pressing questions, but providing more detailed descriptions and narrowing confidence intervals is possible.

Perhaps most critically, the linkage between emissions and temperature increase needs greater understanding. There is no greater policy need than a carbon tax, and the carbon tax level should be set at the best estimate of the social cost of carbon. Although a sub-optimally low carbon tax would be superior to no carbon tax at all, there may be no greater human need than knowing how much emissions will lead to how much temperature increase. Of course, temperatures will be heterogeneous over the surface of the entire planet (including sea surface temperatures), which only accentuates the need for better models, more computing power, and more resources and human capital to achieve these goals.

If humankind does not address climate change soon, and decisively, there is no telling what human society will look like in just a decade or a few decades. If resources shortages predicted by climate models bear out, if people begin to fear for future supply and resort to self-help and violence to secure resources, and if the resulting disorder makes people fearful that their governments can no longer keep the peace, then it is no exaggeration to say that human civilization could become unrecognizable.

7.4 BIOLOGICAL DIVERSITY

A recent credible estimate of the number of species on Earth is 8.7 million,[17] of which scientists have only cataloged 1.2 million.[18] Estimates have ranged from under 1 million to 100 million, but methodologies have improved over time, even in the financially spartan field of ecology. Of the 1.2 million, we have a good understanding of domesticated animals, but of the rest? We scarcely have any knowledge of how the million cataloged-but-poorly-understood species exist within their ecosystems, how they affect other ecosystems, and how they affect or are affected by humankind.

The *ways* in which biodiversity provides value to humankind have been catalogued. These catalogs vary a bit, but most are grounded in economic theory and practice. Importantly, these catalogs accommodate the vast unknowns of which humans may not even yet be aware. Figure 7.1 below is illustrative.

To take just one of the productive uses, one of the better-researched ones, consider the medicinal value of plants and animals. Of the 150 highest-selling pharmaceutical products in the United States, over half are either unaltered natural products or

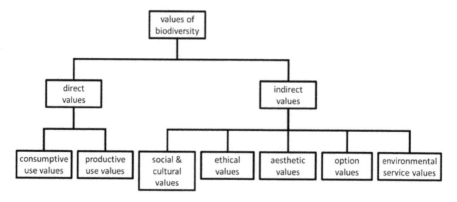

FIGURE 7.1 Categories of values for biodiversity
Source: 8 Main Values of Biodiversity.[19]

derivatives of natural products, many of them plants found in tropical rainforests.[20] How valuable is that?

Valuation of the pharmaceutical value of naturally-occurring organisms is a fraught endeavor. Uncertainties abound, including those having to do with the economics of the global pharmaceutical industry, but also pertaining to the low probabilities of discovery of a useful compound, combined with the often exceptionally high value of cures for deadly diseases. Conservative lower-bound estimates are in the billions (medicines derived from tropical forests),[21] while less constricted estimates are into the hundreds of billions.[22]

But while these estimates of the value of biodiversity are admirable attempts to place a dollar value on that which is otherwise ignored in policy, they ultimately fall short. Attempts to take known species and their known applications, and extrapolate them ultimately fail to see the value of the whole system, and a variety of other synergies that occur with expanded knowledge. Oversimplifying a bit (but not that much), these attempts take the known instances of pharmaceutical success and multiply them by the number of known species, guessing that if we knew all of the species with pharmaceutical value, we would have some multiple of pharmaceutical products. The problem with such thinking is missing how these entire systems work, how species work together (or against each other), and how humankind exists within these complex systems and networks of living organisms. It is like noticing that trees provide oxygen, plants and animals provide food, and then multiplying that by a large number, hoping to catch all human needs satisfied by all organisms, not noticing that, however, trees, plants, animals and the entire ecosphere works together in ways not yet understood, that support the entire system. Extinguishing species that are parts of the system without any understanding of the role of those species is dangerous.

What knowledge are we losing? The Biosphere 2 project, a $200 million (in 1992 dollars) effort to house eight people in a completely enclosed three-acre system for two years failed miserably, terminating early despite injections of aid. Some quipped that "[n]o one yet knows how to engineer systems that provide humans with the life-supporting services that natural ecosystems produce for free."[23]

With perhaps just one-seventh of the world's species in existence known to humankind, and with therefore very little understanding of how the systems of species work, human ignorance of biodiversity falls under the category of unknown unknowns. That is no reason to ignore them. The reason that capitalism has on net imposed so much harm on the global environment is the human propensity to rush headlong forward without sufficient appreciation of the environmental consequences. How many species we are inadvertently extinguishing is not only a moral imperative, but one of self-interest.

7.5 THE AMAZON RAINFOREST

Strictly speaking, concerns and uncertainty pertaining to the Amazon rainforest could be nested under the topic of climate change or biodiversity. But so existentially important is the Amazon's role in regulating the planet's climate that it warrants a whole program of research on its own. The Amazon hosts about 10–15 percent of all terrestrial species on Earth,[24] and absorbs about two billion tons of CO_2 annually,[25] about 5 percent of human-caused emissions. Fires, logging, drought, and other stresses reduce the capacity of the Amazon's massive trees and ancient and rich soils to absorb CO_2. A more menacing prospect is that climate-induced droughts, coupled with increased logging and fires, could cause enough tree mortality that a "dieback" could be self-reinforcing. The Amazon has long been understood to have its own weather systems, and a large enough loss of forest could further reduce rainfall, leading to more dieback, further reducing rainfall, and so forth.[26] The end result could be that most of the Amazon could settle into a much less biodiverse and much less carbon-absorptive grassy savanna, but only after it had released billions of tons of carbon it had stored over millennia. In short, the Amazon could turn from a CO_2 sink to a source.[27] Given that the Amazon stores an estimated 150 to 200 billion tons of carbon,[28] the importance of studying the Amazon becomes clear: if a massive Amazon "dieback" occurs, it could be the single largest climate catastrophe of all.

The frightening prospect of a massive Amazon forest dieback has been studied, modeled, and tested, and as ever, climate scientists are careful to balance scientific rigor with the alarming consequences of failing to heed their science. The Met Office Hadley Centre for Climate Science and Services that Margaret Thatcher championed, one of the top climate research institutions in the world, has been modeling the Amazon for decades but also undertook a synthesis of all seventeen of the models that treated the Amazon specifically, the "Climate Model Intercomparison Project." What Hadley found was that the possibility of an Amazonian rainforest dieback was very sensitive to changes in South Atlantic ocean temperatures, which affect the length of the dry season, which affects tree resilience.[29] In other words, a slight change in ocean temperatures led to a slight lengthening of the dry season which, as it turns out, has a profound effect on the forest's ability to withstand climate change. Large-scale models have the advantage of scale and perspective, but may not account for local conditions, such as soil. Subsequent research focusing on soil conditions has been more pessimistic, showing the Amazon is suffering from other soil imbalances that affect the ability of trees to absorb CO_2.[30] Models also do not explain why the amount of carbon sequestered in Amazon soils is decreasing, even without disturbance.[31] The threat of a multiyear drought hangs over the Amazon, as that would swamp the small nuances of dry season length in the Hadley models, as the dry season length would essentially be extended over years, not months. Paleoclimate analysis suggests that these droughts, which have occurred more frequently than expected, would far exceed the most pessimistic of projections of climate models.[32] And, as if to mock the painstaking detail of climate models, the massive increases in illegal burning in the rainforest under the administration of Brazilian President Jair Bolsonaro, threaten to render all of the projections moot. Forest resilience decreases rapidly once patches of burned forest infiltrate previously healthy forest.[33]

Climate change is itself diminishing the resilience of the Amazon by rendering it less resilient, but it is not known how much. Unlike the threat of climate change generally, there is no margin for error. There is no possibility of an engineering fix to compensate if the Amazon flips from being the largest carbon sink in the world to the largest source of emissions in the world. There will be no replacement for the biodiversity lost to a switch from rainforest to savanna. The Amazon is a component of climate research, but quite likely the most important one, given its vital role in the planet's carbon cycle, and given its apparent fragility, made more so by Brazilian politics. The need to understand it is of existential importance to human civilization.

7.6 THE ECONOMICS OF THE ENVIRONMENT

It is not enough to study the Earth and its many complex systems, and how humans affect this world and vice versa. And it is not enough to develop a system of warnings about certain human activities, processes, and products that might disrupt a balance struck between human activity and the world that supports it. In capitalist economies, *most* tradeoffs are couched in monetary terms. There are very few binary decisions, by firms or governments, so balances must be struck. Striking a balance requires some common metric for weighing advantages against disadvantages, and for comparing options. And for better or for worse, the common metric that dominates in a capitalist system is money. A push to make environmental considerations more prominent in all kinds of decision-making *must* include a push to study the economic implications of all kinds of changes to the nonhuman biota in the world. This is especially true since the fundamental tenet of this book is that private interests, private firms, and private energy must be the engine that drives humankind to a more sustainable relationship with the planet.

It is important, however, to keep in mind the role of economics in decision-making. More so in government than in private firms, important decisions are made for a variety of reasons, of varying weight. Certain values are very difficult to reconcile with monetization, such as the human value placed on the mere existence of a species. Humankind *might* not suffer materially from the loss of one of the seven endangered species of sea turtles. It may, but how it might is unknown. Humankind may not suffer materially from the brutal hunting by Japanese, Icelandic, and Norwegian boats of whales. But the amount of activism, politicking, shaming, and campaigning over the course of nearly a century now suggests that some humans place a very high value on the welfare of whales. At the same time, Japanese whalers seem to place a high value on their ability to hunt them. In the aboriginal context, cultural considerations are important, though they hunt for whales in numbers smaller by orders of magnitude. The abolition of whaling, when it finally happens, will not turn on economic effects or valuations.

With that in mind, it is worth turning to how environmental considerations are to be incorporated into decision-making processes such as (but also well beyond) cost-benefit analyses. The difficulty is that environmental "goods" are not priced – a market and political failure that this book seeks to correct – and therefore lack an anchor as to how much they are valued by humans. The value of clean air, clean water, a wetland or many wetlands, safe drinking water, biological diversity, and many other environmental amenities remain difficult to ascertain.

Economists have gamely worked at valuation of environmental harms. A variety of techniques, refined over decades of research and experimentation, provide some substitutes – imperfect substitutes, to be sure – for market activity and market prices. For example, for lack of an explicit market price for clean recreational water, economists can measure the difference in visitation, and the difference in how much visitors are willing to pay to visit. Alternatively, economists also ask people directly, "how much would you be willing to pay $_ for cleaner water?" The latter, survey-based method, "contingent valuation" has been refined and refined and refined for decades. Contingent valuation studies are still viewed with some skepticism – sometimes based on misunderstandings of the method – but has been deemed robust enough for some of the largest environmental damages cases, including the environmental damages from the explosion of the Deepwater Horizon.[34]

Perhaps most importantly, economists have developed functional categories of environmental values. If economists can classify the different reasons that humans value environmental goods, then the techniques for measuring them can be refined. Consider the following framework for deriving the value of a specific wetland, which may provide many forms of value for humans. The classifications of the environmental benefits are accompanied in Figure 7.2 below with examples of how those benefits are enjoyed in the context of a wetland.

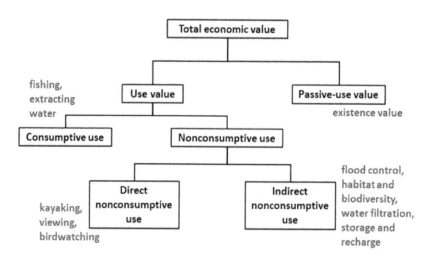

FIGURE 7.2 Categories of wetlands benefits
Adapted from Valuing Environmental Goods and Services: An Economic Perspective.[35]

A typology of environmental benefits, or goods, such as that shown in figure 7.2, is so important because not only does it serve as a checklist of benefits that must be taken into account, it serves as a research agenda. Economists have been at work on quantifying every aspect of this typology of benefits. More progress has been made on some than others.

A mountain of more work awaits, because the cornerstone of the proposals in this book are environmental taxes. The work of valuing myriad environmental outcomes is required to support, transparently and credibly, a system of environmental taxes. Some of the environmental taxes proposed in this book are not proposed to be Pigouvian, in part because there is not enough information to know what the environmental damages are. For environmental taxation to have credibility, they must at least be anchored, if not precisely calibrated, to actual environmental damages.

But even this is a tip of an iceberg of work to be done. How humans, firms, organizations, governments, and other actors move through and affect the planet is vital to understanding how to repair the broken relationship between humans and Earth. To take just one example, climate modeling comprises only one conceptual half of integrated assessment models, which combine environmental and economic impacts. Climate policy demands some comprehension of how humans will react, and economic analysis is a key component of that quest for understanding.

As it always has, thought leadership must emerge from sound economic research. The economic profession has been active in policing what is perceived, at least by a mainstream of economic thought, as transgressions of acceptable economics. There was William Nordhaus's insult of Nicholas Stern's report calling for a high carbon tax.[36] There was also a comprehensive, controversial 1997 study of the world's ecosystem services that placed the value at $33 trillion per year.[37] The study was enthusiastically received in some quarters,[38] but also came under withering criticism from economists for, among other reasons, the $33 trillion figure being larger than the world's GDP at the time.[39] Although cited over 20,000 times, and although the article has brought needed attention to the problem of economic valuation, the $33 trillion is not widely accepted. The economic profession has always been and will foreseeably be, concerned with credibility. Of the several knowledge bulwarks that must be reinforced to guide future economic development in a capitalist system, the economic profession is certainly one of them. Among other things, the development and implementation of environmental taxes, a cornerstone of this book, must be informed by interdisciplinary environmental economic research.

7.7 CLIMATE ENGINEERING, PRIZES, AND INTERNATIONAL LABORATORIES

The stark reality is that climate change is already upon us, and there is no longer the possibility of avoiding it altogether. Concentration of atmospheric carbon dioxide has shot past the symbolic 400 parts per million, and is higher than it has been at any time in the last 800,000 years. The last time CO_2 reached current levels was more than 3–5 million years ago, when the temperature was 5° to 7° F higher and the sea level was 16 to 130 feet higher than they are currently.[40] And while other greenhouse gases such as methane or nitrous oxide (N_2O) are more powerful, carbon dioxide is extremely long-lived in the Earth's atmosphere: at least a century, so that at any given time, the *stock* of CO_2 in the Earth's atmosphere cannot be quickly changed, even if current emissions are reduced quickly (which has obviously not been the case thus far, not even in Sweden).

There are two realities that humankind must now face: the need to *adapt* to climate change, and the need to undertake some form of *climate engineering* to try and manage the Earth's atmosphere for the effects of climate change. Climate engineering subdivides into two categories: (i) technologies to reduce the amount of solar radiation reaching the Earth's atmosphere, referred to as "solar geoengineering" or "solar radiation management," and (ii) technologies to actively capture CO_2 from the ambient air and store it indefinitely, referred to as "carbon removal," or "negative emissions technology," or "NETs." Both solar geoengineering and NETs are large-scale human interventions that attempt to deal with the fact of excess greenhouse gases in the Earth's atmosphere.

That is most certainly *not* to say that humankind can dispense with reducing emissions of greenhouse gases – switching to renewable energy sources, planning infrastructure around lower energy needs, and finding ways to be more efficient with energy. Rather, the need to engage in these additional palliative measures is a recognition that it is already too late to rely *solely* upon emissions reductions. A certain amount of warming and ocean acidification has already been baked in, and the risks posed by climate change have already reached levels that, in retrospect, are alarmingly high. Humankind must try to adapt to whatever is already on its way, and it must also try to reduce the burden by finding a way to deal with the extant greenhouse gases. It is already too late to do anything but adopt an "all-of-the-above" approach to climate change, which must include hedging by adaptation and climate engineering.

This book will only treat the need for government intervention for climate engineering. Although environmental knowledge is vitally important for adaptation, in my view only climate engineering suffers sufficiently from market failures that warrant some *large-scale* government intervention. Adaptation measures will continue to be driven by local needs and local capacities, as they should be. Some coastal states and communities do an excellent job of preparing for climate change just by simply mimicking some natural defenses, by restoring sand dunes and replanting resilient native dune grasses. But because of the wide variety of adaptation measures for the wide variety of adaptation challenges, this is a suite of palliative measures that are best left to local and state governments.

The environmental knowledge to engage in climate engineering, on the other hand, is a global public good, in that such knowledge is, perhaps quite literally, saving the planet for humankind. There is no excluding anyone from the protection of such an endeavor, not even climate change deniers. In fact, climate engineering, even more so than the other forms of environmental knowledge suggested in this book, requires some international cooperation. Individual national governments can and must develop policies and appropriate funds for research and development of climate engineering strategies. But national policies must be building blocks for a global effort. Knowledge of how to tinker with the Earth's atmosphere to reduce the threat of climate change is not only a global public good, but also necessitates – particularly in the case of solar geoengineering – considerable effort in reaching agreement on managing some of the known and the unknown risks. This part of the book suggests some strategies for achieving some international cooperation.

Negative emissions technologies are technologies to remove CO_2 from the ambient air and sequester it. They can be simple: planting trees is one example. They can be simple, but with a technological push: planting trees genetically engineered to grow quickly and take up a large amount of carbon dioxide, would be another example. They can be fully engineered, as some "direct air capture" technologies rely on chemical processes to soak up ambient carbon dioxide. A potentially endless number of ways to absorb carbon dioxide from the atmosphere exist. In 2018, a National Academy of Sciences (NAS) panel, in a 369-page report,[41] using the term "technology" broadly, focused on five techniques:

- Coastal blue carbon, the management of coastal land and wetlands to increase the amount of CO_2 taken up by vegetation in these areas;

- Terrestrial carbon removal and sequestration, land use to increase CO_2 uptake or storage, such as tree-planting or agricultural soil management practices that preserve the massive amount of carbon stored in soils;
- Biomass energy with carbon capture and sequestration, the combusting of organic matter for energy, but with a method of capturing and storing the resulting CO_2 emissions;
- Direct air capture, the chemical absorption of CO_2 from the ambient air;
- Carbon mineralization, the acceleration of natural "weathering" processes in which CO_2 is bonded to certain minerals.

Given the nearly infinite possibilities, the NAS panel focused on these five techniques, because these were either safe (with minimal adverse consequences), or economical (deployment at a reasonable cost), or capable of capturing a large amount of CO_2. Unfortunately, none of these five are all three.

Direct air capture offers the greatest potential to capture large quantities of CO_2, but it is expensive, and decades of research have not substantially reduced costs, which the NAS panel reported at \$600/ton of CO_2. It could even include some aspects of the Republican plan to capture CO_2 emissions from coal-fired power plants, though there are a shrinking number of those. Managing agricultural soils to preserve carbon and reduce emissions is inexpensive and part of existing programs offered by the U.S. Department of Agriculture, but despite fairly generous subsidies, have attracted a limited number of participants. Moreover, it is hard to know if these practices are actually carried out, as monitoring would be required for periodic on-the-ground verification. High monitoring costs make it difficult to execute at large scales for many farms. Biomass combustion with carbon capture and storage is available at moderate cost, provided that the biomass can be made available without compromising the supply of food, or without inducing deforestation for the purpose of generating biomass. Moreover, the capture of resultant CO_2 is still inefficient.

There is clearly no perfect NET solution. While research must continue and redouble, it is discouraging that the safest NET, direct air capture, has been the subject of research for decades, and is still very expensive. If cost and scalability were the only problems, then solar engineering might be a better approach.

Like NETs, solar geoengineering has been proposed in several different forms. Solar geoengineering can be done by depositing reflective aerosols into the lower stratosphere, about 35,000 to 70,000 feet above sea level. If those aerosol particles reflected just 1 percent of the incoming sunlight back into outer space, it could reduce by half the "radiative forcing" or warming effect of a doubling of CO_2 concentrations.[42] Aerosols could be delivered by aircraft, only slightly more advanced than regular commercial aircraft, which routinely fly at the lower end of the range of altitudes at which aerosols would be placed. Better still, the cost of delivering these stratospheric aerosols is in the range of \$10 billion per year, relatively speaking a very low cost. It would be important, however, to view that cost as a long-term commitment, because if there were a stoppage of aerosol deposits, then the Earth's temperature, which had been artificially suppressed by the reduced sunlight, would spike, with resulting damages from a sudden change in climate catastrophically high. Solar geoengineering can also be carried out by manipulating clouds. Marine cloud brightening is the adding of aerosols to clouds that whiten them, so that they reflect more sunlight. Cirrus clouds can be thinned, also by the deposition of aerosols, to allow more radiation, reflected off the Earth surface, to escape into space instead of being trapped in Earth's atmosphere and allowed to warm the planet. Both of these latter cloud-based techniques are less predictably effective. Because they focus only on clouds, which are nonuniform, they create uncertainty in terms of their effects on weather.

And therein lies the catch with solar geoengineering, which is inexpensive and probably effective: the side effects in terms of weather changes are uncertain. Apart from the likelihood (high likelihood in the case of stratospheric aerosol deposition) that they will reduce temperatures, the other effects on weather are unknown, and difficult to predict. Even if the weather side effects were certain, they would be viewed as unfavorable by some community in some country, somewhere, causing potential opposition.

In fact, the low cost and high effectiveness of solar geoengineering raises concerns that a rogue country or even a rogue billionaire individual could undertake it on their own, raising serious questions about the attendant risks. Legal scholars have called for international agreements to govern the research and implementation of solar geoengineering, to try and keep this activity under control.[43] International cooperation would also be useful in advancing a research agenda, but there has been little progress on this front.

Both solar geoengineering and NETs raise one other issue: if either or both of these climate engineering techniques are effective, what is the point of reducing emissions? In the case of solar geoengineering, there are still very serious consequences to leaving intact a high concentration of atmospheric CO_2, some of which may still be unknown. One known consequence is that oceans will continue to absorb excess CO_2 and continue to become more acidic, threatening all marine life in ways still poorly understood. But even solar geoengineering could make life bearable for humankind. Some environmental advocates have thus worried that success on this front might lead to complacency.[44] Economists might call this a moral hazard problem, a disregard of risk when protected from its consequences. This fear is not unfounded, but so severe is the climate crisis, that this fear no longer justifies inaction. As President Obama's chief science advisor, John P. Holdren, put it, "Because the increasing damage to human well-being from continuing rapid climate change is becoming impossible for citizens and policy-makers to ignore, a frantic search for every available way to abate that damage is likely soon."[45]

For both solar geoengineering and NETs, NAP panels offered recommendations for moving ahead with research. Of course, I humbly second the recommendations of these distinguished panels. But I add two other proposals, in the interest of attracting more human capital into these vitally important areas.

First, I propose a different incentive for innovation, complementing the current prevailing systems of intellectual property protection: a system of *prizes* for achieving certain specified technological breakthroughs in NETs and solar geoengineering. Prizes for innovation specify a set of conditions for an outcome, and commit an award for the first to achieve that outcome under the specified conditions. Prizes were actually the dominant method of rewarding inventive effort in eighteenth-century Europe but over time, gave way to mechanisms better suited to smaller breakthroughs, such as patents and targeted research and development funding.

One prominent prize has been offered privately, by Virgin founder Sir Richard Branson. His "Virgin Earth Challenge" is a $25 million prize for a "commercially viable" technology that is capable of removing one billion carbon dioxide (CO_2)-equivalent tonnes of GHGs every year for ten years.[46] Discouragingly, it had not yet been awarded as this book was being written, thirteen years after its launch. The American energy generation company NRG supports a $20 million prize for a technology that can convert emitted CO_2 into a useful product, such as a building material.[47] The U.S. Department of Energy has for several years issued challenges for a variety of energy-related outcomes. Smaller prizes were offered for small-scale hydrogen fueling and BTU sensors, but the Department now holds contests with multimillion dollar prizes for solar energy,[48] hydropower,[49] marine hydrokinetic energy,[50] and a suite of all-around renewable energy and energy efficiency innovations.[51]

Prizes offer important advantages over more common methods of inducing innovation. Firstly, a prize defined as a climate outcome is by design technology-neutral or method-neutral. The point of a prize is to define the desired outcome in advance and leave the methods to would-be contestants, minimizing government interference and bias. A prize at least keeps the objective front and center, providing a measure of transparency as to the desired outcome.

Secondly, unlike patenting, discovered knowledge in a prize contest enters the public domain, available for others to build on. Issuing a patent for an invention creates a monopoly on that knowledge, so that the fruits of that invention are the property of the patentee. Building on the discoveries of a patent thus depends on the willingness of the patentee to license her technology, which is sometimes not forthcoming. Upfront, patents are less expensive to governments because the compensatory mechanism is not money, but the conferral of a benefit – the monopoly on the patented knowledge. But the social cost of a patent is the potential lockup of critical information. Patent holders are under no obligation to allow their technology to be put to use. In light of the urgency of climate change, this could be disastrous.

Thirdly, a prize-based policy of inducing innovation opens up the creative process to the widest possible variety of innovators. Particularly for NETs, it could be useful to attract a broad variety of ways to sequester carbon dioxide, given the many different ways that the carbon cycle naturally transforms CO_2 into stored carbon. The Virgin Earth challenge has not yet produced a winner meeting its ambitious goal, but it could be that a better approach to NETs would be to find a large number of smaller-potential carbon uptake technologies. It could well be that the potential for NETs is to generate a broad variety of carbon removal techniques, that might be deployed in a broad variety of places and circumstances, with the hope that the sum of all reductions amounts to something meaningful. Given the monitoring challenges associated with reducing emissions and promoting carbon uptake in agriculture, a prize contestant may offer a monitoring technology that enables accurate measurements. With prizes, there is no breadth constraint on ideas.

I offer a second additional proposal: the establishment of several international climate engineering research labs, possibly each dedicated to one or more negative emissions technologies, or dedicated to studying impacts of solar geoengineering. This form of environmental knowledge pertaining to climate engineering differs from the other forms discussed above, in that it involves, for lack of better terms, both basic and applied research. Fundamental scientific processes must be studied and understood, but deploying climate engineering technologies is an engineering challenge.

Establishing mandates for climate engineering labs require some infringement of the general injunction in this book against governments making technological choices. Opening a lab requires government decision-makers to make choices about which strategies to pursue. While prizes leave open the possibilities for "dark horse" technologies that have somehow eluded the leading researchers in the world, research labs must inevitably narrow themselves by having a stated mandate. The best that can be said for such intervention is that they can still be science-driven. This section of the book draws upon the work of panels convened by the National Academy of Sciences, which have done an admirable job of combing the extant research and identifying the most promising strategies, along with their advantages of disadvantages. In addition to those, some labs may have more open-ended mandates, allowing greater creative freedom at the expense of a few million more dollars. In any case, the dire situation of climate change will require this much government intervention. Not only must some basic research questions be answered, but climate engineering technologies must be shepherded to large-scale deployment in a matter of years, not decades.

Fortunately, a precedent exists for the kind of basic and applied innovation that must happen quickly: Bell Laboratories. In the past century, Bell Labs scientists and engineers not only discovered some of the most transformative ideas in technology but also found ways to reduce them to practice and make them commercially useful.[52] Bell Labs scientists developed the world's first semiconductor solar cell (a precursor to the photovoltaic cell), communications satellites, fiber optic cables, the cell phone system, the first modern operating system UNIX, the remarkably enduring computer language C, and perhaps most importantly, the transistor. Bell Labs scientists have won the Nobel Prize in Physics thirteen times.[53]

Bell Labs is such a useful model because it accentuates the importance and offers lessons for the development of human capital. Well before social scientists began to study the effect of spatial relationships on creative relationships, Bell Labs designed workspaces to maximize the collaborative potential of talented researchers. Researchers were not divided into silos by specialty or function, as they are in universities, but were grouped so that basic scientists were near applied scientists, theoreticians near experimentalists, physicists near chemists, and engineers near metallurgists. Bell Labs developed possibly the most productive stock of human capital in history because it was effective in *growing* it. Former U.S. Energy Secretary Steven Chu, one of the thirteen Nobel Prize-winning Bell Labs scientists, managed to obtain funding from a moribund U.S. Congress to establish several "Energy Innovation Hubs," labs charged with undertaking high-risk, high-reward technologies with the potential to transform energy production, transmission, and consumption. As an example of the resulting innovation, one of the hubs, the Joint Center for Energy Storage Research, has been working on alternative battery technologies, and has launched a startup company that has demonstrated a battery that runs twenty to forty times as long as a lithium ion battery of the same power.[54]

Prizes and energy labs introduce a surprisingly attractive opportunity for international cooperation. Signatories to the Paris Agreement[55] on climate change have committed funding to the development of climate technologies, through the Technology Mechanism established under the original United Nations Framework Convention on Climate Change (UNFCCC).[56] The Technology Mechanism has thus far been ineffectual, staffed by political figures rather than people with technical expertise.[57] Rather than heed an open-ended and amorphous call for cooperation, prizes and research labs offer an opportunity to bring substantive and technical issues into international negotiations, by necessity drawing in more technologically adept people. A global system of prizes and research labs also offers an opportunity for every country to benefit, facilitating broader agreement. Broad participation would be especially important in an agreement on governing solar geoengineering research and experimentation and ultimately, deployment.

There is even a precedent for an internationally governed network of independent research laboratories: the Consultative Group for International Agricultural Research (CGIAR). CGIAR is an international research organization charged with conducting research on, and development of, agriculture for purposes of reducing poverty, hunger, nutritional imbalances, and environmental degradation.[58] Each of the 15 research centers around the world is dedicated to some aspect of agriculture and development, such as African rice, biodiversity, forestry, tropical agriculture, and food policy. Perhaps most relevant, CGIAR represents a joint international effort to improve agricultural and food outcomes through intensive research. Researchers come from around the world, and benefits accrue to every country in the world.

A similar network of research centers for climate engineering questions might focus on a variety of important areas, including different climate engineering technologies, or their environmental impacts, ocean chemistry, other natural processes that capture and sequester atmospheric carbon dioxide, agricultural practices or enabling technologies. And as with CGIAR, worldwide recruitment effort for climate change research would take advantage of the scale economies of inventive effort, as research laboratories could more easily assemble the critical mass of talent needed. Research laboratories can be both the locus and the source of the human capital needed to combat climate change. Recruiting researchers from around the world could moreover provide some political stability.

A conscious effort to build up a new human capital stock requires capacity building, and a structure for doing so. The Technology Mechanism can still serve as the funding vehicle, but the Technology Executive Committee charged with implementing the Technology Mechanism must recruit laboratory directors with substantive expertise rather than political connections. Lab directors must be given a broad grant of independence, latitude and, most critically, funding. A reconfiguration of research institutions, even if breaking from extant practice, seems consistent with the UNFCCC and the enabling Cancun Agreement.[59]

7.8 A NEW CAPITAL POLITICAL ECONOMY

For as long as there have been clashes over environmental law and policy, worldwide, there has been this political economic advantage enjoyed by polluting industries: there has always been so much more at stake in polluting than there has in the cessation of polluting. There has always been money to be made while polluting, and there has been decidedly less money to be made in finding ways to reduce pollution, or more generally any kind of environmental knowledge. Part of this effect, as argued in Chapter 5, has been the lack of any prices on pollution. But another part of this effect, and crucial to remedying the lack of pollution pricing, is simply human ignorance. In order for new industries to arise that seek to profit from environmental protection or restoration, there must be a *demand* for those goods and services – hence, a system of environmental taxes. But there must also be a *supply* of knowledge to stock those industries – hence the call for the generation of more environmental knowledge. Changing the political economy that has allowed anachronistic polluting industries to persist must include changing what people know.

Capital in the form of physical assets is a powerful economic and political force. Whatever economists say about sunk costs, it is universally true that people and firms expend effort to protect what they have. Human capital in the form of knowledge is also a powerful economic and political force, perhaps more so. If a policy clash could be reduced, in a political economy tradition, to one stock of capital against another, it is manifest that polluting industry will triumph over environmental protection almost all the time. But because there is inexorable private funding for the former, and only public funding for the latter, there must be a concerted push for funding and incubating the latter. The political economy of pollution will not change unless the human capital balance changes.

Notes

1. GARY S. BECKER, A THEORETICAL AND EMPIRICAL ANALYSIS, WITH SPECIAL REFERENCE TO EDUCATION 17 (1994).
2. GARY S. BECKER, A THEORETICAL AND EMPIRICAL ANALYSIS, WITH SPECIAL REFERENCE TO EDUCATION 170 (Table 4, showing income differentials for high school and college graduates); 224 (Table 17, showing higher incomes for college graduates. Although the *marginal* returns to a college education have not always been historically higher than the *marginal* returns to high school education, the marginal returns to college education have always been positive) (1994). *See also* CLAUDIA GOLDIN & LAURENCE KATZ, THE RACE BETWEEN EDUCATION AND TECHNOLOGY 78–79 (2008) (Table 2.5, showing positive returns to college schooling).
3. Theodore W. Schultz, *Investment in Human Capital*, 51 AM. ECON. REV. 1 (1961).
4. GARY S. BECKER, A THEORETICAL AND EMPIRICAL ANALYSIS, WITH SPECIAL REFERENCE TO EDUCATION 17–21 (1994).
5. *See, e.g.*, Theodore W. Schultz, *Capital Formation by Education*, 68 J. POL. ECON. 571 (1960).
6. ADAM SMITH , AN INQUIRY INTO THE NATURE AND CAUSES OF THE WEALTH OF NATIONS 351 (1776).
7. Kevin M. Murphy & Robert H. Topel, *The Value of Health and Longevity*, 114 J. POLIT. ECON. 871, 872 (2006).
8. *See, e.g.*, MATTHEW D. ADLER, MEASURING SOCIAL WELFARE: AN INTRODUCTION (2019).
9. Dale Jorgenson & Barbara M. Fraumeni, *The Accumulation of Human and Nonhuman Capital, 1948–84, in* The MEASUREMENT OF SAVING, INVESTMENT, AND WEALTH 228 (R. E. Lipsey & H. S. Tice eds., 1989).
10. Chester Dawson, *Canadian Oil-Sands Producers Struggle*, WALL ST. J., Aug. 19, 2015, at A1, http://www.wsj.com/articles/oil-sands-producers-struggle-1440017716 [https://perma.cc/DG8V-L9LZ].
11. Heather Richards, *We Are Much Less Safe' 4 Lessons From Deepwater Horizon*, E&E NEWS, Apr. 17, 2020.
12. James West, *MIT Climate Scientist's Wife Threatened in a Frenzy of Hate*, MOTHER JONES, Jan. 13, 2012, http://www.motherjones.com/environment/2012/01/mit-climate-scientists-wife-threatened-frenzy-hate [https://perma.cc/3WRQ-9P84]; *Climate scientists barraged with death threats*, CLIMATEWIRE, July 7, 2010; *Climate Scientists Receive Death Threats*, ABCNEWS.COM, May 24, 2010, http://abcnews.go.com/WNT/video/climate-scientists-receive-death-threats-10729457 [https://perma.cc/4Q8P-A47K].
13. Am. Geosciences Inst., NSF Geosciences Directorate Research Support Funding by Division, https://www.americangeosciences.org/geoscience-currents/nsf-geosciences-directorate-funding-institution-type [https://perma.cc/VTL7-CZPD].

14. Am. Geosciences Inst., Federal Research Funding of the Geosciences (1970-2017), Total Research Funding of the Geosciences, https://www.americangeosciences.org/sites/default/files/currents/Currents-137-FederalFunding_1970-2017.pdf (showing about $4.4 billion in 2016) [https://perma.cc/G62S-J3UN].

15. Matt Hourihan & David Parkes, Federal R&D Budget Trends: A Short Summary 12–13 (2019).

16. Nicholas Stern, *The Structure of Economic Modeling of the Potential Impacts of Climate Change: Grafting Gross Underestimation of Risk onto Already Narrow Science Models*, 51 J. Econ. Lit. 838, 838–39 (2013) ("Scientific evidence over the past decade on the scale and nature of the potential risks from human-induced climate change is becoming still more worrying: rapidly rising emissions and concentrations; impacts appearing more rapidly than anticipated' major features omitted from models, because they are not currently easy to characterize, look still more threatening …").

17. Camilo Mora et al., *How Many Species Are There on Earth and in the Ocean?*, 9 PLOS Biology e1001127 (2011).

18. Lee Sweetlove, *Number of Species on Earth Tagged at 8.7 Million*, Nature, Aug. 32, 2011.

19. *8 Main Values of Biodiversity* (no date), http://www.yourarticlelibrary.com/biodiversity/8-main-values-of-biodiversity-explained/30156 [https://perma.cc/2BEJ-FDV8].

20. Nat'l Acad. Press, Perspectives on Biodiversity: Valuing Its Role in an Everchanging World 49 (1999).

21. Robert Mendelson & Michael J. Balick, *The Value of Undiscovered Pharmaceuticals in Tropical Forests*, 49 Econ. Botany 223 (1995).

22. David W. Pearce & Seema Puroshothaman, Protecting Biological Diversity: The Economic Value of Pharmaceutical Plants, Centre for Social and Economic Research into the Global Environment (Univ. Coll. London, 1993).

23. Joel E. Cohen & David Tilman, *Biosphere 2 and Biodiversity: The Lessons So Far*, 274 Sci. 1150 (1996).

24. Jose A. Marengo et al., *Changes in Climate and Land Use Over the Amazon Region: Current and Future Variability and Trends*, 6 Front. Earth Sci. 228 (2018).

25. Roel J. W. Brienen, Oliver L. Phillips & Roderick J. Zagt, *Long-term Decline of the Amazon Carbon Sink*, 519 Nature 344 (2015) (0.42-0.65 x 10^{15} g/yr = 2.02 tons CO_2).

26. Delphine Clara Zemp, *Self-Amplified Amazon Forest Loss Due to Vegetation-Atmosphere Feedbacks*, 8 Nature Comm. 14681 (2017).

27. Peter M. Cox et al., *Acceleration of Global Warming Due to Carbon-Cycle Feedbacks in a Coupled Climate Model*, 408 Nature 184 (2000).

28. Jose A. Marengo et al., *Changes in Climate and Land Use Over the Amazon Region: Current and Future Variability and Trends*, 6 Front. Earth Sci. 228 (2018).

29. Peter Good et al., *Comparing Tropical Forest Projections from Two Generations of Hadley Centre Earth System Models, HadGEM2-ES and HadCM3LC*, 26 J. Climate 495 (2013).

30. Katrin Fleischer et al., *Amazon Forest Response to CO_2 Fertilization Dependent on Plant Phosphorus Acquisition*, 12 Nature Geosci. 736 (2019).

31. Henirique Barros & Philip M. Fearnside, *Soil Carbon in Decreasing under "Undisturbed" Amazonian Forest*, 83 Soil Sci. Soc. Am. J. 1779 (2019).

32. Luke A. Parsons et al., *The Threat of Multi-Year Drought in Western Amazonia*, 54 Water Res. Rsch. 5890 (2019).

33. Henrique S. Barros & Philip M. Fearnside, *Soil Carbon Stock Changes Due to Edge Effects in Central Amazon Forest Fragments*, 379 Forest Ecology & Mgmt. 30 (2016).

34. See, e.g., Catherine L. Kling, Daniel Phaneuf & Jinhua Zhao, *From Exxon to BP: Has Some Number Become Better Than No Number?*, 26 J. Econ. Persp. 3 (2012).

35. Kathleen Segerson, *Valuing Environmental Goods and Services: An Economic Perspective*, 1–25, *in* A PRIMER ON NONMARKET VALUATION (P. A. Champ, K. J. Boyle & T. C. Brown eds., 2017).

36. William D. Nordhaus, *A Review of the Stern Review on the Economics of Climate Change*, 45 J. ECON. PERSPECTIVES 686, 688 (2007).

37. Robert Costanza et al., *The Value of the World's Ecosystem Services and Natural Capital*, 387 NATURE 253 (1997).

38. William Roush, *Putting a Price Tag on Nature's Bounty*, 276 SCI. 1029 (1997).

39. Nancy Bockstael et al., *On Measuring Economic Values for Nature*, 34 ENVTL. SCI. TECH. 1384 (2000); Roefie Huetting et al., *The Concept of Environmental Function and its Valuation*, 24 ECOLOGICAL ECON. 31 (1995); Richard B. Norgaard & Collin Bode, *Next the Value of God, and Other Reactions*, 25 ECOLOGICAL ECON. 37 (1998).

40. Rebecca Lindsey, *Climate Change: Atmospheric Carbon Dioxide, National Oceanic and Atmospheric Administration*, NOAA: CLIMATE.GOV (Aug. 1, 2018), https://www.climate.gov/news-features/understanding-climate/climate-change-atmospheric-carbon-dioxide (showing 2017 level at 405 ppm).

41. NAT'L ACAD. PRESS, NEGATIVE EMISSIONS TECHNOLOGIES AND RELIABLE SEQUESTRATION: A RESEARCH AGENDA (2018).

42. HARVARD PROJECT CLIMATE AGREEMENTS, GOVERNANCE OF THE DEPLOYMENT OF SOLAR GEOENGINEERING 19–21 (2019).

43. Jane Long & Edward A. Parson, *Functions of Geoengineering Research Governance*, (UCLA Sch. of Law Pub. Rsch. Paper No. 19–42, 2019), https://escholarship.org/content/qt54c158tt/qt54c158tt.pdf [https://perma.cc/V2VP-NQVK].

44. Albert C. Lin, *Does Geoengineering Present a Moral Hazard?*, 40 ECOLOGY L.Q. 673 (2013).

45. HARVARD PROJECT CLIMATE AGREEMENTS, 5.

46. Virgin Earth Challenge, *Removing Greenhouse Gases from the Atmosphere* (no date), https://www.virgin.com/content/virgin-earth-challenge-0 [https://perma.cc/YG3M-P4GJ].

47. XPrize, *NRG Cosia Carbon Xprize* (2020), https://carbon.xprize.org/prizes/carbon [https://perma.cc/L2H3-6V5Z].

48. U.S. Dep't Energy, Off. Energy Efficiency & Renewable Energy, About the Sunshot Prize (no date), https://www.energy.gov/eere/solar/about-sunshot-prize [https://perma.cc/33NH-R2QB].

49. U.S. Dep't Energy, Off. Energy Efficiency & Renewable Energy, Energy Department Announces the Grand Prize Winners of the FAST Prize Competition (Oct. 8, 2019), https://www.energy.gov/eere/articles/energy-department-announces-grand-prize-winners-fast-prize-competition [https://perma.cc/6F6R-WLKH].

50. U.S. Dep't Energy, Off. Energy Efficiency & Renewable Energy, About the Wave Energy Prize (no date), https://www.energy.gov/eere/water/about-wave-energy-prize [https://perma.cc/NDJ3-629T].

51. U.S. Dep't Energy, American-made Challenges (no date), https://americanmadechallenges.org/ [https://perma.cc/2R4U-49RL].

52. JON GERTNER, THE IDEA FACTORY: BELL LABS AND THE GREAT AGE OF AMERICAN INNOVATION 341 (2012).

53. Ryan Francis, *Nobel Prize Latest in Long Line for Bell Labs*, NETWORK WORLD (Oct. 7, 2009), http://www.networkworld.com/article/2869896/lan-wan/nobel-prize-latest-in-long-line-for-bell-labs.html [https://perma.cc/4L46-EMGX].

54. David Iaconangelo, *Tesla's Ex-storage Chief on Trump, Musk, and the "Holy Grail,"* ENERGYWIRE (May 15, 2020), https://www.eenews.net/energywire/2020/05/15/stories/1063138901.

55. Framework Convention on Climate Change, *Adoption of the Paris Agreement*, Dec. 12, 2015, U.N. Doc. FCCC/CP/2015/L.9/Rev.1 http://unfccc.int/resource/docs/2015/cop21/eng/l09.pdf [https://perma.cc/9WA5-SMFT].

56. United Nations, United Nations Framework Convention on Climate Change, Art. 4, para. 5 (1992), https://unfccc.int/resource/docs/convkp/conveng.pdf. [https://perma.cc/A8E8-TFCY].

57. Heleen de Coninck & Shikha Bhasin, *Meaningful Technology Development and Transfer: A Necessary Condition for a Viable Climate Regime, in* TOWARD A WORKABLE AND EFFECTIVE CLIMATE REGIME 451–64 (S. Barrett, C. Carraro & J. de Melo eds., 2015).

58. *See, e.g.,* Consultative Group Int'l Agric. Rsch., How We Work, Strategy (2020), https://www.cgiar.org/how-we-work/strategy/ [https://perma.cc/3P22-SAPG].

59. Framework Convention on Climate Change, *Report of the Conference of Parties on its Sixteenth Session*, Art. 123, Dec. 10, 2010, https://unfccc.int/resource/docs/2010/cop16/eng/07a01.pdf (vaguely providing for "a network of national, regional, sectoral and international technology networks, organizations and initiatives … ") [https://perma.cc/NF6B-SNUV].

8

Looking Before Leaping

The nature of capital investment is that an upfront expenditure is made with the hope of producing a stream of benefits over time that more than pay for the initial expenditure. Capital investments are thus risky, because that stream of benefits may not materialize. The economic environment may deteriorate, induced by new patterns of trade or a technological advancement creating fresh competition. Or the legal environment may darken, if it is later discovered that the production process is harmful, or if the product is harmful in a way that was unknown at the time of investment. When those economic or legal threats present themselves, owners of capital rally to preserve the value of their capital. The bigger the capital, the stronger the rally. When capital owners attempt, through legal, political, or extra-legal means to protect their capital from these changes, they are said to engage in *rent-preserving* activities. The result is a costly policy conflict.

Tolerating some rent-preserving activities is part and parcel of a functional democracy operating under the rule of law. But legal rules and institutions have unwittingly *increased* both the frequency and the costliness of policy conflicts over the operation of harmful capital. They have done this in two ways. First, legal rules and institutions have bloated the stock of physical capital, and with it, the human capital intertwined with it. Sometimes the human capital is much more important than the physical capital. Once bloated, any policy conflict over the discovery of some latent harm will be more costly, because of the larger investment. Second, legal rules and institutions have served to protect extant capital, physical and human, from competition, from regulation, and generally acted to *insure* the owners of that capital from downside risk. As capital owners have grown accustomed to protections, they have become more comfortable making larger investments, betting that law-makers will eventually see them as "too big to fail," and worthy of taxpayer protection or helpful legal intervention. Ex post protections from regulation act as ex ante incentives to invest.

The freedom to choose investments without interference is critical to competition and the discovery of new technologies. Risk-taking is critical to capitalism. Some lawmakers seem to have some rough sense of this, though with some dangerously misguided oversimplifications. Nevertheless, with this sense in mind, lawmakers have developed a complex set of legal rules and institutions that are meant to incentivize this kind of risk-taking. Subsidies for the oil and gas industry is one example. While it may have been justifiable to compensate prospectors for dry holes a century ago, it is inexcusable now. Not only is it just making it more difficult to transition to a lower-carbon economy, but it is an inexcusable waste of taxpayer money. There are other ways in which legal rules and institution excessively incentivize capital investment. This chapter provides a few more examples.

The second way in which legal rules and institutions bloat capital stock is by excessively protecting it. Again, a rule of law society must tolerate this to some extent, as attacking capital by arbitrary government rulemaking would chill investment. But that does not mean that legal rules and institutions need to *insure* capital investors from changes in economic or legal conditions, much less from improvident mistakes. As between a firm contemplating investment and a regulatory agency, it should certainly be the case that the investor should have better information about the potential perils of the investment.

In trying to encourage capital investment by attenuating risk, lawmakers have gone too far in the other direction. Too often, capital investors *discount* risk. Too often, the expectation of being protected or bailed out means capital investors are often gambling with public money or public welfare. In a sense, capitalism has become less capitalist and more socialist, as legal rules and institutions have pushed the risk of failure or harm away from capital investors and onto the general public.

Parts of the strategy for correcting this imbalance have already been proposed: a system of environmental taxes that are credibly based on scientific evidence of harm, and credibly based on economic methods of pricing that harm. Another part of striking the correct balance, however, requires that some guardrails be in place to make sure that some environmental due diligence be undertaken before *some* large or important capital investments are made; only *some* of the large or important capital investments, because I do not propose, and there is no appetite for, any sort of a capital investment police. What I propose here is the strengthening of some existing guardrails, and the changing of some existing rules. My contribution is that I reintroduce these as part of my call to repair capitalism.

It may strike the reader that these proposals are narrow and modest. But that is as it should be, as erecting guardrails and slowing capital investment should be cautiously undertaken, perhaps only where there have developed strong suspicions about certain industries, certain practices, and certain areas of law. Also, slowing down capital investment is slowing down those mechanisms of capitalism that make it effective in quickly transforming an economy. Slowing down capital investment too much would be counterproductive. Indeed, some environmentally restorative technologies, and climate engineering technologies need to ramp up quickly. With that in mind, I here propose a set of measures that build on existing legal mechanisms, address the most glaring omissions, or narrowly correct the most obvious distortions. This is not a comprehensive list of what should be done to mandate a hard look before investing a large amount of money in capital. But like other parts of the proposal in this book, it is a start. And this explicit treatment serves as a reminder, even in a fervent race to save the human habitability of the Earth, that a headlong rush to letting capital investment get too far in front of human knowledge is inviting trouble in a way that ought to be familiar.

8.1 REPEALING ENERGY SUBSIDIES

Oil and gas subsidies under U.S. law are not objectionable because they benefit the oil and gas industry. Indeed, low energy prices benefit consumers as well. Oil and gas subsidies are objectionable because they incentivize the formation of excess capital in those industries. This bloated capital stock has made those industries rigid and inflexible. Rather than adapt, uncompetitively rigid industries resort to political machinations. It is long, long past time that this junk food for capital in the oil and gas industry be cut off.

As introduced already in Chapter 3, oil and gas firms can not only deduct against income the "intangible drilling costs" or "IDCs" of preparing a well, but they can expense them in the first year, instead of spreading them out over a period of years. IDCs include costs such as ground-clearing, surveying, supplies and chemicals, drilling mud, cement, and the wages of workers involved with preparing a well. IDCs account for 60 to 90 percent of the total drilling cost,[1] although "integrated oil companies," large companies with extraction, refining, and distribution capacities, can only expense 70 percent of their IDCs.[2] The rationale for allowing IDCs to be expensed immediately was that it was a form of compensation for the risky activity of drilling, which inevitably resulted in many failures, or "dry holes." But thanks to three-dimensional seismic analysis, horizontal drilling and hydraulic fracturing, dry holes have become rare. In 1961, 39 percent of all of the 44,000 oil and gas wells drilled were "dry," or insufficient to profitably produce; by 2011, that percentage figure had fallen to 10 percent.[3]

Another oil subsidy is the percentage depletion allowance, which allows an oil firm to deduct a certain amount of extracted oil against income, essentially exempting a certain percentage of oil from tax. The rationale for the allowance was that the reserves were themselves a large part of what could be considered the assets of an oil company, analogous to the "wasting assets" of a nonoil business. Allowing oil companies the ability to treat some of their unextracted oil as capital seemed to Congress to be equalizing tax burdens across industries. But how much? Any limits on deductible amounts were based on fair market value, which proved to be difficult to estimate, given the unknowability (back then) of the extent of the reserves.[4] So Congress passed a "percentage depletion" allowance, which allowed oil and gas firms to deduct up to 27.5 percent of their gross income as capital, *even if that amount exceeded the amount of investment by the firm.*[5] Oil and gas firms were allowed to deduct over time a total amount of money as capital in excess of whatever they spent in extraction. Over about seven decades, Congress gradually narrowed the percentage depletion allowance, so that it now stands at 15 percent of gross income, and is limited in other ways.[6]

There are a number of smaller subsidies for oil and gas firms. One is the ability for independent (again, no majors) oil and gas firms to amortize over just two years the geological and geophysical expenditures for the exploration of fossil fuels.[7] Again, like IDCs, this is just the ability to deduct an otherwise nondeductible expense, and acts as an incentive to explore by inflating the upside, a payoff that faces a smaller tax. There are also tax credits – not deductions – for enhanced oil recovery costs, producing oil and gas from "marginal wells," and for "tertiary injectants," all three meant to prolong the life of wells that would otherwise be unprofitable to operate.

Fiscally, none of these would be a significant infusion to a U.S. Treasury in need of more than just nickels – the Joint Committee on Taxation estimated just about $1 billion per year for all three subsidies combined.[8] But the effect of these subsidies, mostly operating to the benefit of small, independent operations, is significant, and may be incentivizing significant investment. The API-commissioned study suggested that activity might decline substantially if these subsidies were curtailed.[9] As environmental awareness, climate change, and alternative technologies have emerged, the enthusiasm for low fossil fuel prices is out of place. But the subsidies, some now over a century old, remain in place.

Those concerned about the climate crisis would not apply the same treatment to the many subsidies that apply to "clean" energies, or noncarbon energies, or to any number of technologies, products, and practices that represent some divergence from a fossil fuel-centered world. There are federal tax credits for the purchase of plug-in electric vehicles,[10] production credits for renewable energy sources,[11] and investment tax credits for renewable energy equipment and facilities,[12] to name just a few. If this were a book *just* about saving the global environment, then retaining these subsidies might make some sense. This is especially true given the economic arguments that some "catch-up" subsidization is needed for alternatives to fossil fuel energy to gain equal footing in terms of research and human capital. Indeed, investment subsidies under the 2009 American Recovery and Reinvestment Act are credited with helping to usher in a wave of renewable energy investments, most explicitly aimed at reducing the cost of renewable energy capital.[13]

But if capitalism is to be taken seriously, this is mistaken thinking. It is politically more expedient to subsidize "good" industries than it is to tax "bad" industries, but it is less efficient and less effective.[14] Among other problems with the pushing-on-a-string effectiveness of trying to prop up all that is supposedly good, subsidizing "good" industries promotes the excessive formation of capital, whereas a tax on a negative environmental externality is capital-neutral.[15] Promoting capital investment in non-fossil fuel energy sources fails to apply what we learned from our past mistakes in promoting fossil fuel energy sources. How do we know this is the "right" energy technology? What will happen if information emerges pointing to alternative energy sources that are even cleaner? Promoting the formation of capital in specific renewable energy technologies runs the risk of locking in these technologies for longer than would be optimal, and runs the risk that efforts to usher in newer and even better technologies will be met with resistance by the owners of this capital.

In the context of energy policy, a much more effective and efficient policy tool than subsidization is a carbon tax. While subsidization may work more quickly by injecting money immediately, the price effect at the margins should be roughly the same: in a competitive electricity market, taxing a natural gas firm by three cents per kilowatt-hour should have the same effect as giving a wind firm an extra three cents per kilowatt-hour. A healthier capitalism requires that governments be minimalists in terms of supporting private goods, and it conversely requires that it vigorously police negative externalities. The capitalist solution to an externality is to tax the bad, *not* subsidize all that is thought to be good, because that determination often changes.

8.2 ACCELERATED COST RECOVERY REFORM

In the United States, just about every asset that can be depreciated is listed in two tables over ten pages of IRS Publication 946. Depreciation is the deduction from income of the cost of the asset over a period of years, reducing the amount of taxable income in the years in which a deduction for depreciation is claimed. The idea is one borrowed from financial accounting: a "true" statement of a firm's financial standing requires an accounting for the degree to which its assets are "wasting," or losing value over time, as they perform their functions. From an income tax perspective, the notion of the "matching principle" was developed so that taxpayers could adjust their taxable income to account for the implicit loss of value of their capital assets. Without this concept of depreciation (or amortization, for intangible, nonphysical assets such as patents), a taxpaying firm or individual would have to pay the full tax on their income in any given year, and then, when the capital asset is actually retired, deduct against taxable income that year the loss suffered by the asset throughout its years of service. Whether this is characterized as inequity or inefficiency, a consensus emerged that rather than concentrate a possibly very large deduction in one, final, penultimate year, the taxpayer should be able to *depreciate*, or spread that deduction over the life of the asset, taking a small deduction each year. But how is the taxpayer, or the Internal Revenue Service (IRS) supposed to know ahead of time when the capital asset will be retired?

At least for tax purposes, that answer is answered in Tables B-1 and B-2 of Publication 946, in which the asset lives for each of the 140 categories are set out. The taxpayer finds its capital asset in the table and reads across the number of years over which it can be depreciated. The question that immediately leaps to mind when reading Tables B-1 and B-2 is this: "How did the IRS arrive at these numbers?" Granted, the useful lives of capital assets can be very heterogenous, dependent as they are on a variety of factors, so the IRS might be forgiven for not getting the asset lives exactly right. But if one had any familiarity with any of the asset classes listed, there is a good chance that she would be surprised at the assumed brevity of the stated asset lives. A shorter asset life means that the taxpayer can spread the deduction out over a smaller number of years, take larger deductions early on and smaller (or zero) deductions later on, and more cash in the early years than it otherwise might. The taxpayer might be able to use the extra cash for other uses in the meantime, like invest in more capital. Shorter asset lives mean tax deferrals, and cash up front. The subsidy is effectively an "interest-free loan."[16]

A long, long time ago, the goal was to have the depreciation period, or the "recovery period" or "asset life," approximate the useful life of the asset, so that tax depreciation mimicked the economic exhaustion of the value of the asset. For most of the early history of depreciation, the Bureau of Internal Revenue (the predecessor to the IRS) relied heavily upon what taxpayers claimed in terms of asset lives. A baseline used by the Bureau early on was to simply adopt whatever accounting practices taxpayers used, subject to some determination of "reasonableness."[17] The Bureau sought to standardize asset lives and publish them in "Bulletin F," the early equivalent of Tables B-1 and B-2. Bulletin F asset lives were still based on estimates in tax returns, with the result that they were shorter than what actual lives turned out to be. This did not trouble the Bureau, not yet concerned about the revenue implications of fast depreciation schedules.[18]

By 1954, an idea took hold: that capital investment was the key to economic growth. An influential paper in 1946 by Evsey Domar argued that under some restrictive assumptions, GDP was proportional to capital investment.[19] The result was the Harrod-Domar model (including British economist Roy Harrod, who had propounded a similar idea), which enjoyed some prominence for its elegant simplicity. Domar followed up in 1953 with a paper arguing that capital investment could be stimulated by allowing taxpayers (mostly corporate taxpayers) to accelerate their depreciation.[20] The one overriding political priority for passage of the Revenue Act of 1954[21] was stimulation of capital investment. The House Ways and Means Committee reported:

> More liberal depreciation allowances are anticipated to have far-reaching economic effects ... The acceleration in the speed of the tax-free recovery of costs is of critical importance in the decision of management to incur risk. The faster tax write-off would increase available working capital and materially aid growing businesses in the financing of their expansion. For all segments of the American economy, liberalized depreciation policies should assist modernization and expansion of industrial capacity, with resulting economic growth, increased production, and a higher standard of living.[22]

The problem is that there was no evidence of this. There still isn't. The literature on the drivers of economic growth is too large and complex to summarize here, but suffice it to say, the broad claim that liberal depreciation schedules generate more capital investment which generates economic growth is completely unsupported. The Harrod-Domar model was never meant to serve as a general model of economic growth. Domar himself said so.[23] Capital investment in physical assets does not just grow and grow and grow, ad infinitum. Even in the context of lesser developed countries, in which labor is abundant and capital more of a limiting factor, the Harrod-Domar model has not held up well, billions of dollars having been poured into lesser developed countries with little to show for it.[24] No single ingredient magically grows an economy, although subsequent models of economic growth have incorporated technological progress,[25] the development of quality institutions,[26] and human capital.[27]

But once an attractive-sounding, simple idea takes hold on Capitol Hill, it becomes difficult to uproot. A further acceleration of depreciation was enacted in 1958, including a new section, 179, which allowed an additional first-year deduction of 20 percent for tangible personal property with a useful life of six years or more.[28] More "reform" was in the works. Economist Walter Heller testified before the House Ways and Means Committee in 1959 against generous depreciation allowances, lamenting that

> Accelerated depreciation singles out investments in fixed assets for preferred tax treatment. Capital intensive industries are favored over labor intensive industries. Industries which invest in steel, brick, and mortar receive a substantial tax bounty while those which rely heavily on intangible capital and brainpower go more or less empty handed. Is this the type of stimulus that will give the greatest boost to the growth rate and provide the pattern of growth best suited to our national needs?[29]

A political preference for short depreciation schedules persisted, even as the Treasury Department tried to systematize them. A comprehensive 1961 study combined information from surveys, tax returns, and engineering studies and produced a detailed list of expected asset lives, grouped by the Standard Industrial Classification System. Depreciation rates were set at the thirtieth percentile of the distribution of estimated asset lives, ensuring that for tax purposes, depreciation would be *on average* faster than the actual devaluation of the asset. That still wasn't good enough, however. The passage of the Economic Recovery Tax Act of 1981[30] created an entirely new and still shorter system of asset lives in the form of the Accelerated Cost Recovery System (ACRS). In so doing, Congress doubled down on the still-unsubstantiated notion that accelerated depreciation generated economic growth. Perhaps even more troubling, all pretense of anchoring asset lives to any estimate of the actual useful lives of assets was discarded. The Senate Finance Committee report accompanying the legislation explained that the new ACRS are "generally unrelated to, but shorter than, present law useful lives."[31] As the late tax scholar Marvin Chirelstein put it, "Congress' stated aim was to stimulate investment in plant and equipment, and with this overriding goal in view it simply discarded accuracy of measurement as an objective for tax law to pursue."[32]

Again, most economists viewed this move towards further acceleration of depreciation with dismay. A letter from over 200 economists, including several Nobel Laureates, expressed chagrin over the economic distortions that would be wrought. In a letter titled "Public Statement on Depreciation Reform," the economists wrote:

> [The] Accelerated Cost Recovery System would lead to enormous distortion in investment decisions, shifting funds away from their most productive uses and into less productive, tax favored areas. The distortions ... could severely impair our economies productivity growth by diverting capital away from its most productive uses ... .[33]

Indeed, the point has been made repeatedly, with every retreat into the political jungle, that any tax preference is a distortion in the sense that it will draw resources away from more productive uses and towards tax-favored investments. In time, accelerated depreciation would become just one of many tax incentives for capital investment, so the study and opposition to accelerated depreciation per se fell out of favor, in favor of other tax incentives and subsidies. In general, the notion that a government could grow an economy by reducing the cost of capital, and more specifically through accelerated depreciation, has never had empirical support. Economist Robert Eisner opined to the House Ways and Means Committee in 1959 that

> It has been argued higher depreciation allowances will encourage investment and growth. This is ultimately a difficult and subtle issue to settle. We can, however, easily point out that most of the arguments that have been advanced in this regard in support of accelerated depreciation are irrelevant and incorrect.[34]

The aggressiveness of ACRS was scaled back somewhat by the Tax Reform Act of 1986 which put into place the Modified Accelerated Cost Recovery System, or "MACRS." But the mythical elixir of capital investment as the secret ingredient to economic growth lives on. It continues to manifest itself in a variety of economic policies, including a general tolerance for short asset lives in depreciation schedules. It has launched an economic ideology which, despite a lack of evidence, persists to this day and continues to distort capital investment decisions. Revisiting the general notion of accelerated depreciation as a stimulant for economic growth is long overdue.

The notion that political considerations have a place in determining the asset lives contained in Tables B-1 and B-2 is troubling. Back in 1959, Walter Heller noted that in addition to three fundamental purposes of the income tax system,

> a series of important but costly supplementary duties [have been] imposed on the income tax: ... to enlarge the flow of resources into particular industries or channels

in pursuit of specific national policies, e.g., into domestic oil and gas and other mineral resource exploration, presumably for national defense purposes.[35]

If political goals in the accelerated depreciation schedules is a fait accompli, then it must certainly be appropriate to revisit these goals, especially in light of previously unappreciated environmental considerations. What exactly is the case for continuing to channel federal taxpayers' dollars into the oil and gas industries? Or even more broadly, what is the case for subsidizing investment in physical assets? By now, the reader is well-accustomed to, and perhaps even weary of, my focus on the oil and gas industries. But even while appreciating the benefits of low energy prices, looking at an industry that has benefited so spectacularly from taxpayer largess seems a logical place to start on Tables B-1 and B-2. In it we find asset class for category 13.0, Offshore Drilling, which is described as "includ[ing] assets used in offshore drilling for oil and gas such as floating, self-propelled and other drilling vessels, barges, platforms, and drilling equipment and support vessels such as tenders, barges, towboats and crewboats . . . ." For this category, the stated class life is 7.5 years, and the faster MACRS recovery period is 5 years. Does this equipment sound like they are designed to last five years? MODUs that cost $500 million? Offshore drilling rigs and production rigs typically last 30–40 years, depending on the quality of the maintenance and exposure to rough conditions. Back in 1986, the 600 rigs then in service had an *average* age of over 20 years.[36] Proposing a *specific* asset life to replace the 5/7.5 figures would seem a bit arbitrary, especially in the absence of some guiding principle for lengthening asset lives in Tables B-1 and B-2 generally. Suffice it to say, such short asset lives for offshore drilling assets are perversely short, and substantial increase is warranted. Given the one thing that is known with certainty, that the oil and gas industries are central in contributing to the existential crisis of climate change, the asset lives of offshore oil and gas assets must certainly be longer than average when compared with other physical assets listed in Tables B-1 and B-2.

Oil and gas pipelines continue to be constructed, and continue to be controversial, in part (though there are several weighty objections raised by landowners and Native American tribes) because their expense and long expected life lock in fossil fuel consumption for decades, possibly for their expected life of fifty years.[37] The asset life and MACRS depreciation period for oil and gas pipelines are, respectively, fourteen and seven years. With the climate crisis nearing (or perhaps past) a time of reckoning, subsidizing and committing to a fossil fuel for such a long period of time is reckless. It is even economically reckless, as at some point well before five decades have passed, fossil fuel usage will be prohibited or extremely costly, and the pipeline will become just another anachronistic asset stranded in a climate-changed future.

Appreciating the benefits of low energy prices, it has become clear that low energy prices does not necessarily mean low *fossil fuel* energy prices. Renewable energy prices might be higher, or possibly not. But efficient allocation of factors of production and capital investment would require that this tax preference be reversed into a tax disadvantage. While a "level playing field" may be illusory, it is certainly possible to recognize this short asset life as a preference over other forms of capital investment.

Category 00.4, Industrial Steam and Electric Generation and/or Distribution Systems, includes most fossil fuel-fired power plants. The asset life for that class is twenty-two years, and the MACRS recovery period is fifteen. That is a tax preference worth reducing as well, as 88 percent of the coal-fired power plant capacity in the United States was constructed between 1950 and 1990,[38] most far exceeding the fifty-year expected lifespan. Natural gas-fired power plants vary in expected life, but are mostly in the range of twenty to thirty years.[39]

As is the case with repealing the oil, gas and coal subsidies, it is important to treat all energy subsidies equally. The asset lives of certain renewable assets should be reevaluated. Certain renewable energy assets can be depreciated over five years,[40] generally a shorter life time than their actual lives, at least for large projects. If politics is fair game in depreciation, then certainly by virtue of these technologies generating carbon-free electricity, treating them more favorably than fossil fuel assets would seem to be in order, so an increase may not need to be as great. Certainly, many climate advocates and a fair number of rigorous economists would argue for keeping in place short recovery periods for renewable energy assets. Keeping in mind the Acemoglu-Aghion argument that some catch-up subsidization may be necessary to boost the renewable energy industry, it is important also to bear in mind the path-dependency of capital investments, and how it might be even more important to keep open competition for renewable energy technologies. The five-year MACRS recovery period is keyed to section 48(a)(3)(A) of the Internal Revenue Code, which specifies the qualifying forms of renewable energy technologies. Again, its smacks of picking winners.

In addition to reviewing just the environmentally problematic capital investments in Tables B-1 and B-2, it is worth rethinking the notion of accelerated depreciation generally. Why, even if accelerated depreciation actually stimulates capital investment, should capital investment be stimulated? If anything, accelerated depreciation only contributes to a problem of "lock-in" of capital assets, and making the economy less nimble. A healthy capitalism requires the free flow of factors of production, and made-to-order asset lives under a gerrymandered accelerated depreciation regime only distort the flow of capital; increasingly, away from their highest and best uses and towards anachronistic capital.

There is also the problem, raised by Heller and many others subsequent, that privileging physical assets imposes a burden on nonphysical assets, such as human capital. At least in the United States, expenditures for higher education are not even deductible, placing it at a disadvantage vis-à-vis everything listed in Table B-1 and B-2. There are some reasonable practical justifications for this, but it still serves as a stark contrast with the allowance of immediate deductibility of intangible drilling costs for oil and gas wells. Not only is human capital formation denied the tax preferences embodied in Tables B-1 and B-2, it is denied some common protections afforded other commercial transactions. It is harder to finance a college degree than it is to finance many, many other capital assets. Student loans for higher education in the United States are financed on terms generally less favorable than home mortgages, let alone the generous debt financing enjoyed by most large corporations, especially utilities. Student loan debt is not dischargeable in bankruptcy. While this book stops short of proposing subsidization of higher education (except in the area of developing capacity in the Earth and Environmental Sciences), it is at least worth *reducing* the tax advantages of physical assets vis-à-vis higher education.

More than sixty years after economists first complained of the economic distortions created by accelerated depreciation, it is time to resurrect the argument against accelerated depreciation. Other tax benefits may also warrant reconsideration. I limit my complaint to accelerated depreciation. A healthy capitalism does not need subsidies for the acquisition of capital, but rather has the economic fundamentals that incentivize private actors, of their own volition and foresight – to acquire capital. It might be difficult to encourage the kind of broad, publicly good human capital typical of higher learning, but a healthy capitalism would at least refrain from burdening it in the myriad ways that the United States does. In particular, given what we know about the productive value of human capital – that is likely an order of magnitude more valuable than physical capital[41] – it is counterproductive to be disfavoring human capital investments. Most of all, the pressing environmental crises point sharply away from subsidizing many physical assets listed on Tables B-1 and B-2, so eliminating those preferences is a small, overdue step.

8.3 IMPROVING THE NATIONAL ENVIRONMENTAL POLICY ACT

American environmental statutes are uniquely, comically, wordy. But there is one American environmental statute that is short and effective. In terms of legal impact, possibly no American environmental statute has had quite the impact of the rail-thin National Environmental Policy Act, or "NEPA." One hundred and eighty-seven countries have adopted some form of the NEPA mandate, the performance of an environmental analysis for any proposal for a project taking place under the aegis of some federal agency.[42] NEPA is possibly the most important and effective guardrail against environmentally dangerous capital investment.

NEPA is the "look before you leap" statute, requiring as it does the examination of the consequences of actions by federal agencies before taking them. It is precisely what is needed to slow down certain large capital investments. The larger the capital investment, the greater the potential for environmental impact, and the greater the need for some environmental investigation. That is as it should be and is in keeping with a theme of this book: that capital creates its own political economy, and the larger the capital, the larger the political economy. For smaller projects, NEPA provides several possibilities for smaller, less ambitious, and less searching environmental analyses. That too, is as it should be.

NEPA has no substantive mandate, only a procedural one. NEPA only requires, before any federal agency carries out, finances, assists, or permits any project (or continues to do so), that it conduct an environmental impact statement (EIS) setting out the significant environmental impacts of the project, the alternatives to the project, and "any irreversible and irretrievable commitments of resources which would be involved in the proposed action should it be implemented."[43] For smaller projects, a scaled-down analysis, called an "environmental assessment" (EA) may be substituted for the full-blown EIS, provided that it culminates in a "finding of no significant impact." But NEPA does not require that any proposed project be defunded or denied permitting because the environmental impacts are so large or so objectionable. It does not even require that agencies choose the best environmental alternative. Courts have held that NEPA only requires agencies to arrive at a "reasoned decision."[44] NEPA has relied very much upon the desire of federal agencies to avoid embarrassment by allowing destructive projects to go forward.

For such a skinny statute, and for a statute with only procedural obligations, NEPA has had a very broad and deep impact. The leasing of federal public lands for fossil fuel extraction, which accounted for about a quarter of fossil fuel sales in the U.S., including over 40 percent of coal sales, generally requires some NEPA analysis at each stage.[45] But well beyond fossil fuel leasing, so many large capital projects require a federal permit from one or more agencies, even projects that take place on just private property may still require a permit from a federal agency to, for example, supply electricity, or perhaps one that will ruin a wetland. The result is that many projects – particularly large ones – will likely necessitate an EIS, or the less burdensome EA. The EIS/EA requirement, though not substantive, has created a field of employment in environmental consulting, one of the few industries that profit from studying the environment. NEPA contains, in a microcosm, very much of what a more sustainable capitalism should look like.

Just the mandate to perform an EIS has had a profound institutional effect on agencies. Whereas an agency such as the Federal Highway Administration was once staffed predominantly by engineers, the mere requirement that the administration look at the environmental impacts has necessitated the hiring of ornithologists (birds), ichthyologists (fishes), herpetologists (amphibians), other types of zoologists, and many other types of biologists. The forced diversification of a work force has made federal agencies much less myopic in terms of the necessity of projects that once would have been deemed routine and uncontroversial. Just the requirement that an EIS include consideration of alternatives has necessitated the hiring of researchers versed in other modes of transportation, such as transit and bicycling. In short, NEPA has been extremely effective in changing the orientation of huge federal agencies just by forcing them to expose themselves to alternative points of view. The effect would be considered insidious by antienvironmentalists.

Complaints about the burdensomeness of NEPA's requirements are not necessarily groundless: many complex EISs take years to complete. But for large, complex projects, the environmental analysis *should* be consummately thorough. Good planning and environmental analysis ahead of the project proposal has always shortened the NEPA process. That is as it should be: NEPA should be providing an incentive for proponents to start thinking about the environmental consequences at an early stage, and not just as an afterthought, after all the contracts have been put out to bid and awarded. For some perspective, less than one percent of all NEPA analyses have involved an EIS; the others have undergone the less rigorous EA or been excluded from substantive analysis altogether from "categorical exclusions," sometimes broad categories aimed at truly environmentally benign actions. So the burdensomeness complaint is a bit overblown.

What could NEPA do better to scrutinize large capital investments that might have hidden but significant environmental impacts? Some fairly subtle changes might produce profound changes in NEPA practice. The goal would *not* be to aggravate complaints about how NEPA slows projects down; the goal would be to ensure environmental impacts are studied thoroughly for large, environmentally disruptive projects, to avoid future collisions between capital and environment.

First and foremost, NEPA must require that federal agencies make reasonable efforts to evaluate the effects of projects on climate change. The challenge is formidable, since a line must be drawn between those impacts deemed "significant" – the threshold for NEPA analysis – and what is not. Is the leasing of a coal mine that will ultimately produce a hundred megatons of CO_2 emissions over its lifetime a "significant" impact when greenhouse gas emissions worldwide total about six Gigatons annually? Perhaps.

Several NEPA pitfalls require some navigation. First, NEPA requires not only estimation of the "direct impacts" of a project – in the context of climate change, the emissions from the doing of the project itself – but also the "indirect impacts," those impacts that are removed in time and/or distant, but are "reasonably foreseeable."[46] Courts seem to have settled on the proposition that for the extraction of a fossil fuel, the combustion of that fuel is "reasonably foreseeable" and therefore should be part of NEPA analysis.[47] So the NEPA analysis accompanying the approval of a coal mine lease on federal land should include an estimate of how much emissions would result from combustion of the mined coal.[48] However, the approval of an oil or gas pipeline might not require consideration of emissions, if there is some uncertainty as to the end use.[49] For natural gas pipelines built for the purpose of supplying power plants, an estimate of emissions is required,[50] although there is less certainty than for extractions, because the pipeline proponent does not necessarily know *how much* natural gas will flow through the pipeline during its lifetime.

A bit more fraught are questions of whether a project might have some economic effects, such as when construction of a pipeline or an export terminal might induce more fossil fuel production because of the lower transportation costs. Courts have been much less clear about the need for estimates of second-order effects, even when they are fairly routinely made by other agencies such as the U.S. Energy Information Administration, and even when the agency itself makes similar estimates in the NEPA analysis. The Federal Energy Regulatory Commission (FERC) has analyzed second-order effects that are beneficial, such as the prospect that natural gas pipelines might displace the use of fuel oil. It has, in the same analysis, disingenuously disclaimed any ability to project the increase in natural gas production.[51]

With respect to these less straightforward, but still very feasible estimates, some standards of analysis are badly needed, not only to ensure adequate deliberation, but also, as Michael Burger and Jessica Wentz have argued, some consistency across federal agencies.[52] Energy markets, in particular, are well-analyzed, and attempts to estimate induced demand and supply can be readily tackled. Others might not be so. But some concerted effort to draw lines would benefit all agencies, and improve the NEPA process.

Another area in which agencies, again most prominently FERC, attempt to shade their NEPA analysis, is disaggregating and separating projects, even when close in time and geography, in order to minimize the perceived impacts. FERC actually sought to divide up different segments of a pipeline in order to minimize the environmental impacts.[53] NEPA requires that the environmental impacts of "related actions" be considered together, but other than in egregious cases, courts have been reluctant to compel agencies to aggregate their NEPA analyses.

And finally, the question of "significance" in the context of climate change also begs for line-drawing. Requiring every single federal action with even the most trivial impacts on climate change is self-defeating. Picking a threshold above which an impact is "significant" could be contentious, but a reasonable starting point is the threshold for reporting greenhouse gas emissions to the EPA under the Greenhouse Gas Reporting Program (from which the Greenhouse Gas Inventory is compiled), which is 25,000 tons of CO_2-equivalent. Any source emitting less than that is deemed to be of insufficient interest. It could also be that a federal project should have a carbon footprint larger than that in order to warrant a separate NEPA analysis.

There are a good many repairs needed for NEPA with respect to climate change, and the foregoing is just a preliminary to-do list. But so much of the fossil fuel economy in the United States takes place with the permission of one or more federal agencies. At a minimum, the federal government can assume responsibility for allowing greenhouse gas emissions permitted under its authority.

A second way to strengthen NEPA would be to tighten up the standards by which federal agencies can shorten the process by just performing an environmental assessment, or EA, or the ways they invoke "categorical exclusions," or "CEs." CEs are categories of federal actions established by rulemaking which are deemed to have very small environmental impacts, and for which an agency can forego an EIS or an EA. The vast majority of CEs pertain to perfectly routine tasks with almost no environmental impacts whatsoever, such as the construction of hiking trails in a National Forest, or the construction of bicycle lanes or noise barriers on a federal road. However, even if a CE applies, a federal agency might still have to perform an EIS or an EA if any "extraordinary circumstances" (also established by rulemaking) exist. So a hiking trail may require an EIS or EA after all if, for example, the trail passes through the nesting area of an endangered species. CEs represent about 95 percent of all NEPA processes, and EAs about 4 percent.

The Deepwater Horizon tragedy itself was not caused by lax NEPA analysis, but rather lax regulation and incredibly poor judgments. But Deepwater Horizon is emblematic of what has gone wrong with NEPA analysis in the context of large programs of multiple activity, with environmental hazards. At any given time, thousands of oil and gas leases are actively tapping into the Gulf of Mexico.

Gulf of Mexico "deepwater" drilling – defined as more than 1,000 feet in depth – had been taking place for decades when the Deepwater Horizon exploded. It is true that drilling for oil in the Gulf of Mexico in general has been extensively studied, so it might have seemed sensible to avoid the repetitive, and probably redundant analyses that might accompany every lease or drill permit. Perhaps with that in mind, the regulatory agency at the time, the Minerals Management Service, did not perform a full-blown EIS for the advent of deepwater operations in the Gulf of Mexico. It conducted an abbreviated EA, and made the finding that "[m]ost deep-water operations and activities are substantially the same as those associated with conventional operations and activities on the continental shelf." And yet, MMS seemed to acknowledge that technology was proceeding apace, and that it was having trouble keeping up, but then concluding that it "necessitates flexibility," (meaning permissiveness):

> New and unusual technologies for deepwater activities are evolving rapidly. Most of the MMS's operating regulations were written prior to the rapid increase in deep-water activities, and advancements in technology typically outpace the regulation revision process. As a result, MMS has seen and is expecting to see more operator requests for alternative technologies and departures from the regulations. The uniqueness of deepwater operations and its environment compared to traditional shelf activities necessitates flexibility in the regulations to permit these development operations to proceed in deepwater areas of the Gulf.[54]

It also acknowledged in the EA that should an oil spill occur in deep waters, containment and cleanup efforts would face challenges not present for a spill on the shallower, nearshore continental shelf:

> As industry rapidly expands operations into deeper waters with technological advances, all parties involved are attempting to assess what could happen if a spill were to occur. In the deepwater OCS, there will be different sources, potentially larger magnitudes and, because of the possible locations and types of oil that could be spilled, different fate and effects.[55]

Risks are amplified further when dealing with little-studied environments. Indeed, the point of NEPA is to understand little-studied environments before committing to disturb them. And yet, it was not until 1984, a full ten years after the first Gulf of Mexico deepwater rig had been drilled, that scientists accidentally discovered "chemosynthetic communities," ecosystems that depend upon seeps of carbon from the ocean floor to support microbial life, which forms the bottom of a bottom-dwelling food chain that had never previously been known to humankind. At the time of the 2000 EA, the MMS had mapped forty-three chemosynthetic communities, but acknowledged that "the depth limits of discoveries probably reflect the lack of exploration." In other words, the MMS had no idea where there might be other chemosynthetic communities, but was going ahead with dense development anyway, settling for a self-enforced rule that drilling take place at least 1,000 feet away from *known* chemosynthetic communities.[56] Studying chemosynthetic communities might even yield secrets to absorbing CO_2.[57]

Herein lies the danger that NEPA was intended to curtail: the comfortable assumption that small (or maybe even not so small), incremental technological changes, viewed by themselves, never seem like "new or unusual technologies." Exactly when did it become routine to extend a pipe down as far as 10,000 feet, into extreme water pressures, and to drill into unpredictable bedrock, for oil or gas at unknown pressures? NEPA was meant to be the bulwark against heedlessly embracing new technologies without first careful consideration of the environmental impacts. An EIS might not have predicted or prevented Deepwater Horizon, but it would have ensured that capital investments were made only after a careful analysis.

A third way to strengthen NEPA to provide a more deliberative process preceding major capital investments has to do with the statutory language "irreversible and irretrievable commitments of resources which would be involved in the proposed action." An EIS must identify these before a federal agency action proceeds, but what does that mean?

Under current interpretations, those resources that are irreversibly or irretrievably committed are ecological ones. Given NEPA's attention on the impacts on the environment, it is unsurprising that the focus is on ecological resources, and not money. That is made clear in an EIS for a pipeline project on federal land, permitted by the U.S. Bureau of Land Management:

> An irreversible or irretrievable commitment of resources refers to impacts on or losses to resources that cannot be recovered or reversed. Examples include permanent conversion of wetlands, or loss of cultural resources, soils, wildlife, agricultural, and socioeconomic conditions.... The monetary investment by Overland Pass is *not* considered to be an irreversible or irretrievable commitment of resources.[58]

While this is a sensible interpretation of an ecology-focused statute, the NEPA process should encompass a new, expanded application of this provision, possibly necessitating a statutory amendment. This exercise in thinking about what is at stake before committing to it, should include an examination of the capital investment involved. Monetary investments *are* sometimes irreversible, just because of the political economy of large capital expenditures, as this book has set out. Large capital investments should thus be a legitimate source of inquiry in NEPA reviews because they amplify the risks that environmental impacts will be long-lived. Expensive capital tends to be, for political reasons, long-lived.

This might seem an odd line of inquiry to take under NEPA, or for a reviewing court to undertake, since economic analysis is not the bailiwick of courts. But nor was it environmental impacts, until NEPA came along and required courts to decide whether agencies had been sufficiently diligent in examining environmental impacts. NEPA also requires that agencies evaluate the cumulative impact of "reasonably foreseeable future actions regardless of what agency (Federal or non-Federal) or person undertakes such other actions,"[59] and to include "similar actions, which when viewed with other reasonably foreseeable or proposed agency actions, have similarities that provide a basis for evaluating their environmental consequences together."[60] Reasonable foreseeability even extends to what other agencies, and other governments, state and local, might do. So too, could reviewing agencies consider reasonably foreseeable private capital decisions. So too, could judges evaluate economic suppositions as they do ecological ones.

Some worry that NEPA could slow down investment in renewable energy or energy storage projects that are vital to the fight against climate change. Wind or solar projects can be, like fossil-fuel energy projects, large-scale enterprises with a large environmental footprint. The Vineyard Wind offshore wind project in New England waters has been delayed not only by Donald Trump's superstitions about wind energy, but by demands for more careful NEPA review by commercial fishermen. Environmentalists and climate advocates worry that this presents an obstacle to renewable energy development when humankind can ill-afford delay. But those careful NEPA reviews are necessary. Among other reasons, NEPA plays a vital role in ensuring the serious consideration of alternatives. A more careful examination of the environmental downsides of large-scale solar photovoltaic energy projects might lead to the conclusion that effective deployment of solar energy is not best accomplished by large projects, but by the installation of arrays on millions of rooftops. Or it might not. Whatever the merits of any energy project, NEPA is the guardrail ensuring that the environmental downsides are examined and considered. As Albert Einstein once said, "We can't solve problems by using the same kind of thinking we used when we created them."

NEPA is an effective law, consistent with robust capitalism. NEPA is a guardrail against the kind of lurch that American capitalism took in pursuing certain industrial paths without adequate consideration of the environmental consequences. Towards rejuvenating and transforming capitalism to be more sustainable, NEPA needs some strengthening.

8.4 TOXIC SUBSTANCE REGULATION REFORM

While the manufacture of potentially toxic substances is not necessarily a highly capital-intensive enterprise, the way it is undertaken in the United States does represent an example of doing before thinking about environmental consequences. The long persistence of some substances, such as perfluoroalkyl substances, or "PFAS," means that manufacturing some chemicals is a long-term commitment. Some balance is necessary, as the use of chemicals is ubiquitous in modern society. Many chemicals are substitutes for other chemicals found to be dangerous. Some are meant to solve environmental problems, such as methyl tertiary butyl ether, or "MTBEs," a replacement for lead in gasoline. A technological push to develop climate technologies, such as techniques for carbon removal, will likely involve the development of new chemicals. So as with other steps to more carefully scrutinize capital investments, some balance is necessary.

But the balance has been struck poorly in the regulation of chemical substances in the United States (and in Europe, until recently). The 1976 Toxic Substances Control Act, or "TSCA," purported to put into place a regulatory scheme whereby EPA would gradually over time collect up and inventory all of the potentially harmful substances being placed into commerce in the United States. For the more than 60,000 chemicals already in commerce then, EPA was not required to review the harmfulness of chemicals, and while manufacturers were required to report the existence of the chemicals – that is how EPA learned of the 60,000 preexisting chemicals – they were not required to provide any information about the harmful properties of those chemicals. The pre-1976 chemicals were "grand-fathered" into a presumption of safety.[61] EPA could embark upon a program of regulation if it could demonstrate the existence of an "unreasonable risk," a standard that was not defined in the statute, nor by regulation. The case *Corrosion Proof Fittings v. EPA*[62] filled the vacuum in a way that effectively ended regulation of existing chemicals. In a stunning opinion, Circuit Judge Jerry E. Smith held that "unreasonable risk" required that EPA undertake the "least burdensome, reasonable regulation required to protect the environment."[63] The opinion struck down a rule by EPA to ban asbestos, a substance known for decades to be highly carcinogenic, a death sentence for the approximately 3,000 cases per year in the United States, 90 percent of which can be attributed to manufactured asbestos exposure.[64] It came after EPA had spent ten years compiling a regulatory record thousands of pages long to support its ban. After addressing only five existing chemicals in the first fifteen years of TSCA (including asbestos), EPA never attempted another one.

EPA had a bit more leverage, but only a bit, in regulating new, post-1976 chemicals. Manufacturers were required to submit "premanufacturing notices" to EPA ninety days before a new chemical was to be placed into commerce, but was not required to provide any testing data on harmfulness. EPA can require testing, but must still show "unreasonable risk" by either showing toxicity or high exposure levels,[65] burdens that have been high in practice. Just over 2,000 chemicals had been subjected to "significant new use rules."[66] Several thousand other chemicals have been managed by EPA somehow, often by consent decree, and often difficult to see.[67]

While TSCA was meant to require EPA to create some sort of inventory of new substances that may be toxic, it has created a backlog that will be practically impossible for EPA to clear, unless considerably more resources are allotted to EPA. Having required testing on only 300 of the approximately 62,000 pre-TSCA chemicals,[68] EPA simply does not have the capacity to find out very much about the rest.[69] How is EPA to develop consistent tests that evaluate the dangers of tens of thousands of chemicals? In the face of an overwhelming workload, EPA's default position is, in the absence of data, to assume the best.[70] As a result, EPA does not even know how many chemicals are circulated in commerce. There are an estimated 84,000 chemicals in the TSCA inventory, and approximately 8,000 are manufactured at volumes of 25,000 pounds per year or more.[71]

Mass ignorance of the toxicity, mutagenicity, persistence, bioaccumulativity and carcinogenicity of tens of thousands of chemicals is concerning because of our matching ignorance of how these chemicals affect human health and other life forms. In theory, EPA has the authority to order testing of a new chemical if a broad public will be exposed to it.[72] But not only has EPA been reluctant to invoke this authority, there are myriad exposure pathways that have been completely overlooked. As Environmental Defense Fund scientist Richard Denison has said, "Every time we look for more, we find more."[73] On the flame retardants that were routinely embedded in older furniture that have been identified as endocrine disrupters, developmental neurotoxins, and possibly carcinogens,[74] Denison notes

> Every time you sit on an upholstered item, a little bit of dust puffs out, and that dust includes those chemicals. That is a pretty clearly established pathway for chemical exposure that we didn't ever really think about.[75]

What else don't we know?

Another grandfathered chemical, the patriarch of a large family of chemicals known as perfluoroalkyl substances, or "PFAS," originated in military applications, before it was applied to ordinary household products by DuPont. After a $670 million settlement for harms from DuPont's dumping of a particular PFAS, perfluorooctanoic acid, or PFOA, into water sources near Parkersburg, West Virginia – *with longstanding knowledge of the dangers*[76] – DuPont ceased production of the incriminating PFOA, but began production of substitutes, suspiciously similar in chemical structure. EPA now regulates PFOA and some other PFAS, but mostly in terms of establishing thresholds under the Safe Drinking Water Act and identifying land that is contaminated by PFAS for purposes of the Comprehensive Environmental Response, Cleanup and Liability Act.[77] Unfortunately, the PFAS problem has already spiraled out of control, as PFAS are a class of as much as 6,000 different chemicals. Every human being except those living in the remotest parts of the world has PFAS in their blood. The fact that EPA is just getting its arms around one or two of the PFAS that chemical manufacturers produced is underwhelming. The only way that more will be learned about PFAS is through continuing litigation.

TSCA was amended in 2016, in the Frank R. Lautenberg Chemical Safety for the 21st Century Act,[78] named for the New Jersey Senator who passed away in 2013 after working for years on TSCA reform. The 2016 Act did not go as far as REACH, but did give EPA more authority to require testing, effectively overruling Judge Smith's decision to find the "least burdensome" regulation, and making clear that a cost-benefit analysis was not necessary to initiate testing requirements and regulation.[79] EPA was also mandated to develop a list of "high priority" substances for which it would conduct risk evaluations,[80] and was required to identify vulnerable populations.[81] However, while EPA has more authority to require testing under the Lautenberg Act, the Act still leaves a great deal of discretion to EPA as to when to require more information from the manufacturer. In publishing a rule setting out the guidelines under which EPA intends to carry out its section 5 mandate to *review* new chemicals,[82] EPA received many comments. This is unsurprising because much turns on when EPA will require information from the manufacturer. A considerable amount of back-and-forth by EPA, buffeted by comments by the American Chemistry Council on the one hand, and the environmental group on the other hand, led to some vacillation on the part of EPA, ending with a final rule that commits EPA to "focus on uses for which manufacturing, processing, or distribution in Commerce is intended, known to be occurring, or reasonably foreseen to occur."[83] This language was helpfully suggested by the American Chemistry Council to limit the circumstances under which EPA would consider risk.[84] In so doing, EPA turned away from considering past uses and circumstances, which was a concern because of the haunting presence of some chemicals persisting in the environment.

This is not, however (at least in my view), a case of EPA playing the role of industry enabler. It is truly difficult to strike a balance on what to review or not. The fundamental problem with TSCA that the Lautenberg Act fails to fix is the burden of understanding the risks of chemicals. Nonsensically, it places the burden on EPA even though it is industry that is clearly in a better position to study and provide information. Compiling information about chemical substances would require a fraction of the cost and effort if industries were required to provide information upfront with an application to begin manufacture. An aggressive EPA could opt to make expansive use of its authority to require testing, but the statute may not provide it sufficient cover to survive lawsuits from industry. From an informational stand-point, EPA is in the same knowledge vacuum in which it sat before the Lautenberg Act. It has been estimated that in order for EPA to work out its backlog, it would take about 50 years just to study a priority list of 500 chemicals, and 1,500 years to study the existing 84,000 chemicals, along with new ones coming along each year.[85]

Even catching up would be inadequate. The Lautenberg Act does not fix a fundamental problem with toxics regulation: that it approaches risk on a single chemical-by-single chemical basis. Very rarely is testing done (when it is done) in light of interaction with other chemicals,[86] with the result that how chemicals are reacting with other chemicals to affect our health is an almost complete unknown.[87] What else don't we know?

This de facto presumption of safety, now rebuttable under the Lautenberg Act but not easily so, must be reversed. The European Union has done so with pesticides and chemicals sold in the EU. Starting in 2005 (and 2001 for pesticides), the Registration Evaluation Authorization and Restriction of Chemicals (REACH) has required manufacturers to submit testing data *before* commencing manufacture, showing that the new chemical was safe. It reversed the burden of proof and placed it on the manufacturer, before the new chemical could be manufactured in large quantities or placed into the market.[88] The new REACH mandate contains exclusions and exemptions to keep the regulatory mandate from being intractable. For example, very small production volumes are exempted (as they are under TSCA),[89] as are research and development activities,[90] a list of exempted substances (such as limestone)[91] and "substances that are considered to cause minimum risk because of their intrinsic properties."[92] There is also an emphasis in REACH on persistence and bioaccumulativity (the propensity of a chemical to accumulate in living organisms), as concentration standards are set out to determine whether a chemical should be subjected to special regulation.[93] It may take time for REACH to fully realize its potential to gather information, but it will probably be less than 1,500 years.

REACH provides an example of what TSCA *should* look like. That is not un-American: the Food, Drug and Cosmetics Act of 1938 and the Food Quality Protection Act of 1996 require a demonstration of safety by the producer before it can be sold for consumption. Granted, exposure to risk through food is different from exposure to risk from a wide variety of products, such as carpeting, furniture, and nonstick cookware. But the risks of chemicals, compared with the costs of evaluating them, is too great to ignore. The American Chemistry Council would certainly complain about the burdens of testing. But REACH has not been particularly controversial, nor have decades of proactive (if imperfect) food and drug regulation. The industry complaint that testing new chemicals would be burdensome, remains an untested proposition.

8.5 LARGE LEAPS

This chapter sets out some cautionary steps before capital investing. They unfortunately will interfere sometimes with a push to reorient capitalism to an environmentally and economically sustainable form. While humankind faces existential environmental crises, it could also be catastrophic to rush off too madly in another direction without studying the destination. Chemical misadventures with MTBE and PFAS should have reinforced that lesson. It is vitally important that certain barriers to capital investment be reduced, but not all of them. Albert Einstein has been reported (inaccurately, as it turns out) to have said, "everything should be made as simple as possible, but not simpler."[94] That might be applied to the current human predicament to enjoin us to "change our economy to an environmentally and economically sustainable form as fast as possible, but not faster."

Notes

1. Wood Mackenzie Consulting, Impacts of Delaying IDC Deductibility (2014–2025), prepared for American Petroleum Institute, July 2013, https://www.api.org/~/media/Files/Policy/Taxes/13-July/API-US-IDC-Delay-Impacts-Release-7-11-13.pdf [https://perma.cc/ZKV6-6EVW].

2. Tax Reform Act of 1986, Pub. L. No. 99–514, 100 Stat. 2085 (codified as amended at I.R.C. § 291(b)(a)(A)).

3. Cong. Rsch. Serv., Oil and Natural Gas Industry Tax Issues in the FY2013 Budget Proposal 3 (n.8) (Mar. 2, 2012).

4. Owen L. Anderson, *Royalty Valuation: Should Royalty Obligations be Determined Intrinsically, Theoretically, or Realistically?*, 37 Nat. Res. J. 547 (1997).

5. 26 U.S.C. § 613A (1997).

6. Anderson.

7. 26 U.S.C. § 167(h) (2020).

8. Joint Comm. on Tax'n, Estimates of Federal Tax Expenditures for Fiscal Years 2019–2023 24 (Table 1) (Dec. 19, 2019).

9. Wood Mackenzie Consulting, Impacts of Delaying IDC Deductibility (2014–2025), prepared for American Petroleum Institute, July 2013, https://www.api.org/~/media/Files/Policy/Taxes/13-July/API-US-IDC-Delay-Impacts-Release-7-11-13.pdf [https://perma.cc/ZKV6-6EVW].

10. 26 U.S.C. §30D (2020).

11. 26 U.S.C. §45 (2020).

12. 26 U.S.C. §48 (2020).

13. Pub. L. No. 111–5, 123 Stat. 115 (2009) (Section 1603) *as amended* by Section 707 of the Tax Relief, Unemployment Insurance Reauthorization, and Job Creation Act of 2010, Pub. L. No. 111–312. Solar, fuel cells, geothermal, wind, hydro, biomass, marine and hydrokinetic energy sources qualify. 26 U.S.C. §45(d)(1), (2), (3), (4), (6), (7), (9) & (11) (2010).

14. Shi-Ling Hsu, The Case for a Carbon Tax: Getting Past Our Hangups to Effective Climate Policy 53–59 (2011).

15. Shi-Ling Hsu, The Case for a Carbon Tax: Getting Past Our Hangups to Effective Climate Policy 41–45 (2011).

16. Robert Eisner, *Business Investment Preferences*, 42 Geo. Wash. L. Rev. 486 (1973).

17. U.S. Treas. Dep't, Bureau of Internal Revenue, Bulletin F Depreciation and Obsolescence (1920)

18. Eugene Grant & Paul T. Norton, Depreciation 90 (1955).

19. Evsey D. Domar, *Capital Expansion, Rate of Growth, and Employment,* 14 ECONOMETRICA 137 (1946).

20. Evsey D. Domar, *The Case for Accelerated Depreciation,* 67 Q.J. ECON. 493, 509 (1953).

21. P.L. 83–51 (1954).

22. H.R. No. 1337, 83rd Cong., 2nd Sess. 1954 U.S. Code & Admin. News 4048 (1954).

23. WILLIAM EASTERLY, THE ELUSIVE QUEST FOR GROWTH 28 (2001).

24. WILLIAM EASTERLY, THE ELUSIVE QUEST FOR GROWTH 34–42 (2001).

25. *See* Robert M. Solow, *A Contribution to the Theory of Economic Growth,* 70 Q. J. ECON. 65 (1956); Robert M. Solow, *Technical Change and the Aggregate Production Function,* 39 REV. ECON. & STAT. 312 (1957).

26. Douglass C. North, *Institutions,* 5 J. ECON. PERSP. 97 (1991).

27. *See, e.g.,* Theodore W. Schultz, *Capital Formation by Education,* 68 J. POLIT. ECON. 571 (1960); Theodore W. Schultz, *Investment in Human Capital,* 51 AM. ECON. REV. 1 (1961).

28. Technical Amendments Act of 1958, Pub. L. 85–866, 72 Stat. 1606 (1958), title II, § 204(a) (1958).

29. Walter Heller, *Some Observations on the Role and Reform of the Federal Income Tax,* 1 Tax Revision Compendium, House Comm. On Ways and Means, 86th Cong., 1st Sess. 181, 186–87 (1959).

30. Pub. L. 97–34, 95 Stat. 172 (1981).

31. S.Rep. No. 144, 97th Cong., 1st Sess. 48 (1981).

32. MARVIN A. CHIRELSTEIN, FEDERAL INCOME TAXATION 162 (9th ed. 2002) ("Most would agree, I think, that at least since the enactment of the 1954 Code, the depreciation allowance . . . has reflected a Congressional policy of encouraging growth and expansion."); MICHAEL J. GRAETZ & DEBORAH H. SCHENK, FEDERAL INCOME TAXATION: PRINCIPLES AND POLICIES 343 (4th ed. 2002) ("Depreciation allowances often have been used not to just measure income, but also as a subsidy to affect the overall investment in plant and equipment for fiscal and economic policy reasons."); WILLIAM A. KLEIN, JOSEPH BANKMAN & DANIEL N. SHAVIRO, FEDERAL INCOME TAXATION 613 (12th ed. 2000) ("Congress has deliberately provided taxpayers with a deduction that is generally in excess of the anticipated decline in value of the asset, in the hope of thereby stimulating investment."); Michael J. Graetz & Alvin C. Warren, Jr., *Income Tax Discrimination and the Political and Economic Integration of Europe,* 115 YALE L.J. 1186, 1225 (2006) ("One standard method for combating recessions, for example, is to increase depreciation allowances or to provide tax credits for new investments in plant and equipment. The United States often has used these techniques in efforts to stimulate its economy.").

33. ROBERT S. MCINTYRE & DEAN C. TIPPS, INEQUITY AND DECLINE: HOW THE REGAN TAX POLICIES ARE AFFECTING THE AMERICAN TAXPAYER AND THE ECONOMY (1983).

34. Robert Eisner, *Effects of Depreciation Allowances for Tax Purposes, House Committee on Ways and Means,* 2 Tax Revision Compendium House Comm. On Ways and Means, 86th Cong., 1st Sess. 181, 793 (1959).

35. Walter Heller, *Some Observations on the Role and Reform of the Federal Income Tax,* 1 Tax Revision Compendium, House Comm. On Ways and Means, 86th Cong., 1st Sess. 181, 182–83 (1959).

36. Jon Rask, *Drilling Rate Economics: Day Support, Constraint for Life of Offshore Drilling Units Needed,* OFFSHORE, May 1, 2001, https://www.offshore-mag.com/drilling-completion/article/16759042/drilling-rig-economics-day-rate-support-constraint-for-life-of-offshore-drilling-units-needed [https://perma.cc/XEB9-WD54].

37. The lives are perhaps longer. *See, e.g.,* Jordan Wirfs-Brock, *Half Century Old Pipelines Carry Oil and Gas Load,* INSIDE ENERGY, Aug. 1, 2014, http://insideenergy.org/2014/08/01/half-century-old-pipelines-carry-oil-and-gas-load/ [https://perma.cc/4BHA-UFHN].

38. U.S. Dep't Energy, *Energy Information Admin., Most Coal Plants in the United States Were Built Before 1990* (2017), https://www.eia.gov/todayinenergy/detail.php?id=30812 [https://perma.cc/W2AB-4V5X].

39. Mike Sonnenberg, *Natural Gas-fired Power Plants Are Cheaper to Build*, MKT. REALIST, Jan. 13, 2015, https://marketrealist.com/2015/01/natural-gas-fired-power-plants-cheaper-build/ [https://perma.cc/K8BY-YG5C].

40. 26 U.S.C. §48(a)(3)(A) *as amended* (2019).

41. Dale Jorgenson & Barbara M. Fraumeni, *The Accumulation of Human and Nonhuman Capital, 1948–84, in* THE MEASUREMENT OF SAVING, INVESTMENT, AND WEALTH 227–86 (R. E. Lipsey & H. S. Tice eds., 1989); Michael S. Christian, *Human Capital Accounting in the United States, 1994–2006*, SURVEY CURRENT BUS., June 2010.

42. UNITED NATIONS ENVTL. PROGRAMME, ENVIRONMENTAL RULE OF LAW 2 (2019).

43. NEPA §102(C), 42 U.S.C. §4332(C) (1970).

44. Sierra Club v. U.S. Army Corps of Eng'rs, 701 F.2d 1011, 1030 (2d Cir. 1983).

45. U.S. DEP'T ENERGY, ENERGY INFO. ADMIN., SALES OF FOSSIL FUELS PRODUCED FROM FEDERAL AND INDIAN LANDS FY 2003 THROUGH 2014 (2015).

46. 40 C.F.R. § 1508.8(b) (2016).

47. Wild Earth Guardians v. Off. of Surface Mining, Reclamation & Enforcement, 104 F. Supp. 3d 1208, 1230 (D. Colo. 2015); Wilderness Workshop v. U.S. Bureau Land Mgmt., 531 F.3d 1221 (10th Cir. 2008); San Juan Citizens Alliance v. U.S. Bureau Land Mgmt., 326 F. Supp. 3d 1227, 1244 (D.N.M. 2018).

48. COUNCIL ON ENVTL. QUALITY, EXECUTIVE OFF. PRESIDENT, MEMORANDUM FOR HEADS OF FEDERAL DEPARTMENTS AND AGENCIES, FINAL GUIDANCE FOR FEDERAL DEPARTMENTS AND AGENCIES ON CONSIDERATION OF GREENHOUSE GAS EMISSION AND THE EFFECTS OF CLIMATE CHANGE IN NEPA REVIEW 13 (2016), https://perma.cc/QP7E-7PUM.

49. Otsego 2000 v. Fed. Energy Regulatory Comm'n, No. 18-1188 (D.C. Cir. July 16, 2018); Birckhead v. Fed. Energy Regulatory Comm'n, No. 18-1218 (D.C. Cir. June 4, 2019).

50. Sierra Club v. Fed. Energy Regulatory Comm'n, 867 F.3d 1357 (D.C. Cir. 2017).

51. *See, e.g.*, FED. ENERGY REGULATORY COMM'N, ROCKAWAY DELIVERY LATERAL PROJECT AND NORTHEAST CONNECTOR PROJECT FINAL ENVIRONMENTAL IMPACT STATEMENT 4–215 to 4–217 (2014) (predicting that pipeline will lead to decrease in fuel oil use, displacing 11,357 MT CO2e daily); FED. ENERGY REGULATORY COMM'N, CONSTITUTIONAL PIPELINE PROJECT AND WRIGHT INTERCONNECT PROJECT FINAL ENVIRONMENTAL IMPACT STATEMENT 4–256 (2014) (anticipating some displacement of greenhouse gases from burning fuel oil).

52. Michael Burger & Jessica Wentz, *Downstream and Upstream Greenhouse Gas Emissions: the Proper Scope of NEPA Review*, 41 HARV. ENVTL. L. REV. 109 (2017).

53. Del. Riverkeeper Network v. Fed. Energy Reg. Comm'n, 753 F.3d 1304, 1308–09 (D.C. Cir. 2014).

54. U.S. DEP'T INTERIOR, MINERALS MGMT. SERV., GULF OF MEXICO DEEPWATER OPERATIONS AND ACTIVITIES, ENVIRONMENTAL ASSESSMENT II-65-66 (2000).

55. U.S. DEPT. OF THE INTERIOR, MINERALS MANAGEMENT SERVICE, GULF OF MEXICO DEEPWATER OPERATIONS AND ACTIVITIES, ENVIRONMENTAL ASSESSMENT II-52 (2000).

56. U.S. DEPT. OF THE INTERIOR, MINERALS MANAGEMENT SERVICE, GULF OF MEXICO DEEPWATER OPERATIONS AND ACTIVITIES, ENVIRONMENTAL ASSESSMENT IV-4 (2000).

57. *See, e.g.*, Julie Ponsard et al., *Inorganic Carbon Fixation by Chemosynthetic Ectosymbionts and Nutritional Transfers to the Hydrothermal Vent Host-Shrimp Rimcaris Exoclata*, 7 ISME J. 96 (2013).

58. U.S. DEP'T INTERIOR, BUREAU LAND MGMT., OVERLAND PASS NATURAL GAS LIQUIDS PIPELINE FINAL ENVIRONMENTAL IMPACT STATEMENT 7–1 (2007) (emphasis added).

59. 42 C.F.R. § 1508.7 (2012); U.S. ENVTL. PROT. AGENCY, SUMMARY OF THE NATIONAL ENVIRONMENTAL POLICY ACT, https://www.epa.gov/laws-regulations/summary-national-environmental-policy-act [https://perma.cc/GB9Q-8MWC] ("NEPA's basic policy is to assure that all branches of government give proper consideration to the environment prior to undertaking any major federal action that significantly affects the environment.").

60. *Id.* § 1508.25(a)(3) (2012).

61. ROBERT POOL AND ERIN RUSCH, IDENTIFYING AND REDUCING ENVIRONMENTAL HEALTH RISKS OF CHEMICALS IN OUR SOCIETY: WORKSHOP SUMMARY 33 (2014).

62. 947 F.2d 1201 (5th Cir. 1991).

63. 947 F.2d 1201, 1215.

64. Am. Cancer Soc'y, *Key Statistics About Malignant Mesothelioma*, https://www.cancer.org/cancer/malignant-mesothelioma/about/key-statistics.html [https://perma.cc/GLA3-GEKC].

65. 15 U.S.C. § 2605(a) (2016).

66. U.S. GOV'T ACCOUNTABILITY OFF., GAO-13-249, TOXIC SUBSTANCES: EPA HAS INCREASED EFFORTS TO ASSESS AND CONTROL CHEMICALS BUT COULD STRENGTHEN ITS APPROACH 21 (2013).

67. ROBERT POOL & ERIN RUSCH, IDENTIFYING AND REDUCING ENVIRONMENTAL HEALTH RISKS OF CHEMICALS IN OUR SOCIETY: WORKSHOP SUMMARY 34 (2014).

68. ROBERT POOL AND ERIN RUSCH, IDENTIFYING AND REDUCING ENVIRONMENTAL HEALTH RISKS OF CHEMICALS IN OUR SOCIETY: WORKSHOP SUMMARY 33 (2014).

69. *See, e.g.,* John S. Applegate, *Bridging the Data Gap: Balancing the Supply and Demand for Chemical Information*, 86 TEX. L. REV. 1365, 1383 (2008).

70. *See, e.g.,* Sheldon Krimsky, *The Unsteady State and Inertia of Chemical Regulation Under the US Toxic Substances Control Act*, PLOS BIOLOGY, Dec. 18, 2017.

71. U.S. GOV'T ACCOUNTABILITY OFF., 10 n.12.

72. 15 U.S.C. § 2604(a)(2)(A)–(C) (2016).

73. ROBERT POOL AND ERIN RUSCH, IDENTIFYING AND REDUCING ENVIRONMENTAL HEALTH RISKS OF CHEMICALS IN OUR SOCIETY: WORKSHOP SUMMARY 10 (2014).

74. *See, e.g.,* Lucio G. Costa et al., *Polybrominated Diphenyl Ether (PBDE) Flame Retardants: Environmental Contamination, Human Body Burden and Potential Adverse Health Effects*, 79 ACTA BIOMED 172 (2008).

75. ROBERT POOL AND ERIN RUSCH, IDENTIFYING AND REDUCING ENVIRONMENTAL HEALTH RISKS OF CHEMICALS IN OUR SOCIETY: WORKSHOP SUMMARY 10 (2014).

76. Nathaniel Rich, *The Lawyer Who Became DuPont's Worst Nightmare*, N.Y. TIMES, Jan. 10, 2016, at 36.

77. U.S. ENVTL. PROT. AGENCY, EPA PFAS ACTION PLAN: PROGRAM UPDATE (2020).

78. Pub. L. 114-182, 130 Stat. 448 (2016)

79. 15 U.S.C. § 2604(a)(3)(A) (2016).

80. 15 U.S.C. § 2505(b)(4)(A) (2016).

81. 15 U.S.C. § 2617 (2016).

82. 15 U.S.C. § 2604(a)(1)(B)(ii)(I) (2016).

83. U.S. Envtl. Prot. Agency, *Procedures for Chemical Risk Evaluation Under the Amended Toxic Substances Control Act, Final Rule*, 82 FED. REG. 33726, July 20, 2017.

84. Valerie J. Watnick, *The Lautenberg Chemical Safety Act of 2016: Cancer, Industry Pressure, and a Proactive Approach*, 43 HARV. ENVTL. L. REV. 373, 397 (2019).

85. Sheldon Krimsky, *The Unsteady State and Inertia of Chemical Regulation Under the US Toxic Substances Control Act*, PLOS BIOLOGY, Dec. 18, 2017.

86. Joseph M. Braun & Kimberley Gray, *Challenges to Studying the Health Effects of Early Life Environmental Chemical Exposures on Children's*, PLOS BIOLOGY, Dec. 19, 2017.

87. Liza Gross & Linda Birnbaum, *Regulating Toxic Chemicals for Public ad Environmental Health*, PLOS BIOLOGY, Dec. 17, 2017.
88. Council Regulation No. 1907/2006, Registration, Evaluation, and Authorisation of Chemicals, Title II, Ch. 1, Art. 6 (EC).
89. Council Regulation No. 1907/2006, Registration, Evaluation, and Authorisation of Chemicals, Title II, Ch. 1, Art. 6 (EC).
90. Council Regulation No. 1907/2006, Registration, Evaluation, and Authorisation of Chemicals, Title II, Ch. 1, Art. 9 (EC).
91. Council Regulation No. 1907/2006, Registration, Evaluation, and Authorisation of Chemicals, Annex IV (EC).
92. Council Regulation No. 1907/2006, Registration, Evaluation, and Authorisation of Chemicals, Title I, Ch. 1, § 7(a) (EC).
93. Council Regulation No. 1907/2006, Registration, Evaluation, and Authorisation of Chemicals, Annex XIII (EC).
94. ALICE CALAPRICE, THE ULTIMATE QUOTABLE EINSTEIN 384–85 (2011). Einstein actually said, in a 1933 lecture, "It can scarcely be denied that the supreme goal of all theory is to make the irreducible basic elements as simple and as few as possible without having to surrender the adequate representation of a single datum of experience."

9

Conclusion

While Adam Smith did not name it, he identified capitalism as something profoundly different, something that would break feudalism, and something that would generate wealth previously unimaginable. To argue that something so transformative could happen without royal edict or conscious purpose, driven only by self-interest, was heretical. But it is a big and consequential mistake to leap to the conclusion that capitalism is "natural" and self-executing. It became a canard that all capitalism needed was "free" markets, unspoiled by government interference. Markets depend upon rules and institutions for governance. Capitalism is more than markets alone, and requires more by way of governance. Even in Smith's eighteenth-century England, there still had to be "tolerable administration of justice."[1] Capitalism was then, is now, and will always be dependent upon the selective coercion of legal rules and institutions. For example, the enforcement of promises requires the coercion of courts, or at least norms broad enough to be institutional in nature. And contracts would never be made unless contracting parties could understand clearly what was being exchanged. Expectations about commonly traded goods and services is required for capitalism to exploit economies of scale, and that inevitably requires some coercion.

What is more, the rules and institutions that govern capitalism must evolve along with capitalism itself. Laws, institutions, and norms sometimes seem to change very slowly relative to technological and organizational changes under capitalism. But when the stakes are high enough, changes occur. For example, the way that governments (including monarchs) once incentivized discovery was through a prize system, described in Chapter 7. Although I argue that climate technologies are a special case for which prizes would be appropriate, it has generally been less effective than the more modern patent system. Prizes are limited by the difficulties of financing research, and also place the responsibility of making technological choices into the hands of government. Centralizing priority-setting never seems to yield the innovative results that have become commonplace in capitalist society. Creativity never seems to be the product of directed, concentrated effort; the questions asked at the beginning of research rarely seem to be the ones that are ultimately answered by discovery. Prizes were eventually replaced by a patent system, which grants a patent holder a monopoly to utilize a novel idea that has been shown to be useful in practice. The relatively lower cost of obtaining a patent relieves the financing problems, and there is no need to prioritize discovery needs, as there is in a prize system. But a monopoly on knowledge can be abused, and patent law has had to evolve to minimize those pitfalls, and remains in need of constant updating. The emergence of "patent trolls," individuals or firms that acquire a patent without any good faith intent to make use of a patented technology, has necessitated changes in patent laws,[2] though require still more.[3]

Antitrust law has also changed along with changing economic realities and changing schools of thought. Antitrust laws were enacted in response to the emergence of monopolist titans,[4] were vigorously enforced for a time, withered under assault in the late twentieth century to almost nothing, and now seems to be regaining currency again. Federal antitrust enforcement in the United States, breaking from European practices, underwent a dramatic retrenchment under assault from Robert Bork and the University of Chicago School of laissez-faire economic governance.[5] But with consolidation in many industries and the unnerving wealth and power of finance and technology companies, the pendulum has started swinging the other way. Even Chicagoans have begun to question how much deference to accord titans. University of Chicago economist Luigi Zingales, at odds with some of his colleagues but by no means an outlier, opined in a commencement speech that "The world has changed, and inevitably the Chicago position has to change, too."[6] So too, again, will antitrust law. Industrial concentration and economic inequality has had a profound impact on economic thought generally. On the failure of the large financial institutions that led to the 2008–09 global financial crisis, no less a socialist than Alan Greenspan offered: "In 1911 we broke up Standard Oil. So what happened? The individual parts became more valuable than the whole. Maybe that's what we need."[7]

Environmental law, however, has not evolved quickly enough in response to changing times and emerging knowledge. Technologies and markets have moved too quickly for agencies and hapless legislators to keep up. Worse, rules and institutions have been manipulated to speed humankind's headlong rush toward environmental catastrophe, just to prolong benefits to a relatively small group of polluting firms. Capital investments, physical and human, made early in the fossil fuel industries have cumulated, and have now become a behemoth. Capital investments have also allowed consolidation of the agricultural sector so that much of the productive capacity of the United States is within the control of a handful of powerful producers. The fossil fuel and agricultural industries are not as large and dominating as say, the finance industries or the big five of technology, Apple, Alphabet, Amazon, Facebook, and Microsoft. But they have established dominance over their small but vital fiefdoms within the United States and to a lesser extent, worldwide. Changes in environmental law must pass through these fiefdoms, and the incumbents are not budging. Humankind has thus driven itself to an environmental precipice because the rules and institutions that protect human society from its own environmental folly have not kept pace.

While getting a late start, humans have made some progress over the past decades in curbing the environmental effects of these industries. Environmental law, in the United States and worldwide, has made significant strides in addressing many of the most obvious and harmful problems. Lead has been removed from gasoline in most countries, so it has ceased to poison through airborne transmission, though it lingers in soil. Asbestos is used sparingly. Harms and death from environmental causes has at least slipped behind spectacular failures of public health in poorly governed countries, including the United States. But for the most part, environmental law has been harvesting low-hanging fruit, the environmental problems most clearly in need of remedy, and not all of them at that. Much, much more is needed.

9.1 MINIMALIST, CAPITALIST ENVIRONMENTAL GOVERNANCE

Bruce Scott, in *Capitalism: Its Origins and Evolution as a System of Governance*, explores the long history of capitalism, in all its forms. The depth of Scott's dive into a wide variety of experiences with capitalism over the centuries provides him with the perspective to note the tradeoffs of government control over capitalist enterprise:

> [G]overnments have to be willing to delegate power to economic actors while holding them accountable, at a minimum, to pay taxes. Too much delegation could lead to the perversion or even destruction of such a system, for example, with an oligarchic takeover. At the other extreme, too little delegation would cripple its capacities for innovation and the generation of increasing incomes and tax revenues.[8]

In one adroit paragraph Scott captures what is wrong with under-regulation and over-regulation; what is wrong with the United States and what is wrong with China. Capitalism is a social construct and requires serious discussion of the advantages and disadvantages, costs and benefits of one set of capitalist preferences as compared with another. The forms of capitalism are shaped by political choices even if, as in the case of China, the choices are severely constrained. Clearly, Americans have opted for an American brand of capitalism, Western Europeans have opted for a different brand of capitalism, Scandinavian countries yet another. Prosperous Singapore has opted for yet another, and under authoritarian rule no less, albeit light-years away from Chinese authoritarianism. The many varieties of capitalism are testament to the weightiness of the political choices made in shaping it, worthy of serious and sober debate, carried on widely. Too often we hear from both self-professed advocates for "free markets" or for "socialism" without acknowledgement of the complexity of markets and governance.

Reigning in the environmental harms of capitalism is tricky because it requires balance, and must be backed by good governance. Both seem to have become scarce. It is true that government could, in a well-intentioned (or not) effort to correct market failures, create other market failures or distortions, and even exacerbate existing ones. There is certainly precedent for those pathologies. But if one were keeping score, the costs of under-regulation have far exceeded those of overzealous government.[9] I have argued that the many failures over the centuries have been political. Democracy and capitalism, while not necessary conditions for each other, are vitally important to each other. Capitalism cannot remain healthy unless democratic institutions are healthy, and vice versa. This book demurs on the political reforms that are probably necessary, but by depicting a future governance regime that is environmentally sustainable, I hope this book plays a role in actualizing the needed reforms.

If the form that capitalism assumes is shaped by political choices, is there any such thing as a "level playing field"? Even if finding a level playing field is too epistemically fraught, it is still worth trying to achieve a *more* level playing field. That is to say, it may be too difficult to identify the perfect, but it is possible to identify the good, and still more feasible to identify the bad. It is abundantly clear that capitalism in its twentieth-century American form has been very, very good to fossil fuel industries and industrial farms (though not small farms), and continues to be so. The consequence has been a continuing and now existentially dangerous environmental harm in the form of climate change. Even if the ideal of a level playing field is impossible to identify, it is possible to identify *tilted* playing fields, and try to right them, in the interests of maximizing the chances that factors of production will migrate to their highest and best uses. Certainly, subsidies tilt playing fields, distort factor markets and likely produce inefficient allocations of capital. Also, allowing an industry to externalize environmental harms is distortionary, generating inefficiencies by pushing factors of production toward unnecessarily harmful uses.

This book is a diagnosis and a proposal. The diagnosis is that capitalism has rushed off too exuberantly in the direction of fossil fuel production and consumption, and in the direction of externality-filled industrial agriculture. Although these directions were the result of political choices, it seems a bit overstated to say that they were by *design*. Political choices were informed only by a desire to grow, and to do more with more energy, without appreciation of the consequences. "Design" implies there was a plan. There was no plan.

And having careened down this industrial path, it has now become difficult to change course. The reason that capitalism has been so difficult to control in terms of its environmental harms is because capital investments can cumulate so quickly. Unfortunately, they have cumulated very quickly in industries that produce large environmental costs. The environmental consequences have now become clear, but the capital investments that have been made in these behemoth sectors are irreversible, and could be stranded were a global transformation to occur.

The proposal is that capitalism be reoriented to rescue humankind from environmental catastrophe. That choice has been hidden because incumbent polluters have obscured it, having much physical and human capital invested in the status quo. Capitalism need not be reinvented or reimagined; a sustainable capitalism would operate very much as it currently does. In fact, a sustainable capitalism would be a more efficient and prosperous capitalism than is currently the case, having relieved people of the environmental damages too commonly suffered, and having eased the anxiety of climate change.

The cornerstone of this book's proposal is that the environmental harms created by these industries – and others – be taxed on per-unit of harm basis. Far too long have these harms been uncounted and therefore ignored, and therefore unnecessarily suffered. Just the internalization of these harms will shift economic activity towards sectors, industries, methods, processes, firms or just individuals that can meet the underlying human demands at a lower environmental cost. In a healthy capitalist society, factors of production – money, equipment, materials, technology, human resources, and other productive assets – flow freely. Environmental taxation is the price signal to migrate these forms of capital away from environmental harmful uses towards environmentally benign or restorative uses.

In addition, this book proposes to fill a knowledge vacuum with respect to the environmental and ecological effects of human activity. A research and learning agenda for the Earth and environmental sciences is a daunting mission, but the only alternative is continued ignorance. Efforts must start somewhere, and thankfully, they would not start at zero. For the money that has been invested in learning about the Earth and the way humans occupy it, humankind has learned much. Just the discovery of climate change could save human civilization, if humans act on that knowledge.

Finally, this book proposes some modest steps towards fixing what is an Achilles heel of capitalism: the tendency for physical and human capital to cumulate, to build on each other, and to erect a political obstacle to reform. There may be some good reasons to encourage the formation of capital, but it has become necessary to more carefully scrutinize some capital investments. For federal projects or federal-permitted projects, the National Environmental Policy Act must be strengthened to build in more serious reviews at certain critical points in the process. This is even true of renewable energy projects, given the time commitment involved. Second, subsidies, especially fossil fuel subsidies, and including renewable energy subsidies, should be eliminated. If renewable energy is to be supported, it would be more productive to tax the externalities of fossil fuels, and to fund expansion of the knowledge base for renewable energies. Finally, tax incentives for capital investment, most notably accelerated depreciation provisions, must be curtailed. The ad hoc handing out of capital cost discounts, industry by industry, sector by sector, firm by firm, is clearly not the way to stimulate economic growth, not even environmentally benign economic growth.

9.2 WHY ENVIRONMENTAL GOVERNANCE MUST BE MINIMALIST

Fundamentally, this book is a call for a minimalist environmental capitalism. The proposals in this book may not seem minimalist to today's self-professed libertarians, but that is because many of them take the extreme view that government should be limited to the bare minimum of cops and courts, and that courts should be limited to enforcing contracts. That is a delusion that hampers the emergence of a libertarian government that is actually practical. Bruce Scott wrote that his "manifesto" was that "Capitalism requires indirect governance through formal regulation. The alternative to formal regulation is not informal regulation, it is chaos."[10]

The self-assumed party of small government, the Republican Party, seems to see no conflict between arguing for small government and subsidizing the oil and coal industries. That grand illusion must be called out, and Republicans must be labeled for what they are when they seek to prop up the fossil fuel industries at all costs: socialists. It is also an implicit subsidy to grant a right to pollute with impunity. Free license to pollute inefficiently shifts capital resources from less harmful uses to polluting ones. Again, minimalist government does not mean *no* government. Freedom to pollute is no less socialism than tax subsidies.

In the context of environmental governance, Scott's conception of "regulation" can be many things. The proposals in this book represent the *minimum* amount of government required to reorient capitalism and avoid a calamitous collision with the ecological constraints of living on Earth. The reason they seem to be a heavy lift is because environmental harms have been ignored and suppressed for so long, and so broadly. Climate change has been a calamity a century in the making, and climate dialogue and policy actively suppressed for half a century already. A minimalist capitalist environmental governance that protects and restores the global environment focuses on the environmental harms, and not the processes or technologies or firms or industries that produce them. Except in the case of extremely dangerous pollutants, and otherwise hard-to-tax pollution, minimalist capitalist environmental governance imposes taxes on pollution that reflect the cost of that pollutant's harm, not for the purposes of punishing the polluter, but for the purpose of allocating society's resources efficiently.

What are the alternatives to a minimalist capitalist environmental governance? The relatively complex and prescriptive regulations that characterize much of modern environmental law provide an example. They have not been unsuccessful; far from it, they have generally saved much more in terms of avoided environmental harm, than they have cost in terms of pecuniary loss to industry and their consumers. Clunky, complex environmental statutes have been made to work by resourceful agencies that have found ways, within the confines of state and federal administrative law, to reduce the most egregious environmental harms while maintaining a "tolerable justice" for polluters.

But what prescriptive environmental laws have not done is spur development of alternatives. They have not unleashed a capitalist revolution of new ways of meeting consumer demands. They did not, except in very indirect ways, launch a new generation of electric motor vehicles. They did not induce a revolution in rooftop solar energy that threatens the entire, ossified model of regulated electric utilities. And they had nothing to do with the explosive development of meat alternatives, invading the world's hamburger fiefdoms.

Another alternative to minimalist capitalist environmental governance, a greater threat to capitalism than prescriptive environmental regulation, is the specious notion that governments can fund certain technologies that will solve environmental problems. We have already seen how easily this becomes a boondoggle, industrial grifters duping gullible politicians and vaulting themselves into the titan class, then using political clout to foreclose competition from worthier entrepreneurs and worthier technologies. That government can affirmatively do something to save humankind is a dangerous delusion. People, groups, and corporations operating under capitalist systems must save humankind. This surprisingly extends to realms other than environmental law: the favorable tax treatment of physical assets, biased for reasons unrelated to anything having to do with the environment, is an unwitting accomplice to environmental spoliation.

At bottom, a minimalist capitalist viewpoint is a recognition of the proper role of government, centered upon preventing harm and avoiding as much as possible pretenses of government doing good deeds. It is simply impossible, even if corruption could be curbed, for government to do a systematically better job of inventing, changing and transforming than atomized private entrepreneurs. There is a vast epistemic difference between learning that $PM_{2.5}$ (fine particulate matter) is harmful, and deciding on the best way to reduce $PM_{2.5}$. The former is challenging – hence the need to ramp up environmental knowledge – but the latter is a fundamental market decision with an almost infinite number of choices. The saying that "governments are bad at picking winners, and losers are good at picking governments" is incomplete. The logically necessarily complement is that comparatively speaking, governments have been reasonably competent at identifying harm.

I am not naïve about the long odds against reducing the amount of heavy-handed government intervention when some legislator gets wind of a silver bullet that happens to coincide with the provision of political benefits. That is a political problem for which I have nothing new to contribute in the way of solutions. This book is a rearticulation of what has gone wrong with capitalism, why it harms the global environment, and why humankind has found it so hard to stop. It serves as a reminder to those who favor small government of *why* they should favor small government, and also as a reminder to those who worry about environmental degradation of the tools they have at hand to curb it. It is a reminder to both groups of what they have in common.

9.3 WHY ENVIRONMENTAL GOVERNANCE MUST BE CAPITALIST

Capitalism must undergo transformation, and transformation must entail, painfully, unfortunately, failure. Obviously, failure occurs everywhere, in any system, but it is most prominent in capitalist systems. That is not coincidence, or evidence of the cruelty of capitalism; the flip side of success is necessarily failure. This symmetry is the genesis of Schumpeter's notion of "creative destruction," central to capitalism. What makes for competition, and what makes capitalism work is the possibility that businesses might fail. There is a saying, while it somewhat caricatures the Catholic faith, that is nevertheless apt for this purpose: "Capitalism without failure is like Catholicism without hell."[11] What has indeed gone wrong with capitalism is that political choices have worked to insulate firms from failure.

That large corporations fail may be hard to imagine, as an endless parade of large corporations march on Washington with hat in hand, begging for money and privilege, and not just in the time of COVID-19. It has been discouraging to watch as the United States federal government spends trillions and trillions of taxpayer dollars rescuing corporations that have recklessly gambled their solvency for higher returns, crisis after crisis after crisis. The big three of the airline industry, Delta, American, and United spent a total of $34 billion in stock buybacks[12] over a five-year period, rewarding shareholders instead of preparing a rainy day fund for unexpected shocks to business; they received a total of $16.2 billion in federal aid relating to the COVID-19 crisis.[13] Airlines, energy companies, and other businesses cited the unforeseeability of COVID-19; but was it really, after outbreaks of its close cousins SARS and MERS?

The fact that the United States federal government has time and time and time again attempted to *insure*, with taxpayer dollars and environmental forgiveness, firms that have fully deserved the fate of a final dissolution in bankruptcy, is not evidence that capitalism is dead. After all, small businesses such as restaurants fail quite often. The behavior of the United States federal government is evidence that American capitalism is faulty, and that American democracy is faulty. Still struggling against market obsolescence, coal companies, with Donald Trump's abetting, have taken to invoking culture wars as a means of securing financial and political support, even as low renewable energy prices and lower natural gas prices inexorably drive coal companies out of business. Oil companies, too, succeeded in at least rallying handfuls of Republicans to try and get the Federal Reserve and the White House to pressure investment houses not to give up on oil and gas companies. Such rugged individualism!

Fortunately, there are limits to the ability of the federal government to muck up markets by insuring failing businesses and indulging in crony capitalism. Coal production will probably eventually cease in the United States, even without any environmental regulation or climate policy. More coal-fired power plant capacity was retired under the Trump Administration than under President Obama's second term, despite some deregulatory efforts, and even attempts to add subsidies to coal production.[14] While the big three American automakers were beneficiaries of the support of the George W. Bush administration's hydrogen fuel cell initiative, Toyota eventually won the technological battle, and became the dominant seller of popular hybrid electric passenger vehicles. And at least the 2008–09 global financial crisis did claim one prominent victim: Lehman Brothers, the fourth-largest investment bank in the United States at the time, was allowed to fail. It would be a little oblivious to say that competition is alive and well. But apart from a sob-story political culture, there are as yet few reasons to think that capitalism has been completely deprived of its threat of failure.

The upside of failure in capitalism is its dynamism, a key element of competition. Competition spurs innovation, which necessarily induces change. Sometimes the forms of competition are unfortunate, such as the race to Congress for taxpayer money or legal privilege. Sometimes competition produces monopoly or oligopoly that defeats competition itself, and sometimes it leads to predatory behavior. But even if competition is ugly, it more often than not produces change, and more often than not the change benefits consumers. Again, certain guardrails on competition are necessary, as even Chicagoans are realizing. All in all, competition is more robust and more productive under capitalism than under any alternative, and innovation is concomitantly more frequent and more disruptive.

Nothing is more central to capitalism than the price system, and this too, is a reason that capitalism is indispensable to a global effort to repair humankind's relationship with the environment. The environmental effort required will be herculean, requiring the vast coordination of resources accomplished by the hyper-coordination of resources, ideas, and human initiative. Towards this end, nothing communicates more efficiently the cost of environmental harm than an environmental tax. Even an intensely capitalist system must still include some prescriptive regulation; technological and other knowledge constraints preclude a system of *purely* environmental taxes. Moreover, some harms are so great that pricing them would be unseemly. But in terms of marshalling the maximum amount of resources, ideas, and human initiative, there is no replacement for the price system, which is the *only* way to connect the possibly far-flung and disparate bits of a successful enterprise.

Finally, scale production is a strength of capitalism that is needed for a transformation to a sustainable capitalism. It is true that the People's Republic of China has demonstrated an amazing ability to produce many things at huge scales. China built an incredibly large stock of coal-fired power plants very quickly, at one point in the 1990s adding as much coal-fired capacity in a single year as the United Kingdom *ever had*. Separating out the admiration of that productive effort from the appalling ends of that effort, it is still dubious to conclude that a state-centered effort was required. Certainly, a national mandate for development of electric capacity focused attention. But especially in such a large and heterogeneous country as

China, putting the necessary resources together required the incentives that only a price system could have accomplished. It was no stroke of managerial genius – if that is the right word, for such a terrible project – that got so many coal-fired power plants built. It was the capitalism within a state-capitalist country responsible for this feat.

Left unmolested, prescriptive environmental regulation would continue to improve environmental conditions globally. But the central thesis of this book is that because of massive capital investments already made over the course of more than a century, a game of catch-up environmental knowledge acquisition and environmental regulation is doomed. Capitalism has worked so powerfully and relentlessly to build up and maintain a global economy predicated on environmental degradation, that there is no other means available to change its course. At this late hour, there is only fire to fight fire.

9.4 GLOBAL ENVIRONMENTAL CAPITALISM

If there is a limit to capitalism's ability to address environmental problems, it is the political difficulty of addressing environmental problems *globally*. The most pressing environmental problems are global in nature. Climate change certainly is, but so is the production of pollutants that may travel long distances, some of them persistent and long-lived substances that can impose harm for decades. Capitalism can solve coordination problems within groups, and perhaps in enlightened countries, but can it solve global coordination problems?

A solution to the global coordination problem ventures outside of the bounds of my central thesis because capitalism, by itself, has no acceptable solution to the problem of global coordination. There will thankfully *not* be a global government, with one single type of capitalism. What a future of environmental capitalism holds, hopefully, is a polyglot of multiple forms of environmental capitalism, each tailored to the unique culture and historical context in which it arises. One *unacceptable* answer is that global capitalism will involve the dominance of one or a few global corporate hegemons, able to subvert local governance prerogatives by coercion. That would venture too close to authoritarianism in order to be sustainable.

While capitalism cannot itself solve the global environmental coordination problem, it can create the stable building blocks that can effectively support international coordination. International coordination could simply insinuate itself in existing institutions, such as the United Nations. Or it might begin anew in some other institution. Whatever form global environmental coordination takes, it will require stable, prosperous countries as parties to agreement and coordination. Inequality among countries must decrease in order for coordination to be robust and lasting, and for better or for worse, capitalism offers the best hope. Robust and trusted institutions must replace corrupt ones, and capitalism must be allowed to thrive within.

Capitalism can also create focal points for global negotiation and coordination: prices. Capitalism being foremost a system of governance based on prices, if enough countries adopt some form of the minimalist, capitalist environmental governance proposed in this book, those prices – preferably environmental taxes – could at least serve as a focal point for international coordination. At present, global negotiations over climate change seem riven by difference.

9.5 DISLOCATION

The capitalism feared by Marx, Polanyi, and lamented by modern writers such as Speth, Alperovitz, and Heilbroner, seems to have the quality of a runaway train, mowing down everything in its path, until finally it runs out of track and plummets over a precipice. The thesis of this book is this: humankind's situation with respect to the global environment that sustains it is so dire that only a runaway train, redirected to point away from the precipice, can save human civilization. If an economically and environmentally sustainable capitalism takes root and reconciles human existence with the rest of life on this planet, we can worry about what comes next. But there is one consequence of the proposals of this book that must be considered now: the dislocation caused by a minimalist capitalist environmental governance.

Throughout this book examples of the power of capitalism have *all* involved successful ventures with very serious downsides that, thanks to the path-dependency of capital investment, tend to get overlooked or swept under a rug. American railroad development used something like slave labor and settled an American West with no real plan and consequently, chaotic and ill-considered land development. Global finance firms have seized an *enormous* fraction of the world's wealth without obviously increasing social welfare anywhere. Oil and gas development has boomed worldwide and has delivered energy to almost every single corner of the globe, but now seems to be pushing human civilization over a precipice.

The proposals in this book, representing a minimalist capitalist solution, would claim its own casualties if fully funded and carried out. The retrenchment of industries that are finally made to pay for the harm they cause will result in dislocation. Many will lose jobs. The human capital of millions will suddenly become obsolete. Many coal miners, and many subsea engineers, derrickmen, and roughnecks who worked on offshore oil platforms will have to figure out a way to ply their skills elsewhere. Many farmers that simply cannot grow profitably without overfertilizing, or without a way to handle animal manure, may simply have to abandon farming. Many of these workers formed entire communities in places where these industries were the sole or dominant source of economic activity. Many of those communities would be at risk under a minimalist, capitalist environmental governance.

Polanyi and others worried that capitalism would undermine social institutions upon which capitalism depended, and also that it would ruin the environment, upon which capitalism also depended. In that view, social institutions and the environment sit side by side, both underpinnings of society and of capitalism. Indeed they are, and indeed they are both threatened by an unguided, runaway capitalism. But what if protecting and restoring the global environment threatened some social institutions? That is the argument that has been propounded by many industries facing new environmental regulations.

To be sure, even if all of the proposals in this book were fully funded and carried out, the dislocation caused would be large, but not so large as a fraction of the overall economy. And retrenchment does not mean extinction, as both fossil fuels and agriculture will remain vital to any future society. It is difficult to project how industries respond to higher costs, but it seems safe to say that fewer people would be employed in fossil fuel-specific and agricultural industries.

In actual fact, agriculture in the United States has been contracting for over half a century, with farmworkers falling from 10 million in 1950 to 3.2 million by 2000.[15] The retrenchment has not been due to environmental laws, but because of technological changes,[16] and because of industrial consolidation that has placed more and more control into fewer and larger firms.[17] A U.S. Department of Agriculture report in 2005 noted

> Those who remained in agriculture increased their efficiency by expanding and specializing their operations to take advantage of economies of scale, or by identifying niche markets to maintain profitability. Others moved out of farming and into other enterprises or occupations, or combined farming with off-farm work, with other family members tapping different sources of income. In some cases, farming has become a secondary occupation, providing a preferred lifestyle rather than a primary source of income. Certainly, not all adjustments have been voluntary or preferred.[18]

Fossil fuel industries have been subject to different economic forces. Crude oil chronically suffers price volatility, caused by demand shocks, hurricanes, geopolitical conflict, and a variety of other foreseeable and unforeseeable events. Natural gas prices have also fluctuated since deregulation, but the advent of fracking has pushed prices to historically low levels. Coal has steadily declined, shedding 4,500 jobs just during the Trump presidency.[19] Consider the following 2018 employment statistics for the United States energy industry.

Table 9.1 provides some perspective about what a shift in energy sources would involve. All of the jobs listed in the first three columns are specific to fossil fuels, a total of over one million jobs in the United States alone. But were, for example, a carbon tax to reduce jobs in those first three columns, many of those would migrate to one or more of the four columns on the right, as lost electricity generation from coal would be replaced by another fuel source. A carbon price would also spur additional job growth in an already-growing energy efficiency industry: workers developing advanced HVAC systems and upgrading traditional HVAC systems,

TABLE 9.1 *U.S. employment in energy industries*

	Coal	Natural Gas	Petroleum	Solar	Wind	Battery Storage	Smart Grid and Grid Moderni- zation
Mining and Extraction[20]	55,905	162,928	308,681				
Transmission Distribution and Wholesale Trade (excluding construction and electricity)[21]	36,385	147,233	110,370			62,910	45,125
Electricity Generation[22]	86,202	141,930		242,343	111,166		

Data: National Association of State Energy Officials and the Energy Futures Initiative, The 2019 U.S. Energy & Employment Report (2019).

and workers building and installing renewable heating and cooling systems total over 700,000 jobs.[23]

Granted, many workers, possibly a great majority, would be unwilling or unable to make such a switch. Mining and extraction jobs would not translate to any analogous job in the renewable energy industry. Managing natural gas processing stations and storage facilities does not necessarily prepare a worker to take advantage of a growing job market involving battery storage technologies. Retraining could be difficult and costly. But the magnitude of such change should not be confused with the end of American prosperity. In the first three months of the COVID-19 pandemic, over forty-two million Americans filed new unemployment claims.[24] What is at stake in the fossil-fuel specific and agricultural industries is a fraction of that.

That said, the fossil fuel and agricultural industries occupy uniquely powerful political niches, and may represent obstacles to progress indefinitely, so some compensation or assistance in a creative form is worth considering. Legislation enacting all or parts of this proposed minimalist, capitalist environmental govern-ance might usefully include some compensation for those suffering job loss, or assistance in finding new employment. That is easier said than done, as even the relatively few remaining places in which coal mining is economically important may be *communities*, with social networks that may be vitally important. Older workers may strongly resist learning a new trade. But there are only two alternatives to offering help: (i) *not* offering help, and (ii) allowing anachronistic industries to continue. Both of those options are on full display, and they do not show well.

Refusing to assist with retraining or help with dislocation is the default policy, especially in capitalist societies in which self-reliance is considered an important value (such as the United States). Compensation or assistance also poses practical problems: once an industry or a group of workers receive compensation for job loss above normal unemployment benefits, then it becomes difficult to see where to draw the line. But there is precedent: the GI bill has assisted millions of Americans in securing higher education. A bit more controversially, the Trade Adjustment Assistance Program helps workers losing jobs due to international trade. Qualifying workers (they must apply to the Department of Labor) can apply for an extension of unemployment benefits, plus help with retraining and relocation. It has been hobbled by a lack of funding, which is perhaps politically understandable given American politics. But as many scholarly works have now documented, the chronic, persistent and steadfast refusal to help those losing jobs has created a new underclass in the United States. Work by Anne Case and Nobel Laureate Angus Deaton showed a startling *decrease* in life expectancy driven by economic decline in certain parts of the United States affected by changing international trade patterns. It occurred *only* in the United States.[25] Unless the United States is politically willing to adopt a much broader and more robust safety net such as that of Canada or Sweden, a more effective program to help with dislocation would appear to be a lesser "evil."

9.6 CAPITALISM RENEWED

I have acknowledged at several junctures in this book that these proposals are a heavy lift. Many modern writers despair that no political or economic system currently known to humankind can actually change the course of human civilization soon enough to save anything worth saving. Speth worried as he wrote his trilogy in the early 2000s, that the political conditions for a transformation of new values, priorities, policies, institutions were "not at hand and won't be for many years."[26] Complicating further the prospects for effective action is the need for international coordination, which is even more difficult than decisive domestic action. The economic and social inertia is massive, and the political will for change nowhere to be seen.

The economist Herb Stein, chief economic advisor to Presidents Nixon and Ford, once quipped, "if something cannot go on forever, it will stop."[27] Many, many have noted the grave environmental crises now facing humankind, and I need not repeat them here. At some point, countries, systems, alliances, or large chunks of human civilization will fail because they lack the resources needed to carry on, suffering some failure precipitated by the cessation of ecosystem services that had come to be vital, but inadequately protected by law. The only question is how much human civilization will have deteriorated by the time that humankind acts to decisively repair its relationship with the Earth. There is probably no such thing as "too late" for the Earth itself, as it will continue to carry millions of species until the Sun expires. What is "too late" for humankind depends on one's perspective, but there is certainly going to be some point at which the vast majority of surviving humans lament, "I wish we had thought of this earlier."

Whether from ashes, or from just a state of advanced environmental deterioration, some human society will transform, and if necessary, rebuild. What will that new society look like?

Authoritarianism is certainly an option, perhaps the default one in times of privation. Climate change or some other environmental catastrophe could consign humankind to some post-apocalyptic future where too many governments have collapsed for failure to provide the most basic government services. In a power vacuum, authoritarians can temporarily halt the chaos. But history strongly suggests authoritarianism eventually fails, though the Soviet Union managed a seventy-two-year run through terror. Centralized control of assets by authoritarian states is never successful because it is impossible to stamp out pockets of renegade capitalism. Authoritarian states such as China and Singapore, on the other hand, have persisted because of their tolerance of capitalism.

What seems inevitable, then, is that capitalism will persist. Mercantilist impulses are too ingrained in human nature for it not to be a prominent part of any future society, anywhere. If nothing else, capitalism must be successful because socialism will inevitably be unsuccessful. Smaller-scale communitarianism is as important a human impulse as mercantilism. But in terms of allocating resources and conveying information on a large scale, there is no substitute for prices. And in terms of coordinating the deployment of resources, there is no substitute for capitalism.

If human civilization were to suffer a truly apocalyptic fall, it might seem unlikely that capitalism could rise from the ashes. Capitalism, after all, requires peace and tolerable justice, if not low taxes. But capitalism can emerge locally, borne as it has in the past out of existential security threats. As Bruce Scott has documented, it is no accident that the earliest successful experiments with capitalism occurred in places like Venice, England, and the Netherlands, places with security concerns.[28] Venice may be the first jurisdiction to have allowed joint stock ownership, in the form of *commenda*, partnerships with one active member and one financial sponsor. By virtue of its favorable trading location and its innovative advances, Venice had grown to the size of Paris and thrice the size of London by 1330.[29] While the early United States was rich in resources, it suffered continually from security threats, and it had the benefit of Alexander Hamilton's innovations in national finance, giving capitalism a boost in the fledgling country.[30] By contrast, early states that enjoyed relative security were often governed by authoritarian rulers, untroubled by outside threats and able to focus on oppression of their subjects. Unfortunately for Venice, trading wealth produced rich families that eroded democratic and economic gains by controlling assets, which produced an authoritarian regime that unwound Venice's economic gains.[31] So although authoritarianism seems to be a natural response in times of disorder and existential threat, it is actually capitalism that has historically provided security through prosperity. In a future with fractured state powers, those adopting capitalist systems will outcompete those that do not.

Scott also observes that capitalism has arisen in societies with relatively poor factor endowments.[32] In contrast to resource-poor Venice, the Netherlands, and England, large and resource-rich China never even broached capitalism until about 1980. The southeastern states of the United States were endowed richer soils and exploited slaves, and were far less capitalist, and still remain poorer than northeastern ones. And is it an accident that two of the most successful capitalist countries, Sweden and Israel, have risen improbably high above their limited factor endowments? Sweden has abundant water, but lacks fossil fuel reserves and an agriculturally friendly climate. Israel lacks both fossil fuels (at least historically) and water, and faces multiple and continuing existential threats. Sweden has clearly emerged as the country that has best adapted its affluent lifestyle to a small carbon footprint, and Israel has become the world's leader in water conservation and efficiency. It is not even as if these countries have developed world-beating technologies; it is just that they have allocated just the right amount of resources, it seems, to solving their most pressing resource problems. Swedish and Israeli governments could not aid in developing technologies or industries, because they did not have the money. Is necessity the mother of invention, or capitalism?

All of this is so transformative that it is hard to believe that it could actually happen. To repeat my assertion in the first chapter, hope may not be a sufficient condition, but it is a necessary one. History is replete with instances in which the impossible suddenly becomes the inevitable, without ever being just plain probable. During the 2008–09 global financial crisis, Congress went quickly from incredulous to imperative in authorizing the expenditure of the then unheard-of amount of $700 billion as part of the Emergency Economic Stabilization Act of 2008. (That figure seems quaint compared to the trillions spent in response to the COVID-19 crisis.) What confronts humankind is something more destructive in the long run, and worthy of recognition as a crisis. And the package of proposals in this book will not cost trillions of dollars.

Instead of looking more closely, it might be worthwhile to zoom out, to gain some perspective of the glimmers of hope that now quite regularly infiltrate the business news. While governments flail in the United States, Brazil, and Australia, business leaders are taking tentative steps not so much to affirmatively *change* the world, but to prepare for a carbon-limited world. Several examples have been mentioned in this book: Blackrock, Harvard, and Israeli water companies have all moved in a direction that provides greater resilience in the face of climate change. Tesla, Walmart, meat substitute companies and Swedish energy companies are reducing emissions. In the deep red state of Texas, where oil and gas reign supreme, and whose junior senator once said that Democrats were lying about "so-called global warming,"[33] firms are transitioning quickly – at least more quickly than the rest of the United States – to an electricity grid with large amounts of renewable energy sources. By 2020, Texas had installed nearly 30 Gigawatts of wind energy capacity, five times that of California.[34]

Only in Texas can you get paid to run your dryer at night, the product of *negative* electricity rates produced by wind turbines running all night. The Houston-based investment bank Tudor Pickering, a leading financier of the shale revolution, will begin focusing on renewable energy investments.[35] And Broad Reach Power LLC, a Houston-based energy storage company that has refused renewable energy subsidies and opposes their enactment, has initiated a plan to construct 150 megawatts of battery storage capacity in Texas to add value to the Lone Star state's large wind capacity.[36]

These and countless other private initiatives, undertaken in the absence of regulation or an environmental tax, represent a growing recognition that change is coming. Individually, each instance can be dismissed as inconsequential or exceptional, but viewed in the collective, strongly suggest an increasingly broad conviction that an environmental reckoning is at hand (if it has not already passed).

It is hard to believe, but there was a time that Milton Friedman thought himself the underdog, and his ideas unripe for popular acceptance. He wrote, in an introduction to *Capitalism and Freedom*, of his view of policy advocates such as himself:

[O]nly a crisis – actual or perceived – produces real change. When that crisis occurs, the actions that are taken depend on the ideas that are lying around. That, I believe, is our basic function: to develop alternatives to existing policies, to keep them alive and available until the politically impossible becomes the politically inevitable.[37]

The purpose of this book has been to introduce a set of policies that will dramatically reduce the amount of environmental degradation, and perform some environmental restoration, so as to make human living on Earth indefinitely sustainable. No policy proposed in this book is novel. But these policies have not been pitched as part of an effort to use capitalism to *save* human civilization on Earth. There is some ideological tension that has long separated those who believe on the one hand, in the wealth creation powers of capitalism and, on the other hand, those who are deeply concerned about degradation of the environment. In time, it will be necessary for those two groups to put aside disagreements and recognize their common cause.

Notes

1. Douglas A. Irwin, *Adam Smith's "Tolerable Administration of Justice" and the Wealth of Nations*, 67 SCOTTISH J. POLIT. ECON. 231 (2020).
2. America Invents Act, P.L. 112–29, 125 Stat. 284 (2011).
3. *See, e.g.*, Paul R. Gugliuzza, *Patent Trolls and Preemption*, 101 VA. L. REV. 1579 (2015).
4. *See, e.g.*, John B. Kirkwood & Robert H. Lande, *The Fundamental Goal of Antitrust: Protecting Consumers, Not Increasing Efficiency*, 84 NOTRE DAME L. REV. 191, 202 (2008); Robert H. Lande, *Wealth Transfers as the Original and Primary Concern of Antitrust: the Efficiency Interpretation Challenged*, 34 HASTINGS L.J. 877, 900–01 (1982). Sherman himself warned that "[no problem] is more threatening than the inequality of condition of wealth, and opportunity that has grown within a single generation out of the concentration of capital." 21 CONG. REC. 2460 (statement of Sen. Sherman).

5. ROBERT BORK, THE ANTITRUST PARADOX: A POLICY AT WAR WITH ITSELF 61 (1978); Reiter v. Sonotone, 442 U.S. at 343 (1979).

6. Daisuke Wakabayashi, *A Challenge to Big Tech and Antitrust Thinking in a Surprising Place*, N.Y. TIMES, Sept. 16, 2019, at B1.

7. Alan Greenspan, Address at C. Peter McColough Series on International Economics: The Global Financial Crisis: Causes and Consequences (Oct. 15, 2009).

8. BRUCE SCOTT, CAPITALISM: ITS ORIGINS AND EVOLUTION AS A SYSTEM OF GOVERNANCE 603 (2011).

9. For example, a cost-benefit analysis of the Clean Air Act showed benefits exceeding costs by a ratio of 30 to 1. U.S. ENVTL. PROT. AGENCY, BENEFITS AND COSTS OF THE CLEAN AIR ACT 1990–2020, THE SECOND PROSPECTIVE STUDY (2011), https://www.epa.gov/clean-air-act-overview/benefits-and-costs-clean-air-act-1990-2020-second-prospective-study [https://perma.cc/VTC6-KEL8].

10. BRUCE SCOTT, CAPITALISM: ITS ORIGINS AND EVOLUTION AS A SYSTEM OF GOVERNANCE 611 (2011).

11. Nick Timiraos & Jon Hilsenrath, *The Fed Break Taboos to Prop Up Economy*, WALL ST. J., Apr. 28, 2020, at A1, (quoting Howard Marks, Oaktree Capital Management LP).

12. Delta Airlines spent $11 billion of free cash on stock buybacks since 2013, and American Airlines $12.4 billion and United Airlines $10.8 billion since 2014. Andrew Bary, *Politicians Want Clampdown on Stock Buybacks. What That Means For Investors*, Barron's (Mar. 22, 2020), https://www.barrons.com/articles/companies-halt-stock-buybacks-as-a-result-of-the-coronavirus-and-politics-51584908991 [https://perma.cc/X9NN-HY9R].

13. The three airlines received $5.4 billion, $5.8 billion, and $5 billion, respectively. Tom Otley, *These Airlines Have Received a Bailout*, BUSINESS TRAVELLER (May 21, 2020), https://www.businesstraveller.com/features/these-airlines-have-received-a-bailout/ [https://perma.cc/3E8B-D8ZL].

14. Benjamin Storrow, *More Coal Has Retired Under Trump Than in Obama's Second Term*, E&E NEWS, June 22, 2020.

15. U.S. DEP'T AGRIC., ECON. RSCH. SERV., FARM LABOR SURVEY (2001). The Farm Labor Survey stopped estimating the number of family farmworkers beginning in 2001, and stopped counting agricultural service workers in 2012.

16. CAROLYN DIMITRI ET AL., U.S. DEP'T AGRIC., ECON. RSCH. SERV., THE 20TH CENTURY TRANSFORMATION OF U.S. AGRICULTURE AND FARM POLICY 6 (2005), https://www.ers.usda.gov/webdocs/publications/44197/13566_eib3_1_.pdf?v=5364.1 [https://perma.cc/8ARZ-GAC2].

17. Testimony of Keith Collins, before Subcommittee on Agriculture, Rural Development and Related Agencies, Committee on Appropriations, U.S. Senate (May 17, 2001), https://www.usda.gov/oce/newsroom/archives/testimony/2005-1997files/051701co.html [https://perma.cc/PX3P-KLLL].

18. CAROLYN DIMITRI ET AL., U.S. DEP'T OF AGRIC. ECON. RESEARCH SERV., THE 20TH CENTURY TRANSFORMATION OF U.S. AGRICULTURE AND FARM POLICY 12 (2005), https://www.ers.usda.gov/webdocs/publications/44197/13566_eib3_1_.pdf?v=5364.1 [https://perma.cc/8ARZ-GAC2].

19. Benjamin Storrow, *More Coal Has Retired Under Trump Than in Obama's Second Term*, E&E News, June 22, 2020.

20. NAT'L ASS'N STATE ENERGY OFFICIALS & THE ENERGY FUTURES INITIATIVE, THE 2019 U.S. ENERGY & EMPLOYMENT REPORT 4–5 (2019).

21. NATIONAL ASSOCIATION OF STATE ENERGY OFFICIALS AND THE ENERGY FUTURES INITIATIVE, THE 2019 U.S. ENERGY & EMPLOYMENT REPORT 101 (Table 34) (2019).

22. National Association of State Energy Officials and the Energy Futures Initiative, The 2019 U.S. Energy & Employment Report 52 (Table 18) (2019).

23. National Association of State Energy Officials and the Energy Futures Initiative, The 2019 U.S. Energy & Employment Report 130 (2019).

24. Lance Lambert, *Over 42.6 Million Americans Have Filed for Unemployment During the Coronavirus Pandemic*, Fortune (June 4, 2020), https://fortune.com/2020/06/04/us-unemployment-rate-numbers-claims-this-week-total-job-losses-june-4-2020-benefits-claims/ [https://perma.cc/36Z6-E3PS].

25. Anne Case & Angus Deaton, *Rising Morbidity and Mortality in Midlife Among White Nonhispanic Americans in the 21st Century*, 112 PNAS 15078 (2015).

26. James Gustave Speth, America the Possible: Manifesto for a New Economy 11 (2012).

27. A Symposium on the 40th Anniversary of the Joint Economic Committee: Hearings Before the Joint Economic Committee, Congress of the United States, 99th Cong., 1st Session, Jan. 16 & 17, 1986, p. 262.

28. Bruce Scott, Capitalism: Its Origins and Evolution as a System of Governance 602 (2011).

29. Daron Acemoglu & James Robinson, Why Nations Fail: The Origins of Power, Prosperity, and Poverty 152–54 (2013).

30. Ron Chernow, Alexander Hamilton 351–59 (2004).

31. Daron Acemoglu and James Robinson, Why Nations Fail: The Origins of Power, Prosperity, and Poverty 152–54 (2013).

32. Bruce Scott, Capitalism: Its Origins and Evolution as a System of Governance 602 (2011).

33. Evan Lehmann, *Cruz Accuses Democrats of Lying About "So-called Global Warming,"* ClimateWire (Nov. 19, 2015).

34. Am. Wind Energy Ass'n, *AWEA State Wind Energy Facts* (2020), https://www.awea.org/resources/fact-sheets/state-facts-sheets [https://perma.cc/XZ7K-XYE9].

35. Naureen S. Malik, *Shale Advisor Tudor Pickering to Start Clean Tech Research*, Bloomberg Green (June 3, 2020).

36. Edward Klump, *Q&A Storage CEO on Coronavirus, Trump and Federal "Constraint,"* EnergyWire (June 23, 2020).

37. Milton Friedman, Capitalism & Freedom xiv (3d reprinting, 2002).

Index

Lightning Source UK Ltd.
Milton Keynes UK
UKHW021828091221
395377UK00009B/675